David Benedictus was born in Kensington during the Munich crisis and was educated at Broadstairs, Eton, Balliol and Iowa.

After a brief spell as a private tutor, washing up at Butlin's and writing scripts for the COI, he became a story editor of 'The Wednesday Play'. He went on to be a television drama director, theatre director and novelist and now lives in Twickenham. He is commissioning editor for drama series at Channel 4.

The Absolutely Essential Guide to London

DAVID BENEDICTUS

SPHERE BOOKS LIMITED

First published in Great Britain by
Sphere Books Ltd 1984
27 Wrights Lane, London W8 5TZ
2nd edition 1986
Copyright © 1984, 1986 by David Benedictus
Reprinted 1987

TRADE
MARK

Set in Baskerville

Printed and bound in Great Britain by
Collins, Glasgow

To those who love London absolutely

Acknowledgements

Apologies to those who would have liked to be on this list and aren't; also to those who would have preferred not to be and are; also to those whose names may have been mis-spelled.

Olive Ainge; Lucy Antrobus; Yvonne Antrobus; Bruce Baker of Wisconsin; Andrew Barr; N. W. Bate; Jared Bernstein; Ann Bodek; Jill Brooke; Henrietta Browne-Wilkinson; Simon Calder; Emily Carey; R. Cleaver; Danny Cohen; Paul Corballis; John Crockett; Lesley Cunliffe; Krsto and Celia Cviic; Rex Darne; Johan van Der Brugge; Tony Elliott; Ann Fitzgerald; Marion Foon; Jane Forman; John & Sheila Frisby; Alan Gavunin; Kate Gilchrist; Gary Gillman; Anne Gobey; David Goldberg; Daniel & Benjamin Goldstein; Elliott Graham; Nicky Henson; Jane Heslop; Bill Hootkins; Rachel Ingals; Angela Jones; Joyce Jones; Florine Katz; C. L. E. King; Julie Kirk; Martin & Ruth Landy & friends; Nirion Lauritz; Roger Lloyd Pack; Neil Mann; Peter Marcan; Sara & Charles Michell; Bru & Roger Myddleton; Lena O'Connor; Mimi O'Grady; Mark Penfold; Paul Petzold & Jane; Michael Phillips; Clay Randall; Edward J. Reardon; Benedict & Sara Rich; Carole & Richard Savage; Rosemary Anne Sisson; Richard Slee; Hilary Smith; Len Still; Sue & Nick; T. H. Swad; Diana Tamblyn; Nina Thomas; Angelica Toynbee-Clarke; Geoffrey Tufts; Ann Valery; Lizzie Webb; Gerald Wells; M. Wiltshaw; Miki van Zwanenberg; Jill Zilkha & friends.

Particular thanks to Nicola Head, Elaine Merris and Julia Simpson for cheerfully typing over and above the call of duty.

Introduction

'There was this man', said the Israeli taxi-driver, turning round because in his opinion our reactions were more interesting than the road ahead, 'and he dreamed that he was dead. And he went to heaven – in his dream, you understand – and it was wonderful, lots to eat and drink, angels and harps and clouds and so forth. So when he woke up he was no longer afraid to die. But when he really did die some years later, and duly went to heaven, it was like an enormous railway waiting room, nothing to do at all. So he complained to God. "When I was here before it was great, food and drink and angels, all that sort of thing, and now just look at it." "Ah well," replied God, "before you were a tourist, now you're a resident." '

This story was told us by the Israeli taxi-driver to illustrate how tourists get quite the wrong impression of this country. But if I were to refer the story to London I would reverse it. London is a great city to be resident in, hell for tourists.

I mean, think about it. Peering through the railings at the Changing of the Guard, quivering for hours in the draughtiest part of the Marylebone Road to see waxworks, for heaven's sake, and then queuing again to be served a pale imitation of American food by a surly Italian waiter . . . Then back to your hugely expensive hotel room, in which you are invited to polish your own shoes, and make your own cup of instant coffee, before settling down to watch bowls on television. You came here for the theatre? All you get to see is *No Sex Please We're British*. You came here for the museums? They've imposed admission charges. You feel like a drink to cheer yourself up? Ah, but you'd forgotten the licensing laws. Poor old tourist, ripped off left, right and centre, by cabbies, ice-cream vendors, hostesses, and – unkindest cut of all – by the authors of guides who have told you what a wonderful time you're going to have.

So you may. The galleries, the museums, the music, the city scapes, the food, compare with any city in the world, but only if you know where to find the best. I hope this book will enable you to do just that.

As a resident I hope you will find my London guide absolutely essential, as it claims to be. It contains a hell of a lot of information, and just as much prejudice to stimulate or infuriate. Use a contribution form – they're at the back of the book – to argue with me, or to share your enthusiasms. Let us not rest until together we have created the *ultimate guide book*.

One drawback. There can be no such thing as an ultimate guide book because the concept of the ultimate is of something transcendental and unchanging, and London changes even faster than I can write about it. So be indulgent towards me if you find the Chinese restaurant closed, the cheerful publican replaced by a monster, the architectural treasure demolished, or the steak full of gristle. I'm only human. ('What kind of excuse is that?' snarls one of Beckett's characters.) I set out to please and inform and if, with considerable help – see the Acknowledgements – I have done so, that is reward enough, so long as my royalties are paid puntually.

How to use this book

Ideally you should buy two copies, so you can keep one copy open at the index while roaming freely through the text of the other copy. But in any case don't ignore the index. While the main body of the book is arranged alphabetically, you can only find out at a glance if your favourite statue is included, or if I have missed your best fanlight or foot scraper by using the index, in which the best in each category is emphasized in heavy type. You will also find a list of recommendations by area, and a bibliography, although specialist books will be mentioned under the appropriate heading. There are omissions. I am entirely ignorant about lacrosse, for instance, so you will find no information on lacrosse. Isn't it better to be ignored than confused? It goes without saying that I haven't received payment for any entry, and that I have never advertised my presence in any establishment in order to solicit favourable treatment. No, I move in silence like the night, my cape of anonymity my one protection.

And when the book has outlived its usefulness I shall not be at all offended if you hang its numerous pages on a nail in your smallest room. Or fold them up to make spills, or shred them for hamster bedding. Authors are not vain creatures; nor are they allowed to be. Once, after addressing a Zionist ladies' luncheon club, the chairperson called for questions. There was only one question. An old lady at the back snapped out: 'What did he say his name was?'

David Benedictus
November 1985

African Food

The best African food is at the *Calabash* (downstairs at the African Centre, 38 King Street, WC2; 01-836 1976). You eat regional dishes of West Africa, chicken in coconut milk (from Zanzibar), beef stew with spinach and palm-nut (Zaire), and rice, black-eyed beans, cassava, and yams till they're coming out of your ears. Pepperpot soup will make your eyes spin and blow the top off your head. You could end up looking a mess. Nonetheless at about £8 a head with friendly service you could go further, even to Africa, and fare worse. Occasional cultural activities, if you don't regard eating as cultural.

A new and already successful African vegetarian restaurant is the *Bambaya* (1 Park Road, N8; 01-348 5609), located in a converted dairy. Including black American food means you can enjoy fish chowders and from the Caribbean such delicacies as Ackee with salt fish, and Sah-Bah (prawn and aubergines). As you would expect, African stand-bys (rice, black-eyed peas, plantains and tropical fruit) are always available.

Toddie's (241 Old Brompton Road, SW5; 01-373 8217) is run by Quasline from Sierra Leone. Specialities such as Joloff Rice, Palava Sauce and Gari. Also live jazz every night and rejuvenating cocktails.

At the *Afric-Carib* (1 Stroud Green Road, N4; 01-263 7440), it is Nigeria in Finsbury Park. The pepper soup is even hotter than the Calabash equivalent. Okra, yam, plantain and maize are used, and there is a take-away at street level with an informal restaurant below. As you might suppose, West Indian food is also featured. Friendly.

For take-away African food visit *Ras Catering Co-op* (108 Goldhawk Road, W12; 01-749 9714).

Best African Food: The *Calabash*.

Airports

The statistics are impressive. Twenty-nine million passengers a year pass through *Heathrow*, the busiest airport in the world. (Gatwick is fourth.) More than £20,000,000,000 worth of foreign trade each year, and during the peak period of the summer months at least 2,400 departures a week. Even these figures will appear faulty when the new terminal opens.

I had thought that Heathrow was efficiently organised, and that the design of the place showed some flair, but that was before (a) I travelled via Terminal 3 which deals with the Third World and is

1

three times as squalid as 1 or 2, and (b) I experienced the beauty and imagination of Changi Airport, Singapore, and realised what was possible. The best feature about Heathrow is the underground link to Central London. The worst feature is the treatment of Third World visitors by customs and immigration.

Alleys

The most remarkable alley in London has to be *Brydges Place*, WC2, which runs between St Martin's Lane and Bedfordbury. It measures 200 yards by (at its narrowest point) 15 inches wide. Since the buildings on either side are tall and dark and since the sun never pierces the crack in the surface of London, walking along it is not unlike falling down a well sideways.

The most beautiful alley is *Goodwin's Court*, also running between St Martin's Lane and Bedfordbury. Wrought iron gas-holders illuminate a marvellous row of gently serpentine bow-front houses – shops, of course, originally. A plaque announces: 'Goodwin's Court (replacing Fishers Alley) first appeared in Rate-Books in 1690 and it seems probable that the houses of the Court were erected in that year. LCC Survey'. Inside, however, these houses are a little disappointing.

Magnificent and unexpected is *Gentleman's Row*, Enfield. This footpath, which blossoms with bronze plaques, is flanked by enchanting houses from the 16th, 17th, 18th and 19th centuries. On the other side of the path gardens run down to the Brent with its iron footbridges and ingenuous ducks.

The gas-lit *Exchange Court*, WC2, where William Terriss, the actor-manager, was stabbed, is alarming but not so alarming as the little yards and alleys around Aldgate, where the ghosts of Jack the Ripper's victims cry out for retribution.

Post Office Alley, Strand-on-the-Green, W4, is too cute for its own good; like something on a film set. *Crown Passage*, St James's, SW1, has elements of cuteness, but Chubby's Sandwich Bar and Supersam Snacks present a healthily vulgar front to passers-by.

Bankside is rich in alleys, including *Clink Street*, running between towering warehouses and the site of the Old Clink Prison, run by the Bishops of Winchester and *very* dank and unpleasant, *Cardinal Cap Alley*, which has somehow survived unchanged in shape since the 16th century and was named after Wolsey, one of those Winchester bishops, and *Rose Alley*, on the site of the Rose Theatre, where Shakespeare trod the boards. On both sides of Borough High Street – but principally the east – the Strand and St James's are courts of much interest. *Middle Temple Lane* does qualify and is dignified and historical.

Also recommended are *Crown Passage* and *Harrow Passage* in Kingston; *Church Path*, Mortlake, from which you can listen to one of the oldest peals of eight bells in the country; *Holland Path*, W8, where you get a good class of voyeur watching the schoolgirls, and various sinister alleys running west off Bishopsgate, EC2.

Best Alley: *Goodwin's Court*, WC2.
Worst Alley: *Cons Street*, Waterloo.

P.S. Read: *London Lanes and London Alleys, Byways and Courts*, two books (1930 and 1924 respectively) by A. Stapleton.

All-Night Eating

(a) Grand

The *Carlton Tower* and the *Kensington Hilton*, catering as they do for jet-lagged foreigners who find Greenwich Mean Time as confusing as pounds, shillings and pence used to be, will provide food at all hours – even, if nagged, to non-residents. The *Strand Palace Hotel* serves snacks as a matter of course, but beware of the spaghetti.

Sunrise's (3 Long Acre, WC2; 01-936 2816) is just the place for a pepper steak at a quarter to two in the morning. It continues to serve respectable breakfasts from 2 a.m.-6 a.m.

(b) Not so grand

Wurst Max (75 Westbourne Grove, W2; 01-229 3771) is lively. Open till 4 a.m. You can eat hot sausages and sauerkraut – in the garden if it's a balmy summer's night. Also take away.

Calamities (104 Heath Street, NW3; 01-435 2145) serves hamburgers to hungry Hampstead intellectuals till 3 a.m., while *Up All Night* (325 Fulham Road, SW10; 01-352 1998) does the same until 6 a.m. for famished Fulham fops. Chinese somnambulists walk to the *Diamond* (23 Lisle Street, WC2; 01-437 2517) – Cantonese food till 4 a.m.

(c) Basic

Mick's Cafe in Fleet Street might look squalid to most of us, but journalists seldom notice their surroundings unless paid to. The *Pie Stand* at Chelsea Bridge is popular with taxi drivers and famous for its brown sauce. The *Kiosk* at Caxton Hall and the *Beigel Shop* in Brick Lane attract a better class of insomniac than the *Wimpy* opposite King's Cross Station, which is depressing. Many of the *Kentucky Fried Chicken* branches open 24 hours a day for their battery customers, who throw the chicken bones on the ground for my dogs to crunch up. Their apple pies are all right.

Harry's (6 Kingly Street, W1; 01-734 8708) is open until six in the morning for proletarian foods such as cottage pie and cauliflower cheese.

Don't forget that the Lebanese seldom go to bed. Consequently two Lebanese restaurants *Maroush* (21 Edgware Road, W2; 01-723 0773) and *Fakhreldine* (85 Piccadilly, W1; 01-693 3424) are almost always open – but the *Baalbek*, the *Byblos*, the *Olive Tree*, and *The Lebanese Restaurant* close by midnight. As for the Chinese – well, I have always been able to find hot food in Chinatown (in and around Gerrard Street, W1) night and day, though even at three in the morning parking can be a problem.

Best all-night eating: *The Beigel Shop*.
Worst all-night eating: *Kentucky Fried Chicken*.

P.S. Most posh hotels run room service throughout the night, but that's a very extravagant way of getting a club sandwich!

All-Night Petrol

South West London:
Chelsea Cloisters Garage, Sloane Avenue, SW3. (01-589 1226)

West London:
Shepherd's Bush.
Chiswick Flyover (under it).

North West London:
Esso, Camden Road, NW1.
Esso, 617 Finchley Road, NW3.
Cavendish Motors, Cavendish Road, NW6 (01-459 0046).
Station Supreme, 63 Fortune Green Road, NW6 (01-435 2211).

North London:
Mount Pleasant Filling Station, 39 King's Cross Road, WC1.
City Petroleum, 276 Upper Street, N1.

South East London:
Heron Garage, 430 Old Kent Road, SE1.

Suburbs:
City Petroleum, London Road, Kingston.

It's always worth considering converting to diesel fuel. Diesel engines are fifty per cent more efficient than petrol, and can run on a variety of fuels (after-shave might be worth a try in extremis), all of which are lead-free. But then you have to ask a cabbie for a 24-hour diesel garage – there's one at Shepherd's Bush.

Best all-night petrol: Whichever one you get to in time!

Arcades

When Lord George Cavendish and his architect, Samuel Ware, built the *Burlington Arcade* between 1815 and 1819, they declared it was 'for the gratification of the publick and to give employment to industrious females'. Some said though – ungratefully – that it was to stop the rabble throwing rubbish into Lord George's garden next door. However, the gallery lighting flattered shop and shopper alike and it was a success, although by the 1870s, Dickens reported that it was principally tenanted by 'bonnet-makers, ladies' bootmakers, and sellers of knicknacks'. In 1930 Beresford Pite recast the Piccadilly entrance, replacing Ware's original façade with 'cynically outrageous baroque' – a characteristically trenchant description by Sir John Summerson. Supposedly it is patrolled by beadles in liveries and top-hats, who are recruited from ex-soldiers of the 10th Hussars. I say supposedly, because they have been invisible on my last two visits. Their duties are to ensure good behaviour within the precinct, which means no undue whistling, humming, hurrying, or unfurling of umbrellas. When does humming become undue? Beadles know.

The oldest arcade – just – in London is the *Royal Opera Arcade* and it is a particularly handsome one. It formed part of Her Majesty's Theatre, the largest theatre in the country, designed by M. Novosielski and completed by Nash in 1817. A fire gutted it in 1867 – 'sparks and burning fragments fell like so much hail in front of the Clubs in Pall Mall'. Now Her Majesty's has crossed the road and, on the site of the opera house in which Mr Carl Rosa first offered British audiences operas sung in English, New Zealand House – that imperturbable monolith – now scrapes the sky. But the Royal Opera Arcade survives intact. Nearly intact. The eastern side is given over to the neon-lit picture windows of the Bank of New Zealand.

Two arcades run between Piccadilly and Jermyn Street. On the site of the Brunswick Hotel, where Louis Napoleon lived incognito as the Comte d'Arenberg from 1846, the *Piccadilly Arcade* looks like an elaborate Regency toy but it was not erected until 1910. The upstairs rooms scarcely appear large enough to house normal-sized people;

maybe they don't. The balloon-like illuminated shop-numbers do nothing for the hanging lights (and vice versa) but there are some interesting shops.

The modern *Prince's Arcade* (architecturally undistinguished – ceilings too low, lanterns too large) features the traditional arcade mixture of sweet shops, crafts, opticians and travel agents. But you can get ecclesiastical vestments and classy men's footwear in this short arcade, as well as delicious plain chocolate truffles from Lessiter's.

The *Royal Arcade*, running between 28 Old Bond Street and Albemarle Street, was opened in 1880, damaged in the blitz, and has recently been restored. High Victorian taste is exemplified in the allegorical Bond Street frontage. A lady with bare bazooms is handing a roast lizard to a boy carrying sheaves of corn and wearing a hat with a ribbon in it. The shops scarcely live up to the expectations engendered by this entrance.

The worst arcade in London is the *Brompton Arcade*, running south from Knightsbridge. On my last visit the dress shop was holding a savage sale, the porcelain dog in the window of the hat shop had a broken foreleg, and the matchbox seller was slumped on a milk crate. But the *Halkin Arcade* (Motcomb Street to West Halkin Street) is a very different matter. Almost every establishment in the exuberant precinct shimmers with 20th century chic.

Mr Chiu, whose gallery is in the Marquis de Sade Bauhaus taste, was one of the pioneers of Deco when he opened his shop. He sold several of those bronze and ivory nudes (usually by Chiparus or Preiss) for £100, making a profit of about £20 on each. 'Twenty years ago it was clever – very imaginative and advanced, now it's like Biba. I buy only what I like – I mean what are we here for? – but not everything I like. I mean people you see in the street you quite like to go to bed with them, but you don't break your heart over it.' Mr Chiu is disenchanted over many things. He sees no style, no elegance around; style being the ability to create your own consistent taste, elegance the ability to make others wish to emulate it. He is even disenchanted with *Halkin Arcade*.

Best Arcade: *Halkin Arcade*, SW1.
Worst Arcade: *Brompton Arcade*, SW1.

Arches

My distaste for arches dates back to my schooldays when I was forced to take regular runs to the viaduct (known as the Arches) which carried trains from Slough to Windsor. I had flat feet – or fallen arches – and, had it not been for Timothy Pitt-Miller dragging me along by my scruff I would never have made it.

Drive up the A1 (Holloway Road) on a wet Friday evening during the late autumn rush-hour, and even the Gresham Ballroom and the Fairplay Amusements Arcade will do little to raise your spirits, for you know that you are about to undertake the slow haul up *Archway Road*. Originally the road was carried through a tunnel, but less than three years after completion the entire structure collapsed. Astonishingly no one was injured. Thereafter a road replaced the tunnel with an archway to carry Hornsey Lane traffic – the first arch (Nash 1813) being replaced in 1897 with the present lofty edifice. Though the large cream bosses and the wrought iron wheels have a kind of portentousness, this is nc⁺ a sight for smarting eyes. Ask 100 Londoners the name of the most celebrated London arch, and I would guess that no more than ten of them would name the *Archway*. Most would cite *Marble Arch*; a few *Admiralty Arch* or *Wellington Arch* (otherwise known as *Constitution Arch*). *Marble Arch*, built (1828) by Nash for £75,000 and inspired by the Arch of Constantine in Rome, was too narrow (so the story goes) for its intended purpose, the ingress and egress of the state coach to and from Buckingham Palace, and was moved to the north-east corner of Hyde Park in 1851 at an additional cost of £4,340. For the move each stone had to be numbered. Marble Arch now contains a police station in the attic.

Upon *Wellington Arch* (Decimus Burton, 1828) where Peace now drives her chariot, the Duke once rode his horse. *Admiralty Arch* (Sir Aston Webb, 1910) was built as part of the National Monument to Queen Victoria.

These three massive chunks of masonry are not to my taste, but they do provide a certain formal dignity to a ride up Park Lane or along the Mall, and they are safe from bureaucratic vandals. I mention this because, as recently as 1962, Philip Hardwick's *Doric Arch* at Euston Station which with 'columns of gigantic girth opened a vista to the railway world beyond' (Dickens) was demolished for reasons beyond logic. Not that it had more than symbolic significance, travellers having always used a smaller side-gate.

Three historic London arches deserve to be mentioned. *St John's Gate* in Clerkenwell is part of what once was the Old Priory of the Knights Hospitallers. Even older is the archway to *Richmond Palace*, rebuilt by Henry VII from the smoking ruins of Sheen Palace. Above the archway is the room in which Queen Elizabeth died – so they say – and in the courtyard through the arch Shakespeare's players performed to her shortly before her death. Well, the bricks remain and very mellow they appear in the elegant setting of Richmond Green, even if the graffiti-writers have been at them.

Oldest of all is the Norman archway of *Merton Priory*. As with *St John's*, Clerkenwell, and *Richmond Palace*, the archway is just about all that survives of the original structure. Not discovered until 1914, the archway was re-erected next to the Church of St Mary, itself full of charm and boasting a Norman door inside the north porch, in Melrose Road. It is all a Norman arch should be, and its poignant isolation (well, a garage has been erected close by) seems to speak of the vanity of human aspirations.

There are others. Nash may have gone OTT with *Marble Arch* but his archway entrance to *Cumberland Terrace* is classical elegance frozen in stucco. In a recent book Bill Grundy calls the archway entrance to the *Natural History Museum* 'positively horrendous' and calls for a government health warning to be prominently displayed: 'This doorway can damage your eyesight'. What rubbish! To me it's enchanting. Alfred Waterhouse, the architect of Mancunian Gothic, was employed, and he selected a Romanesque Rhineland style with prefabricated terracotta facing. There are eight rows of barley-sugar twist columns on either side of the front door, which also boasts eight concentric arches, a frieze of improbable beasties, and a Moorish chequerboard effect. The hand-rails and lamps are integrated into this fantasy. Entering the museum under this arch has to be an adventure. Once inside the vision is equally exciting.

The entrance archway to *Waterloo Station* (by J. R. Scott, overlooking Waterloo Road) is a huge memorial to 585 employees who died in the war. The horrors of war are graphically displayed, broken bodies, gaunt faces. But the delights of peace are nowhere apparent. The survivors look not so much triumphant as exhausted; there is one surviving child – asleep. Over the entire sculpture Britannia with two admirers hovers, and incorporated within the design, clouds, lightning bolts, funeral torches, a helmet, a spear, and a clock may be found. Remarkable.

Best London Arch: *Cumberland Terrace, NW1.*
Worst London Arch: *Knightsbridge Barracks* (Sir Basil Spence, see next entry).

Architecture

London architecture is both instantly recognisable and entirely unpredictable. It is the brick of the early Victorian terraced houses in Islington, Bloomsbury and Southwark, it is the villas in Parson's Green and the suburbs, it is the gloomy philanthropy of the Peabody Estates. It is the stucco of the Nash terraces, the wit of the Palladian Lodges, the fantasy of the Victorian Gothic. It is the domestic friendliness of iron balconies and fanlights, and the public arrogance of railway stations. It is statues everywhere.

There were periods of great speculative building which produced the handsome London squares, and periods of disastrous speculative vandalism which pulled them down again – whatever happened to *Portman Square*? The Great Fire of 1666 destroyed four-fifths of the City. The Great Fire of 1676 destroyed most of Southwark, and the great fires of the Blitz savaged much of South London, the Docks and the City. The first fires made way for Wren and Gibbs and Dance, Vanbrugh and Hawksmoor, men of vision and taste, the later fires made way for towers of concrete and glass which could not be lived in, but could be borrowed against.

Had it not been for *St Paul's* surviving triumphantly in the midst of chaos and proving beyond argument that when men aspire to God they become as gods, architects might have forgotten what they were there for; fortunately a few – very few – remembered. But it is salutary to compare the *Chelsea Hospital*, built by Wren and Hawksmoor for the pensioners, with the *Knightsbridge Barracks*, built by Sir Basil Spence some 250 years later for serving men; salutary and dispiriting. And so often the charmingly eccentric churches along the Marylebone Road are crushed by flyovers and skyscrapers. The pretty façade of the *Victoria Palace Theatre* is insulted by *Portland House* behind, and what madness possessed the BBC when they erected their yellow brick offices behind *All Souls'*, Langham Place, I cannot imagine. Much of what isn't molested or raped is destroyed – and anything which is charming and unpretentious is vulnerable to the mad eyes of the office developer.

Later in this book you may find architecture dealt with in greater detail under such headings as Crescents, Big and Small Houses, Palaces, Squares, Cathedrals, Churches, Underground Lines and Stations, Streets, Modern and Commercial Buildings etc., but just now let me nominate:

Best architecture: The *Wren Churches*.
Worst architecture: *59/67 Portland Place*, where one fifth of an Adam Terrace has been sliced off through pediment, pilaster and all, to squeeze in a 1930s building of total mediocrity.
I can recommend the excellent book *A Guide to the Architecture of*

London by Edward Jones and Christopher Woodward (Weidenfeld and Nicolson £12.95 and £8.50) and the classic *Georgian London* by John Summerson (3rd Edition Barrie and Jenkins, 1978).

Art Deco and Art Nouveau

There are two centres for the decorative arts. *Halkin Arcade*, which I've mentioned under Arcades above. And a small group of shops in the Fulham Palace Road just north of Putney Bridge, including *L'Odeon*. Tragically the *Packard Factory* at Osterley on the Great West Road was demolished by a flying bomb and the *Firestone Factory* by developers, but at least the fine *Gillette Factory* with its striking (!) clock tower (designed by Sir Banister Fletcher) remains.

Many Art Deco cinemas have somehow survived (with or without Wurlitzers), the best being the cathedral-like *Granada*, Tooting (Mitcham Road) with marble, stained glass lit from behind, and Gothic everywhere it can be squeezed in. It can seat four thousand disciples. Bingo is played there. The splendid *Finsbury Park Empire*, now the *Rainbow*, has Moorish settlements around the screen. The *Twickenham Odeon* is a deco gem, down to the green illuminated exit signs, but has been empty for some time. The *Richmond Odeon* has been chopped in three.

To buy Art Nouveau I strongly recommend *Galerie 1900* (267 Camden High Street, NW1; 01-485 1001), or the *Fine Art Society* (148 New Bond Street, W1; 01-629 5116). But London has nothing to compare with the glorious metalwork at the entrances to the Paris metro. A nice example of a family house in this taste is *115 Howard's Lane*, Putney, SW15. It has stained glass and a huge dragon weather-vane (q.v.).

Best Art Deco: The *Granada Tooting*.
Best Art Nouveau: *Whitechapel Art Gallery*.

Art Galleries

If it's pictures you're after, it has to be the *National Gallery*. Titian, Leonardo, Turner, Reynolds, Fra Angelico, Tintoretto, Rubens, Rembrandt, Vermeer, El Greco, and a superb selection from the French School, these are just some of the artists who make this collection a celebration of the optimism of the human race. But the quality and the scope of the pictures on display does not ensure that a visit to the *National Gallery* is necessarily a success. It's not unlike being tied down with silken ropes and having vintage champagne dripped onto your head while Mozart plays incessantly in the background and a pedigree Pomeranian licks your toes. If sensibly you decide to 'do' one room per visit, you still have to walk blindfolded through the others or risk premature artistic ejaculation. The Velasquez room is too cool; the Impressionist room next door too hot and the pictures are unimaginatively hung.

When the *Tate* stirs itself it can mount an exhibition of international repute, but it has been going through tough times since it destroyed its splendid extension and forfeited much of the goodwill that went with it. There is much that is impressive at the *Tate*. Hogarth and Blake and the civilised English painters of the 19th century, who painted as they lived, with style and decorum; Matisse and Picasso ('that brute Picasso' – Evelyn Waugh); and the best of the modern Brits – Bacon and Hockney, Peter Blake and Freud. But many of the post-war acquisitions look jaded, and Warhol and Pollock and Liechtenstein do not deserve their wall space.

The *Royal Academy* (Burlington House, Piccadilly, W1; 01-734 9052) is an institution. It has an annual dinner when the critics are castigated for being out of touch, and a Summer Exhibition at which the said critics get their own back. It's a shame that so few of the leading British artists are members, but it's a joy when it concentrates on a Really Big One, such as 'The Genius of Venice'. Norman Foster has been hired to redesign the Upper Galleries, where contemporary exhibitions will feature.

Compare the eccentric formality of *Burlington House* with the *Dulwich Picture Gallery* (College Road, SE21; 01-693 5254 – closed daily for lunch, so be warned), London's oldest public art gallery and designed by Sir John Soane. This is what J. C. Smetham wrote in 1891:

'How kind! How civil! How silent! You write your name in the visitors' book, and see that yesterday John Ruskin was here . . . All is sober and uncrowded, and well-lighted and profoundly still . . . The keeper of the Gallery comes and peers at you over his spectacles. He is not quite sure in his little room which are the pictures and which are the visitors, and he's come to see.'

The design, which incorporated a mausoleum containing the bodies of the principal benefactor of the gallery and his friends, is superb. What if the pictures are not so fine? There is always a Rembrandt, a Gainsborough, a Claude Lorraine and a Guido Reni which redeem the rest. The Reni, in which John the Baptist is depicted as young and handsome, is as fresh and unexpected as the day it was painted.

To qualify for inclusion in the *National Portrait Gallery* (round the corner from the *National Gallery*) you have to be famous or royal and ten years dead. It has been computed that since several of the works on display are crowd scenes there are some 45,000 faces on view at this gallery, and what a fascinating place it is! The photographs – Beardsley with his bony nose and spatulate fingers, Thomas Hardy so grey and undistinguished – are often even more illuminating than the portraits, but the whole exhibition is an essential reminder that these people, Henry Moore and Henry VIII, Sir Thomas More and Sir Thomas Beecham, John Donne and T. S. Eliot, lived. History being about chaps (geography is about maps), this is the best place to go and study history.

The *Hayward* (South Bank, SE1; 01-261 0127) is a building of notorious hideousness, concealed within the serpentine coils of the South Bank complex. For some years it has featured Arts Council Loan Exhibitions of considerable significance. With the loss of the GLC and its grant its future is once more at risk. As I write, it has closed, and I don't mind. The *Whitechapel Art Gallery* (adjoining Aldgate East tube station) has a fine terracotta façade in the art nouveau taste; inside it is light and it was designed in 1901 by C. Harrison Townsend on a desperately reduced budget. The recent rebuilding and expansion incorporating an additional site have been entirely successful. The *Courtauld's* move to Somerset House should by now have taken place. The inevitable loss in charm and intimacy should be balanced by much increased wall space to enable more of the *Courtauld's* riches to be shared with us. Other recent changes: The *Mayor Gallery* (22a Cork Street, W1; 01-734 3558) has opened a back room for the heavy mob. *Nigel Greenwood* has commandeered a new space at 4 New Burlington Street, W1; (01-437 3795). The *Wolfson Galleries* at the *British Museum* have opened, and so has the *Diorama* (14 Peto Place, NW1; 01-487 3598 – a building with an intriguing history). *Anthony Reynolds* (37 Cowper Street, EC2; 01-608 1516) lords it over the biggest commercial space in London, and other new galleries to be watched include the *Fabian Carlsson* (160 New Bond Street, W1; 01-409 0619) and *Edward Totah* (first floor at 13 Old Burlington Street, W1; 01-734 0343). Modern galleries which are (almost) always worth a visit include *Angela Flowers* (11 Tottenham Mews, W1; 01-637 3089), the *Lisson Gallery* (66 Bell Street, NW1; 01-262 1539), and *Blond Fine Art* (22 Princes Street, W1; 01-437 1230). The *Barbican* is a pleasure to browse in – always assuming you can find it. For photographs: The *Photographers' Gallery* (5/8 Great Newport Street, WC2; 01-240 5511); for cartoons, the *Workshop* (83 Lamb's Conduit Street, WC1; 01-242 5335); and to buy old masters, *Thomas Agnew* (43 Old Bond Street, W1; 01-629 6176).

The pictures on display along Piccadilly and the Bayswater Road on a Sunday are usually of great hideosity, nor do their clients enjoy champagne or canapés. Many of those selling the pictures are not, as you might suppose, the artists, but merely salesmen for the mass producers. Be warned! The *Serpentine Gallery* (Kensington Gardens, W2; 01-402 6075) mounts two summer shows of the works of young and little-known artists. There are altogether far too many of these to choose from. The *Queen's Gallery* (Buckingham Palace Road, SW1; 01-930 4832) is an easy way to see pictures from the royal collection within the royal palace.

My favourite gallery – indeed one of my favourite places in the world – is the *Marianne North Gallery* in Kew Gardens. Marianne spent her life (1830-1890) travelling throughout the world to paint flowers and trees in their natural habitat. After a successful London exhibition of her paintings, which are fanciful and exuberant, she decided that they belonged to the nation and had her friend, James Fergusson, design a special gallery to house them. In the Gallery, marvellously intimate and colourful, hang 832 examples of her work, with panels from the barks of the different trees she encountered. What a glorious place!

Best Art Gallery: (for pictures) *The National Gallery*.
Best Art Gallery qua Gallery: *Dulwich Picture Gallery*.
Most Interesting Gallery: *National Portrait Gallery*.
Nicest Gallery: *Marianne North Gallery*.
Worst Gallery: (for pictures) *Royal Academy Summer Exhibition*.

If you've only the time or the inclination for one picture try:
National Gallery: 'Young Woman Standing at the Virginals' (Vermeer). (Room XI).
National Portrait Gallery: 'The Brontë Sisters' (Branwell Bronte). (Room XXI).
Tate Gallery: 'Swan Upping' (Stanley Spencer).
Dulwich Picture Gallery: 'John the Baptist' (Guido Reni).
Wallace Collection, Hertford House: 'The Swing' (Fragonard). (Room XVIII).
Sir John Soane's Museum: 'The Rake's Progress' (Hogarth). (The Picture Room).

Arts and Crafts

Liberty's in Regent Street ('Tudor revival at its most exuberant') is the Mecca of arts and crafts. Founded in 1857, it still retains something of its original quaint earnestness, and bearded artisans in open-toed sandals may still be seen flashing Barclaycards amongst the Paisley shawls and leather rhinoceri. At the *Portmeirion Shop* (5 Pont Street, SW1; 01-235 7601) look out for old patchwork quilts and brass bedsteads.

However, good quality crafts can be bought at the *National Theatre Craft Market*, outside the theatre (telephone M. Meakin 01-928 2033 x 344 for details), at a fraction of the prices charged in the stores. There are prints, jewellery of the 1930s, pots, hand-knitted jumpers and home-made sweets, patchwork, herbs, and much else that is wholesome and ideologically sound.

Specifically British crafts may be viewed at the *British Crafts Centre* (43 Earlham Street, WC2; 01-836 6993 – Tuesday, Friday and Saturday) and at *Naturally British* (13 New Row, WC2; 01-240 0551); exhibits are for sale, as they are at the *Design Centre* in the Haymarket. Here the emphasis tends towards what Betjeman calls 'ghastly good taste'. For healthy vulgarity try *Petticoat Lane*. The *Arts and Crafts Shop* in Abbey Road, NW8 (junction of Belsize Road) will attempt to mend, alter or repair anything with good grace. But I recommend *Swallow Art Suppliers* (100-108 Battersea Rise, SW11; 01-228 0314) as the best for painting accessories. Also recommended: *Yarncraft* (112a Westbourne Grove, W2; 01-229 1432) for the homey weavey set and *Hobbyhorse* (15 Langton Street, SW10; 01-351 1913).

Best arts and crafts: The *National Theatre Craft Market.*
Worst arts and crafts: Those pottery ewers you see in florists' shops.

Arts Centres

Arts should not properly be in centres. Administrators like to put them there so that they can keep an eye on them, and performers rather like them so that they can be fed and wined without having to emerge into the rain. But once you have a centre with an ocean of wall space the problems begin. What to hang on them? What to put on in your two or three theatres/cinemas/concert halls? What if – as is invariably the case – there just isn't enough worthwhile 'art' to go round? Inevitably what there is is diluted, and standards begin to fall. More seriously, audiences come to believe that because the building (rightly in the case of the Barbican called a 'complex') is so splendid, all that goes on in it must be artistically splendid too. Peter Brook, a bright lad, has realised this and takes his plays to drill halls and African villages and traffic islands and wherever.

The best arts centre in London is probably the *Riverside* in Hammersmith. It is friendly and tatty and seems to get some of the best – if not the most reputable – of the visiting companies. As a result it lives on a financial tight-rope, and its circumstances have become even more dire since the loss of its grant and its innovative director, David Gothard, replaced by Charlie Hanson, who is riding an under-fed tiger. Its cinema is like a wrecked set from *Citizen Kane*.

The *ICA* in the Mall is full of loonies. On my last visit there I was subjected to an improvised concert of great banality followed by a horror film in three dimensions. The radical book store was not much of a comfort. The *Concert Hall* is either suffocating (with the windows shut) or noisy (with them open). But the snacks are wholesome.

The *Barbican* is a monster. Apart from Trevor Nunn and his immediate entourage, the entire staff work underground, like creatures in a novel of the future. That would matter less if the air conditioning worked better. However the acoustics in the Concert Hall have now organised themselves and it's a very pleasant place to listen to and watch – sight-lines are excellent throughout the Barbican – music being made. The Barbican boasts the best safety curtain and by no means the best food in London.

The *National*, like the Royal Shakespeare Company at the Barbican and Stratford, is very hot on production values. Their shows are impeccably mounted and competently acted. But the choice of plays is sometimes alarming. *Jean Seberg* was as great a disaster as *The Mysteries* was a triumph. The new policy of turning actors into producers is like asking models to take photographs or corpses to become undertakers. The ambiance, as they say, is very agreeable, but the chocolate cake is to be avoided, though the restaurant these days is pretty good.

Best arts centre: The *National*.
Worst arts centre: *Television Centre*.

Auctions

An auctioneer: 'One who admires *all* works of arts' – Oscar Wilde.

The credibility of the big London sale-rooms has recently taken a tumble. *Sotheby's* (34 New Bond Street, W1; 01-493 8080) is no longer British-owned. *Christie's* (8 King Street, SW1; 01-839 9060) – that is to say a top executive of that firm – confessed to announcing high prices realised by paintings which had been bought in. The purpose, of course, was to set artificially high levels for future sales. The effect –

dishonour and disgrace (but no sackings or resignations). In the light of such a scandal, the matter of buyers' premiums (a sly way of upping the commission for the auction house) seems of less consequence. *Christie's* have premiums of 8% plus VAT, but none at South Kensington. *Sotheby's*, *Phillips* (7 Blenheim Street, W1; 01-629 6602), *Bonham's* (Montpelier Galleries, Montpelier Street, SW7; 01-584 9161) et al hold their premium at 10% plus VAT of 15% on the 10%. But these are not honest methods, nor is it quite proper to do what many big sale-rooms do, i.e. start the bidding at £500, say, on a lot with an unannounced reserve of £2,000.

Despite these sententious carpings, it is still worthwhile, as a vendor, using the major London houses – the four mentioned above – if you have a masterpiece requiring international exposure. (In 1984 at a *Sotheby's* London sale the highest price ever paid for a work of art – £8,140,000 for an illuminated 12th century edition of the Gospels – was secured.) Also, for specialist items, such as art nouveau and art deco, model soldiers, antiquities, postcards, textiles, cameras, gramophones and records, and so on. The best place to sell general goods is *Bonsor Pennington's* of Eden Street, Kingston (01-546 0022). For some reason goods sold in their spacious salerooms (too hot in summer and too cold in winter) seem to raise some 15% more than anywhere else. Although they do not exact a premium their commission rate (17½%) is hefty.

My favourite hunting grounds for bargains have been *Phillips* in Marylebone (Hayes Place next to Lisson Grove, NW1; 01-723 2647), and *Harvey's* (14 Neal Street, WC2; 01-240 1464) in Covent Garden. *Phillips* is junky with vast job lots of glassware, toys, books and so on; you need to be sharp and quick, for the auctioneer rattles through the lots at 120-150 per hour. At *Harvey's* the 'antiques' and furniture come first, but the bankrupt stock 'by order of the sheriff' is where the real bargains are to be had. You want fifty gross of leather uppers? Harvey's is the place to get them, though parking is a serious problem. The auctioneer at Harvey's used to regale you with selections from Broadway musicals, but has become a bit solemn since they moved to their smart new premises. Extremely cheerful is the *Lots Road Galleries* (71 Lots Road, SW10; 01-352 2349). If you bring goods in on Wednesday they will sell them the following Monday and pay two days later. But there is a drawback. They have imposed an outrageous minimum 'commission' of £9 per lot, plus insurance and storage, so that when I sold a variety of goods recently at Lots Road, though the stuff sold for over £200, I was sent a cheque for a little over £60. Beware . . .

There are numerous other sales in London. Here are a few:

Frank G. Bowen (15 Greek Street, W1; 01-437 3244). Bankrupt stock including office furniture fortnightly.

Camden Auctions (The Salerooms, Hoppers Road, The Green, N21; 01-886 1550). Not in Camden at all, but Southgate. Fortnightly sales of private goods.

Dowell Lloyd (118 Putney Bridge Road, SW15; 01-788 7777) used to be amazingly squalid with mould hanging from the ceilings of a dank basement. Recently refurbished. A treasure-trove of mixed junk. Fortnightly.

Forrest's (79/85 Cobbold Road, E11; 01-534 2931). Fortnightly all-day sales under the arches of a railway bridge. An experience.

General Auctions (53/65 Garratt Lane, SW18; 01-870 3909). Bicycles, typewriters, electrical goods, jewellery, tools, brassware, bankrupt stock, W.H.Y. Every Monday at 10 a.m.

R. F. Greasby (211 Longley Road, SW17; 01-672 1100). London Transport and British Airways lost property along with tradestock. Fortnightly.

Heritage Auctions (4-6 Ellsworth Street, E2; 01-739 7348). Monday and Thursday evenings. *Very* mixed effects.

Kelly Poster (5 Falcon Grove, SW11; 01-228 1375). Fortnightly on Wednesdays. Efficiently organised. Mediocre stuff.

Moore's (217-219 Greenwich High Street, SE10; 01-858 7848). General antiques at weekly sales.

North West London Auctions (Lodge House, 9/17 Lodge Lane, N12; 01-445 9000). Weekly on Mondays at 5 p.m. Good quality antiques and household goods.

Best auction for buying: *Christie's*, South Kensington (no premiums).
Best auction for selling: *Bonsor Pennington's*.
Worst auction for buying and selling: *Southall horse sales*.
Worst auction for selling: *Lots Road*.

Ballet

Except that now it's called dance.

The Essential Guide to London commented harshly on the wrinkled decline of the *Royal Ballet*. Obviously it was an influential book, because now Anthony Dowell has taken over as dancer/director. Brian Shaw is an established star, Wendy Ellis a new talent, things will surely improve. Elsewhere Siobhan Davies may still be confidently recommended, and Michael Clark, who has diversified, should be watched whenever he stays in one place long enough to be watched. *Extemporary Dancers* have been known to go rather over the top, but they deserve praise for taking risks. *London Contemporary Dance* at The Place are as energetic as ever; Paul Taylor's 'Esplanade' was special. *Festival Ballet* under its new Danish director has disposed of Patricia Ruanne, its star, and Dr Grinaldi, its medic. Rash. *Ballet Rambert* has enhanced its reputation in an exciting time for terpsichores. The two intriguing new London companies are the *Union Dance*, who are equally adept at Indian classical ballet and modern contemporary and jazz dance. *Geographical Duvet* believe in taking dance onto the streets and spent five days last summer dancing their way across London.

Lindsay Kemp, a descendant of Will Kemp, the clown in Shakespeare's company, remains a unique general of a unique company. He produces, designs, directs and dances. John Spradbery, his regular lighting designer, is a genius too. If you have never seen Kemp, move fast. The *Sadler's Wells Theatre*, at which his company last performed in London, is being developed into a massively modern, glass-fronted Arts Centre.

You will not be surprised that this time I nominate:

Best Ballet Company: *Lindsay Kemp.*

Banks

After Edward I was unwise enough to expel the Jews, control of the money supply passed to *Lombards*; hence Lombard Street, the centre of banking today. And what a business to be in during the seventies and early eighties! As interest rates rose, so did profits; the inheritance is a mass of shining edifices (the Nat West Building supreme) which o'ertop the city's churches, and even St Paul's, proving that religion is all very well so far as it goes, but it doesn't get half as near to God as money does.

Indeed there are few good banks in London. In almost all of them the cashiers sneer openly when you ask them for money, they close when you need them to be open (a few now open on Saturday mornings), and their much advertised cash points are not to be trusted. The *TSB* remains open till 4 p.m. on weekdays, the *Giro Bank* keeps normal post office hours, and *Co-op* customers can cash cheques at some *Co-op* branches, but if you are desperate for cash at an unsociable hour, try Heathrow or the various Bureax des Changes (see below).

Now for the exceptions. *Hoare's*, with only two branches, is a venerable family bank offering the sort of services the big five used to offer. Its head office, at the sign of the Golden Bottle in Fleet Street, is a dignified architectural delight. *Lloyds Bank* in St James's Street is well-proportioned in the manner of one of the adjacent London clubs. *Barclays*, just off Park Lane, is a remarkable example of lysergic gothic, while the *Nat West* in Victoria Street, SW1 displays, above a model house, two stone squirrels hoarding nuts. *Drummond's Royal Bank of Scotland* in Spring Gardens, Trafalgar Square, is the only drive-in bank. *Coutts* seem to care.

I had one pleasant bank manager, who sang tenor in *Belshazzar's Feast* at the Albert Hall, and another, Mr Bate, who was sympathetically inclined, but nothing can erase the dreadful memory of Mr L who, holding up a huge pair of scissors, brought to him specially by his secretary, announced: 'I want you to watch this' as he sliced my Barclaycard in half. I crawled from *Barclays* a broken man, my voice an octave higher than when I went in. Mrs Barley has done what she can to restore my masculine pride, Mr Riddlestone found my account gently humorous, and Mr Camber is fond of the word 'incorrigible'.

Scattered throughout the railway and underground systems – there's one at Waterloo – and in various tourist spots, bureaux de change have been mushrooming. They are useful in a crisis but charge 5% for cashing cheques, and take no chances.

Best bank: *Hoare's*.

Beer

See under Pubs.

Benches

The very essence of a bench is that it should not draw attention to itself. But it is hard not to take pleasure from the benches along the *Victoria Embankment*. At their ends are iron camels rampant, which match, I'm sure, the camel in the *Embankment Gardens* (see under Statues). As consoling is the circular bench around the tree in *Oriel Place*, NW3. Very fine – except that you are not allowed to sit on them – are the striped benches along the walls of the striped dining room in the Adam-designed *Apsley House*, the home of the great Duke of

Wellington and choc-a-bloc with his loot including a vast (11 feet high) naked (all but a fig-leaf) statue of Napoleon in white marble by Canova.

The traditional benches in the *Great Chamber* in the Inner Court of the Law Courts are good solid oak with good solid carved feet. Sitting on them does not make you a bencher; you need to be a senior member of one of the four Inns of Court to merit that honour. The benches in the shadow of *Paper Buildings*, Middle Temple, are sheltered, elegant, and inspirational to work on. Sitting on a bench in a *McDonald's* hamburger restaurant is anything but inspirational. Like as not it will throw you off again. This discourages customers from lingering too long over their grub. When the new *Euston Station* was built there was a public outcry because no benches had been provided. Commented a spokesman: 'They would make the place look untidy.' There are a few there now, but quite inadequate. Very few in any of the stations, come to think of it.

Best benches: *Victoria Embankment*.

Betting Shops

The mid-sixties were not great just for photographers and property developers. Punters had the time of their lives as well. It was possible in *Olympia* – which is where I then lived – to find a betting shop which would happily offer one third the odds for a place in a race even if the favourite was odds on. These were the years in which the big money men like Mr Bird and Mr Bull made their fortunes; with no tax to be paid there was really no excuse for losing. Things are now sadly changed. There is little point in shopping around, for most betting shops offer the same odds. Only at the race tracks does the punter have any advantage, for there the tax is a mere 4% instead of 10%.

Currently the distressing odds on offer for place betting are as follows:

6 or 7 horses: ¼ the odds
8 or more horses, non handicap, favourite odds on: ⅙th the odds
8 or more horses, no handicap, favourite odds against: ⅕th the odds
8-11 horses, handicaps: ⅕th the odds
12-15 horses, handicaps: ¼ the odds
16-21 horses, handicaps: ⅕th the odds, 4 places
22 and more horses, handicaps: ¼ the odds, 4 places

If you can find a betting shop offering better odds than these, go there. It will not, however, be one of the big conglomerates. A few, including *John Ponder* in Goodge Street, have reduced the tax to 8%.

Amongst the major bookmakers off the racecourse the only shopping around to be done is in the ante-post market. But this is also the area in which the bookmakers have traditionally made the greatest profits. There is no justification for a two year old being quoted during the winter at less than 12/1 for a classic.

The old established family firm of *Heathorn's* has now been taken over by the more recently established family firm of *Coral's*. *Esal's* and *Marshall's* have gone the way of all horse-flesh. The big three control more and more of the high-street betting shops. With punters soon to be able to sip coffee and watch TV while losing their money, profits should continue to soar for bookmakers.

At the racecourse (q.v.), it can be profitable and fun to shop around, but few of the bookmakers in the ring are prepared to take each way bets, although account customers can always bet each way. Things are more favourable for the punter in Australia, where huge sums are punted every weekend. There is no tax paid by the punter, the odds are more favourable to him or her and ¼ the odds for a place (1st, 2nd, 3rd) are always available, even with the favourite odds on. The punter can also watch on the race-track live television coverage of other meetings, so that during the course of an afternoon at Warwick Farm, Sydney, I had 24 opportunities to make my fortune. (Not that I did!)

The only way you can hope to win without psychic powers is to bet once in your lifetime, hugely, to win, tax paid, on a horse that is well fancied. There is the story of a very rich man at Monte Carlo, who asked the management if they would remove the limits for him to bet that evening. The casino manager asked, was he standing at the tables or sitting? Sitting, said the croupier. In that case, said the manager, let him bet as heavily as he wishes. Evelyn Waugh, in whose collected letters this anecdote may be found, commented correctly that all the casino feared was one massive bet on an even chance. The moral is clear.

My favourite betting shops are those in which I have won. These include *William Hill* in Shepherd Market, W1 and *Mecca* in South Molton Lane. Most betting shops take cheques to £50 with credit cards. A disastrous development! Amazingly in Acton there is a betting shop called *James Joyce*, and several other shops called *A Stallion*. *Mecca* welcome the enjoyable Placepot bets.

Bicycles

On a bicycle you can pedal 1,600 miles – or you *ought* to be able to – before you have used the energy equivalent to one gallon of petrol. No wonder then that cycling has become popular both as a sport and as a healthy and economical form of transport. Currently there are six monthly and weekly magazines devoted to cycling – *Bicycle Action* being the most entertaining. To buy a bicycle I recommend browsing through the *Bicycle Buyers' Bible* (published by UKBMK) or the catalogues produced by *Chicken & Son* (Bisley Works, Landpark Lane, Kensworth, Dunstable, Beds LU6 2PP), by *Ron Kitching* (Hookstone Park, Harrogate, Yorks), and by *Freewheel* (275 West End Lane, London, NW6; 01-450 0768).

With prices as high as £1,200 for a bike it can be worth shopping around. I can happily recommend *London Bridge Cycles* (Railway Approach, SE1; 01-403 1690), *Brixton Bikes* (433 Coldharbour Lane, SW9; 01-733 6055), *Condor Cycles* (144/148 Gray's Inn Road, WC1; 01-837 7641), *F. W. Evans* (77/79 The Cut, SE1; 01-928 4785 with a branch in Kingston, where *Pitfield Cycles* is also recommended), *Rohan's Cycles* (451/455 Rayner's Lane, Pinner, Middx; 01-868 6262) and the posh *Cycle Logical* (136/138 New Cavendish Street, W1M 7FG; 01-637 5960).

For repairs, go to *The Bicycle Workshop* (23 Portobello Green, 281 Portobello Road, W10 5TZ; 01-960 6651) – but they don't carry BMX spares. The places to practise track-racing are *Paddington Recreation Ground* (Randolph Avenue, W9; 01-624 1688) and *Herne Hill Recreation Centre* while the *Eastway Cycle Circuit* (Lee Valley Park, Temple Mill Lane, E15; 01-534 6085) not only has the best flat – as opposed to banked – cycle track in Europe, but plenty of bikes to hire when you drive there. To avoid punctures just squeeze *Muddy Seal* into your inner tube. To hire a bike try *Dial-A-Bike* (18 Gillingham Street, SW1; 01-828 4040) or *Bike UK* (Lower Robert Street, Charing Cross, WC2; 01-839 2111 with branches in King's Cross and Putney); expect to pay about a fiver a day.

If you want to take a cycle on London Transport, you must pay a child's fare. On British Rail a charge is only levied during rush hour, but you may *not* take a bike from Finsbury Park to Moorgate, or back again.

Essential for London cyclists is a guide published by the *London Cycling Campaign*. This contains 16 pages of route maps and at 90p (£1.10 inc p&p), a mere 5p up in 3 years, is a snip. Contact the *London Cycling Campaign*, 3 Stamford Street, SE1 9NT. A membership of the campaign (£2 annually) entitles you to a newsletter, discounts, insurance, and a chance to fight for pedal-power.

Birds

There are extraordinary birds to be observed even in London. A greenish warbler was confirmed in Dollis Hill, and a cormorant was reported floating on the Thames by an apparently sober onlooker, while in our forty-feet urban garden my wife has identified goldcrests, siskins, and a flock of long-tailed tits. Any of the London reservoirs are worth watching, and south London is especially honoured by magpies, jays and crows. In *Tower Hamlets Cemetery*, Southern Grove, E3, over one hundred species of birds have been recorded. The *London Natural History Society* at the *Natural History Museum* (01-589 6323) has a strong ornithological section, and organises field meetings and weekend trips. The *London Wildlife Trust* (2 Nelson Mandela Street, NW1; 01-403 2078) co-ordinates conservation within the city.

Adjacent to London are *Broxbourne Woods*, Herts (nightingales and nightjars), *Epping Forest* (redstarts and tree pipits), the *Hilfield Park Reservoir*, Herts (a multitude of ducks and gulls), the *Perry Oaks Sewage Farm* (west of Heathrow – waders and plovers), the *Queen Mary Reservoir*, Ashford, Middlesex (gulls, grebes, terns), *Rainham Marshes*, Essex (waders), the *Rye Meads Sewage Works*, Herts, (ducks and warblers), the *Staines Reservoir* (waders, terns, and a flock of black-necked grebe), and *Walton Heath*, Surrey (warblers and great grey shrike). Within the London A-Z area the following sites are particularly rewarding;

Barn Elms Reservoir (access only by permit from the Thames Water Authority, New River Head, Rosebery Avenue, EC1); turn east along Merthyr Terrace, SW13 – the tenth best ornithological site for wildfowl in Britain.
(a)   Winter: duck including smew.
(b)   Spring and autumn: waders and terns.

Beddington Sewage Farm (access only by permit from Beddington Sewage Treatment Works, Beddington Lane, Croydon, Surrey); near Hackbridge Station.
(a)   Summer: yellow wagtail, snipe, redshank.
(b)   Other seasons: waders, snipe, short-eared owls, green sand-pipers.

Regent's Park (Baker Street Underground)
(a)   Spring: willow warbler, chiffchaff, whitethroat, lesser whitethroat, spotted flycatcher.
(b)   Autumn: pied flycatcher, redstart, wheatear, warblers, finches, thrushes, pipits, redpoll, tree sparrows, brambling.

Stoke Newington Reservoirs (no access but easily visible from the aqueduct bridge); Lordship Road, near Manor House Station.
   Winter: tufted duck, pochard, great crested grebe. (These waters stay ice-free longer than others in the London area, so that in hard weather a congregation of birds gathers here.)

Walthamstow Reservoirs (access only by permit from the Thames Water Authority, see under *Barn Elms*); the twelve reservoirs are best approached from Ferry Lane (Tottenham Hale Station). The heronry may be seen from Coppermill Lane (Walthamstow Station).
(a)   Winter: tufted duck, smew, great crested grebe.
(b)   Summer: heron, great crested grebe.

Wimbledon Common/Putney Heath (free access). Various heath and woodland birds, especially rich in the summer months.
   Finally, don't forget the bird sanctuary in St James's Park.

Best London bird-watching: *Barn Elms Reservoir.*
Worst London bird-watching: *Any underground car-park.*
Best London birds: *Greenfinches.*
Worst London birds: *The highly volatile ravens at the Tower.*

Blue Plaques

William Ewart MP, founder of the free public library, had the idea in 1863. A year later, after the scheme had been predictably rejected by the government, it found favour with the Royal Society of Arts, who commented that memorials to persons 'eminent in the arts, manufactures and commerce' might give pleasure to 'travellers up and down in omnibuses etc.' who would thus beguile 'a not very rapid progress through the streets'. How little London has changed! A hundred years after Ewart had his brainwave, he too was commemorated by a plaque at 16 Eaton Place, SW1.
   By 1981, 438 official plaques had been erected in London besides those rogue plaques put up by individuals and societies. Over one

hundred blue plaques are to be found in Westminster, while, at the time of writing, Barking, Enfield, Havering, Hillingdon, Kingston and Waltham Forest cannot muster one plaque between them.

The memorial to *Arthur Lucan* ('Old Mother Riley') at 11 Forty Lane, Wembley was opposed in 1978 by the Conservative GLC member for Brent North who claimed that the Labour controlled Council wanted the plaque 'as a misguided effort to curry popular favour'. But music hall entertainers have fared well as have insignificant British artists. *Karl Marx's* plaque has been smashed on two occasions and he now has one high up on the wall at Leoni's Quo Vadis Restaurant in Dean Street, Soho. *Lenin* received one when 16 Percy Street, W1 where he stayed in 1905, became the Royal Scot Hotel in 1972. The previous building on the site had been a vicarage!

A recent letter to the Times complained that, while Southwark commemorated the sites of the *White Hart* and *Queen's Head* inns in Borough High street with plaques, the Tabard, celebrated by Chaucer in 'The Canterbury Tales' was ignored. I took this up with the librarian at the John Harvard Library, who explained that copper plaques were regularly stolen and that it would be replaced with porcelain. 'Historic Southwark' has been extremely conscientious in identifying its most interesting features. Other boroughs take note!

The 'best' blue plaque can only be a matter of taste. How gratifying that *Annie Besant*, organiser of the Match Girls, is remembered at 39 Colby Road, SE19. Similarly commemorated are *Mark Gertler* (32 Elder Street, E1), a brilliant but tormented artist, *Harry Relph*, alias *Little Tich* (93 Shirehall Park, NW4) who had an extra finger on each hand and still made folk bellow with laughter, *Violette Szabo GC* (18 Burnley Road, SW9), who gave her life for the French Resistance and *Chaim Weizmann* (67 Addison Road, W14), who helped to win the Great War and found the state of Israel.

The blue plaque on Chatham House, St James's Square, SW1, commemorates three Prime Ministers. The worst plaques must be those naming *John Dryden* (Gerrard Street, W1), *Joshua Reynolds* (Great Newport Street, WC2), and *Lady Di* and *Topham Beauclerk* at Great Russell Street, WC2. All are attached to the wrong houses. But perhaps the most ill-advised plaque, in the light of later events, is that to *Charles de Gaulle* (14 Carlton Gardens, SW1). In the words of Winston Churchill: 'He had to be rude to the British to prove to French eyes that he was not a British puppet. He certainly carried out this policy with perseverance'. For further details see Caroline Daker's excellent *The Blue Plaque Guide to London* (Macmillan).

Bollards

Most Georgian bollards were made from disused cannon, their mouths blocked for ever with cannon balls. This, a 19th-century version of swords into ploughshares, accounts for the traditional shape, which may be seen in excellent repair in *India Street*, EC3, at the north end of *Old Barge House Alley*, Blackfriars, and elsewhere throughout London. Most London bollards date from the years immediately after Waterloo, the battle, many thought, to end all wars. Two fine old bollards marked 'SOMMERS TOWN 1817' may be spied in *Pancras Road*, and in *Great Suffolk Street* and profusely scattered around *Bankside* and *Borough Market* are bollards marked 'Clink' with the date either 1812 or 1825. These originate from the Clink Pavement Company. A magnificent row of seven old bollards stands guard over *Puma Court*, beloved of Dickens, and just off *Commercial Street*, E1.

There are bollards shaped like antique rockets in the *Strand*, and bollards made from shells outside the *Imperial War Museum*. In *Gracechurch Street*, EC3, the bollards are inset with coats of arms, and in *Cavendish Court*, W1, they are extremely suggestive. *Gough Square*, EC4, where Dr Johnson's House stands amidst the alien concrete, is generously sprinkled with attractive examples, but amongst the worst bollards, those in and around *Leicester Square* (a square which defies anything anyone seems able to do to improve it) are reminiscent of amputated limbs, or plastic pencil-sharpeners, or both. The ugly ones in *Tottenham Street*, W1 (corner of Tottenham Court Road) appear to unscrew though I haven't yet succeeded.

I am indebted to a Barclays' bank manager for directing my attention to some of the above. A bank manager who is tired of bollards is tired of life.

Best bollards: *India Street*.
Worst bollards: *Leicester Square* and *Browning Road, E11*.

Bookshops

The British book business, worth about £1.15 billion in 1984, is undergoing an upheaval. The chains have taken over from the independents, 36% of whom, it is claimed by the Bookseller's Association, are trading at a loss. Thus we find *Hammicks* with seventeen shops in the UK, *Webster's*, a subsidiary of *W. H. Smith's* with fifteen shops, and *Penguin* with eight shops. The *Blackwell Group*, who have over 75% of the academic market, have 52 shops, *Pentos*, with *Hudson's*, *Dillon's* and *Athena* under its wing, 81 shops, and *W. H. Smith* with some 25% of the whole market. Latest on the scene is *Tim Waterstone* with six London shops and a turnover of £7m in 1984. His policy is to stay open till 10 p.m. seven days a week and to sell books from the minority publishers as well as the posh ones. Cheekily, he set up shop next door to *Foyle's*. Other London based companies include *Hatchard's* with six outlets (a good and glitzy one in Richmond). *Hatchard's*, part of the Collins group, has recently purchased the *Claude Gill* shops. The original *Hatchard's* (187 Piccadilly, W1; 01-439 9921) is the oldest bookshop in London, architecturally delightful and awash with enthusiasm and new fiction; it is not easy to leave such a bookshop empty-handed.

The *Kilburn Bookshop* (8 Kilburn High Road, NW6; 01-388 7071) will 'get anything', and at the celebrated *Heywood Hill Bookshop* (10 Curzon Street, W1; 01-629 0647) they not only know their books but have also read them. Those who report that 'it is not what it was' may be referring to the days when Nancy Mitford served there. Some confuse it with the *High Hill Bookshop* (6 Hampstead High Street, NW3; 01-435 2218) which combines great enthusiasm for local authors with impressive knowledge of literature and the trade.

Maggs in Berkeley Square (No 50, 01-499 2501), which is very grand and has a good line in private press books and autographed letters, is a family concern par excellence. Their shop is haunted but the ghosts seem to be a little soporific these days (see under Ghosts). *Maggs* and *Bertram Rota* (4 Savile Row, W1; 01-734 3860 – strong in first and limited editions) have been staunch in their continuing campaign against the Ring, more active in the world of book auctions than elsewhere. The most remarkable examples of antique manuscripts and texts can be found at *Quaritch* (3 Lower John Street, W1; 01-734 2983).

Dillon's (1 Malet Street, WC1; 01-636 1577), the academic specialist, has possibly the most knowledgeable staff of all and a carefully selected and arranged stock. *Grant and Cutler* (11 Buckingham Street, WC2; 01-839 3136) is excellent for foreign language books. *Mandarin Books* (22 Notting Hill Gate, W11; 01-229 0327) is chaotic, but you will find books there that you will find nowhere else. Thus *Compendium* (234 Camden High Street, NW1; 01-485 8944/267 1525). At *Compendium* you can buy American literature, African books, and various subversive publications, intended to change the world – whether for better or worse seems immaterial. If you wish to change the world cheaply, try *Collet's London Bookshop* (64/66 Charing Cross Road, WC2; 01-836 6306), one of dozens of bookshops which have given this undistinguished street (besides St Martin's School of Art) a real raison d'être. Visit *Waterstone's* (121/125 Charing Cross Road, WC2; 01-434 4391) with other branches, (including one at 99/101 Old Brompton Road, SW7; 01-581 8522/3), for good general stock and friendly service, *Collet's Penguin Bookshop* (64-66 Charing Cross Road, WC2) for every Penguin title in print, and some out of print, and *Silver Moon* (68 Charing Cross Road, WC2; 01-836 7906) for feminist books, wholefood cakes and herbal tea. *Books Etc*. (120 Charing Cross Road, WC2; 01-379 6838, and other branches) has a good stock of popular titles.

And what about *Foyle's:* (191-121 Charing Cross Road, WC2; 01-437 5660). Christina's policy towards her staff and the antiquated system, which makes it almost impossible to buy and pay for books without giving up your entire holidays so to do, make a trip to *Foyle's* an experience many would not like to repeat. Once, when I asked at the enquiry desk for Richard Clutterbuck's book on the urban guerilla, I was sent to the natural history department! Recently *Foyle's* has taken to classifying books on the shelves by publisher, leading to further mayhem. However it is only fair to add that *Foyle's* stock is one of the wonders of the world, and that, where any normal bookshop would have two or three copies of books about Ruskin or Czechoslovakian wildlife, *Foyle's* will have thirty-seven. Life without *Foyles* would be blander and duller and less frustrating.

Finally in Charing Cross Road don't forget *Zwemmer's* at 76-80 (01-836 4710), unparalleled for books on the fine arts. Nearby is *Bondy* for miniature books, (16 Little Russell Street, W1; 01-405 2737), and *Cecil Court*, which is worth half an hour of anybody's time. Amongst intriguing shops there is *Dance Books* (9 Cecil Court, WC2; 01-836 2314). This of course is conveniently near to Floral Street, where everybody dances, and the *Coliseum*, where ballerinas do. Actors go to the *Samuel French Theatre Bookshop* (52 Fitzroy Street, W1; 01-387 9373) which contains a vast selection of playscripts as well as sound effects, records, and books on the theatre. Horsey people clip clop to *J. A. Allen* (1 Lower Grosvenor Place, Buckingham Palace Road, SW1; 01-834 5606), a charmingly decorative little place. The best shop for 20th century first editions is *Bell, Book & Radmall Ltd* (80 Long Acre, WC2; 01-240 2161). *Baldur Books* (44 Hill Rise, Richmond; 01-940 1214) is run by Eric, an eccentric who once invited me to take over the shop. He sees bookselling as a branch of the social services – 'they spend 30 years hunting down a book and then buy it from me for sixty pence!'

28

Two excellent children's bookshops in the area are *Langton's* (Church Street, Twickenham; 01-892 3800 – adult books too), and *The Lion and the Unicorn* (19 King Street, Richmond; 01-940 0483), where there is a mat for children to sit on and a wide range of picture books. *Al Sagri* (26 Westbourne Grove, London, W2 5RH) is for Arab books; the *Virago Bookshop* (34 Southampton Street, WC2; 01-240 6638) is for Virago Press books in particular and feminist books in general. *Forbidden Planet* (23 Denmark Street, WC2; 01-836 4179) is for sci-fi and comics while their branch at 58 St Giles High Street, WC2 (01-379 6042) is for material on films and TV. The *Pan Bookshop* (158 Fulham Road, SW10; 01-373 4997) is open seven days a week, till 10.30 p.m. on weekdays and *Peter Eaton* (80 Holland Park, W11; 01-727 5211) has one of the best stocks of second-hand books in the West End. For legal, naval and military subjects try *Francis Edwards* (83 Marylebone High Street, W1; 01-935 9221, also Charing Cross Road) in splendid new purpose-built premises. The *Costume Bookshop* (Queen's Elm Parade, Fulham Road, Old Church Street, SW3) is best for costume and *The Travel Bookshop* (13 Blenheim Crescent, W11) is best for – wait for it! – travel. The *Owl Bookshop* (211 Kentish Town Road, NW5; 01-485 7793) and *Central Books* (37 Gray's Inn Road, WC1; 01-242 6166) are recommended for general stock. *Ian Sheridan's Bookshop* in Sunbury, just a hop from Hampton Court, is rather special.

Then there is *W. H. Smith*, who probably sell more books than all other British bookshops put together. I was not too polite in *The Essential Guide to London* about *Smith's* bookselling, but it has certainly improved in the last few years. Of course the emphasis is still on best-sellers, and middle-of-the-road books, but lay-out in the larger branches is sensible, and a worthwhile selection of hardback fiction is usually available. The manager at the Richmond branch is rude.

This is an engrossing and substantial area for study. I conclude by recommending:
(a)   *Bookshops of London* by Diana Stephenson (Roger Lascelles £3.95), and
(b)   The highly idiosyncratic *Drift's Guide to all the Secondhand and Antiquarian Bookshops in Britain* (£4.50 plus 45p post and packing from BCM Driffield, London, WC1 3XX or from bookshops). Just one sample quote: 'Major contender for most irritating bookshop in London. Goes in for third degree, overprices the wrong books and waxes eloquent. He is in the middle of writing his memoirs and uses the customers as a test bed. It must be the only shop in Britain where sales shoot up when the owner is away.'

Best London Bookshop: *Waterstone's* (various branches).

Worst London Bookshops: Remaindered stock in short-lease premises with emphasis on books of soft focus nude photography.

Bottlenecks and How to Avoid Them

The worst bottlenecks in London are:

(a)   Westway/Marylebone Road/Euston Road

What makes this bottleneck particularly depressing is the continuing views of planners' blight as you sit sniffing the carbon monoxide. The underpass proved a waste of time and money. How to avoid it?

(Going east) up Cosway Street, right into Shroton Street, left up Lisson Grove, right into St John's Wood Road, right into Park Road, into Regent's Park at Hanover Gate, left around the Outer Circle, out of the park at Gloucester Gate, left along Parkway, right along Camden High Street, left along Crowndale Road into Pancras Road, and through to King's Cross.

(Going west) into Regent's Park at Park Crescent, left along Outer Circle, out of the Park at Hanover Gate, right along Park Street, left along Lodge Road, left along Lisson Grove, right along Church Street, straight over Edgware Road (by the cinema), left around Paddington Green, right into the Harrow Road and follow the signs for the A40(M).

(b)   Knightsbridge

Should be avoided whenever possible, either by use of South Carriage in Hyde Park (enter either at Exhibition Road or Park Close) or via Beauchamp Place/Pont Street/Chesham Place/Chapel Street into Grosvenor Place.

(c)   Hammersmith Flyover and the Great West Road

Can best be avoided by using (going west) Hammersmith Bridge, turning right along Lonsdale Road/The Terrace/Mortlake High Street and the Lower Richmond Road, recrossing the river (if you wish to) at Twickenham Bridge and so to the M4 or – better since it's usually clear – the M3 and the M25. The same system works just as well going east.

(d)   Hampstead's Heath Street and Fitzjohn's Avenue

Can be desperate. Frognal Lane, Frognal and Lower Terrace may be your salvation (a pretty route anyway). Use West End Lane rather than Finchley Road to get to Frognal Lane, but don't try it on Friday evenings at all.

(e) Staples Corner, where the Edgware Road crosses the North Circular

There is a way of avoiding this mess, but, alas, I'm sworn to secrecy. The North Circular is quite the worst London road for traffic (worse even than the South Circular), but for journeys which skirt North London there seems no sensible alternative. Get a decent stereo set in your car and let Mozart's flute concertos ease away your cares.

(f) Archway Road, N6

Bad going north and south. Use Highgate Hill/Highgate High Street/North Road and North Hill.

(g) Southampton Row

This may be avoided by the cunning use of Bloomsbury Square, Bedford Place or Montague Street, and Russell Square.

(h) Old Kent Road and New Cross

Use Rotherhithe New Road/Evelyn Street and Creek Road to Greenwich (or the same in reverse). This is usually a worthwhile diversion, especially during the rush hours.

(i) Streatham High Street

Travelling north between midday and 3 p.m. Don't.

As a general rule it saves petrol (and pollution) to switch off your engine if you're likely to remain static for more than thirty seconds.
   Safe journey.

Boules

You may be surprised to hear that the curious activity indulged in by Gauloise-smoking, bereted, French bit-part actors has spread to London. I mean boules. All you need is chutzpah and steel balls to play successfully and more than 140 teams compete for the London Standard Boules Championship, held in Battersea Park. If there are other venues this side of the channel perhaps you'll be kind enough, in the interests of accuracy, to let me know.

Bowls

There has been a revolution on the greens. Television and

sponsorship have produced money and money has produced a generation of young players. The best thing about bowls is that you don't have to be fit. It is not a class sport, but it does have its prejudices; men and women have separate clubs. There are three kinds of bowls, flat greens, federation bowls and crown greens. In London and the South flat greens are used.

Once you have your set of woods – they have glamorous names such as Tyrolites, Lignoids, Jackfinders and Henselites and come from *Thurston's* (220 Camden High Street, NW1; 01-267 5367) and *Sullivan & Co* (Dept B1, 1334 Greenford Road, Greenford, Middlesex; 01-422 2347) – which should last your lifetime, bowls is one of the cheaper sports. It is ideal, of course, for those who no longer care to leap around. The most select club is the *Royal Household Club*, whose members are the royal staff at Windsor Castle and Buckingham Palace and who bowl at Home Park, Windsor. One of their regular fixtures is with another exclusive club, the one at Wormwood Scrubs Prison.

The City Institutions play at *Finsbury Circus Gardens*, but the most famous London club is *Paddington*, a green glade amidst the concrete jungle. For full details the English Bowling Association (2A Iddesleigh Road, Bournemouth. Tel 22233) should be contacted. Or subscribe to *Bowls International* (85p) or *World Bowls* (80p). It is remarkable that in Britain more people play bowls at 2,660 clubs than any other sport.

Best Bowling: *Paddington*.

Brasseries

Properly a 'brasserie' means a brewery (q.v.). It came to mean a café, often near a railway station serving food and drink to those on their way to or from work. A brasserie should at least serve hearty refreshment in a casual atmosphere, ideally with a long chrome-edged bar for those in a hurry. It should be open from early morning to late at night. Not many of the so-called London brasseries would qualify. And an *authentic* brasserie also serves Alsatian food, such as onion soup, sausages with mustard, herring with potato salad, that sort of thing. And it does not impose a minimum charge. I would cite seven contenders for the most agreeable brasserie, in alphabetical order, thus:

Café Pelican, (45 St Martin's Lane, WC2; 01-379 0309). It's unusual for a London Electricity Board showroom to convert into a café, but this one did successfully. The chef, Gerard Mosiniak, is from Alsace, which is an enormous plus. You can eat at the long bar, washing down your charcuterie or baguette sandwiches with a French beer called Pelican, or rather more grandly at the commodious restaurant at the back. Marvellous patisserie by the ex-pastry-cook of the Dorchester, but the mange touts had been cooked in stale butter. Jazz and music of the 20s and 30s entertains you (if you find such music entertaining), and the roast beef is superb.

Camden Brasserie, (216 Camden High Street, NW1; 01-482 2114). Spacious and functional with excellent straightforward food at about £14 per head. Everything freshly cooked to order and those elegant shoe string chips, which children complain about (they get washed away by the ketchup) but grown-ups prefer.

Criterion Brasserie, (Piccadilly, W1; 01-839 7133). This too contains a bar and a restaurant and, considering that Charles Forte does not hail from Alsace, is most authentic with cassoulet, French sausages and so on. What is spectacular is Thomas Verity's design. Marble and malachite and lapis lazuli under a ceiling of gold mosaic – lord knows what they'd make of it in Alsace but it is a very welcome addition to the pathetic quality of Piccadilly Circus establishments.

The Hermitage, (19 Leigh Street, WC1; 01-387 8034). Here, encouragingly close to a major railway station – King's Cross/St Pancras – is a neighbourhood cafe upstairs with an intimate room downstairs. Although the menu is more ambitious than at a traditional brasserie (monkfish, skate in black butter, that sort of thing), the hours of 9 a.m. to 11 p.m. are authentic and so is the price (about £11 a head).

La Brasserie, (Brompton Road, SW3, 01-584 1666). Actually modelled on *La Coupole* and *Paris Flo*, this has round the wall benches, mirrors, fans in the ceiling, and two long bars – just like the Parisian version of the real thing (viz Brasserie 1920 at the Gare du Nord). It opens at 8 a.m. and stays open to midnight. Most of the food is of Alsatian origin – pig's trotters grilled in mustard and vinegar, tranche of lamb with haricots – and the prices are fair, though the wine seems a bit rich.

Soho Brasserie, (23/25 Old Compton Street, W1; 01-439 9301/3758). In several details the *Soho Brasserie* loses marks. It does not open until noon. It closes for three hours in the afternoon. It is not particularly cheap. It is alarmingly trendy. The waitresses kept looking over my shoulder when taking my order to see if anyone better had come in. So, after a while, did I! But the food is fine, and the atmosphere is not only accurate, but ideal for Old Compton Street. And people seemed delightfully cheerful there despite the crowds.

Surinder's Café Brasserie, (43 Hereford Road, W2; 01-221 9192). Open 9.30 a.m.-11.30 p.m. Tuesday to Saturday, this intimate and informal café is near enough to Paddington Station to qualify. But a set menu (£8.50) and cherry cheesecake are not much to do with brasseries, though the chef's friendliness is pleasant. I'm not even sure a brasserie should have a chef; a patron instead, I suspect.

On the whole I prefer brasseries to hamburger (q.v.) joints, and the new fashion is to be welcomed, don't you think?

Best Brasserie: *Café Pelican*.

P.S. There are a score or more co-called 'brasseries' in London (many of them Indian) which I have not dealt with in this section, because, although they might claim to, they really *don't* belong.

Brass Rubbing

As a congenial, harmless and even modestly interesting hobby, brass rubbing is ideal. There is only one drawback; what to do with the pictures you produce?

The *London Centre* is at St James's Church, Piccadilly, W1; (01-437 6023), which is open every day of the year from 10 a.m. to 6 p.m. (on Sundays midday to 6 p.m.). There is a small charge (about £2.50) but this includes the cost of all the materials you will need and some basic instructions. Get rubbing . . .

An exhibition at St James's of old church brasses includes Celtic designs from the Books of Kells and Durrow and historical subjects such as Robert the Bruce and the Black Prince.

An alternative brass rubbing centre is *All Hallows Church*, Byward Street, EC3.

Best Brass Rubbing: *St James's Church*, Piccadilly, W1.

Bread

If you think a baguette is where you put the baby to sleep, this entry is not for you.

Harrods can offer the customer 130 kinds of loaf, though none of them is baked on the premises, but since you normally eat only one at a time, I recommend either *Dugdale and Adams* (3 Gerrard Street, W1; 01-437 3864) for their French loaves, *Bonne Bouche* (22 Bute Street, SW7; 01-584 9839) for their black bread, *Justin de Blank's Hygienic*

Bakery (46 Walton Street, SW3; 01-589 4734) for its entire range, or the *Bamboo Grove Wholefoods* (100 Park Avenue, NW10; 01-965 8549) for its granaries. *Goswell Bakeries Ltd* (Caxton Street North, E16; 01-474 6141) which also specialises in 'natural' breads, will deliver. *W. H. Summers* (323 Fulham Road, SW10; 01-352 8286) bakes bread throughout the day. The best Jewish bread for Friday nights (if you can't bake it yourself) comes from *Grodzinski* (13 Brewer Street, W1; 01-437 6007 and other branches). And at *Perry's Bakery* (151 Earl's Court Road, SW5; 01-370 4825) you can buy excellent bread and buns along with Bulgarian pastries.

If I had to choose one I would go for *Dugdale and Adams*, which has a fan club of passionate office workers whose lunch time would be drab indeed without their daily fix. The bread is cooked in 100 year old Vienna ovens with low ceilings and steam injection. They supply Buckingham Palace and many Soho restaurants.

Best Baker: *Dugdale and Adams*.

P.S. Mother's Pride thick white sliced makes quite the best fried bread.

Breakfasts

It goes without saying that any of those establishments described under Brasseries (see above), except for the *Soho Brasserie*, will serve you a worthwhile breakfast. Here though I'm dealing with specialists. In the past I have recommended the *Connaught's* breakfast (Carlos Place, W1; 01-499 7070). They make a marvellous kedgeree but on my last visit it was served hot around the edges and stone cold within, and on a previous visit they refused to serve one of my friends, an eminent writer who was wearing a polo-neck instead of a suit and tie like the rest of us, and then tried to charge me for the coffee I'd drunk before being thrown out; no, that really won't do. Also they should itemise the bill. *Claridges* (Brook Street, W1; 01-629 8860) was far more welcoming, but alas, the kedgeree wasn't up to much.

For the perfect breakfast, it's necessary to travel east. The *Quality Chop House* (94 Farringdon Street, EC1 – no 'phone) is the place. Polished wooden pews house night-shift workers, Fleet Street reporters, and gents from the city offices studying the racing form. Breakfast special advertised on the blackboard may include kippers (£1.30 the pair), haddock fillets (perfect for breakfast at £1.45) or fried liver with bubble and squeak (£1.35). Eddy Enrico has followed in his father's footsteps by serving these splendid collations for 42 years; on the window he is described as a 'Progressive Working Man's Caterer' and so he is.

Other recommendations: the *Regent Palace Hotel* (12 Sherwood Street, W1; 01-734 7000) is where chefs congregate for breakfast on their mornings off; you can get porridge at *Diana's Diner* (30 Endell Street, WC2; 01-240 0272) and Coopers Marmalade with excellent coffee at the *Betjeman Room* in the *Charing Cross Hotel* adjoining the station. Black pudding and fried bread may be enjoyed at *Arthur's Restaurant* in Smithfield (60 Long Lane, EC1; 01-600 8243) while at the *Fox and Anchor* (115 Charterhouse Street, EC1; 01-253 4838) order the Full House at £2.95 – a massive fry-up. Kidneys as well as kedgeree are on the menu at another pub, the *Albert* (Victoria Street, SW1) though you may have to rub shoulders with MPs, drooping after an all-night sitting.

Peter's (59 Pimlico Road, SW1; 01-730 5991) which is spanking clean opens at 7 a.m. and does egg and bacon or splendid bangers, just like mother used to cook them (or better depending on mother).

Upmarket is the Hyatt Carlton Tower's *Chelsea Room* (Cadogan Place, SW1; 01-235 5411). Here you have privacy and a choice of newspapers with either an English breakfast at £7.50 or a continental breakfast at £5.50. Both excellent. Fifty pence less for both kinds of breakfast is charged at *Pavillion* (Grosvenor House, Park Lane, W1; 01-499 6363); you eat amidst pillars and a jungle of plants. At the *Sheraton Park Tower* (Knightsbridge, SW1; 01-235 8050) in an Edwardian ambiance you can have not just the continental (£4.50) or English (£6.75) or buffet (£5.75) breakfast, but a breakfast which will involve you in a rumpsteak with a fried egg on top (£9.75). I have excellent reports of *The White House Hotel* breakfasts, though the service is slow, and dreadful reports of breakfast at *Brown's Hotel* (Dover Street, W1; 01-493 6020). Confirm or deny please. According to the *Good Food Guide*, whose reports can often be accurate, the best breakfasts are to be had at the *Coffee House* of the *Inter-Continental Hotel* (1 Hamilton Place, W1; 01-409 3131). Maybe.

For more tender stomachs, the continental breakfast is recommended. Coffee, brioches, croissants and sympathy may safely be enjoyed at *Sagne* (105 Marylebone High Street, W1; 01-935 6240) where there is a mural of Lake Geneva (why not?), at *Maison Bertaux* (28 Greek Street, W1; 01-437 6007 closed Mondays) and at *Patisserie Valerie* (44 Old Compton Street, W1; 01-437 3466), which is the place for dewy-eyed lovers tucking into French croissants while recalling crumpled sheets.

Also recommended: *Bacon and Eggs* (South Molton Street, W1),

La Campannia (5 Vigo Street, W1; 01-734 8353), *The Cherry Top* (Paddington Street, W1), *Chubbies* (22-23 Liverpool Street, EC2; 01-283 3504) and the *Old Burlington* (140 Old Burlington Street, W1; 01-734 6177).

Sunday brunches are particularly trendy at *Le Caprice* (Arlington Street, W1; 01-629 2239) – smoked salmon and scrambled eggs (£4.50); at *Truffles* (Portman Hotel, Portman Square, W1; 01-486 5844) – Okra Seafood Gumbo with rice (£5.50); and at *Le Soufflé* (Hotel Intercontinental, 1 Hamilton Place, W1; 01-439 3131) which boasts a Michelin Rosette.

More modest, old-fashioned, friendly and kosher is the *Cosmo* (5 Northways Parade, NW3; 01-722 2627) and, in the heart of Hackney, *Quinns* (138 Columbia Road, E2; 01-739 9090) does a Sunday breakfast at £2.50 for the Columbia Road market traders. Excellent breakfasts may be had at the *Pont Street Cabbie Shelter* (and other cabbie shelters). But these are *not* open to the public.

Best Breakfast: *Quality Chop House* (down market).
Hyatts Carlton Tower Chelsea Room (upmarket).
Best Brunch: *Cosmo.*

Breweries

No doubt about the best brewery in London. The accolade goes to *Young's Ram Brewery* in Wandsworth High Street. Not only is there a beautiful brewer's house attached to the brewery and a friendly tap with real ale, but in the back yard you may meet several geese beak to beak, as well as Gertie the goat and, naturally enough, a ram. There is also a golden one on the weather-cock. From this brewery there is a horse-drawn delivery (by dray horses) to establishments within three miles.

Whitbread's Brewery in Chiswell Street, EC1 incorporates a courtyard enclosed by well-restored 18th century buildings. But the most intriguing feature of the Brewery may be found in the *Porter Tun Room*, an impressive place in which to give a banquet, for it boasts a king-post roof, sixty feet high. Also at *Whitbread's* is the *Speaker's Coach*, built in 1698, and portraits of the first three Samuel Whitbreads painted by Reynolds, Gainsborough and George Richmond.

Another fine old brewery is *Truman's* in Brick Lane E1, against whose wall grows a fine fig tree. Both the building – residential as well as commercial – and I suspect, the tree, are late Regency.

Best Brewery: *Young's Ram Brewery.*

Bridges

William Overs was a ferryman at the point where the old Roman Road from the coast met the Thames. Though business was good (for in the 10th century there were still no bridges over the river) he was mean as hell, and conceived an ingenious idea for cutting down on the housekeeping. If he pretended to be dead, the family would go into mourning and fast, at least for a day or two. He pretended to be dead, and was appalled when his family at once proclaimed a feast to celebrate the event. At the feast he rose from his recumbent posture in a state of high moral disapproval, but one of the guests, an oarsman, alarmed by this supernatural vision, struck him on the head with an oar and killed him instantly. Mary, the ferryman's daughter, sent for her boyfriend – her late father had disapproved of the lad and forbidden him the house – but in his haste to be with his beloved he spurred his horse so violently that he toppled off, receiving injuries which proved fatal. Disconsolate, Mary used the profits of the ferry to found a convent to which the Church of St Mary Overie, later St Saviour's, later Southwark Cathedral, was attached, and in due course, there being no ferryman, London Bridge was built on the site.

(This story is such an entertaining one that I included it under B for bridges so that you wouldn't have to wait until F for ferries (q.v.) where it more properly belongs).

There were many London bridges after the original wooden one (an arch of which is preserved in the London Museum). The first stone one, 180 feet further down the river than the original one, was built to the order of Henry II between 1176 and 1209. On it were houses and shops, with a chapel in the middle. At either end were gates on the spikes on which the heads of traitors were exposed.

The water rushed around the piles of the 19 narrow arches making the bridge a danger to shipping and a challenge to young men for whom 'shooting' the bridge was an excellent, if dangerous, sport.

The old bridge was replaced in 1831 by a granite structure, designed and built by the Rennie family at a cost of two million pounds. All the London bridges have been subjected to horrific traffic jams, and Rennie's bridge proving inadequate, *London Bridge* was exported to Lake Havasu City, Arizona, being replaced by the present bridge of pre-stressed concrete (Harold K. King 1972). There were unkind rumours that what the consortium of businessmen thought they were buying was *Tower Bridge*. One arch of Rennie's bridge may be seen in Kew Gardens.

There are 26 bridges between Teddington and the Tower. (A 27th is to be built below the Tower at Thamesmead.)

Tower Bridge may not be beautiful ('steel skeletons clothed with stone' was the architect's description), but it has raised and lowered its twin bascules, each weighing 1000 tons, some half million times since the bridge was built almost a hundred years ago. The pedestrian way was such an attraction to suicides that it had to be closed but recently it has been redeveloped as a tourist attraction.

Waterloo Bridge, a clean and graceful design by Gilbert Scott, completed in 1939, is renowned more for the view from than the view of it ('earth hath not anything to show more fair . . .'). *Albert Bridge*, a cantilever and suspension affair (R. W. Ordish 1873) looks especially glamorous at night and has more distinction than most of the Thames bridges. Myself, I have a silly fondness for *Hammersmith Bridge*, a suspension bridge designed by Bazalgette furnished with statues underneath where there shouldn't be statues – there was money left over from the subscriptions – and over-elaborate lights on top; but it works.

Richmond Bridge is a fine old bridge, 250 years old, beautifully proportioned and perfectly placed where the river curves. It looks best from the water, however, or from a couple of hundred yards up the Surrey bank.

Despite the claims of *Tower, Waterloo, Albert, Hammersmith* and *Richmond* bridges, and with a happy sigh for Telford's retractable iron bridge at St Katharine's Docks, I think the prize belongs to *Rennie's* five-arched stone bridge over the Serpentine. Everybody loves it and the views from it, and rightly so, but driving over it you scarcely notice it. Since we've lost two of *Rennie's* bridges, we should treasure this one.

There are numerous bad bridges, *Vauxhall* and *Hungerford* railway bridges, *Battersea* (Bazalgette again) and *Cannon Street* are without much distinction. Many dislike the railway bridge between Strand-on-the-Green and Kew; I like it for its iron soul. Another fine iron bridge crosses the Regent's Canal at *Camden Lock*; this too makes few claims to beauty and so achieves it.

Recently, London lost a bridge. The old iron railway bridge at *Blackfriars* was removed by a giant Dutch crane in one fell swoop. The 12 sixty-foot piles remain, and British Rail has capped them with concrete and painted them bright red, like amputated stumps still oozing blood. A prize should be offered for the most imaginative use of these staunch survivors.

Best Bridge: *The Rennie Serpentine Bridge.*
Worst Bridge: *Cannon Street Railway.*

Brothels

I am sorry to be unable to make any recommendations in this category. My research for the previous edition of this book – *The Essential Guide to London* (Sphere Books 1984, something of a Collector's Item by now) – was so traumatic that I was unable to stiffen up my sinews sufficiently to provide my readers with the information they have so cheerfully paid for.

It may be useful though to know the law whether you are in the business of supply or demand. Prostitution per se is not illegal. Soliciting, loitering with intent and kerb-crawling are. If you sit at the window of your house seductively and people are encouraged to come up and see you sometime, why, that's just fine. But if two of you share a room and take money for 'it', that's a brothel. Cynthia Payne, once brothel-keeper, is now a Personality. Willie Donaldson once a 'pimp', is now a deservedly successful writer. *King's Cross* in general, and *Argyle Square* in particular, have been cleaned up. (How strange that *King's Cross* in Sydney, Australia and *King's Cross* in London should both specialise in this form of therapy.) The girls nostalgic for the past, have drifted back to Bayswater and Soho. Sussex Gardens and Great Windmill Street, to be exact. The boys still hang around the 'meat-rack' at Piccadilly Circus, but the threat of AIDS is a powerful detumescent. Even the licensee of the *Silver Cross* (33 Whitehall, SW1) denies my claim that he has a licence from Charles I to run a brothel. Heigh-ho.

As they say in the Good Food Guide, more reports please. See also under Prostitutes.

Budget Restaurants

Bad food is never cheap. The nastiest food I have eaten in London recently has been in the *Café* at the Victoria Coach Station, but there the surroundings are so squalid that even the best food would seem unappetising. There is a strong argument for an automat in such a place, where the constant demand is for conveyor-belt type food. Similar remarks could apply to the food at many of our most popular tourist attractions, although Madame Tussaud's has put its house in order.

The *Churchill Theatre*, Bromley, the *Oval House*, Kennington, the *Royal Festival Hall* and the *National Film Theatre* are a good deal better than the *Natural History Museum*, and *Young Vic* or the *Albery Theatre*. The *National Theatre* has an excellent restaurant, but the snacks are poor (especially the chocolate cake) and the coffee is weak.

Your only chance to eat substantially and well for a pound or so is to opt for fish and chips (q.v.), baked potatoes with various fillings (at Spud-U-Like branches) or an unfashionable pub, but the best quality food at modest prices may often be found at those theatres, art galleries and cinemas that take the trouble to cater. The best was, and is, the *Lyric Theatre Buffet* (King Street, Hammersmith, W6; 01-741 2311) where soups, stews, baked potatoes, salads and cakes are all excellent. About £4 a head.

The *Everest Café* in Portobello Road serves huge mountains of succulent food on oval meat dishes from a varied menu ranging from fry-ups through roasts to curries. You need not pay more than £3 or so.

The four *Cooke's* eel and pie houses, one at 41 Kingsland Road, E8 (01-254 2878), one at 48 Goldhawk Road, W12 (01-743 7630), one at 9 Broadway Market, E8 (01-254 6458) and one at The Cut SE1, (01-928 5931) are crowded, unlicensed, and excellent value at no more than £3.50 a head. At the first you sit at marble tables and the cabaret consists of live eels in a tank; at the others it's wooden benches and formica surfaces.

Nontas (16 Camden High Street, NW1; 01-387 4579) is bustling and friendly and serves home-made sausage and meat loaf, toasted cheese and jugged hare, all at genial prices. *Luba's Bistro* (6 Yeoman's Row, SW3; 01-589 2950) is wonderfully left bank and unchanged from the fifties. It would be no surprise to find Juliette Greco being nihilistic here. The food is . . . robust, and the stuffed mushrooms are especially good.

It's noisy, unlicensed (but no corkage if you bring your own), the kitchen is entertainingly visible, and the lavatories don't always flush – but then you can't have everything!

The best pancake houses (it's smart to call them crêperies) are *Astrix* (329 King's Road, SW3; 01-352 3891) and *La Crêperie de L'Ecluse* (3 Chalk Farm Road, NW1; 01-267 8816), where onion soup, sausages, moules and such are on the menu along with the pancakes. I don't recommend *galettes* (buckwheat pancakes) which are not unlike shoe-leather for texture and shredded wheat for flavour.

Luigi and Paolo have two snack bars, one in Blenheim Street, adjacent to Phillips Auctions, one at 21 Woodstock Road, W1; (01-629 5039). Both are excellent, and notable for good humour and custard tarts.

Vegetable samosas at *The Jerusalem Restaurant* (150 Shaftesbury Avenue, WC2; 01-836 7145) are a sensational thirty-pence worth and the fish-cakes at *The Sea-Shell* (see under fish and chips), big, round and stuffed with white fish and pepper but no potatoes, are superb value at 40p.

Since travel is so expensive I append a list of budget restaurants, divided by area. Prices per head are approximate of course. Bon appétit!

Recommended:

E2	*The Cherry Orchard* 241 Glebe Road, 01-980 6678. Vegetarian, open air, lovely salads and cakes.	£4.50
E8	*Cooke's Eel and Pie House* 41 Kingsland Road, 01-254 2878. See text.	£3.00
SE1	*Cooke's Eel and Pie House* The Cut (opposite Old Vic), 01-928 5931. See text.	£3.00
W1	*Luigi and Paolo* Blenheim Street. Also at 21 Woodstock Road, 01-629 5039. See text.	£3.50 £3.50
	Bafta 195 Piccadilly, does members and guests proud.	£3.50
	Rupert Street Junction 7 Rupert Street, 01-734 2079. Converted carriages of The Brighton Belle. Barbecued chicken wings, potato skins with bacon and cheese etc.	£5.00
	L'Artiste Musclé 1 Shepherd Market, 01-493 6150.	£6.00
W2	*Everest Café* Portobello Road. See text.	£3.00
W6	*Lyric Theatre Buffet* King Street, 01-741 2311. See text.	£4.00
W9	*Linda's* 4 Fernhead Road, 01-969 9387. Includes Vietnamese specialities.	£5.00
WC1	*Mille Pini* 33 Boswell Street, 01-242 2434. Excellent Pasta.	£5.00
	Swiss Coffee House 38 Lamb's Conduit Street, 01-405 7950.	£4.50
WC2	*Diana's Diner* 39 Endell Street, 01-240 0272. Home-made steak and kidney pie, sausages and mash etc.	£3.50

NW1 *La Crêperie de L'Ecluse* 3 Chalk Farm Road, 01-267 8816. £4.00
See text.

Nontas 16 Camden High Street, 01-387 4579. £4.50
See text.

The Sea Shell 33/35 Lisson Grove, 01-723 8703.
See text.

NW5 *Le Petit Prince* 5 Holmes Road, 01-627 0752. £6.00
Notably couscous and home-made ice-cream.

NW6 *The Olive Branch* 267 Kilburn High Road, 01-625 8734. £5.00
Humous, fish dishes, crumbles, pretty music and
atmosphere.

SW3 *Astrix* 329 King's Road, 01-352 3891. £4.50
See text.

Luba's Bistro Yeoman's Row, 01-589 2950. £6.00
See text.

Picasso 127 King's Road, 01-352 4921. £3.00
Nice snacks.

Foxtrot Oscar (silly nudging title) 79 Royal £6.00
Hospital Road, 01-352 7179.
Cheap champagne, filling foods, salads.

SW5 *The Hot Pot* 6 Kenway Road, 01-373 1256. £3.50
Extra-large portions.

The Pot 5A Hogarth Place, 01-370 4371. £6.00
Rabbit casserole, cheap wines, provençal atmosphere.

SW11 *La Bouffe* 13 Battersea Rise, 01-228 3384. £4.95
Classy, set menus from

SW14 *Carlo Dimingos* 201 Upper Richmond Road East, £5.00
East Sheen.

A few post-scripts. Always watch out for minimum charges, some of
which apply only during rush-hours. For non-smokers, ASH (27-35
Mortimer Street, W1; 01-637 9843) has a booklet listing 69 eating
establishments where smoking is not permitted.

I have not yet listed here restaurants serving specifically ethnic
food. They will be found under their appropriate listings (see under
Restaurants). You should also check under Brasseries, Breakfasts,
Pub food (under Pubs) and Salad Bars.

A useful guide, published annually, is *Eating Out in London* (Time Out). *The Good Caff Guide* by M. Fletcher and *Just a Bite*, the Egon Ronay Guide may also be helpful, but try my recommendations first!

Best Budget Restaurant: *Lyric Theatre Buffet.*
Worst Budget Restaurant: *Victoria Coach Station.*

Buses and Bus Routes

Like a nut being nibbled at by a squirrel, London's bus services are being encroached upon from the suburbs by privatisation. London Regional Transport first handed the 81 route (Hounslow to Slough) to Len Wright Travel – Mr Right perhaps. Now another 40 routes are to be offered up to tender. By April 1986 8,000,000 bus miles (5% of the total) will have been contracted out.

In the meantime, we continue to live with what we've got. Let us take the good ones first. The 7 meanders through the back streets of Ladbroke Grove in the general direction of Oxford Circus with a cheerful disregard for schedules. The 11 strikes out boldly from Chelsea to the City and has even made it on occasions. (London bus drivers are a determined race; if their route required them to terminate at the source of the Nile they would certainly get there in due course and probably in convoy.) The 44 is useful, connecting London Bridge and Vauxhall Stations with the Battersea fringe theatres (q.v.) and the heart of beautiful downtown Battersea. The 53 is a common occurrence but always comes when you are awaiting something else; the 221 is much admired by connoisseurs. As for the 185, it is admirably regular and frequent, but, frustratingly, does not go anywhere much. The following may be recommended: 7, 11, 15 (very scenic), 16, 24, 53, 74, 88, 134, 159, 185, 221 and 227. Also all Bayswater Road buses.

Now for the bad news. The 2 and 2B are disasters. The 9 seldom comes, which is a shame, because it is such a useful route and takes in the best bits of Kensington. By the time the 22 arrives one is so relieved (a sixty minute wait is not unusual) that one smiles all the way from Putney to Liverpool Street. I have waited an hour and a half for a 176 (it was raining) and the notorious 54 seldom if ever completes its journey. The 53 (Camden Town to Plumstead) has to cope with the interminable Elephant and Castle – Old Kent Road stretch and often can't. The 104 and 187 hibernate for ten months of the year, and the 68 is virtually extinct despite a World Wildlife Fund Appeal. The '*Bloody 33*' is only described so rudely, because it always comes when one wants a *90B*. While prepared to be convinced that one-man manning is an improvement on the Driver/Conductor syndrome, I have my doubts. Is it (a) safe or (b) sensible: How, for instance, can a driver check that the right fare has been proffered or paid?

Bus tours around London are organised by London Transport (01-222 1234), by London Crusader (01-437 0124) and by Harrods (01-730 1234) whose coaches are the most exquisitely commodious. Then there are the Culture Buses (01-834 6732) which have stops at which you can board or disembark outside twenty cultural hotspots. The trip, which costs £3.50 (£2 for children) starts at a not particularly cultural venue, Baker Street tube, and runs every twenty minutes, with a commentary from 9 a.m.

Best Bus Route: *15* east to west, north of the river taking in the City and Limehouse.

Worst Bus Routes: *37* east to west, south of the river and *137* north to south, through the West End (RIP).

P.S. Carl Davis's *Variations on a Bus Route* selected the *31* for special attention. Does he know something we don't know?

P.P.S. The GLC Central Zone Travelcard which enables you to mix tube and bus travel on a single ticket is a welcome innovation.

P.P.P.S. Hunt down *A History of London Transport* by T.C. Baker and R.M. Robbins (two vols 1963 & 1976). It's indispensable.

Buskers

If Ken Livingstone is remembered for nothing else he will be remembered with gratitude by London commuters for his efforts to legalise the life-enhancing activities of the London buskers. I do not know what happened to the charming fellows in fezzes and aprons who used to do silly dances in *Leicester Square*, nor to the celebrated escapologist who performed there to cinema queues. Maybe he tried to escape once too often. However a sighting of an escapologist in Portobello Road has been reported and he may indeed be – let us hope he is – the same one. But in *Green Park*, *Tottenham Court Road*, *Waterloo* and *Charing Cross* tube stations, in the *King's Road* next to Safeways and above all in *Covent Garden*, buskers have never been so numerous, so talented and I hope so profitable. The latest fashion is for saxophones with taped rhythm backing. They can be heard above the traffic, and are easily transportable.

To busk in *Covent Garden* (the *Piazza* outside the *Actor's Church* is the prime location, but you can also be busked these days in *King Street* and *James Street*) you need a performer's licence (details from the *Covent Garden Community Association*, 45 Short's Gardens, WC2; 01-836 5555). There is now an annual festival of street entertainers (as they are rather grandly called) with *The Vicious Boys* winning last year's prize and deserving to.

A new and welcome development is the young man who not only accompanies himself as he sings *Streets of London* on the Circle Line, but gives a brief but well-informed guide to places of interest adjacent to each station.

Butchers

The qualities I look for in a butcher: blue and white tiles, men in striped aprons with no fingers missing, a cashier partitioned well away from the meat, a willingness to prepare a crown, or obtain mutton, or sell boiling fowl or capons, or find good solid marrow bones for dogs. Surprisingly there are a great many such butchers in London. But a new kind of butcher has emerged, a specialist who supplies restaurants and private clients with meat prepared for cordon bleu standard cooking. Marc Beaujeu will roll pork with prunes, alternate layers of veal and shallot or pistachio stuffing, create sophisticated hamburgers for expatriate democrat Professors on sabbatical from Stanford. At *Boucherie Lamartine* (229 Ebury Street, SW1; 01-730 4175) he does all this and, even more importantly, ensures that the quality of meat he serves is the best available. His beef is Aberdeen Angus, his lamb comes from the west country, his rabbits from his own garden in Sussex, his game from Newbury, his chickens from Bresse. On Fridays and Saturdays he has the weekly French imports – Bombay ducks (unobtainable elsewhere), poulets fermiers, both white and yellow, boudins blancs and toutes choses.

By common consent the best of the old-fashioned butchers is *C. Lidgate* (10 Holland Park Avenue, W11; 01-727 8243) who passes all these tests with ease but who also sells fresh poultry and game and sensational sausages and pies. *Bailey's* and *Allen's* in Mount Street, W1 run them close. *J. Bailey* (116 Mount Street, W1; 01-499 1833) is a glazed symphony to dead birds and beasts but, since they also serve free range poultry and eggs, one cannot regard them as callous. They claim to be the oldest poulterers in the country and have Royal Warrants dating back 150 years. *R. Allen & Co* (117 Mount Street, W1; 01-493 0238) is also recommended though a pound of best fillet will set you back over £7. *Slater & Cooke, Bisney & Jones*

(67 Brewer Street, W1; 01-437 2026) are unusual in that they provide special counters for separate meats. It's a splendidly clean, air-conditioned place where a request for haggis will not faze them. Haggis and baby goat have been spotted also at *John Lane* (6 Walkers Court, W1; 01-437 8903). Good kosher butchers include *M. Taylor* (31 D'Arblay Street, W1; 01-437 4119) and *I Zell* (14 Newburgh Street, W1; 01-437 2176). *Robert Portwine* (24 Earlham Street, WC2; 01-836 2353) is for connoisseurs with a distinction made between 'gammon' and 'corner gammon'. *Harrods Food Hall* (Knightbridge, SW1) provides wonderful food for the eye and particularly where the game, displayed feathered and furred, is concerned. It's not just shopping, more a lecture in natural history. A correspondent writes of Harrods Food Hall: 'In the area where the Melton pies and similar articles are sold, I saw a salesman who looked like a ruddier version of Basil Rathbone spend at least five minutes discussing the merits of a piece of black pudding with a Scot and his wife'. Harrods, who have always enjoyed spectacular challenges claim that their own brand sausages will not split on the barbecue. (Pity. I like the split bits best!)

Recommended:
Leadenhall Market (for value and freshness), *Bifulco* (St John's Wood and Frith Street) for Italian cuts, also crowns and saddles of lamb, chicken kiev and fresh quail on Thursdays.

Randall & Aubin (16 Brewer Street, W1; 01-437 3507), for calves' tongues and feet, brains and tripe, lambs' testicles, quail, pheasant, woodcock and snipe plucked to order, *Bartholdi* (4 Charlotte Street, W1; 01-636 3762), for smoked meats, *J. & J. Dalli* (78 Brewer Street, W1; 01-437 8870), for Toulouse and Marquez sausages and *Fenn's* (Unit 6 Covent Garden, WC2; 01-379 6427), for game and venison. London's first organic butcher is called just that *Organic Butcher* (217 Holloway Road, N7; 01-609 7016). All David Mullen's meat is free range and guaranteed free of chemical additives. Similarly at the excellent *Wholefoods*, 24 Paddington Street, W1 (01-486 1390).

The Bromley branch of *Manson's* is recommended, but not other branches, and it's worth considering that on Saturday afternoons from about four o'clock onwards *Murray's* (9 Church Street, NW8; 01-723 6245) sell off assorted cuts at plebeian prices. *Sainsbury's* branches are dependable. *Dewhurst's* put too much colouring and such into their mince.

Best Butcher: *Boucherie Lamartine*.
Best Traditional Butcher: *C. Lidgate*.

Butterflies

One of the most beautiful places in London is the Butterfly House at *Syon Park*, Brentford (01-560 0881). You walk into what appears to be a large tropical conservatory and all around your head flutter these fragile brightly coloured bits of nonsense. They fly in pairs but appear to have no knowledge that there is such a thing as evil in the world. Any insects that might mean them harm are kept down through the co-operation of baby quail, and the whole environment has the surreal atmosphere of a dream. Children love it. A second area devoted exclusively to British butterflies (that should please the National Front!) has just opened. There is also a modest display of stick insects, locusts and so forth, the prize exhibit being a red-legged tarantula which just sits there looking glum. The souvenir shop sells quality goods, and you can buy pupae of tortoiseshell butterflies which you take home to increase the population spread of these enchanting creatures. You can study the extraordinary complexity of lepidoptera in the display cases, but dead butterflies are no substitute for live ones.

Dead ones may also be viewed on the walls of *G. Dionysus* the Greek restaurant in Heath Street, Hampstead, and can be bought in the shop next to Sainsbury's in Streatham. A variety of live butterflies may be seen in London cemeteries including the following species: Common Blue, Large Skipper, Peacock, Orange Tip, Tortoiseshell and Wall. If your enthusiasm for butterflies extends that far you should visit the Isle of Wight and the Channel Islands where the air pulsates with butterflies' wings.

On the first night of Peter Brook's production *U.S.* for the RSC at the Aldwych a butterfly was removed from a matchbox and a match applied to its wings. The RSPCA threatened to take Mr Brook to court. He explained to them that the butterfly only *appeared* to be burned, but that, if anyone was told, a butterfly would in fact be burned the following night.

Best Butterflies: *Syon Park*, Brentford.

Buttons

There are two wonderful button retailers in London: *The Button Queen* and the *Button Box*. The former (19 Marylebone Lane, W1; 01-935 1505) specialises in rare and antique buttons, while the greatest strength of the latter (44 Bedford Street, WC2; 01-240 2716) is in supplying buttons in modern materials, many of which are weird and wonderful. It is no big thing to remove your dreary high street store buttons from your off-the-peg purchase and replace them with something astonishing from the *Button Box* which also operates in Covent Garden Market on Tuesday and Wednesday and on Saturday in Camden Lock.

Cabaret

Off the streets and into the pubs they go, clowns and zanies, surrealists and satirists, high (quite often), wide (occasionally) and handsome (rarely). There is so much alternative culture around that the real thing begins to seem just a little, well, alternative. There is no point in naming the venues. The weekly listings magazines Time Out and City Limits, do that quite adequately. But a list of some of the names of the better known cabaret performances may be instructive. In no particular order then: Johnny Immaterial, The False Dots, Joan Collins Fan Club – I've seen it and it's *revolting!* – Otiz Cannelloni, Morris Minor and the Majors, the Jam Tarts, Eric the Transalvanian (sic) Egg Man, the Meccano Club, Rev Robert Righteous Indignation, Sensible Footwear, Podomoffski, Mr Nasty, Anne Rabbit, The Brown Paper Bag Brothers, Johnny Hubcap and the Axles, Randolph The Remarkable, Slattery Branch Irrigation System, and the Screaming Abdabs.

The campest cabaret act in London is Bloolips, a song-and-dance queen act, involving Gloriana Piana, Diva Danny, Marge, Lavinia Co-op, Precious Pearl and Bette Bloolip herself. The targets are predictable. Politicians, the pop industry, consumerism, the BBC, Channel 4 (even!), sexual stereotypes, vicars, Australians, trendies, journalists, men and so on. A few of the acts are brilliant. The Vicious Boys, Stefan Bednarczyk, and Oscar Maclennan should not be missed, particularly the last-named. Most struggle hard aping the style of the latest alternative to make it to the big time. The big time is the Edinburgh Fringe en route to television.

The most amusing way to keep up to date with the cabaret acts is at the *Comedy Store*, in Meard Street until three years ago, now at 28 Leicester Square, WC2; (01-839 6665). The idea has a beautiful, though gruesome simplicity. The compère (probably Jim Barclay) introduces new acts or acts trying to look new. The audience drink (entrance is £5, drinks are 65p) and heckle; if they don't like the act it gets the gong. Only the tough and the deserving survive, and after such a baptism, they should be ready for anything. The sadism/

masochism begins at midnight on Saturdays; doors open at 11. The old *Comedy Store* got so crowded the fire officers closed it down. The new one is not much bigger, so arrive early.

Best Cabaret: *The Comedy Store*.

Canals

The best and one of the very few London canals is the *Regent's Canal*, an extension of the Grand Union Canal from Paddington to Wapping and completed in 1820. The junction of the two canals is Little Venice, a peaceful area of gardens, houseboats and plane trees, to the west of Maida Vale. To walk from the M4 motorway to Wapping would be a major undertaking (you have to go underground for half a mile at Islington) but there are stretches of canal packed with interest and even beauty. Between Yeading and West End are green fields with buttercups. It is still pastoral at Alperton. Between the cemetery of Kensal Green and the prison of Wormwood Scrubs it ought to be gloomy, but is picturesque. Behind St Pancras it's even better and where it passes through London Zoo anything can happen. Several firms offer trips along the canal, notably *Jason's* (60 Blomfield Road, W9; 01-286 3428), the oldest in the business and always great value, *Jenny Wren* (250 Camden High Street, NW1; 01-485 4433), and the *Regent's Canal Waterbus* (information from 01-482 2550). Jason will hire out a narrow boat (£17.50 per head plus wine for a party of twelve), and there is a floating restaurant, *My Fair Lady*, which serves a dinner at 8 p.m. accompanied by a passionate guitar for £14.95 all in.

At *Camden Lock* there is the craft market and *Dingwall's Disco* as well as several life-enhancing shops. At Southall, there is a gas works, a cemetery, and a sewage plant.

Best Canal: *Regent's Canal*.
Read: *London's Canal Walks* by Marie Rodda – free from London Tourist Board Offices.

Canteens

The willingness with which experienced Londoners pay large sums of money for moderate lunches amazes me, when an excellent alternative is available. I mean of course canteens.

It is all a matter of confidence. If you look as though you work for the establishment whose lunch you intend to sample you are unlikely to be asked for your credentials. Only at broadcasting establishments and television companies have things been tightened up somewhat and then, if you can get an appointment with somebody working in the building, you have no further problems about your subsidised lunch. Now it goes without saying that I am not *suggesting* that you should do any such thing as take possession of a pork pie under false pretences – that would be most improper – but it is possible . . .

The best canteen food I have enjoyed was at *Goldsmith's College* in New Cross where Parson's Hat, the chef's special turned out to be a sensationally good haddock and pastry dish. At the *National Film Theatre* canteen, which is first-rate value, the public wander in and out and nobody checks membership cards.

Other recommended canteens: the *Royal College of Art*, the *Barbican Staff Canteen* (the staff eat better than the public and why not?), the *Crown Court* behind Harrods, the *National Theatre* (excellent value and coffee at 10p), the *Civic Centre*, Bromley and the *Liverpool Victoria Friendly Society* building in Southampton Row. The *London School of Economics* canteen is variable. If you are smartly dressed and look like a budding executive there is no reason why you should not survive on the free food available at conferences. The *UK Press Gazette* gives a list of forthcoming press conferences so that, if you have sufficient chutzpah, or a press card, you need not starve.

Best Canteen: *Goldsmith's College*.
More reports please . . .

Car Parks

With rare exceptions expect to pay at least 60p per hour in central London. A rare exception is *Charing Cross Garages* under the arches – if you can get in. *Cavendish Square*, W1 (01-629 6968) is the most expensive at £1 per hour. If you can leave your car outside the centre of town you will do best. The *National Theatre Car Park* and the *Royal Festival Hall Car Park* both charge 50p for 2 hours rising to £5 for 24 hours. If you leave your car at *Richmond Station* you will pay £2.40 for twelve hours and can take a train to almost anywhere you wish to go.

I've had disastrous experiences at *St Martin's Lane* multi-storey and others have no cause to remember the *Whitcomb Street* WC2 car park happily. Here are some other OK parks:

Tower Hill, Lower Thames Street, EC3; 01-626 2082.
London Wall, EC2; 01-628 7468.

Bedfordbury, St Martin's Lane, 01-240 0397.
Hyde Park Underground Car Park (at Marble Arch) 01-723 9825.
Drury Lane, Winter Garden, WC2.
Gunnersbury (next to the underground station).

A list of their car-parks and a map of how to find them may be had from *NCP Head Office*, 21 Bryanston Street, W1; (01-499 7050).

Best Car Park: *Royal Festival Hall.*
Worst Car Park: *Heathrow Terminal 2* (brutally expensive but with a great view of the planes from the roof).

Carveries

See under *English Restaurants*

Cathedrals

St Paul's (see Architecture) is a miracle of course. It is also miraculous that it survived the blitz. On December 29th 1940 incendiary bombs dropped by the Germans intent on destroying the cathedral fell in a circle around it but failed to hit the target. A further bombing raid with high explosive bombs, which must surely have succeeded, was cancelled after an abrupt deterioration of weather over Normandy. In 1941, the Cathedral did receive direct hits by bombs which damaged the high altar and the north transept and blew out much of the glass. But fire-watchers helped to save it from irreparable harm.

A few statistics for those who like them. The dome is second in size to *St Peter's* in Rome; the total area of the cathedral is only exceeded in Britain by the *Anglican Cathedral of Liverpool*. An early church on the site in the 14th century had an overall length of 596 feet (as against 515 feet today) and a spire of at least 480 feet (the dome is a mere 365 feet high). The building of the cathedral, after the old one had been severely damaged in the Great Fire of 1666, was accompanied by massive criticism. Wren's salary was withheld and in 1718, eight years after completion, the great architect was dismissed from his post as Surveyor General.

One of Wren's great achievements had been to surround himself with men of genius – Hawksmoor the architect, Thomas and Edward Strong as stone-masons, Grinling Gibbons as wood-carver and Jean Tijou as ironwright amongst others. Within the Cathedral are monuments to many heroes, including Wellington, Gordon,

Nelson and Sir John Moore, artists, such as Reynolds and Turner, and writers including Samuel Johnson and John Donne. (Nelson's body is preserved in alcohol.) We owe it to them to pay our respects. There is no space here to detail all the glories of *St Paul's*, but if you undertake the climb (627 steps) into the ball at the top of the lantern within the dome, you will be rewarded along the way by a breath-taking view of London from the *Golden Gallery*. And one other requirement: visit the tomb of Sir Christopher Wren (in the third recess within the Crypt) then return to the Nave and follow the instructions which are Wren's epitaph: 'Lector, si monumentum requiris, circumspice' ('Reader, if what you want is a monument, take a look around you.')

I have written of the origins of *Southwark Cathedral* (see under Bridges). The great attraction of this promoted Parish Church (it was inaugurated as a cathedral for the diocese of South London in 1905) is (a) its position and (b) its music.

Almost underneath a railway bridge and bounded on the south by the river, to the west by the Borough fruit and vegetable market, and to the east by the frantic pedestrian commuters on London Bridge, it is in the centre of the action. It too has fine memorials, one to Shakespeare, and others to Shakespeare's actor-brother Edmund, to John Gower, the poet, to Fletcher and Massinger the playwrights, to Lyonell Lockyer, the quack-doctor, to the saintly Bishop of Winchester, Lancelot Andrewes, and to John Harvard, who has a small and tranquil chapel built in his honour. Harvard, a Southwark man who made good and founded an educational establishment somewhere in the colonies, is also commemorated in the John Harvard Library further down Borough High Street. Then there is the music.

Architecturally *Southwark Cathedral* has a bit of everything, but the flavour is predominantly Gothic. The tower is beautiful, but the retro-choir is very special. Recently cleaned and renovated, the columns, spreading graciously into fan vaulting, give one the feeling of stepping into a sunlit coppice.

Westminster Cathedral was inspired – if that is the word – by St Mark's Venice. Officially it is described as being in 'an early-Christian Byzantine style', though Hugh Kingsmill called it 'incipient Turkish bath' and Hesketh Pearson likened its style to 'later Marzipan period'. Well, it has a thrusting campanile (St Edward's Tower) which it is hard to ignore, and from which more grand views may be enjoyed and fascinating stations of the Cross bas-reliefs, carved by Eric Gill, the eccentric typographer. In the cross which surmounts St Edward's Tower is a relic of the True Cross.

Amidst all this grandeur spare a thought for *St George's Cathedral* at the junction of Lambeth Road and St George's Road, for this is the principal church of the Roman Catholic diocese of Southwark; it is also a typical piece of Decorated Gothic by Pugin, the architect of the *House of Commons*, and much restored; and a moment too for the *Ukrainian Catholic Cathedral of the Holy Family in Exile*, Duke Street, W1.

Best Cathedral: *St Paul's*.
Worst Cathedral: *Westminster Cathedral*.

Cats

> For he keeps the Lord's watch in the night against the adversary
> For he counteracts the power of darkness by his electrical skin and glaring eyes
> For he counteracts the Devil, who is death, by brisking about the life
> For in his morning orisons he loves the Sun and the Sun loves him
> For he is of the tribe of Tiger
>
> From *Jubilate Agno* by Christopher Smart (1722-1771)

The most remarkable cat in London is *Binks*, a huge tabby. Binks (1921-1926) resided at Bates, the hatters, of 21a Jermyn Street, W1, where he would sit in the window in a top hat with a Turkish cigarette between his rakish lips. He still does, although now he observes the passing scene from a glass case and through glass eyes.

The *fattest* cat in London used to be *Tiddles*, who lived in the ladies' lavatories at Paddington Station. Alas, *Tiddles* too has gone before, and it may not be very long before the lavatories have, to be replaced by Superloos.

The *largest* cat in London, and probably the world, may be seen poised over the Catford Shopping Precinct, back arched as though mousing or sniffing the dogs at the dog track down the road.

Dick Whittington's cat is made of stone and was added to the statue of Dick Whittington on Highgate Hill in 1964. It has its head turned as though listening to the bells from Bow, which supposedly strengthened Dick's resolve to turn back and become a hero in fish-net tights. Whittington was a mercer, wool exporter, royal banker, and four times Lord Mayor. His cat is probably legendary, and his route to the City from his home in Gloucestershire should certainly not have taken him via Highgate. Pedants have suggested that Dick's 'cat' referred to a coal-carrying barge plying its trade between London and Newcastle ('carrying coals to Newcastle').

The *worst* cat in London is the mummified one in the Tiger Tavern (1 Tower Hill, EC3; 01-626 5097). It is surrounded by six rats, though whether it is victim or victor is unclear.

For buyers and sellers of cats (though not real ones) I can recommend Erika Bruce who has a stall in Grays-in-the-Mews Antique Market (1 Davies Mews, W1), and is a confirmed felinophile. Cherry Saltzer's shop, *Catz* (25 Bedfordbury, WC2; 01-836 6513) is another purr-lined paradise. For distressed or stray cats 'phone the *Cats Protection League* (0403-65566).

Best Cat: *Binks*.
Worst Cat: *The Tiger Tavern Cat*.

Ceilings

The finest ceiling in London is that which overhangs the *Painted Hall* at the *Royal Naval College*, Greenwich. The Hall is divided between the Lower Hall, where it was intended that ratings should sit, and the Upper Hall for staff and officers. Above the Lower Hall are painted the royal founders of the Hospital with appropriate emblems; above the Upper Hall Queen Anne with her consort Prince George of Denmark. Painted on the West Wall and completing the Baroque effect is George 1, surrounded by his brood. Sir James Thornhill, who painted this massive hall, and was paid at the rate of £3 a yard for the ceiling and £1 a yard for the walls, was the genius responsible for the grisaille paintings on the inside of the Dome of *St Paul's*, representing incidents in the saint's life, and the original rose-window of *Westminster Abbey*. The ceiling of the *Painted Hall* was decorated between 1707 and 1726 and cunningly restored between 1957 and 1960. The Hall is in continuous use as the Royal Naval College's refectory. The *Chapel Royal* in St James' Palace has a wonderful coffered ceiling attributed to Holbein. You may enjoy it on Sundays at 8.30 and 11.15 between October and Palm Sunday and on 6th January, the Feast of the Epiphany, when gifts of gold and frankincense and myrrh are offered up.

Best Ceiling: *The Painted Hall*, Greenwich.
Worst Ceiling: *The Chamber of Horrors*, Madame Tussaud's.

Cemeteries

Flaubert on Highgate Cemetery: 'Far too neat. These people seem to have died with white gloves on.'

Hugh Meller's *Illustrated Guide and Gazetteer to London Cemeteries* (invaluable) lists exactly 100 cemeteries within the London A-Z map area. They range from half an acre (the *Jewish Cemetery* in Kingsbury Road, N1) to 182 acres (*St Pancras and Islington Cemetery*, High Road, East Finchley, N12). The finest are *Highgate, Brompton, Kensal Green* and *Norwood*, and the oldest *Bunhill* (corrupted from Bonehill) *Fields*.

(a) Brompton

The catacombs have been full for over half a century and their gloomy gates – snakes twining around inverted torches symbolising eternity triumphing over life extinguished – would deter any but the most intrepid. The cemetery is also closed for burials. The finest monuments are both to pre-Raphaelites, Frederick Leyland's tomb, ornately extravant in the arts and crafts style, and the Gothic sarcophagus in Sienese marble memorialising Valentine Prinsep. Other notable residents include: Emmeline Pankhurst, Lionel Monckton, Gentleman John Jackson, Sir Squire Bancroft, George Henty, Richard Tauber and Brandon Thomas. One can imagine that crowd enjoying quite a lively party in the hereafter.

(b) Highgate

Wild and overgrown and full of interest. Professor Girouard: 'There is a vast army of Victorian merchants, officers, widows and judges gently crumbling into anonymity beneath ivy and saplings and lushly sinister mares' tails.' The Egyptian catacombs, Julius Beer's mausoleum, based on the original at Halicarnassus, and Karl and Eleanor Marx's memorial (by Lawrence Bradshaw 1956 in the new part of the cemetery) are not to be missed, but there are also: a lion (commemorating a lion-tamer), a horse (commemorating a horse-slaughterer), and a dog which led the mourning procession at his prize-fighter master's funeral. Lying there also: Jacob Bronowski, John Brinsmead, Charles Cruft, George Eliot, William Foyle, Quaritch and Colnaghi, the book dealers, Galsworthy, Radclyffe Hall buried with her first lover, Charles Green, the balloonist, Philip Harben, the chef, Rowland Hill, 'Hutch', Frederick Lillywhite, who introduced round-arm bowling to cricket, Carl Rosa, Mrs Henry Wood, Herbert Spencer, the Rossetti Family and Patrick Wymark (much missed).

(c) Kensal Green

An historic cemetery with the widest range of mausolea, temples, obelisks, caryatids and follies in the country. Lying there: Bartolozzi the engraver, Blondin, who kept on crossing the Niagara Falls on a tight-rope and once on stilts as well, Marc Brunel who built tunnels and his son Isambard, who built bridges, Decimus Burton, Cassell and Murray, the publishers, Cruikshank and Leech, the caricaturists, Hood and Leigh Hunt, the poets, Thackeray, Wilkie Collins and Trollope, the novelists, Sydney Smith, and William Whiteley and James Pope-Hennessey, both murdered under similarly tragic circumstances.

(d) Norwood (the South Metropolitan Cemetery)

Battered by time and vandals, both official and unofficial, *Norwood* has a splendid array of crumbling monuments, including a Doric Temple (for the Ralli family), a fine sarcophagus (for Alexander Berens, linen-draper), and a magnificent monolith (for the antiquary John Britton).

A variegated group of residents include: Isabella Beeton and Mr B., the publisher, Charles Bravo, Sir Henry Doulton, David Cox the younger and Samuel Prout, artists, Sir Henry Tate and James Epps, the man whose splendid contribution to our well-being was to introduce cocoa to Britain.

(e) Bunhill Fields

Specifically for dissenters, *Bunhill* is remarkable for the quality of the men and women who lie there. These include: Bunyan, Blake, Defoe, Quare – the clockmaker, Watts – the hymnwriter, Buxton – the philanthropist, Robert Tilling – the murderer, fourteen assorted Cromwells, and Hugh Pugh, the Welsh Harpist.

The *Royal Hospital Burial Ground* is notable, as you might expect, for the longevity of its inhabitants with two old soldiers who lived to be 112, and William Hiseland (1620-1732) who served eighty years in the army, and married when a centenarian. Also two women who joined the army in masquerade to search for their soldier husbands. One, Hannah Snell, served in the navy too, was once punished with 500 lashes, published her memoirs in 1750, went on the stage and died insane.

Don't miss: the waterfall at *Crystal Palace*; the crocuses at *Golders Green*; the rhubarb at *Mortlake Roman Catholic Cemetery*, and the Muslims with their flowers and joss-sticks at *Tottenham Park*. The five Iranian terrorists who died in the Embassy siege lie in an unmarked grave at the neglected *Woodgrange Park*. *Brockley Cemetery* is renowned for the names of those who lie there. Here are a few: Alberta Codbolt, Absalom Dandridge, Amelia Gossage, Horace Lermit, Alice Pyefinch, Philadelphia Sampson and Benjamin Sloss.

What happened, I wonder, to all the Pyefinches and Slosses? There are only two of each in the current London Telephone Directory.

Best Cemetery: *Kensal Green.*
Worst Cemetery: *Lee Cemetery* (the new section), Verdant Lane, SE6.

P.S. Lambeth Council offers its poorer residents a free cremation service, including a two-line entry in The Book of Remembrance.

Chapels

The *Chapel of the Savoy* squats beside the huge hotel like a small tug half-hidden behind the luxury liner it has been towing into port. It is the official chapel of the Queen (the royal pews to the west end of the Chapel are slightly raised so as to be a few feet nearer to God) and is Victorian, having been rebuilt from a late Perpendicular original after a fire in 1864. It is notable for a stained glass window to D'Oyly Carte, an old wooden roof, and a plaque commemorating a Mr Gosling who died in 1586:

> 'So well inclined to poor and rich
> God send more Goslings to be sich'

According to *Brideshead Revisited* it is a poky little place in which divorced people got married, as Julia tragically does.

The *Chapel-of-Ease* in South Audley Street, built of brick and stone c 1750 is full of charm. Designed by a carpenter (Benjamin Timbrell), it has just the qualities you might expect; artisan and delightful.

Another charming *Chapel-of-Ease* is the one in Vere Street, NW1 attached to *All Souls*, Langham Place. Built by James Gibbs in 1722 it used to be called the *Marylebone Chapel*. It is dedicated to St Peter.

Within the *Holy Sepulchre Church*, Newgate, whose graveyard was once particularly popular with bodysnatchers, is a Musician's Chapel, which has windows celebrating Sir Henry Wood, one-time deputy organist there, John Ireland, Dame Nellie Melba and many other musicians. Characteristically Sir Malcolm Sargent has his own niche in the sanctuary. The Church has a Cecilian Festival every November.

St Paul's contains several chapels; the *Jesus Chapel* to the east of the High Altar, has a memorial to 28,000 Americans who died fighting in the last war. This affects me more than *All Soul's Chapel* which is chock full of marble and dedicated to Kitchener.

I have mentioned the *John Harvard Chapel* (see Cathedrals) but *St Katherine's Chapel* (between Albany Street and the Outer Circle, NW1) is also too little appreciated. Built to Ambrose Poynter's specifications in 1829 and restored in 1952, it was originally part of the ancient Royal Hospital of St Katharine, established by Matilda in 1148. The hospital has returned to the East End but the chapel remains and the Danish community in London worship there. It contains the shields of arms of the 39 Queens of England from Matilda to Queen Mary. Ask the caretaker (in the adjoining hall) to show you round.

The *Chapel Royal* in St James' Palace has been much renovated since it was supposedly built to a Holbein design, but its ceiling still bears a monogram H and A for Henry VIII and Anne of Cleves (see Ceilings).

Another *Chapel Royal* is the one to St Peter ad Vincula on Tower Green; here lie Anne Boleyn and Catherine Howard, also the Dukes of Northumberland and Somerset – all beheaded. Also Lady Jane Grey, the Earl of Essex, the wild Duke of Monmouth, and Sir Thomas More. (Some dispute about this. His head is at Canterbury. His body may be at Chelsea Old Church, outside which his splendid statue in black and gold stands guard.) Within the White Tower, the oldest part of the Tower of London, is the beautiful and peaceful *St John's Chapel* of massive Norman construction. Prayers uttered here have great weight and authority.

Do not miss the *Chapel* at Greenwich Hospital (adjoining the amazing Painted Hall). Rebuilt by James 'Athenian' Stuart with statues and an altar-piece by Benjamin West, it is quite something. Stuart was first a painter of fans, but a visit to Greece changed all that. The Adam brothers owe him a fortune.

One curiosity: the *Chapel of the Holy Rood* above the impressive Gateway of Barking Abbey. And another: the fine Congregational *Islington Chapel* (1888/9 by Bonella and Paul) in Upper Street, now recording studios.

Best Chapel: *St John's Chapel*, White Tower, Tower of London.

Characters

London's most distinguished characters have come from modest homes. *Chaucer* was born in the Vintry, *Sir Thomas More* in Milk Street,

John Donne and *John Milton* in Bread Street. *Defoe* was a butcher's boy, *Pope* came from a linen-draper's shop, and *Browning* was born in Camberwell.

The most public 'characters' in London may be found on Sundays at Speaker's Corner, both speechifying and heckling. (The right of free speech does not, incidentally, apply there, Irish demagogues having been arrested quite recently for arguing that British troops should get out of Northern Ireland.) During the first six months of 1985, heckling at Speaker's Corner became organised to a distasteful extent by extreme right-wing factions, who spoiled the fun.

Most Londoners asked to name a familiar character from the streets would probably mention a sandwich-man who has been seen round the West End for 17 years with his familiar board proclaiming in bold, white capitals: 'LESS LUST FROM LESS PROTEIN: LESS (in yellow) FISH BIRDMEAT CHEESE EGG BEANS PEAS NUTS . . .'

Try as I may, I cannot understand what *Stanley Green* – for that's his name – is trying to communicate. He doesn't approve of too much passion. He knows that protein makes passion. Yet he wants us to eat *less* protein, not *no* protein. Others must be mystified too for, in search of enlightenment, they have bought 58,000 copies of his booklet: 'Eight Passion Proteins With Care' at eleven pence a copy. Misguided he may be. Persistent he certainly is. I don't know if he's serious. It's *just* possible he's a saint.

Then there is the famous *spieler* in Lisson Grove Market. The expatriate New Yorker *John Lahr* has done us all a service by recording his spiel:

'Never mind £35. Never mind £22. I'll make you the envy of everybody here for £10 . . . To see who's kidding and who's bidding to separate the needy from the greedy . . . If I went much lower, I'd be in Tottenham bloody underground . . . We take any money here except matrimony.'

Those honoured with the friendship of *Elena*, otherwise Mrs Salvoni, the manageress of L'Escargot in Greek Street and once of the Café Bleu in Old Compton Street and Bianchi's, would wish me to record her warmth and affection towards the world in general and her customers in particular. Others to be noted should include *Oscar*, the Manager of the Waldorf, a dignified chap who is also – I use the word advisedly – *flamboyant*, for his skill at Crêpes Suzettes is such that he is a fellow of the International Academy of Flambiers, one of only eight so honoured.

But despite the claims of *Stanley Green* and the *spieler*, of *Elena* and *Oscar*, of *'Red'*, the Irish late night snack-seller in Soho, and of metropolitan judges and magistrates (the Master of the Rolls sucks blackcurrant sweets on the bench) the most loved character is the *Queen Mother*, who on the Royal Yacht apparently telephoned to some of the staff: 'I don't know what you old queens are doing, but this old queen could do with a whisky . . .' 85 and still following the horses it has to be . . .

Best Character: *The Queen Mother*.

Cheese

Paxton and Whitfield of 93 Jermyn Street, SW1 (01-930 0259) run a cheese club. You pay £8.60 a month and receive three different cheeses of which one at least will be British. P & W, who also deal deliciously in hams, have realised that in London appreciation of cheese has lagged a long way behind appreciation of beer, with which it is partnered so amiably. Their Stilton is the best in the world and their manager, Mr MacEwen, is one of only four cheese Chevaliers in the country. Besides the cheese club, P & W will arrange educational cheese lectures, organised in conjunction with a local wine merchant, a cheese and wine event, and send out hampers for presents consisting either of cheeses and biscuits or of a more representative selection of comestibles.

Typically *Harrods Food Hall* offers no fewer than 450 cheeses, even if it does take so long to get served that you can watch a Brie ripen as you wait. Try Dolcelatte (Italian) or Chaume or Caprice de Dieu (French). Mr Bowen, the buyer, is also a Chevalier of cheese.

Also recommended: *Mace & Potts* at the corner of the Strand and Essex Street and *Neal's Yard Dairy* where they make it and sell it. It's worth a trip to the *Prince Regent* pub in Marylebone High Street to see their imposing collection of cheese dishes and it's worth reading *The Great British Cheese Book* by Patrick Rance (Macmillan) or *Guide Du Fromage* by Androuet (revised English edition published by Aidan Ellis) on your way.

The *London Cheese Champion* is Dr Guy Mitchell, former head of psychiatry at Great Ormond Street Hospital. He can not only identify every cheese but explain the significance of all those little holes too!

Best Cheeses: *Paxton & Whitfield*.
Worst Cheeses: Anything bought in a supermarket wrapped in a triangle of tin foil with a picture of a cow or a laughing peasant on it.

Chess

> 'Chess: As elaborate a waste of human intelligence as you could find anywhere outside an advertising agency' – Raymond Chandler.
>
> 'It is impossible to win gracefully at chess. No man has yet said "Mate!" in a voice which failed to sound to his opponents better boastful and malicious.'

The sad news is that *Prompt Corner* in Parliament Hill Fields, a chess café where you could suck spaghetti all day while considering the modern Benoni, has closed. I would have been a regular there, had my dog not vomited on the feet of a most serious group of players, who scarcely blinked, even when I mopped round their odorous feet with a sopping rag. In its place is the *Chequers* (18 Chalk Farm Road, NW1). There is chess every night of the week there and at the *King's Head Pub* in Moscow Road, W2, where lightning tournaments are run most amicably, on Mondays. You can also play at the *Hole in the Wall* (12 Sutton Lane, Chiswick, W4; 01-994 4107) which has an intriguing inn sign and the *Black Lion* (2 South Black Lion Lane, W6). The best clubs are *Streatham*, *Morley College*, the *Athenaeum*, and *Richmond and Twickenham*.

The venue for matches in the London League used to be the top room at the *St Bride's Institute*, where, behind glass doors, there is a fascinating library of antique books on chess puzzles and problems. *St Bride's* is ideal for chess, being gloomy, airless and intense. Now games are played at the Bishopsgate Institute. Open air chess is played on *Clapham Common*, and the best chess set is a fine old Staunton downstairs at *Simpsons-in-the-Strand*, for long associated with chess players. Don't miss the chess tiles on the restaurant's exterior, facing the Strand. *Game Advice*, the north London chess centre (1 Holmes Road, NW5; 01-485 5226, closed 2 p.m.-3p.m.) has a huge selection of books, sets, boards and clocks; the specialists for chess computers are *Competence* (263A Eversholt Street, NW1; 01-380 0666) and for antiquarian chess books *Caissa Books* at Stand A 18/19 (01-629 3644) in the basement of *Gray's Antique Market* (1-7 Davies Mews, W1) are recommended.

The best opening for White is the Giucco Piano, and for Black the French Defence.

Chickens

The best chicken in London is the concrete sculpture with mosaic comb and wattles by *John Willett*, which may be found ruling the roost (more precisely Ashmount Junior School) in Hornsey Lane.

The worst chickens in London (though it's scarcely their fault) are the battery birds which end up spitted in the windows of fast food restaurants or spiced up by the late *Colonel Sanders*, who was not himself force-fed, but force-fed millions.

Children's London

At last it has been generally accepted that children are intelligent, that holidays seem long, that television becomes tiresome, and that the children who are admitted free or at half-price today are the ones who will pay full rates and bring *their* own children tomorrow. Almost every museum and gallery in London was involved last Summer in organising events for children. They were usually split into three age-ranges. Here are just a few of them: at the *British Museum* you could hunt the hieroglyphs, at the *Horniman* there was the opportunity to improvise a show with shadow puppets, at the *London Transport* there was table-soccer and finger-printing, at the *Museum of Childhood* a doll-in, at the *Museum of London* an afternoon in a medieval kitchen or a chance to become a Huguenot, at the *Museum of Mankind* an investigation into the crafts of the Indians and Eskimos, with war-games at the *Army Museum*, writing on the wall at the *National Gallery*, disguises at the *National Portrait Gallery*, improvised drama at *Ranger's House*, and all kinds of experiments at the *Science Museum*.

There were children's concerts at the *Barbican*, performances daily in the peripatetic *Bubble Theatre*, animations at the *ICA*, storytelling at the *National Book League*, films (what else?) at the *National Film Theatre*, Punch and Judy and other arena events at the *National Theatre*, sport and magic at the *Picketts Lock Centre* in Edmonton, Marathon Madness at the *Polka Theatre* in Wimbledon, African drumming at the *Queen Elizabeth Hall*, inflatables on the *South Bank* and an open day on waste disposal at the *Victoria Road Transfer Station*, South Ruislip (no, honestly!).

Amidst such a choice – and much of it free – what to plunk for? Study the booklets:

Holiday Fun, distributed free by the ILEA to schools and libraries.

What's On For Youngsters, free with SAE (foolscap) from Information Office, Dept for Recreation, County Hall, SO7.
Snakes and Ladders, 70p from bookshops or £1 by post from Westminster Play Association, 147 Church Street, London W2 1NA; (01-258 3817). Or telephone:
Children's London 01-246 8007
Kidsline 01-222 8070

My favourite children's activities, alas, are none of them free. The *Butterfly House* (see Butterflies) was one. The *Royal Tournament* at Earl's Court – hugely successful – was another. The rock-laser shows at the *Laserium* (01-486 2242; next to *Madame Tussauds*) are magical and mystical. And *Thorpe Park* (down the M3, follow the signs to Chertsey, then to Thorpe Park) is a splendid £3.50 worth. So many and varied are the events there (assault courses, 180° cinema, boat-trips, astonishing models of the world's most famous buildings, displays of falconry, a working farm, roller-skating, a splendid ghost train etc.) that a single day is scarcely enough, even for the most inquisitive child – or adult. Strongly recommended. Nor on any account should you miss the *Waterslide* at Richmond Baths (on the right of the Chertsey Road as it by-passes Richmond). There are four slides from the least frightening, the Corkscrew, to the alarming Black Hole – but none of them, I promise, is *too* scary. Forty minutes at £3.50 is not cheap; but marvellously exhilarating. The best playground for small children, is the *Queen's Park* playground in Kensal Rise.

If you need to feed the little mouths, hamburgers (q.v.) at *Macarthur's* or spare-ribs at the *Texas Lone Star Saloon* (see Mexican Food) could be followed by tea at the *Old Rangoon Pub* (201 Castelnau, SW13, 01-741 9656), where the garden features a duck pond for falling into and a games hut for drying out in. Grown-ups get scones and children choccy bickies with their tea. If you're feeling flush the *Gardens* (99 Kensington High Street, W8; 01-937 7994) is the Derry and Toms roof-garden tarted up with a river and flamingoes. Amazing but over-priced. On Sundays take them to lunch at the *Holiday Inn* (17 Sloane Street, W1; 01-235 4377). After the roasts (excellent value) you can doze while they drown in the handsome pool.

Best children's event: *The Waterslide*, Richmond.

(See also under such entries as Bookshops, Butterflies, Circuses, Farms, Hamburgers, Kites, Mexican Food, Model Boats, Museums, Swimming, Theatres, Toys, Zoos etc.)

Chimney Sweeps

From William Hone's *Table Book* (1826):

> On Monday, the first of May, 1826, the first anniversary dinner of the 'United Society of Master Chimney Sweepers' took place at the Eyre Tavern, St John's Wood, Marylebone.
>
> About eleven o'clock, two hundred of their apprentices proceeded in great regularity through the principal streets and squares at the west end of the town, accompanied by an excellent band of music. The clean and wholesome appearance of the lads, certainly, reflected much credit on their masters . . . the boys were regaled with a substantial repast of roast beef and plum pudding; after which the masters themselves sat down to a very excellent dinner provided for the occasion . . .
>
> Mr Bennett, of Welbeck Street, addressed the company on the subject of cleansing chimnies with the machine, the introduction of which he was confident would never answer the intended purposes. He urged the absolute necessity of climbing boys in their trade; and instanced several cases in which the machines were rendered perfectly useless: most of the chimnies in the great houses at the west end of the town were constructed in such a manner that it was utterly impossible to clear them of soot, unless a human being was sent up for that purpose . . .

The best chimney sweep in London is *Mr A. L. Ashby* (143 Harvist Road, NW6; 01-969 1633) who still uses the old-fashioned brush method and charges a gentlemanly £3.50 a go. But he doesn't send boys up the chimney.

Best sweep: *Mr Ashby.*

Chinese Restaurants

Although Chinese Restaurants, from the humblest take-away to the grandest cordon jaune, remain as consistently good as ever, there is increasing competition from Malayan, Thai, Vietnamese and Korean establishments. What seemed the summit of sophistication fifteen years ago, seems a little vieux jeu today. (Indeed I recall my first sweet and sour pork ball, and it was not unlike my first sexual initiation – I won't go into details – for the horizons that were suddenly opened. Now sweet and sour pork seems just like gristle surrounded by greasy batter in a suspiciously pink puddle.)

The new cuisine in oriental cooking seems to entail wrapping things in lettuce leaves whenever possible and serving those parts of the bird, animal or fish that other chefs cannot reach. One way to find your way around the Chinese puzzle is to join the *Chinese Gourmet Club* (249

Sandycombe Road, Kew, Surrey; 01-940 5714). Another is to try some at least of the score listed briefly below, which list covers, I hope, most of the newer and more enterprising establishments in London while giving a fair geographical spread. I have put them in alphabetical order (although *not* in alphabetical order of Chinese ideograms).

Canton, 11 Newport Place, WC2 (01-437 6220). A busy, brisk, business-like place, open all the hours Krishna gave, and seven days a week. One basic menu, one more discerning. Over 24 varieties of dim sum, none priced at more than £1.40. Predominantly Chinese clientele.

Chiang Mai, 48 Frith Street, W1 (01-437 7444). Particularly recommended for its Pahd Thai and its Chicken, Coconut and Galanga Soup.

Chuen Cheng Ku, 17 Wardour Street, W1 (01-437 1398) and 20 Rupert Street, W1; (separate entrance). A vast emporium of oriental guzzling, seating up to 400 people on several levels. The food comes round on trolleys and when you see anything you fancy, you stop it and try one. Cantonese menu with emphasis on dim sum and sea-food. Good value.

City Friends, 34 Old Bailey, EC4 (01-248 5189/4111). Old established City restaurant specialising in food from the Peking region, such as baked crab with spring onions and ginger and diced chicken in chili sauce. Closed Sundays. Not cheap.

Fung Shing, 15 Lisle Street, WC2 (01-437 1539). Rather chic, svelte even, with mirrors so you can see who else is there unobtrusively. Try eel with coriander or chili, salt, steamed carp, beancurd with crab, that sort of thing. Medium priced.

Green Cottage II, 122a Finchley Road, NW3 (01-794 3833/3969). That rare occurrence, a Chinese vegetarian restaurant, and a pretty good one. No animal fats employed. Try the Nest of Gems, the sweet and sour 'fish' (made of yams), the deep fried wuntun, the Chinese vegetables in lotus leaves, the black straw mushrooms, and – the traditional conclusion – banana fritters. Medium price.

Happy Wok, 52 Floral Street, WC2 (01-836 3696). Just across the street from the Royal Opera House, this is ideal before or after Madam Butterfly. An eclectic menu, featuring Crispy Shredded Beef in a Bird's Nest, and very fresh seafood dishes. Not cheap.

Ho Ho, 29 Maddox Street, W1 (01-493 1228) (with a sister establishment at 20 High Street, South Woodford, E18; 01-989 1041). Classy and spacious with specialities from Peking, Szechuan and Singapore. The Imperial Cold Hors D'Oeuvres is an excellent starter with aromatic duck, king prawns with ginger and chicken with cashew nuts recommended for your main course.

Hunan, 51 Pimlico Road, SW1 (01-730 5712). Julienned cucumber in place of niblets, shredded chicken in sesame dressing, Hunan duck in honey and soya, phoenix chicken, sliced jelly fish are specialities. Drink Dynasty Wine and end with Mei Kwei Lu, a golden liqueur flavoured with wild roses.

Jasmin, 50 Battersea Rise, SW1 (01-228 0336). Starched white linen table cloths and flattering lighting and food attuned to western palates (not many orientals living in Battersea). Some exceptions – i.e. Duck with Jellyfish. The crispy aromatic Peking duck is a succulent stand-by, and the filleted chicken dumpling with spring onions and garlic is excellent so long as you're not the only one to choose it. Not cheap.

Kong Lam, 57 Abbeville Road, SW4 (01-673 2791). Peking cuisine, and a strong recommendation for the under-privileged Clapham area. Hot and sour soup and shrimp with sesame seeds are excellent. Open every day.

Ley-Ons, 56 Wardour Street, W1 (01-437 6465/743 2769). A formidable restaurant, much respected, long-established and reasonably priced (set dinner £5.20). Apparently the only restaurant in London serving sharks' fin dumplings.

Lok Ho Fook, 4/5 Gerrard Street, W1 (01-437 2001). The archetypal Chinatown restaurant, large, renowned, busy and frequently off-hand. Notable for sea-food and the amazing Fried Milk, but most of the food is predictably good.

Memories of China, 56 Ebury Street, SW1 (01-730 7734). Otherwise known as *Ken Lo's Memories of China*, Ken Lo being the remarkable tennis-playing, self-publicising, charming bon-viveur. Excellent Pekinese, Szechuan and Hunan food. Not cheap, but worth it.

Mr Kong, 21 Lisle Street, W1 (01-437 7341). A close neighbour of Fung Shing (see above), this place is named after the chef, and not to be confused with Mr Chung of Greenwich or Mr Tang of Shaftesbury Avenue – both also well worth a visit incidentally. Scallops on the shell, paper-bag salt and pepper spare ribs, oysters in soya and sea bass figure on a menu which is well worth researching. Open till late. Medium price.

Oakwood Palace, Oakwood, 113 Bramley Road, N14 (01-886 6639/3945). An improbable place to include here, but the excellent spare ribs justify a mention.

O Malean Chinese Restaurant, 1585 London Road, SW16 (01-764 2336). Also unfashionably situated, but this is well worth hunting down for its duck with green peppers, its bang bang chicken and its

Manchurian lamb. Toffee bananas, naturally, to round things off. Very fairly priced.

Poon's, 41 King Street, WC2 (01-240 1743) and 4 Leicester Street, WC2; (01-437 1528). Always seem to slip into lists of Chinese restaurants do the two branches of Poon's. I have always preferred the brisk bustling efficiency of the more modest Leicester Square operation – excellent value – to the trendier and rather superior Covent Garden branch, but the food at the latter is usually excellent.

Princess Garden, 8-10 North Audley Street, W1 (01-493 3223). A very smart Mayfair restaurant with chefs imported from Hong Kong and large circular tables to sit at with eleven friends. Hand-made noodles, Pekinese prawns on toast, fish smoked in tea leaves (!), pancakes with red beans and stuffed pork dumplings are recommended, plus, of course, the ubiquitous crispy duck. Not cheap, but then the restaurant cost the owners two million pounds, and they need to get something back . . .

Zen, Chelsea Cloisters, Sloane Avenue, SW3 (01-589 1781). Under the management of Cecil Wu and K. S. Leung, the Chef, this and its off-shoot are about as up-market as Chinese restaurants go. So elegant and sophisticated that I often wonder what I have done to deserve such treatment. Food includes squirrel fish, boned duck web, sautèed asparagus and scallops, bon bon chicken (too polite to call it bang bang here), duck's tongue, jellyfish cold toss, and so on. Obviously necessary to book and to take out a second mortgage. An event however.

Zen Too, 53 Old Brompton Road, SW7 (01-225 1609). See above. If you can't get into the one, try the other. (This is known as the Gabor Syndrome – subtle middle-aged joke.)

Oh, and by the way, Chinese soft and crispy buns of all sorts are available from *Kowloon*, the Chinese bakery, at 21 Gerrard Street, W1; (01-437 1694).

Best Chinese Restaurant: *Happy Wok*.

Chocolates

There have been only two significant moments in my development as a human being. The second was the day I discovered *Bendick's bittermints*. The bittermint is a plain dark chocolate filled with mint and surrounded by foil. A single mouthful and you are participating in the decline and fall of the Roman Empire. It is obtainable from its

HQ, Bendicks, (195 Sloane Street, SW1; 01-235 4749) and other Bendick's branches in Royal Exchange, New Bond Street, Throgmorton Street, and Wigmore Street, W1, as well as most serious-minded delicatessens, but, besides Bendicks, London is choc-a-block with chocs.

Ackerman's Chocolates (9 Goldhurst Terrace, NW6; 01-924 2742) not only do a mischievous line in champagne truffles and noisettes, but they can also supply a chocolate zoo and delectables for diabetics, who deserve a bit of luxury. At *Quirk's* (76 St John's Wood High Street, NW8; 01-586 9525), where you must expect to pay £4 a pound, they enjoy pouring melted chocolate on fresh strawberries. At *Charbonnel et Walker* (1 Royal Arcade, 28 Old Bond Street, W1; 01-629 4396) you can buy a boïte blanche with a greeting spelt out in gold-wrapped chocolates or chocolates for children with animals on top. *Thornton's* (2 The Market, WC2; 01-836 2173) sells handmade chocolates but specialises in toffee, while *Lessiter's Chocolatiers* (167a Finchley Road, NW3; 01-624 5925) have attracted adherents who will be stretched on the rack before they will part with a rum truffle.

On the subject of truffles the best in London, at 25p a truf, come from *Prestat* (40 South Molton Street, W1; 01-629 4838). Actually that is not so expensive. At *Teuscher* near the Rockefeller Center, New York truffles were 92 cents each. (At least the one I ate was and that was when the pound was worth a pound). At *Prestat* one pound carton of Napoleon truffles costs a mere £7.70, but will never be forgotten (incidentally truffles will keep for over six months in a deep freeze). Furthermore *Prestat*, founded in 1908, has exclusive rights to chocolate moulded Paddington Bears. A little bear is £2.50, a giant one £9.50 milk or plain. (Personal shoppers only.) Belgian hand-made chocolates are obtainable from the *Regent Emporium* (8/12 Quadrant Arcade and 80/82 Regent Street, W1; 01-437 4513).

And at Harrods Food Hall join the queue at *Elena's* counter for Leonides chocolates. 'Manon' at £4.90 a pound is a confection of fresh cream, white chocolate, caramel and nuts, and sinful as hell. (You can also buy them at Selfridges.)

The most extraordinary chocolate shop in London is *Rococo* (321 King's Road, SW3; 01-352 5857). Here in the premises once occupied by the Crane Art Gallery, Chantal Cody, an ex-art-student, has opened a kind of chocolate gallery, realising, as I have long argued, that a chocolatier is or should be an artist. Anything can be made to order in chocolate or sugar – an edible engagement ring costs £7.50 – and there's even an edible chandelier.

You can also eat tea there and even buy the furniture which may or may not be made of chocolate.

Best Chocolates: *Bendick's Bittermints*.
Best Chocolatier: *Chantal Cody*.
Worst Chocolates: The confectionary machine, westward District Line, South Kensington, fails to deliver any. *Which* magazine reports that one out of four attempts to get chocolate out of such machines ends in failure, and one out of eight in the loss of money!

Churches

How is it possible to choose between Wren and Hawksmoor, Vanbrugh, Butterfield and Gibbs? Between *St Bartholomew-the-Great, Smithfield*, the oldest parish church in London, and Norman architecture at its noblest with a brick tower and a wooden turret housing a complete ring of bells – though these are never rung lest the patients in Bart's Hospital are disturbed) and the Gibbs baroque of *St Mary-le-Strand*, the finest traffic island in the world? Between the prettiness of *St John's*, Downshire Hill (S.P. Cockerell c 1818), *Hinde Street Methodist Church*, the Victorian Gothic of *St Augustine*, Kilburn (J. L. Pearson 1880) and the high splendours of *St Mary the Virgin*, Bourne Street, SW1 (W. P. Manning 1885) with its small but excellent professional choir? It isn't possible.

St Dunstan's, the medieval church in Stepney Green within its seven-acre country churchyard is miraculous. It escaped the Blitz, which was half a miracle, and it boasts a majestic east window by Hugh Easton, representing the risen Christ above the rubble of the East End. And is it fair to compare *St Magnus-the-Martyr*, rebuilt by Wren (1671-87) whose interior T. S. Eliot described as 'inexplicable splendour of Ionian white and gold', *St Bride's*, the Cathedral of Fleet Street, whose 226-feet Wren spire inspired a local baker to invent the wedding cake (within the Cathedral's bowels were discovered seven earlier churches and 5,000 skeletons), *St Mary Woolnoth*, and *Christ Church*, Spitalfields, two of Hawksmoor's masterpieces, and *St Andrew Undershaft*, named after the Maypole which used to be set up outside it each Mayday until 1517? Then there is *Holy Joe's* (St Joseph's, Highgate Hill) the large and delightfully ugly Romanesque building, like a clumsy adolescent. To choose between them is like choosing between spring and autumn or Donne and Herbert.

So the choice must be instantaneous: *St Ethelburga-the-Virgin-Within-*

Bishopsgate. The virgin saint behaved so impeccably during a 7th-century plague that Bede remarked: 'No person who knew her ought to question but that the heavenly kingdom was opened to her, when she departed this world.' Her brother, *St Erconwald*, was also a saint – that couldn't have been easy – and her father possibly the King of East Anglia. Anyway her church is tiny, merely 56½ feet long and 30 feet high, and dates back to the early 15th century, though the doorway could be even earlier. The west front of common ragstone with a silly little bell-turret on top reminds me of a small bull terrier standing staunchly against the encroaching bulls of Bishopsgate. It survived both Great Wars and the Great Fire but has been much renovated. The organ, described by those who know about such things, as having a mellow tone with an admirable violin diapason and great flute stops, fills much of the interior, and three attractive windows tell the story of the voyage of Henry Hudson, he of the Hudson River, and his gallant crew. Having vicariously shared their adventures you may, by permission of the verger, pass into the tiny garden at the rear of the church. Here pigeons drink from the terracotta bowl of the fountain, this and the octagonal pool around it being the gift of the Billiter Literary Society in June 1923. Even in rough weather the garden may be enjoyed for there's a covered loggia.

Overlooked as it is by skyscrapers and office buildings this must be the most peaceful place in the City of London. On the way out you step over a motto taken from the ancient temple of Aesculapius: Bonus Intra, Melior Exi – 'Come in Good, Go out Better.' *St Ethelburga's Church* is an architectural muddle, unassuming, little written about by the posh church-fanciers, but all the same *one does*.

Best Church (for atmosphere): *St Ethelburga-the-Virgin-Within-Bishopsgate*.
Best Church (for architecture): *St Mary-le-Strand*.
Best Modern Church: *The Scottish Church of St Columba*, Pont Street.

P.S. There are many books on London churches. *The Good Church Guide* (Ed. Anthony Kilmister – Blond & Briggs/Penguin) is a splendid read, with an excellent section on London.

Cinemas

British Film Year came and went and attendances at cinemas looked rather healthier. The TV film industry continues to flourish. There is a deep and mysterious pod of talent amongst the independent companies, several hundred strong, who continue to feed excellent fiction to the television companies – particularly the flourishing Channel 4 – but fail to make much impact on the international markets. Within the London area, however, there remain enough concerned cinema-goers to keep the good cinemas profitable. By 'good' I mean those which offer interesting films in comfortable surroundings and project these films expertly at affordable prices to interested audiences. I shall be specific. The following are good: The *National Film Theatre*, the *Screen-on-the-Green*, the *Screen-on-the-Hill*, the *Screen on Baker Street* and the *Electric Screen* in Portobello Road; the *Gates* at Bloomsbury and Notting Hill; the *Camden Parkway*, the *Curzon* but not the *Curzon*, *West End*; the *Academy*, the *Minema*, the *Everyman*, the *Ritzy*, Brixton Road, the *Roxie*, Wardour Street, the *Rio*, Dalston, the *Scala*, King's Cross and the *Lumière*, St Martin's Lane.

Bad cinemas are those which offer bad films badly projected in minimal comfort to boorish audiences. In such circumstances the price is immaterial; one would be better off at home. Bad, in one way or another, are these: the *Ritz*, Leicester Square, the *Odeon*, Swiss Cottage, the *Cinecenta* cinemas, the *Moulin*, Great Windmill Street, and the *Classic*, Praed Street.

Features of the good ones: The *Curzon*, which is not cheap, and *Gate* 2 are luxuriously comfortable. So are the *Camden Plaza* and the *Lumière*. The *Minema* is delightfully intimate. The *Academy* shows worthwhile shorts and will run a film that is losing money if it believes that it deserves to succeed. The *Ritzy* is fun, but has financial problems too. The *Rio* and the *Roxie* are brave with inventive and even witty double bills. At the *Ritzy* they sell slabs of home made chocolate cake. The *Everyman* is hooked on classics.

The *Screens*, the *Scala*, the *NFT*, the *Gates*, the *Rio*, the *Ritzy* and the *Roxie* are clubs with reciprocal membership arrangements and instant membership. They are in touch with current trends and respect their audiences, not starting their main feature until all the paying public are in their seats. (At a visit to the *Screen-on-the-Hill* the film had been running a half hour when the box office manager rushed into the auditorium and shouted 'Jesus Christ! I've been robbed!'). The S-o-t-H is particularly friendly. Peter Walker, the Manager at the *Camden Parkway* has entrepreneurial flair. During the run of 'A Passage to India' he pursuaded Eric, the newsagent from across the road, to put on a turban, black up, and welcome the audience in pidgin English from the stage. Commented Walker: 'A few extreme lefties said the coloureds wouldn't like it, but the Asians roared their heads off.'

Bad features of the bad ones? The Swiss Cottage *Odeon* has 'scarily situated lavatories'. The *Ritz*, Leicester Square, built by Jack Buchanan, is draughty, over-priced with bad projection and promotion. It has also removed its lovely art deco ladies from its walls. The *Cinecenta*, while sensibly staggering the times of their programmes, have tiny screens which are hard to see and poor sound which is hard to hear. Late night films every night. The *Moulin* shows terrible films. The *Thorn-EMI* circuit duopoly is a continuing scandal and discourages a new generation of concerned cinema-goers. A word of warning: the *Classic Haymarket* has no facilities for wheelchair users. The *Curzon West End* projects out of focus.

The recently opened *Metro* shows in the basement of the dreadful Trocadero development at Piccadilly Circus experimental work by British film-makers and has projecting facilities for video as well as film.

Best Cinema: *The Ritzy*.
Worst Cinema: *The Moulin*. (Censored porn – the worst of all worlds!)

Circuses

> Dame Laura Knight
> Had unusually keen sight
> She could spot a circus clown, they say,
> A couple of miles away. E. Clerihew Bentley

The only remaining regular circus seems to be *Gerry Cottle's*, and, in response to the animal liberationists, they have reduced their animal acts to a minimum (though a circus without animals has lost something of its raison d'être). But *Cottle's Circus* had enough reason for cut-backs. Having been invited to Iran by the Shah for a substantial fee, they ran into a revolution, and that, expensively, was that. Now the slimmed-down circus has a narrative structure – a story about two dancing dolls. Nothing new about this – the Victorian circus had similar narratives.

Gerry Cottle's is a true family circus with an amiable and engaging flavour. A regular venue is Clapham Common.

Best Circus: *Gerry Cottle*.

Clairvoyants

Whether it is auragraph readings, psychic development, electro-crystal therapy, self-hypnosis, or merely old-fashioned clairvoyance you're after, 33 Belgrave Square, SW1 (01-235 3351) should be your first port of call, for this is the centre of the *Spiritualist Association of Great Britain*. In the Conan Doyle Room, decorated with an imposing chandelier and plastic flowers, I attended a public demonstration by *Janet Smithers*, the cheeriest of mediums. She encouraged me to believe that the book you are now reading would be a success, and passed on a message for me from 'Cyril'. *Cyril?* There are meetings at the centre every afternoon (3.30 p.m.) and evening (7.15 p.m.) and the charges are modest. *Paul McElhoney* specialises in apport seances and the production of ectoplasm, but the clairvoyant currently held in the highest regard is *Louis Benjamin*.

My appointment to see a Romany clairvoyant at *Mysteries* (Monmouth Street, WC2; 01-240 3688) got off to a shaky start when they wrote down the date and the time of the appointment incorrectly. When finally I got to see the Romany who had been most strongly recommended (at £12 a throw I needed a strong recommendation) she got my age wrong by eleven years, and just about everything else wrong as well. But a variety of fortune-tellers, using palmistry, psychometry and crystal balls, are available at *Mysteries*, and I may have been unfortunate.

Recently *Doris Stokes* has become a vogue, hiring large halls like the Dominion to demonstrate her psychic powers. She is jolly, and has a thing about polished floors.

If you wish to unravel astrological puzzles for yourself, you may enrol for a course at *The Company of Astrologers*, 6 Queen Square, Bloomsbury, WC1 (01-837 4410). On the other hand for a personal horoscope you could try ringing *Graham Rowe* or *Judith Beech* of the Three Steps Astrological Services on 01-644 7640.

A few other suggestions:
Madame Theodora, specialist in the Magic Mirror – £25 a go, 01-834 5696.
Madame Ghesh, astrology, clairvoyance, palmistry, tarot, every Sunday afternoon at the Leicester Towers Hotel, W2.
Elizabeth Adams, psychic adviser, speaking French, Spanish and Italian can be your 'confident' (sic) – 01-727 6561.
Jackie London, 'spiritual advisor' (sic) 01-458 3515.
J. M. Gandhi, all the usual skills, plus 'personalised talismans' (sic) at

34 Brentmead Gardens, off Twyford Abbey Road, NW10 7DS; 01-965 9541.

You will notice that clairvoyants are lousy spellers – however successfully they may cast them. And a word of warning. Don't expect to receive alarming messages from the beyond. British clairvoyants seem extremely anxious to tell you what you wish to hear. Their messages tend towards vagueness and admit of many interpretations; they never give you the winner of tomorrow's three thirty.

Best Clairvoyants: the *Spiritualist Association of GB.**

*They will also supply you with a list of spiritualist churches in your neighbourhood.

Clocks

Should you find yourself in Fleet Street on the stroke of noon, hurry to *St-Dunstan-in-the-West* (an interesting church anyway, for John Donne was once its vicar and Izaac Walton its vestryman). In a niche stands the only known contemporary statue of Elizabeth I. But the church's chief claim to renown is its clock, removed when the old church was pulled down – Charles Lamb wept to see it go – and returned from sanctuary in St Dunstan's Lodge, Regent's Park, in 1936. The clock (Thomas Harris, 1671) projects over the pavement, and behind the dials stand the two giants variously referred to as 'savages', 'wooden horologists', 'bell-thumpers' and 'Gog and Magog'. The mechanism is basic and the giants strike the bell 'so indolently', writes an anonymous author, although in fact they only appear to strike it, 'that spectators often complained that they were not well up to their work'. Despite this, and despite their being 'nude almost to impropriety' they were universally admired and 'Punch was hardly so popular'.

Other interesting clocks include the apostle clock at the *Horniman Museum*, which has a whole tower to itself, like a pip-squeak *Big Ben* (even pipper and squeaker is the pathetic little thing outside *Victoria Station*); the *Fortnum and Mason's* clock, which chimes the quarters and on the hour the founders trot out to make sure that everything in Piccadilly is as it should be (incidentally, William Fortnum was a footman to Queen Anne); the original Act of Parliament clock in the *George Tavern*, Borough High Street; the much loved *Selfridges'* clock, and of course *Big Ben* himself. The name properly applies not to the clock but to the 13½ ton bell, struck at the Whitechapel Bell Foundry, which happily still survives. A huge fob watch complete with winder overhangs *Arthur Saunders*, watchmaker, of Southampton Row. But the best clock around London has to be the astronomical clock (Nicholas Oursian, 1540) over the Anne Boleyn Gateway at *Hampton Court Palace*. Still working, cunning and beautiful, it is quite a clock. A miniature version of the Hampton Court clock may be seen on the exterior of *Bracken House*, Cannon Street, the building in which the *Financial Times* is published. Time, after all, is money. This clock, by Thwaites and Reed of Clerkenwell, has a conventional face on the reverse side, and this may be seen from the interior of the building.

Two silly clocks. At the *Eccentrics' Club* in St James's is a pendulum clock whose hands move backwards to symbolise that within the club Time is irrelevant. At *World's End*, a fashion boutique in King's Road, Chelsea, is a clock which not only runs very fast backwards but has 13 hours on its dial. That way madness lies. The clock of *St George the Martyr*, opposite Borough tube, has three silvered faces. The one drab face looks out over the residents of Lambeth, who were too mean to cough up enough to deserve better.

Best Clock: *Astronomical Clock, Hampton Court.*
Worst Clock: *World's End, Chelsea.*

Clubs

See under London Clubs.

Cobblers

The best cobbler in London is *C. E. Cham* (132 Allitsen Road, NW8; 01-722 3389). He knows all his customers' shoes by heart and sole; and *H. M. Jordan* in Nugent Terrace. This is a marvellous place, with the ancient signs still on the wall ('Orders executed on the shortest notice', 'Repairs called for and Sent Home', 'The Ole in the Wall – Rapid Boots Repairers – Best English Leather used'). What is more to the point, the shop is still run by the Jordan family, who are consistently helpful and kind, and take the greatest trouble, even on the most modest order.

At 21 Meard Street, Soho, there is *H. Peen*, a maker of boot and shoe-lasts whose workshops can be observed (and very picturesque they are too) through the front window of the fine Georgian house – one of a fine terrace. See also: Shoe Shops.

Best Cobbler: *H. M. Jordan.*

Cocktails

> Cocktails and laughter
> But what comes after
> Nobody knows . . . Noël Coward

The American Bar at the *Savoy* (Strand, 01-836 4343) is for well-heeled old-timers; Harry's Bar at the *Park Lane* (Piccadilly, W1; 01-499 6321) is for Hemingway types, although Harry has been replaced by David. At the Nicholas Bar of the *Café Royal* (68 Regent Street, W1; 01-439 6082) the ghost of Oscar Wilde sips at a weak hock and seltzer and Augustus Johns line the walls, while, if you wish to fantasise that you're meeting Faye Dunaway for a natter about old times, the Palm Court at the *Ritz* with its gold-leaved fountain is the place to be. If you care to get your nose hopelessly entangled in lotus blossoms and water-lilies Trader Vic's at the *Park Lane Hilton* (22 Park Lane, W1; 01-493 8000) is for you, but waiters with too many teeth in Hawaiian shirts (that sounds wrong) are not my scene. I prefer the contemporary style of cocktail bar, such as *The Palm* (539 Battersea Park Road, SW11), *Fridays* (24/26 Great Russell Street, WC1), the *Zanzibar* (30 Great Queen Street, WC2) or *Rumours* (51 Frith Street, W1; 01-734 2738; 33 Wellington Street, WC2; 01-836 0038; 41 Mackennal Street, NW8; 01-722 5009). *Rumours* in Wallington Street has that authentic cocktail air of frivolity with most cocktails priced at £2 between 11 a.m. and 3 p.m. and 5.30 p.m. and 7.30 p.m. Here you may drink a Killer Zombie or a Suffering Bastard, a Dr Funk ('says more about you than American Express') or an Impatient Virgin ('an adventure into the unknown'). Fun, but crowded.

Also recommended: *Masters*, 90 Queensgate, SW7 (01-581 5666) where the cocktails are excellent and the Brandy Alexanders the *best*. *Zee Zees*, 212 Fulham Road, SW10 (01-351 5303). A lively American style cocktail bar with 'home cooking'.

Cyril Ray adjudged that the best cocktail is the Sidecar, so called from the officers of Pershing's Army in Paris, who travelled to Harry's Bar in sidecars. In those days it was equal parts of lemon juice, cointreau and cognac, but they make them stronger than that these days. Set 'em up, Joe.

If you are in the business of mixing your own you will need to visit the *Cocktail Shop* (30 Neal Street, W1; 01-836 5772) where you'll find shakers, straws, swizzle sticks, trays, and appropriately jazzy accessories.

Best cocktail bar: (traditional) Palm Court at the *Ritz*.
(trendy) *Rumours* in Covent Garden.

Coffee

Let's not beat about the bush. *H. R. Higgins* (coffee-man) *Ltd* is my man. His aromatic emporium (42 South Molton Street, W1; 01-629 3913) glows with shafts of golden light reflecting off antique copper containers and his display of old wooden grinders is a delight to the eye. His original coffees include Tanzanian Chagga farmed by the Wa-Chagga tribe who live on the slopes of Mount Kilimanjaro, his Colombian Libano Supreme, exceptionally full-flavoured, and his Nicaraguan Dark Roasted, mild without acidity. Higgins's blended coffees are cheaper than his originals, but the very dark roasted coffees (Santiago, Creole, Sultan and Continental Blends) are to ordinary blends as curry is to mince. Once you have been initiated there is no turning back. Mr Tony Higgins and Miss Audrey Higgins are prepared to lecture on coffee on request.

Marcus Coffee (13 Connaught Street, SW2; 01-723 4020) can offer thirty-two varieties of bean, while at the *Algerian Coffee Stores* (52 Old Compton Street, W1; 01-437 2480) you can buy coffee sacks and coffee machines as well as burgundies, ports, teas . . . and coffee. Their most popular lines are their Esotico ('rich and nutty') and their Velluto Nero ('subtle and silky'). The *Drury Tea and Coffee Company* (1-3 Mepham Street, SW1; 01-928 2551 – also in New Row, WC1; 01-836 2607 and 37 Drury Lane, W1; 01-836 2607) is old fashioned in the best sense. The coffees – 27 beans and blends in three degrees of roasting – are roasted in the Waterloo branch, but ground in the New Row and Drury Lane. While at the *Monmouth Coffee House* (27 Monmouth Street, WC2; 01-836 2572) you can try a cup of coffee on the premises before committing yourself to buying. Although they do not stock a great variety, their coffee is amongst the cheapest in London (£2.70 per half kilo, with lower rates the more you buy). *A. Angelucci* (23b Frith Street, W1; 01-437 5889) has been established fifty years and knows his beans, and at *Coffee Campaign* (52 Acre Lane,

SW2; 01-732 4144) you can be certain that the coffee you buy will not be abetting wicked bosses with rhino whips to exploit starving peasants. Apparently Tanzanian coffee is the most acceptable to grass roots socialists, but that brings us back to the Chagga tribe and Mr Higgins. Also recommended with confidence is *L. Fern & Co.* (27 Rathbone Place, W1; 01-636 2237 and two branches). They've been roasting and blending for ninety years.

At the *Swiss Coffee House*, 38 Lamb's Conduit Street, WC1 (01-405 7950) you can accompany your éclairs with one of the best cups of coffee around.

It is too depressing to list the abomination served in most cafés and canteens; they sully the good name of coffee. Indian restaurants are notorious. The best coffee from a machine comes from the Zanussi machines, which grind as well as heat the coffee, at Channel 4 in Charlotte Street, which could be why the programmes are so laid back.

Best coffee: *H. R. Higgins.*
Worst coffee: In the buffets of British Rail trains.

Concert Halls

It all depends on what you want. *Fairfield Halls* in Croydon is a deeply depressing pile of a place, in deeply depressing Croydon, but the acoustics are superb, the best in London. The *Wigmore Hall* is ideal for recitals and is charmingly staffed, but the dire murals are discouraging. For Mahler and Bruckner and the Last Night of the Proms, the *Albert Hall* is irreplaceable, but 'pack 'em in and hang the sound' seems often to be the attitude. It's like listening to music from within the belly of an elephant. (The freehold of a ten-seater grand tier box at the *Albert Hall* would currently cost you some £150,000.) On the South Bank the choice is between the *Royal Festival Hall* (capacity 3,000 with room for 250 musicians on the platform), the *Queen Elizabeth Hall* (seats 1,100), where the cheap seats are every bit as good as the expensive ones, and the delightful *Purcell Room* (seats 372), where, while enjoying excellent chamber music at half the price of an LP, you may have to suffer from the vagaries of eccentric page-turners.

At the *Barbican Hall* singers are able to exploit the gentlest of pianissimi, and the audience are close enough to the musicians to feel deeply involved in a Brahms love song or Chopin nocturne. The initial acoustic problems have been solved. The worst acoustics in

London are at the *Logan Hall*, University of London. Its atmosphere is unhelpful too.

A fine summer evening at *Kneller Hall*, Whitton, Middx, the home of the Royal Military School of Music, where concerts are given under the stars is unforgettable, but *Kenwood* can be even more seductive. The ornamental lakes, alive with nightingales and kingfishers and owls, form a magical setting for open air music on warm June evenings.

St John's, Smith Square, rebuilt after the Blitz is now used for concerts and lectures. It also has a wine bar. Consulted on the design, Queen Anne kicked her footstool over and snapped: 'Oh why not build it like that?', which the architect did. Nonetheless this Footstool Church has a certain baroque charm and pleasant acoustics.

Best concert hall: *Purcell Room.*
Worst concert hall: *Logan Hall.*

Cosmetics and body care

> *'Le nez de Cleopatre, s'il eût été plus court, toute la face de la terre aurait changé.'* Blaise Pascal (1623-1662)

The Body Shop (six branches since its inception seven years ago) sells only natural lotions, creams, oils, shampoos etc. in refillable containers. They have been recommended to me by a walking advertisement for their properties. *Joan Price's Face Places* (33 Cadogan Street, SW3; 01-589 9062 and 31 Connaught Street, W2; 01-723 6671) allow you to try out their beauty products before parting with good (isn't it always?) money. They are stockists for most of the leading brands, which means that you can compare lipsticks at one counter – a service not readily available elsewhere.

Estée Lauder Cosmetics (71 Grosvenor Street, W1; 01-493 9271) are extremely pricey. To pay such sums to be made more beautiful hints at desperation.

Animal Aid (111 High Street, Tonbridge, Kent; Tonbridge 364546) will let you know which cosmetic firms refuse to abuse animals in their research. Any product marked 'Beauty without Cruelty' is safe, as are *Boots* own brand cosmetics, *Yardley* and *Innoxa*. At *L'Herbier de Provence* (241 Fulham Road, SW10; 01-352 0012) they stock, besides herbs and spices, such invigorating items as essential oils, dried flowers and beauty products. The people who serve you are charming and smell delightful, as does the whole establishment.

The parade of the demi-mondaine in the cosmetic department at Harrods is like something out of de Maupassant.

The *Aetherius Society* (757 Fulham Road, SW6; 01-736 4187) has been mounting a muscular campaign – at least for such an aetherial organisation – to get natural therapies, such as herbalism, homeopathy, acupuncture and osteopathy, within the rigours of the National Health Service. Since waiting lists on the NHS are so extended, this sounds like a harmless way to shorten them.

Best cosmetics: *The Face Place.*

P.S. Are people really deceived by packing such tiny bottles of scent in such large boxes?

Cottages

In Victorian London there was a craze for building miniature houses, often Gothic and usually topped with a tea-cosy of thatch. The most famous of these *fermes ornées* were *Ivy Cottage* at Parson's Green, *Queen's Cottage* in Kew Gardens and *Craven Cottage* at Fulham. One of the few survivors besides *Queen's Cottage* is *Hunter's Grove* in Belsize Lane, NW3, very charming and rather silly as the fashion required. An earlier example is *The Hermitage*, 8 Church Road, Hanwell; with its whitewashed walls and ogival doorway it is reminiscent of a Beatrix Potter illustration. Less fey are the 18th century cottages at *1-6 Pond Square*, Highgate. But the essence of an ideal cottage is that it should be delightful, lived in, and unexpected, and I must therefore refer you to *Lisson Grove Cottages* – follow the alley beside the quaint Lisson Grove post office – described by Geoffrey Fletcher as 'industrial revolution combined with Peabody'. Dated 1855 these cottages are certainly an unlikely survival. So too are *Chester Cottages* and *Sparke's Cottages*, both so improbably sited behind the Royal Court Theatre as not even to figure in the A-Z. Rose-bedecked and winsome, they are nevertheless real working cottages. The terrace of cottages (c 1810) in *Old Palace Lane*, Richmond, next to the White Swan, are best in the bleak midwinter when the crowds of pubby tourists stay at home. *Maunsel Street*, SW1, is another delightful and beautifully maintained terrace. *Canonbury Grove*, N1, is a row of charming cottages – houses almost – beside the New River. The lock-keeper's cottage at *St Pancras Lock* on the Regent's Canal amidst its chrysanthemums appears as isolated as if it were in the depths of the country.

Best cottages: *Chester Cottages*, SW1.

P.S. 'Cottaging' is not hunting for cottages by the way. If you want to know what it is, read *Prick Up Your Ears*, the biography of Joe Orton, by John Lahr, or ask anyone in the Joe Orton Bar at the King Edward VI pub, 25 Bromfield Street, N1. They'll tell you. They may even show you.

Courts

Within the Law Courts in the Strand, there are some 30 courts, including the *Courts of Appeal*, the *Divisions of Chancery, Queen's Bench*, and *Probate, Divorce* and *Admiralty*. You can visit during term-time between 10.30 a.m. and 1 p.m. and between 2 p.m. and 4 p.m. and admittance is free, although in the eighteenth century one had to pay two shillings. To get to *Queen's Bench* you need to be fit – there are many stairs to be climbed. But probably *Probate* is the best bet where entertainment is concerned. As a building, well what can one say? Best perhaps to leave it to E. V. Lucas, who describes the Law Courts as 'the most astounding assemblage of spires and turrets, and gables and cloisters, that ever sprang from one Englishman's brain'.

The public is also admitted to the *Old Bailey*, the court for crimes committed in the London area (Mon-Fri 10.15 a.m. and 1.45 p.m.), located on the site of the dastardly old Newgate Prison – the Court is called the *Central Criminal Court*, the street is Old Bailey. On the first two days of each session the judges carry posies and the court is disinfected with odoriferous herbs either to keep the Plague away, or to overcome the stench of the prison. Free tours of the *Old Bailey* (01-248 3277) and the *Royal Courts of Justice* (01-405 7641) are available daily. See also under Magistrates' Courts.

Crafts

See under Arts and Crafts.

Crêperies

The best pancakes may be enjoyed at *Astrix* and *La Crêperie de l'Ecluse*, but for details of these, see under Budget Restaurants.

Cream Cakes

Here too you must turn the pages and look under Tea Houses/Cream Cakes. There is a method in all this exercise. The purpose is to shape the edge of your appetite for mille feuilles.

Crescents

For several years I lived in the handsomest crescent in London. This was, and remains, *The Paragon*, Blackheath, and consists of a cluster of mansions linked by colonnades, designed by Michael Searles circa 1790, bombed and extensively rebuilt as flats. Before the war it had been unsmart and contained a hotel. Now, with landscaped gardens at the rear, and spell-binding trees and daffodils in the front, *The Paragon* is most attractive. Living there had its drawbacks however. We were not permitted to feed the birds, my dog chased the Air-Vice-Marshal's cat, and children were never conceived nor born on the premises. Adjacent to *The Paragon* and almost as impressive is Morden College, brick almshouses almost certainly designed by Wren.

Very satisfactory is *Pelham Crescent*, which, like much of Belgravia, was built by George Basevi, Sir John Soane's pupil. The houses here and in *Pelham Place* (1820-1830) are exactly as town houses should be with iron railings and balconies, elegant cornices, good, solid front doors, and high moulded ceilings. Gainsboroughs should hang on the walls. Even more to my taste is *Wilton Crescent*, built a few years later. How handsome are the house numbers here and in Kinnerton Street, which cuddles *Wilton Crescent*, and is itself a half-crescent. As Gascoigne, one of London's worst poets, wrote:

I sing Belgravia! that fair spot of ground
Where all that worldlings covet most is found!
Of this stupendous town, this mighty heart!
Of England's frame, the Fashionable part!

The Crescent (1827) in Crescent Grove, Clapham, is quite beautiful. Julius Caesar Czarnikow, the merchant, was once a resident. *Annett's Crescent* at 246-290 Essex Road, N1, is another late Georgian gem, and I have always enjoyed driving round the *Aldwych* which reminds me of a vast plunger for unblocking the drains which embouch into the Thames – Kingsway, of course, being the handle. It's worth a small detour to glance at *Mountford Crescent* in Barnsbury, which boasts particularly handsome 1830 villas. Also in north London glance at the lovely *Keystone Crescent*, just off the Caledonian Road, a little toy of a crescent.

The most spectacular crescent in London is Nash's *Park Crescent*. The rebuilt façades have copied the destroyed ones in every particular, and what finer gateway to a park could there be? But it's a shame that one has to stare at it so balefully from traffic jams, and that so much of it is lit internally with neon. This crescent of 1812 was the first major construction in Parkes' Roman Cement, thus inaugurating the age of stucco. It was to have been part of the largest circus in Europe, but was never completed.

Best crescent: *The Paragon*.
Worst crescent: *Albacore Crescent*, Catford.

Cricket

Well, it has to be *Lord's*, despite everything. And if you want to know why the best answer is to quote from the Autobiography of Neville Cardus (1947):

> A hundred times I have walked down St John's Wood Road on a quiet morning – that's the proper way to enjoy Lord's: choose a match of no importance, for preference one for which the fixture card promises "a band if possible". I have gone a hundred times into the Long Room out of the hot sun and never have I not felt that this is a good place to be in, and if the British simply *had* to make cricket a national institution and a passion and a pride, this was the way to do it, in a handsome hall and pavilion, a resting place for the game's history, with its constitution to be found as much in Debrett as in *Wisden*. I have looked through the great windows on the field of play and seen the cricketers in the heat, moving like creatures in another element, the scene as though suspended in time; the crowd a painted canvas; the blue sky and the green of the trees at the nursery end; the lordly ones slumbering on the white seats of the pavilion, or greatly talking.

I should be happy to abandon the rest of this book and quote Cardus instead. Nor do I believe that any of my readers would demand their money back.

A curiosity of *Lord's*. There are plans afoot to develop the Mound Stand at a cost of several millions. But the view from the Mound has never been much. What is needed is more seating at the Nursery End, where the opportunities for developments are so much greater anyway.

No question but that *Lord's* has lost some of its decorum, and the *Oval* is no longer the plebian playground it once was. There used to be a poet called Cray who sold his cricket poems around the *Oval* for a penny a sheet. It was very much the place for a working-class day out. But the trouble with the *Oval* has always been that the spectator is too far from the action, and there aren't enough trees to soften the gritty landscape of industrial South London.

There is still plenty of village cricket in and around London: *Kew Green*, where the Middlesex colts receive excellent coaching throughout the summer, *Roehampton*, *Richmond Green* or *South Park*, Fulham, are the pleasantest places to watch or play.

Best Cricket Ground: *Kew Green.*

Croissants

A strong black cup of unblended coffee, a hot crisp croissant with black cherry jam like they used to serve – and maybe still do – at the buffet in *Basle Railway Station*, why there's a breakfast fit for heroes!

Unchronicled and unsung (well it doesn't rhyme with anything much) the croissant is enjoying something of a revival, with the opening of, for instance, the *Croissant Show* at the Trafalgar Square end of the Strand, *Croissant Variées* in Fleet Street, and *Le Croissant Shops* at Paddington, Euston, Holborn, Liverpool Street, London Bridge and Waterloo Stations.

There are six places (at least) where you can buy really superb croissants:

(a)   *Maison Sagne*, 105 Marylebone High Street, W1.
(b)   *Maison Bouquillon*, 4 Moscow Road, W2 with a second branch around the corner at 28 Westbourne Grove.
(c)   *Café Matthiae*, Kew Road, Richmond.
(d)   The *Original Maids of Honour*, further up the same road towards Kew Bridge.
(e)   *Paris Croissants*, next to the giant HMV emporium in Oxford Street.
(f)   *Patisserie Valerie* (44 Old Compton Street, W1; 01-437 3466).
But see also the recommendations under Bakers.

A word of warning. Those who are not content to leave well alone have been developing croissants in disastrous ways. While the *Croques Dorés* may be all very fine, the *Pains du Chocolat* are an unfortunate hybrid.

Best croissant: *Maison Sagne.*

Croquet

Although croquet may be played seriously at the *Wimbledon All-England Lawn Tennis Club* and at the *Lansdowne Club* in Berkeley Square and the *Roehampton Club* and in the Dulwich garden of my brother-in-law the QC, the best place for croquet in London, in Britain, and, so far as I know, in the world is the *Hurlingham Club*, Fulham, SW6 (01-736 8411), which is the national headquarters for the game. Here, while bishops' daughters sip china tea under blue and white striped awnings, the clink of a Jacques mallet upon a Jacques ball as a young blade from the Baltic Exchange executes a mischievous roquet upon an Anglo-Indian administrator, indicates that all is well with the Empire. Says the club secretary, Mr D.F.A. Trewby: 'You could scarcely have anything else on these lawns. Two people moving about is all right; bowls would be a crowd!'

Best croquet: *The Hurlingham Club*.

Dancing

Small, rowdy intimate spaces will be found under Discos. Of the grand old dance halls only a handful remain. Largest is the *Empire Ballroom* (Leicester Square, WC2; 01-437 1446). The *Starfleet Band* run the disco and there are two DJs. The *Great Room*, Grosvenor House (Park Lane, W1; 01-499 6363) is the largest dance area available for private hire, and then there is the *Lyceum* (Wellington Street, WC2) run for 40 years as a dance hall by Eric Morley and Mecca, but originally a fine theatre, Wings Theatre, a theatre in which – among other famous productions – Bram Stoker's *Dracula* first saw the light of day. An auction following the final production (*Hamlet*) saw the 846 Circle seats sold for 5d each and the box office fittings of fine mahogany sold in their entirety for ten bob. But that was *not* the final production. In 1985 the *Lyceum* reopened as a theatre with the wonderful National Theatre production of the *Mysteries*.

Perhaps even more celebrated than the *Empire* and the *Lyceum*, is the *Hammersmith Palais* (242 Shepherd's Bush Road, W6; 01-748 2812), the epitome of respectable jitterbugging, where nice young girls in the thirties could go for a bit of rough. The *Hippodrome* (corner of Coventry Street and Charing Cross Road; 01-437 4311) is now a *Peter Stringfellow* disco. Splendid light shows; moving floors and ceilings. Bouncers claim they were required to refuse admittance to customers of the wrong colour and to fat women. If true, contemptible. Mondays are gay nights. Every night is saturnalia. Thés Dansants are held at the *Waldorf* (Aldwych, WC2 01-836 2400).

Through the crack in the gold velvet curtain a glimpse of a bygone age. For a pastiche of the above try *Park's Bar*, 45 Inverness Terrace, WC2 (01-229 3068).

Best Dancing: *The Empire Ballroom.*

Danish restaurants

Not much choice here, but you shouldn't need to eat Danish often. Not that Danish food is unpleasant (though it has rather too much to do with herrings, pickles and sour cream for my palate), but it *is* substantial. A traditional Smorgasbord is available, lunchtimes only, Mondays to Fridays, at *The Causerie*, under the stairs at Claridges (Brook Street, W1; 01-629 8860). There is a duplex 'cold' table (the inverted commas are necessary because some of the dishes are hot) and you start at the top and work down (about £11 a head inclusive). First then you have herrings – inevitable – smoked salmon and such accompanied by Akvavit. Next Frikadeller (meatballs) or Janssen's Temptation (casserole of potatoes, anchovies and cheese) or BikseMad (a kind of hash) or Rulle Polse (spiced pork), or Lever Postej (liver paste and bacon). This should be accompanied by beer, and followed by cheese.

Also try the *Danish Coffee Room* (146 Regent Street, W1; 01-734 7784) for open sandwiches and the *Danish Food Centre* (2 Conduit Street, W1) for pastries, salads, sausages etc.

The Danish are the nicest people in the world and well-dressed, but unambitious and over-weight.

Best Danish Food: *The Causerie.*

Darts

The *Sussex Pub* is the place. At 21 London Street, W2 (01-402 9602) it runs nine teams and counts four internationals amongst its regular players. Other good pubs for darts players include *The Skiddaw* (46 Chippenham Road, W9; 01-286 1264), the *World's End* (459 Kings Road, SW10; 01-352 7992) with matches on Thursdays, and, for the less competitive, the *Angel* (11 Roehampton High Street, SW15; 01-788 1997), which has a charming pub sign (q.v.) and clusters of roses. The *Cambridge Arms* (42 Cambridge Road, Kingston; 01-546 0937) currently boasts two of the best international players amongst its regulars.

Buy your darts from *Lillywhite's* (Piccadilly Circus) or *Stabler's*, the fishing (q.v.) experts, wear a silk shirt (q.v.) from *Turnbull & Asser* with an Old Etonian cravat, allow a sly smile to play upon your features in the manner of Paul Newman, and you'll soon put those pot-bellied beer-swilling northerners in their place.

Best darts venue: the *Sussex*.

Delicatessens/Grocers

It is always delightful in London to find surviving enclaves of those immigrant populations which down the centuries brought variety and energy to an ageing city. The Huguenots in Spitalfields, the Greeks in Soho, the Jews' in Whitechapel . . . and the Italians in Clerkenwell. Some hundred years ago they arrived and still on Sundays you can find Italian families praying, gossiping and marrying at St Peter's Church. Two civilised Italian grocers – olive oil and mortadella, pasta and parmigiano – remain: *Gazzano's* (169 Farringdon Road, EC1; 01-837 1712) and *Terroni's* (138 Clerkenwell Road, EC1; 01-837 1712). Other traditional Italian delights may be brought at *Gastronomia Italia* (8 Tachbrook Street, SW1) and *Pomodoro* (5 Warwick Way, SW1), both in the heart of downtown Pimlico.

In the West End the sad loss of *Jackson's of Piccadilly* has left the top people feeling under-privileged. *Harrods Food Hall* (see also under Butchers) is not quite what it was. It's old-fashioned and appears uninspired but where else can you get them to send a box of kippers to Texas without turning an obsequious hair? *Selfridges* food department (Oxford Street, W1; 01-629 1234) has been improving recently in an unostentatious way. I'm told you can even buy lights for the dog there.

Fortnum's (181 Piccadilly, W1; 01-734 8040) is a rewarding tourist attraction but expensive and not always obliging – despite those tail-coats. They are reluctant to grind less than half a pound of coffee beans, but perhaps one should not ask them to.

Partridge's (132 Sloane Street, SW1; 01-730 0651 and 11 Malcombe Street, NW1; 01-730 0651) stocks groceries of consistently good quality. Smoked salmon is recommended. It is also where Sloane Rangers buy their ham; they slice it very thin and eat it in front of Brookside, preparatory to insulting the au pair and 'phoning mummy in Hampshire.

For delicatessens there is no better place to start than Old Compton Street, not that *Lina Stores* (18 Brewer Street, W1; 01-437 6482) is actually in OC Street, but it is *of* it, and excellent for pasta, parmesan, mozzarella, olive oil, and such. Amongst French delis, one could do worse than *Délices de Gascognes* (3 Hillgate Street, W8; 01-221 4151) with their bisques and terrines, *Hobbs & Co* (3 Garrick Street, WC2; 01-240 5653) and *Justin de Blank* (42 Elizabeth Street, SW1; 01-730 0605) especially for sausages, bread and microwaveable gourmet dinners. In south London *O. Bellusci* (39 South Lambeth Road, SW8; 01-582 9766) is an oasis of delights and *La Ciocciara* (54 Garratt Lane, SW18; 01-874 9529) specialises in homemade pasta. In north London *Le Provençal* (opposite Belsize Park Station, 167 Haverstock Hill, NW3; 01-586 7987 and three other branches) is splendid. *Rogg* (137 Cannon Street Road, E1; 01-488 3386) is open from 7 a.m. on Sundays. Pickled herrings, bagels, gefillte fish, and excellent smoked salmon are amongst their treats. If you are fortunate enough to live in Cockfosters, you already know about *Arkay Cuisine* in Haddon Court Parade (01-449 3847), a splendid deli. You may also know that it opens between 5 p.m. and 8.30 p.m. on Sunday evenings for hot salt beef and mustard. What could be nicer? See also Take-Away.

Best grocer: *Lina Stores.*
Worst grocer: Anywhere with space invaders in it.

Discos

They come and they go. Blink, and it's all changed. If you watch migrating birds on the wing one of the mysteries is how, when one changes direction, all do. Latest trends at the time of writing include the use of video juke boxes and promotional evenings organised by whisky or vodka manufacturers. Some of the latest laser equipment produces effects of stunning beauty. Dancers can turn out to be holograms and vice versa.

Although policy at many clubs is to require membership before admittance, this policy is seldom adhered to. If the club thinks that you have something to offer, you should be able to sweet talk your way past the bouncers. There are several hundred music gigs each week and the intelligent thing to do is buy a listings magazine (*Time Out* or

City Limits), telephone the venue you like the sound of, and, if they seem welcoming, comb your hair and trot along. The best I can offer you is an abbreviated list of these popular clubs which seem likely still be in business by the time you buy (or borrow or steal) this book. Alphabetically then:

Le Beat Route (17 Greek Street, W1; 01-734 1470). Underground and popular – therefore sweaty and crowded. A different policy each night. Equity, Natke, Nurses and Croupiers free – so be warned!

Buzby's (157 Charing Cross Road, WC2). For the young, well-dressed and fashionable. Funk or 60s rock or w.h.y. Not to be missed on Club nights when Philip Salon and his entourage preside over close encounters of a hopeful kind.

Camden Palace (1A Camden High Street, NW1; 01-387 0428). A vast discotheque with equally vast video screen, powerful sound system, and nightly variations (Wednesdays are Twist 'n' Shout). A Gallery restaurant, cocktail bar, and a benign crowd.

Catacomb (Manor House, 317 Green Lanes, N4). The only place for North London rockers.

Crazy Larry's (Lots Road, SW10; 01-352 3518). A lively new reggae club in Chelsea. For £15 you may eat and drink your fill.

Dingles (Fulham Broadway, SW6; 01-385 0834). Almost luxurious with highly competent DJ, cocktails, wine-bar and snacks. Nurses admitted free. Splendid laser effects.

Dingwall's (Camden Lock, Chalk Farm Road, NW1; 01-267 4967). Don't arrive too early or you'll feel like Kafka's K awaiting his trial. Interesting artists; emphasis on blues, sixties music, and American 'roots' bands.

Dougie's (229 Lower Clapton Road, E5; 01-985 9192). Smart reggae club, no jeans or trainers.

Electric Ballroom (184 Camden High Street, NW1; 01-485 9006). Specialises in the same U.S.-influence music as Dingwall's with rockabilly and funk. Energetic. Jazz upstairs (Fridays).

Les Elites (253 Finchley Road, NW3; 01-794 6628). Air conditioned, inexpensive (admission £1 and drinks 50p before midnight) with Ladies Nights on Mondays, Tuesdays and Thursdays. Lively.

Embassy (7 Old Bond Street, W1; 01-499 4793). Highly contemporary music, soul and boogie. Don't come early. Renovated and chic. On Saturdays Astral Flight has three DJs and improbable music.

Fridge (Town Hall Parade, Brixton Hill, SW2; 01-326 5100). Old televisions showing old promos. The owner Andrew Czezowski likes things to be unpredictable and often they are. Note that the *Fridge* has moved from its old location.

Gaz's Rockin' Blues at Gossips (69 Dean Street, W1; 01-734 5736). *Gaz's*, named after Gaz Mayal, blues and reggae expert, is the oldest one-nighter (just about) in London. Spirited, lively, recommended. Other nights at *Gossips* for other trends.

The Harp (327 New Cross Road, SE14; 01-692 4077). A large but unpretentious place with two spaces for dancing and excellent DJs.

Heaven (Under the Arches, Villiers Street, WC2; 01-839 3892). Gay men only except for Thursdays. A dance floor that will take a thousand hunky dancers and a more intimate bar for sweet-talking. Europe's largest gay disco.

Park (38 Kensington High Street, W8; 01-937 7744). Four bars, a restaurant, up-to-date disco, champagne, excellent lighting, lots of au pairs giggling over their cocktails . . .

Phoenix Club (37 Cavendish Square, W1; 01-629 1700). Mainly 50s music and rock 'n' roll under DJ Tom Ingham.

Sol Y Sombra (74 Charlotte Street, W1; 01-580 7719). Founded in 1982 by Dave Hucker, this friendly and welcoming club on two floors has an emphasis on Latin American music (though not exclusively so). Good food, sort of Spanish. Not expensive. Thursdays and Saturdays best. An excellent choice of music from a wide and eclectic library.

Shaftesbury's (24 Shaftesbury Avenue, W1; 01-734 2017/8). Under Gerald Summers this bowling alley turned dance floor is noisy, successful and fashionable with excellent laser-shows. Membership required. Smart clothes.

WAG Club (35/37 Wardour Street, W1; 01-437 5534). Latin, salsa, jazz, good DJs. On Tuesdays TFV (stands for Total Fashion Victim) which may include Doris Day, or, if you're in luck, B. B. King.

Besides the above keep an eye open for concerts at universities, colleges and polys. The bands are often worth hearing and the charge is minimal.

Best Disco: *Sol Y Sombra*.

Doctors etc

The most notorious doctor in London was a Dr John Lettsom, a Quaker of Camberwell, who earned himself £12,000 a year. This was how he did it:

> When any patient calls in haste,
> I physics, bleeds and sweats 'em;
> If after that they choose to die,

Why, what care I? I lets 'em.
But he came to a sorry end.

The best gynaecologist in London is *Bridget Mason*, 25 Weymouth Street, W1; 01-631 1583.

The best osteopath is *Neil Mann*, 8 Becmead Avenue, SW16; 01-769 3267. When you visit him mention this book.

The best VD Clinic is James Pringle House (attached to the Middlesex Hospital) in Charlotte Street where the best consultant is *Dr Duncan Catterall*. The whole system there is efficient, computerised and friendly.

The safest test of psychiatrists is to check whether they bite their fingernails.

The worst doctor in London was the one who took me in for a routine cartilage operation and released me from hospital with a probable lung embolism. Wild horses wouldn't drag his name out of me unless, as Ben Travers put it in *Thark*, there were an awful lot of them.

Dogs

In the porch of *St George's*, Hanover Square (John James, 1724) stand two fine pointers in bronze. They are said to be by Landseer. Either side of the *Battersea Dog's Home* (4 Battersea Park Road, SW8; 01-622 4454, do get your dogs there) two shaggy-haired somethings hold up their paws in supplication. I only wish that the Dog's Home would open at weekends when it's most useful. If you can't find what you want at Battersea, ignore the pet shops, and go straight to *Exchange and Mart*. In the Imperial War Museum, stuffed, is Edith Cavell's dog, *Jock*, looking highly intelligent. In *St Pancras Gardens*, NW1 a stone retriever waits for you to scratch his chilly ears. Outside *The Greyhound* (151 Greyhound Lane, SW16) stands a white greyhound, tail permanently frozen in mid-twitch.

If you have a friend who likes dogs, propose to him/her in *St Pancras Gardens*, marry him/her in *St George's*, Hanover Square, buy him/her a dog at *Battersea* – guaranteed distemper free – and go to celebrate with the hair of the dog down *Greyhound Lane*.

Best London dogs: *St George's pointers*.
Worst London dogs: *those like mine that shit on the pavement*.

Dog Tracks

One evening at the *White City* I offered my usual generous prize to whomsoever could come up with the best anagram of GREYHOUND. To my amazed delight the winner produced 'HEY DOG, RUN!' and the second 'HEY, RUN DOG!'. But, alas, the White City dogs have been swallowed up by the BBC and there's no anagram of that.

The best dog track for food is *Wimbledon;* the best for odds is *Hackney* where the food is basic but the service friendly. *Walthamstow* is becoming fashionable, but the best for atmosphere is *Catford* where all the south London villains go with their jewel-encrusted fancy women. Until recently *Catford* was the only London track to stage 8-dog races. Now sadly they conform. But you may still tickle the ears of the dogs after the races.

Two things when dining at a dog track:
(a)   Book early, especially for the big meetings, and reserve a table opposite the winning post. Far more exciting and can be profitable.
(b)   Place your bets yourself. If you wait for the ladies from the tote to get your bets on for you, you will risk not getting on.

Best dog track: *Catford.*

Domes

There is a fine pair of domes (one with a clock, one with a compass) on the Queen Mary and King William blocks of the *Royal Naval College*, Greenwich. They are by Wren who knew about domes. *St Mary Abchurch* (Abchurch Yard near Cannon Street) is a Wren church and has a magnificent painted dome attributed to both Sir James Thornhill and William Snow. There are three rather half-hearted domes on the *National Gallery* (William Wilkins) in Trafalgar Square. I always enjoy the demi-dome (sliced open like an orange) on *Bush House*, looking north up Kingsway; illuminated at night it makes a bright show. Overlooking London Bridge like a neon-faced nanny is the imposing dome of the *Guardian Assurance Company* building – also known as the Great White Building. This dome, in copper, rises to 160 feet above street level.

The Romanesque domes on *Holy Joe's* (St Joseph's Church, Highgate Hill) are attractively different, but not half as different as the dome on *Westminster Cathedral* (q.v.). The dome which was added to *Brompton Oratory* in 1896 (George Sherrin trying to improve on Herbert Gribble) is a powerful landmark at least, and you could say the same about the domes on *Harrods*, which are best studied from the Chairman's dining room at the IBA. (Name-dropping!). The *Alexandra Hotel*, Clapham South Side (opposite the tube) has one of the most endearing domes in London, a bosom-shaped protuberance with a wrought iron nipple.

The delightful dome roof of the *Diorama*, one of the earliest London cinemas in Camden Town, is at risk. *Greycoat Estates* have received planning permission from the Crown Commissioners to turn the place into an office complex. If they remove the dome they will have me to reckon with.

But when you get right down to it (or up to it) there are only two serious domes in London: *St Paul's* and the *British Museum Reading Room*. Like the whole structure, the dome of *St Paul's* is a miracle. And you should certainly make the effort to climb up to it. Apart from a close look at Thornhill's paintings, you get The View. As Thomas Flood put it:

> The man that pays his pence and goes
>   Up to thy lofty cross, St Paul's,
> Looks over London's naked nose,
>   Women and men;
> The world is all beneath his ken;
>   He sits above the ball,
> He seems on Mount Olympus' top,
> Among the Gods, by Jupiter! and lets drop
>   His eyes from the empyreal clouds
>   on mortal crowds.

As for the dome of the *Reading Room*, Thackeray put it best:

> I have seen all sorts of domes of Peter's and Paul's, Sophia, Pantheon – what not? – and have been struck by none of them so much as by that catholic dome in Bloomsbury, under which our million volumes are housed. What peace, what love, what truth, what beauty, what happiness for all, what generous kindness for you and me, are here spread out! It seems to be I cannot sit down in that place without a heart full of grateful reverence. I own to have said my grace at the table, and to have thanked Heaven for this my English birthright, freely to partake of those bountiful books, and to spread the truth I find there.

Best dome: *St Paul's*.
Worst domes: *National Gallery*.

Dragons

Curious but there are no George and Dragon pubs in London any more. Well no, obviously I must not be so dogmatic – there *must* be George and Dragons, I just don't know of them. (I draw your attention to the Reader's Contribution Forms at the back of this book.) The famous *George Inn*, Borough High Street was once the *George and Dragon*, and there's a splendid – though vanquished – dragon contained within the peal of bells above *Liberty's* (Kingly Street, W1). St George chases him at every quarter and spears him on the hour. On *Horse Guards Parade* is a French Mortar gun used for attacking Cadiz in 1812 – it was then given by the grateful Spanish Government to Prinny who erected it here. It is held in place by a fierce Chinese dragon in cast iron. A contemporary cartoon referred to the whole artefact as: 'The Regent's tremendous thing erected in the Park'. Then there's the huge dragon weather-vane at *115 Howard's Lane*, Putney. And smallish dragons on the roof of the *Liberty Shopping Centre*, South Road, Southall. And the dragons available at the tattoo shop, more or less opposite Waterloo Station. For some 60 years George Burchett kept the business going until 1953 when his son, Leslie, succeeded him. George was prepared to undertake anything, even 'all over jobs' (like Ray Bradbury's *Illustrated Man*) which could take three years to complete. For China dragons visit the *Percival David Foundation*, 53 Gordon Square, WC1 – the finest collection of Chinese ceramics in Europe. The best live dragon is the one which twists and turns through London's Chinatown (Gerrard Street, W1) during the celebrations for the Chinese New Year. It is huge. The newest dragon is the big red one painted on the *Hammersmith Subway* giving us directions with the smoke it breathes.

Best Dragon: *The Cadiz memorial.*

Drama Schools

Outside London the *Bristol Old Vic School* is supreme. Within the metropolitan area the *Mountview* and the *Richmond School*, run by the Misses de Leon are eccentric, the *Central School* and the *London Academy of Music and Dramatic Art* are middle-of-the-road, *RADA* has an established reputation, the *Webber Douglas* is sparky, the *E15* school is well-intentioned, and the *Guildhall* combines music and drama impressively. But the accolade goes to *Anna Scher's* school (Barnsbury Road, N1) , where the children remain unspoiled while their talents are developed.

The little *LAMDA* theatre is admirably purpose built, more versatile than *RADA's* Vanburgh Theatre in Gower Street. A visit to the drama schools' end-of-year productions is altogether more rewarding than watching *Fame*. Beware of cowboy operations however.

Best Drama School: *Anna Scher.*

Driving Schools

Two million driving tests – give or take a mini or two – are carried out each year. Just over half of those tested pass. The test is quite inadequate – it excludes motorway driving and night-driving, and your licence is not much use to you if you only drive during daylight hours on minor roads. The largest school in London (in the world come to that) is the *British School of Motoring* and there have been allegations that the *BSM* has exceeded the permitted number of trainee instructors; for each qualified instructor a school is permitted one trainee. You pay the same rate whichever you get, but short of *asking* your instructor there's no way of finding out whether he/she is qualified or training. Lessons run from 40 to 100 minutes so the rates (about £7-£8 per hour) should be carefully studied to see what you get. An hour's lesson is not much use if you spend half an hour in a jam – preferably go for a suburban school.

Some schools:

ABM (01-840 3443): Fiestas and Starlets. Manual only. First lesson reduced rate.
Acclaim (01-520 0512): Acclaims, Rovers, Metros. Manual only. Door to door. First lesson free.
BSM (01-540 8262): Metros. Automatic and manual. Door to door. First lesson reduced rate.
ISM (01-278 6297): Fiestas, Escorts. Manual only. North London areas. Door to door.
KC Tuition (01-278 1943): Fiestas. Manual only. Door to door. Advanced Motoring courses too.
LSM (01-674 8211): Fiestas. Manual and automatic. 100-minute lessons. Advanced driving courses.
Olympia (01-734 9908): Datsuns and Escorts. Automatic and manual. West London.

Of course a test taken in an automatic car does not permit you to drive a manual. The *RAC* (01-686 2525) has a register of instructors, including those who have passed their own exam.

Best Driving School: *London School of Motoring*.

Dry Cleaning

For any queries concerning dry cleaning and a list of your local dry cleaners, phone the *Drycleaning Information Bureau* on 01-863 8658. They might have warned me against buying that suede jacket at the sale in Edinburgh. £19.95 seemed cheap, until I took it to be cleaned . . .

Embassies

It is not generally known that *3 St James's Street*, a fine edifice with a façade of five arched windows, the home of Berry Brothers and Rudd, wine merchants (q.v.), was once the embassy of the Republic of Texas; well it was. But now Texans have to muck in like everyone else under the eagle eye in Grosvenor Square.

The *Indian Embassy* (Sir Herbert Baker, 1930) has an extremely pretty interior decorated by Indian artists and a reading room open to the public (Aldwych, WC2; 01-836 8484). The *Chinese Embassy* (110 Westcombe Park Road, SE3) despite being a listed building, is the most ramshackle; the *Icelandic Embassy* (1 Eaton Terrace, SW1) the friendliest. The *Czech Embassy* (25 Kensington Palace Gardens, W8) is disconcertingly close to the *Russian* (18 Kensington Palace Gardens, W8) and has hidden cameras clearly visible everywhere. At one of the Far Eastern embassies (I can't remember which but it was in Tufnell Park) I mistook the ambassador for the gardener; most embarrassing. The *Bulgarian Embassy*, they say, is entirely staffed by spies. As you might predict, it is not listed in the phone book. (But see under Secrets.)

Best Embassy: *Indian*.
Worst Embassy: *Italian*.

Emergency Services

The best emergency information service is that run by the *Daily*

Telegraph (01-353 4242). At dinner a discussion arose as to which months of the year are the wettest and the driest (see under Weather). A telephone call and the matter was resolved within seconds. For financial queries, the *Financial Times Business Information Service* (Bracken House, 10 Cannon Street, EC4P 4BY) is excellent. Enquiries on 01-243 8000.

Problem (01-828 8181), *Universal Aunts* (01-730 9834) and *SOS Services* (01-458 3258) pride themselves on getting you out of a hole in a hurry. Once when Binkie Beaumont was on his way to our place to hear the songs of the new musical we hoped he would present in the West End, the pianist discovered that humidity had affected the action of the piano. The notes kept sticking. Panic! *Problem* was roused and, despite it being a Sunday, swiftly sent round a little man with a tin of talc. Hey presto!

Universal Aunts is the oldest established of these organisations; staid and reliable especially in such matters as needlework and au pairs.

SOS Services, who liaise with *UA* on occasion, is the latest of these organisations to get going (July 1982), but can put you in touch with experts in more or less any field in your London postal area. Curtains re-lined with your own material, stuffed ferrets, hired greenhouses, no problem.

If you've been busted, or have urgent need of legal advice, or emotional rescue, try *Release* (01-603 8654 for 24 hour emergencies). If you're contemplating suicide – although it's unlikely you'd be reading this book while doing so – it has to be the *Samaritans* (01-283 3400). Local branches in telephone directories. Their 24 hour centre is at St Stephen's 29 Wallbrook, EC4. I saw a graffito a while back proclaiming: 'Death is nature's way of telling you to slow down.'

Other peculiar problems try:

Capital Helpline (01-388 7575).
International Traveller's Aid (01-834 3925) at the YWCA, 16 Great Russell Street if you're stranded.
Lost Property (London Transport) 200 Baker Street, NW1 (01-486 2496).
Lost Property (Taxis) 15 Panton Street, NW1.
Teledata (01-200 0200) – calls answered in rotation.
Rape Crisis Centre (01-378 3965).

And of course 999 for fire, police or ambulance.

A wonderfully useful book for all repairs is *Mend It* by Richard Ball (pub. Orbis Books £8). This remarkable anthology lists some thousand expert repairers and restorers. Three examples:

Hi-Fi (London Sound, 266 Field End Road, Eastcote, Ruislip, Herts). (Nothing electrical which you can replace for less than £50 is worth repairing, unless the repair is very minor.)
Porcelain (Studio 9, 465 Battersea Park Road, SW11).
Concertinas (H. Crabb and Son, 158 Liverpool Road, N1).
See also under Unusual Shops.

Best Emergency Service: *Samaritans.*
Worst Emergency Service: *Electricity and Gas Boards.*

Employment

For casual labour make your way to Camden Town tube station. Just behind the station at 6 a.m. every morning building labourers foregather to be taken by van to wherever the work may be. No need for national insurance and such. This is strictly cash and those who take the work are predominantly Irish. Local papers and the *London Standard* are best for classified ads. And there's always the *Job Centre* if you're philosophical and an optimist. Plenty of work in Brighton.

English Restaurants

To eat English in London you have several choices. If you are rich or celebrating you can patronise the big London hotels. If you are anaemic and/or hungry you should visit the carveries. If you are trendy and upwardly mobile (or only hope that you are) then there are the pretty places to go to. If you are poor but honest (they usually go together) you have the pubs and the pie and mash places. And if you live in the past there are those grand old stand-bys, *Wilton's*, *Simpson's*, *Rule's* and the *Wheeler's* chain. Let me deal with each in turn.

(a) Rich or celebrating
Michael Quinn, the first British chef ever at the *Ritz* and a splendid guest on Desert Island Discs, has left that most handsome of restaurants and gone to Stratford, that most English of towns. So far as I know only the *Savoy Grill* (Keith Stanley) of the other big hotels boasts or screens its English chef, and only at the London clubs will you find the sort of food which reeks of the gun-room and pepper-and-salt tweeds. The best of these (for food) are the *St James' Club* (7 Park Place, SW1; 01-629 7688) and the *Carlton* (69 St

St James's Street, SW1; 01-493 1164). (See under London Clubs.)

But the big hotels have correctly concluded that what visitors to London want is English food, and that means joints and game and poultry, oysters and sole, soups and puddings and savouries. (You remember savouries?). So now the *Hilton* (Park Lane, SW1; 01-493 8000) runs its British Harvest Restaurant; the *Dorchester* (Swiss chef), the *Connaught* and the *Savoy* have their grill rooms and the *Ritz* will always do you rice pudding and raspberry jam. (On the subject of puddings, whoever invented bread and butter pudding deserves – along with whoever invented flush toilets – a medal. The best ones I've eaten were at *Churchill College*, Cambridge, but the *Connaught's* aren't bad.) All these hotel restaurants deserve house-points for their basics, meat and fish, but lose them for vegetables (delicious salmon with *sauce verte* at the *Savoy* was wrecked by ruined Jersey potatoes) and those dishes which need last minute attention, such as omelettes.

Some specialities:

Connaught: Pheasant, silverside.
Savoy Grill: Saddle of lamb.
Ritz: Sirloin of beef.
Brown's: Roasted dover sole.
Dorchester: Lancashire hot-pot, Irish stew.

Best Hotel Food (British): *Connaught.*

(b) Carveries

The advantage of the carvery for the hotel is that the problems of waiters/waitresses are eased, and there is little wastage of food. The advantage for the customer is that the juice is still in the meat and it is possible (or should be) to choose from which end of the sirloin you wish your slices to come. I think it was the *Cumberland Hotel* (Marble Arch, W1; 01-262 1234) which started the carvery notion, but in those days you, the diner, could carve the meat yourself. Now even at the lower end of the market – *Berni Inns* – carveries exist. Meat is usually wonderful. Crackling on the pork soggy. Yorkshire pudding drear. Vegetables stale. Gravy artificial! Cost from around £5 (*Berni's*) to maybe £12 (the *Cut Above*, Barbican Centre; 01-588 3008). I'm fond of the *Charing Cross Hotel* (Strand, WC2; 01-639 7282) sentimentally because they honoured Betjeman, naming a handsome room after him, and it's reliable fare. The *Trusthouse Forte* chain of hotels has carveries at six branches. Predictable starters and puddings surround the main purpose i.e. the joints, though seasonal special and cold tables are also unnecessarily provided. At £9.25 inc. VAT this is reasonable value. The addresses are:

The *Russell*, Russell Square, WC1B 5BE; 01-837 6470.
The *Cumberland*, Marble Arch, W1A 4RF; 01-262 1234.
The *Strand Palace*, Strand, WC2R 0JJ; 01-836 8080.
The *Regent Palace*, Piccadilly Circus, W1A 4BZ; 01-734 7000.
Heathrow Excelsior, Bath Road, W. Drayton, Middx; 01-759 6611.
Heathrow Post House, Sipson Road, W. Drayton, Middx; 01-759 2323.

The latest carvery is at the *Rubens Hotel* (Buckingham Palace Road, SW1; 01-834 6600) and it is probably the best: they try harder.

Best Carvery: *Charing Cross Hotel*.

(c) Pretty places

The *English Garden* (10 Lincoln Street, SW3; 01-584 7272) is *very* pretty.

In summer you eat in a refined kind of conservatory, in the winter in front of a log fire. Under the same management is the *English House* (3 Milner Street, SW3; 01-584 3002) and while the *Garden* has a seductive Gallic tincture to its English recipes, the *House* uses recipes taken from old recipe books. The desserts are rather special. The originator of these two restaurants is Michael Smith, who completes his stable with *Walton's* (121 Walton Street, SW3; 01-584 0204) where Regency English food features supported by a splendid wine list. The set lunch at £8 is a real bargain. I've always liked *Maggie Jones's* (6 Old Court Place, W8; 01-937 6462), which is wittily named after one of its close neighbours and enhanced with music from a wind-up gramophone. I was present at the launching party many years ago and so feel myself to have something of the status of a godfather. Also managed by the same team is *La Poule Au Pot* (see under French Restaurants), and a new one, *Ware's* (388 King's Road, SW3; 01-352 9669), on the site where Queenie's once was. Excellent for that glorious Anglo-Indian invention kedgeree, liver and bacon, boiled beef and the like. Enjoy the arrangements of dried flowers. Drink from a magnum of wine and pay for what you drink. *Heal's Restaurant* (Tottenham Court Road) is exceptionally pretty and uncrowded. Although near Saatchi's, Channel 4 and the Independent Film Companies, it has not been 'discovered' yet – except by me and a few close friends. The food is elegant, the menu quirkish, the service variable, the atmosphere romantic. Ideal for lunch (indeed it's not open for dinner!). The Chinese radishes with watercress mayonnaise were *not* a great success. The *Refectory* (6 Church Walk, Richmond, Surrey; 01-940 6264) is particularly pretty, being set in the Old Parish Rooms adjacent to the Church. In the summer (you remember summers?) you can sit outside. The food is unusual and succulent, and the English wines, gooseberry, elderflower and such, are not easily obtainable elsewhere – nor would I much want to drink them elsewhere. The *Refectory* prices are low enough to make it available to the fairly poor (and fairly honest). Other pretty ones in brief and alphabetically:

Auntie's 126 Cleveland Street, W1; 01-387 3226 is for wholesome sustaining Victorian food. Modestly priced and well established by now.

Bates 11 Henrietta Street, WC2; 01-240 7600. Informal with live jazz in the evenings and food 'based on hedgerow produce'. It tastes better than it sounds. Crayons and paper tablecloths for budding Lautrecs.

Changing Times 22 North Street, SW4; 01-720 9559. Delicious food which mixes the familiar (roast beef) with the exotic (blue ice cream). Wooden pew benches and school-type tables. Set dinner at £6.95, so the remarks on the *Refectory* (above) apply. A jewel in Clapham's Crown.

Chimes 26 Churton Street, SW1; 01-821 7456. Highly authentic olde English food, wines and ciders.

Greens Duke Street, St James's, SW1; 01-930 4566. Oysters, fish cakes and kedgeree, followed by treacle tarts and suet puddings. Yummy.

The *Perfumed Conservatory* 182 Wandsworth Bridge Road, SW6; 01-731 0732. Intimate, which means, in this context, candle-lit, and interesting which means home-made soups and variations of solid English fare. Recommended despite the name (not too many perfumed conservatories in Wandsworth Bridge Road).

Sheppard's 1 Prince of Wales Terrace, W8; 01-937 3119. A cook who used to be a model and who has a chic sense of style gives *Sheppard's* an engaging ambiance for its excellent English menu. Prices very fair for Kensington.

Yesterday 12-14 Leopold Road, SW19; 01-946 4300/947 8844. Not as pretty as the others in this section but the food is *very* authentic, the ingredients are fresh, and the portions are big.

Best Pretty English Restaurant: *Heal's*.

(d) Pubs – see under Pubs with Food.

(e) Pie and Mash – see under Budget Restaurants.

(f) Stand-bys

Restaurants which survive are obviously doing something right. *Wilton's* has now moved for a second time, to 55 Jermyn Street, SW1; 01-629 9955 but otherwise little changed, and is as aristocratic as ever. Edwardian England is what's on offer with oysters and fish and game.

Simpson's in the Strand 100 Strand, WC2; 01-836 9112 could only lose by bringing itself up to date. Soggy vegetables are part of the fun here; one *always* complained about the vegetables at *Simpson's*. Roast beef and treacle tart are buttresses against radicalism and change. It was always 'done' to tip the carver. Cads don't know this.

The *Baron of Beef* Gutter Lane, Gresham Street, EC2; 01-606 9415 represents the sort of England you find in Hollywood films starring David Niven. Consequently tourists are delighted to find life imitating art. But the sirloin with Yorkshire pud is the real thing.

Rule's 35 Maiden Lane, WC2; 01-836 5314 was created in 1798 and has a colourful theatrical history represented by playbills on the walls. It is supposed that Edward VII was nice to Lily Langtry there, or she to him, or improbably both. The food has certainly improved, if not since then, at least since the first edition of this book appeared. For the *Wheeler's* chain, see under Fish Restaurants.

Best Standby English Restaurant: *Wilton's*.

Epitaphs

In *Alperton Cemetery*, Clifford Road, Wembley, beneath a carving of a 1928 schoolboy, neat and tidy in his uniform there is the following epitaph:

> With a kindly smile and a wave of his hand he has wandered into a better land.

Equally cheerful is the charming goodbye to Isabella David who died in 1954 and lies in *Brompton Cemetery*, Old Brompton Road:

> Have a good sleep, dear.

The intellectual equivalent of such healthy matter-of-factness is the memorial in *Highgate Cemetery* to Professor Clifford, the Atheist. He sums up life thus:

> I was not and was conceived.
> I loved, and did a little work.
> I am not, and grieve not.

As for Susan Dunford in *Pinner Cemetery*, under a life-sized red granite armchair, 1950s vintage, we read that she 'left her chair vacant'. It is hard not to feel admiration for those content to leave this vale of tears with so little fuss and bother. But there are those who are remembered more effusively. David Nieto (1654-1728) lies in the *Old Sephardic Cemetery*, Mile End Road, east London and this sometime rabbi at the Bevis Marks Synagogue is remembered as a:

> Sublime theologian, profound sage, distinguished physician, famous astronomer, sweet poet, elegant preacher, subtle logician, ingenious mathematician, fluent rhetorician, pleasant author, expert in languages, learned in history.

A saint obviously. Mary Page, buried in *Bunhill Fields*, City Road, EC1 was another:

> Here lies Dame Mary Page relict of Sir Gregory Page Bart. She departed this life March 11th 1728 in the 56th year of her age. In 67 months she was tap'd 66 times had taken away 240 gallons of water without ever repining at her case or ever fearing the operation.

Most affecting of course are the epitaphs on children's graves and, in some of the poorer cemeteries these make up a tragically high percentage of the total. In the *Jewish Cemetery*, Kingsbury Road, N1, for example, during the first ten years (1843-1853) of burials, forty-two deaths are recorded, of which seven are still births and the average age of the remaining thirty-five is only thirty-three years. In *St Paul's Deptford Churchyard*, there is a compensatingly cheerful memorial to one Margaret Hawtree, a midwife who died in 1734:

> She was an indulgent mother and the best of wives.
> She brought into this world more than three thousand lives.

Frequently the epitaphs contain awful warnings. The following dire example from the cemetery in *Church Road*, Mitcham, is all too explicit:

> Mary, Susan and Eliza Atwood . . . who were poisoned by eating fungous vegetables mistaken for champignons on the 11th day of October 1808 and died at the ages of 14, 7 and 5 years within a few hours of each other in excruciating circumstances. The Father, Mother and now, alas, an only child, partakers of the same meal have survived with debilitated constitutions and to lament so dreadful a calumny. This monument is erected to perpetuate the fatal events as an awful caution to others, let it be too a solemn warning that in our most grateful enjoyments even in our necessary food may lurk deadly poison . . .

The ultimate in Victorian morbidity, written to commemorate 17-year-old Louisa Waklein who died in 1840 and lies in *Kensal Green Cemetery*, is the following carved on Louisa's stone:

She is mine and I must have her
The coffin must be her bridal bed
The winding sheet must wrap her head
The whispering winds must o'er her sigh

For soon in the grave the maid must lie
The worm it will riot
On heavenly diet
When death has deflowered her eye

And the ultimate in simplicity. In the east cloister of *Westminster Abbey* you may find, if you have a mind to, this tribute:

Jane Lister, deare child.

Finally a non-existent epitaph. Derek Bentley (1934-1953) was wrongly executed for the murder of a policeman. His father wished to have the phrase: 'A victim of English justice' inscribed on his tombstone, but permission was refused. I wonder whose decision that was, and whether it kept him/her awake at night.

Best Epitaph: *Professor Clifford* (see above).

P.S. Much of the above information comes from Hugh Meller's marvellous book *London Cemeteries* (Avebury Publishing).

Estate Agents

It must be pleasant to be an estate agent. Somebody comes in and tells you they wish you to sell their house; you put a photograph of it in the window; somebody else comes in and says they want to buy it; you take anything up to 3% commission on what may be £100,000.

Well, of course, this is a simplification and there is nothing to stop the owner selling his/her house privately and keeping the comission; but it is a curious business. The agent is paid by the seller whom he/she may never meet. But the agent may show the potential purchaser round thirty houses, and never receive a penny piece from him/her.

The concept of the House Shop – the seller pays a fee to have details of his house put up in the shop – has become fashionable. Why should buyers pay such large sums on top of the purchase price when the service they receive can be duplicated by a competent solicitor? As I write the range of house prices in London veers between £15,000 and

£16,000,000 (see under Houses); that is from a South East London terraced property to a mansion on Millionaire's Row. Agents may run a small operation such as *Alan Fisher* in Kennington, whose office staff wear T-shirts, to the momentous *Chesterton's* of Kensington. *Alan Fisher* relies on rapid turnover within the neighbourhood, *Chesterton's* on big buyers from the Middle East, Nigeria and the US and exhibits a willingness to eat sheep's testicles or sleep with Eskimos' wives while concluding a deal.

Flats on the Barbican Estate, Europe's highest residential block, are increasingly popular, with Arthur Scargill and until recently Norman Tebbit resident there, while properties in Limehouse and on the Island (Isle of Dogs) are hugely sought after by those whose work takes them to the London Docks Development Area. Residents who rent accommodation are not at all pleased to find themselves priced out of the market by West End spivs. Another area being talked up by estate agents is 'Chelham' that part of Chelsea and Fulham centred around the New King's Road – Parson's Green doesn't sound at all so grand.

Meanwhile, the plight of the homeless (q.v.) becomes more and more severe.

Not having bought or sold a house for well over ten years my advice on estate agents is based on hearsay, but I have received glowing accounts of the following: *Raymond Bushell, Strutt & Parker, Sturt and Tivendale, Stocker & Roberts* (of Blackheath), *Pye* (of Wimbledon Village) and *John D. Wood*. Less happy reports have reached me concerning *Dutch and Dutch, Gascoigne Pees, May & Co, Ruck and Ruck, Bernard Thorpe & Partners, Benham & Reeves, Stickley and Kent* and *Faron Sutaria*. I must emphasise that I cannot personally substantiate these remarks. More reports please!

Fabrics

Obviously the major stores, including the *John Lewis Partnership, Habitat Conran* and – especially – *Liberty's* should be considered, but a more imaginative approach is to visit *Ian Mankin*, 109 Regent's Park Road, NW1; 01-722 0997 – closed Mondays – or to write to him for a catalogue and samples. The shop specialises in the unusual and the intriguing. Examples? Mattress ticking, butcher's stripes, muslin, unbleached calico, airtex, cotton piqué and suit linen.

Best Fabrics: (cottons and silks) *Liberty's*.
Best Fabrics: (outlandish) *Ian Mankin*.

Façades

The terracotta façade of the *Whitechapel Art Gallery*, recently renovated and extended, is a fine example of late (1901) Art Nouveau design, though it falls a long way short of what the architect, C. H. Townsend, had intended. The façade of *Harrod's*, arrogant in its familiar flower-pot red, and the gothic fantasy of *St Pancras Station* (q.v.) are all very well; the *South Kensington Museums* and the *Houses of Parliament* add grandeur of an eccentric sort to London's streetscapes but there can only be one winner here. The façade of the *Royal Naval College*, originally Greenwich Hospital (Wren) with the witty perspective effect of Queen's House (Inigo Jones) is stunning especially seen across the river from the Isle of Dogs. Also very impressive is the old warehouse building at *St Katharine's Docks*.

Best Façade: *Royal Naval College, Greenwich*. See also Shop Fronts.

Fancy Dress

It is a craze. By being someone else for a night you can Be Yourself. That's the theory, and there are plenty of practitioners to support it.

The traditional suppliers are *Morris Angel & Son* (119 Shaftesbury Avenue, WC2; 01-836 5678) and *Berman's & Nathan's* (18 Irving Street, WC2; 01-839 1651) who deal principally with theatres and television and film companies. As a result they have massive stocks.

Barnum's (67 Hammersmith Road, W14; 01-602 1211) lists in its catalogue seventeen different kinds of comic moustaches and eighteen different beards. They will hire out anything from a false nose to a marquee. Almost next door at the *Carnival Store* (95 Hammersmith Road, W14; 01-603 7824) Mr Stephanides worked hard to turn me into a monk or a monkey; at £10 to hire and £10 deposit it seemed like a cheap transformation. *Escapade* (150 Camden High Street, NW1; 01-485 7384) makes a similar charge.

Both *C. and W. May* (9 Garrick Street, WC2; 01-836 5993) and *Mardi Gras* (54 Browning Road, Manor Park, E12; 01-472 2012) will design and make a costume to meet your private requirements, while at *Call to Arms* (79 Upper Street, N1; 01-359 0501) they specialise in matters military. The most bizarrely intriguing of these emporia is *Theatre Zoo* (28 New Row, WC2; 01-836 3150). They will hire out costumes and wigs perfectly efficiently, but their real love is masks, false feet and hands and fantastical animal costumes. It is not easy to walk past their crowded window without breaking your stride. I append some other recommended suppliers:

The Costume Studio (227 Eversholt Street, NW1; 01-388 4481).
Fancy Dress Shop (24 Hartfield Crescent, SW19; 01-540 4868).
Fantasy Studios (22 Coronet Street, N1; 01-739 1948).
Joker (97 Chiswick High Road, W4; 01-995 4118).
Nite Out Fancy Dress (52 Beulah Road, E17; 01-520 1542) and
West End Costumes (43 Compton Close, NW1; 01-387 5343).

For Children: *Anthea Moore Ede* (16 Victoria Grove, W8; 01-584 8826) is the place to go. And the best costumes can be *seen* at the annual *Notting Hill Carnival* during August Bank Holiday weekend.

Best Fancy Dress: (for grotesquerie) *Theatre Zoo* and (for comprehensive range) *Berman's & Nathan's*.

Fanlights

In early Georgian London a shell-hood was provided above the door of the more substantial houses. It gave Sheraton elegance to the house entrance and some protection from the weather. Later this feature was replaced by the fanlight, although some Edwardian architects re-introduced the shell-hood. An expert can date a house by the patterns of the glazing bars in the fanlights, but it's a rather barren accomplishment. The earliest, though, is at *36 Bedford Row* just east of Red Lion Square. It is the work of Nicholas Barbon. *Islington* is where most of the better examples may be found, Duncan Terrace, Bewdley Street, Canonbury Square, Barnsbury Street, Cloudesley Road and Colebrooke Row in particular. Despite the ponderous claims of the vast fanlight at *Waterloo Station*, with the names of our First World War allies in the cartouches around the arch (q.v.), and the unexpected lunette of the Last Judgement in the gate of *St Giles-in-the-Fields*, I prefer the confident swirls of *1 Ripplevale Grove*, N1 or *3 Lincoln's Inn Fields*. I love the things; really I should start a fan club . . .

Best Fanlight: *1 Ripplevale Grove*, N1.

Farms

There are eight non-commercial farms in London. They are open to visitors. These are the *City Farm*, Grafton Road, NW5; *Freightliners*, Sheringham Road, N7; *Hackney City Farm*, Leslie Road, E5; *Mudchute*

Community Farm, Manchester Road, E14; *Spitalfields Farm*, Buxton Street, E1; *Stepping Stones*, Ben Johnson Road, E1; *Surrey Docks Farm*, Gulliver Street, Woolwich; and the *Vauxhall City Farm*, St Oswald's Place, SE11. The *City Farm* in Grafton Road is close by the headquarters of Inter Action, Ed Berman's Community empire which runs the City Farms Advisory Service and produces a newsletter. The address for both of these is 15 Wilkin Street, NW5; (01-403 0881). The *City Farm* itself is a pleasantly mucky place where the kids can even sit on the pigs if they wish to or the pigs on the children; the same probably applies to the other farms. But sadly the estimable *City Farm* has severe financial problems.

Petersham Farm, Petersham Road, Surrey is rather different: a small working farm-cum-garden-centre on the banks of the Thames, where children are invited to attend such arcane mysteries as the milking of a cow. Recently it changed ownership and bought a goat. Goat's milk may now be purchased there.

At *Thorpe Park Theme Park* (for instructions see under Children's London) there is a splendid working farm. Huge entertainment on a hot summer's day (remember them?) is to watch Sophie, the sow, taking a dip in the village pond. About the same distance from the centre of London is the largest working farm in the Greater London area – *Wrotham Park Estate*, Barnet, Herts, with 2,300 acres of arable land and 200 Jersey cows.

Ferries

Ahoy! And Oho, and it's who for the ferry?
(The briar's in bud and the sun going down):
And I'll row ye so quick and I'll row ye so steady,
And 'tis but a penny to Twickenham Town.

Twickenham Ferry by T. J. H. Marzials (1850-1920)

The ancient *Twickenham Ferry* still operates, though not if the weather is inclement (for Ham House 7-12, 2-sunset). Sandy Scott, the ferryman, uses an outboard motor these days, but will pull on the oars for special occasions. Since the ferry links Ham House (1610 built by Sir Thomas Vavasour) and its marvellous furniture with Marble Hill House (the Palladian Villa built for George II's mistress) and James Gibb's exciting Octagon Room (in Orleans House) this ferry is a perfect adjunct to a warm summer's afternoon out. But a lot of water has flowed under the bridges since there were 40,000 employed ferrymen in London.

The *Woolwich Free Ferry*, rapidly approaching its centenary, carries over three thousand vehicles and twice as many passengers across the Thames each day between 8 a.m. and 8 p.m. Although paddle-steamers were replaced by diesel power in 1963, this remains an agreeable way of crossing the river. Why is it free? Well, the Woolwich people persuaded the Metropolitan Board of Works that if their rates went towards bridges used free by Londoners from other boroughs, there was no logic why *they* should have to pay for their own ferry. The commuter service from Greenwich Pier to Charing Cross leaving at 8.15 a.m. and returning at 5.30 p.m. is worth knowing about. Quite the pleasantest way of getting to work.

For other river trips telephone the Westminster Passenger Service Association, Westminster Pier, Victoria Embankment, SW1 (01-930 2062 and (01-930 4097).

Best Ferry: *Twickenham*.

Fish and Chips

What is remarkable about the *Sea Shell* (33-35 Lisson Grove, NW1; 01-723 8703) is not just that it serves the best fish and chips in London, but that it does so cheaply, has done so for a long time, and should continue to do so. The problems attaching to success – crowds and queues and the temptation to take things easy – have been avoided, and the fish, served with a commendable lack of frills, are as big and crisp and succulent as ever, while the fish cakes, the size of small cannon-balls, delectably peppery, and made entirely of fresh white fish, are the best forty pence worth of nourishment in London. The *Sea Shell* uses ground-nut oil for frying (replaced daily) and serves sole as well as more plebeian fish. The *Sea Shell* has two adjacent establishments: one for take-away customers and one for nobs, who sit amongst nets and chianti bottles, happily gregarious, for the success of the *Sea Shell* often means that tables are shared. The proprietors will even fry your own fish for you at Passover.

There is another *Sea Shell* fish restaurant under the same management at 392 Kingsland Road, Hackney, E8 (01-254 6152).

Grahame's Sea Fare (38 Poland Street, W1; 01-437 3788/0975) serves fish and chips kosher style with batter made from matzo meal. Not only is the fish delicious, but the hospitality is jocular, even chaotic, and it's not a place to hurry away from, except to the Academy Cinema, nearby.

Other establishments that serve take-away fish and chips and may be securely recommended include: *Something Fishy* of Elmers End, the *Rock & Sole Plaice* (sic), 47 Endell Street, WC2 (01-836 3785), *John's Fish Bar* of Thornton Heath, *Belle's Fish and Chips* of Bromley South, *Redford's* of 126 Golders Green Road, NW11 (01-455 2789) and the fish and chip bar on the corner of Harrow High Street and Weald Lane.

Geale's (2 Farmer Street, W8; 01-727 7969), who cook their fish in beef dripping, no longer serve take-away, but their fish are delicious. So too is their apple crumble.

Also recommended: the *Nautilus* (27/29 Fortune Green Road, NW6; 01-435 2532); the *North Sea Restaurant* (7/8 Leigh Street, WC1; 01-387 5892) where chips are included in the price, *Steve's Fish Bar* (246 St Paul's Road, N1; 01-354 0922); *Costa's* (18 Highgate Street, W8; 01-727 4310) and the *Windmill Fish Bar* (211 Kennington Lane, SE11; 01-582 5754). So there's something for you wherever you live.

I have not enjoyed my fish and chips at *Berni Inns* (various branches) nor at the branches of the *Hungry Fisherman* (24 Thurloe Street, 142 Victoria Street, and a very crowded branch at 48 Oxford Street). For grander establishments see under Fish Restaurants.

Best Fish and Chips: The *Sea Shell*.

P.S. For tourists: if you want to be really unpopular try offering an American Express to a crowded fish and chip bar.

Fishing

The Thames is rich in barbel, flounders and smelt upstream of *Vauxhall Bridge* and particularly during the winter months when the boat traffic is diminished. You may even find the occasional trout, but 'Thames Trouting', as it is known, is a specialist art. Pike, carp and bream may be found in *Pen Ponds* in Richmond Park, and particularly large carp enjoy themselves in the warm water from the power station at *Canbury Gardens*. There is a biggie in the lake in *Kew Gardens* too. The largest tench ever caught in Great Britain weighed 11lbs and was landed from a pit at Wraysbury, but it was probably diseased and filled with fluid, so it was not permitted to stand as a record.

George Bennett (Leisure Sport) at 53-55 High Street, Feltham, Middlesex (01-890 1313) can let you have a season ticket to streams and gravel pits in the area, while you can get your Calpac season ticket (£5.75) to nineteen local waters from *Stabler's* (350-352 Garratt Lane, SW18; 01-874 4683). *Stabler's* opposite Earlsfield Station and established almost 100 years has a fine selection of rods, guns, darts, penknives and wellies. I am happy to say it also displays an urgent warning against discarding lead shot, which has been killing swans. Also recommended are *Kennington's* (195 Kennington Lane, SE11; 01-582 3540) and inevitably *Farlow's* of Pall Mall (01-839 2423), who is to fishing what *Purdey's* (57 South Audley Street, W1; 01-499 1801) is to guns (q.v.).

· The *Thames Water Angling Guide* and *Bill Howe's Fishing for Londoners* are the law and the prophets for anglers in London while the *Angling Times* is more useful for those with things to buy and sell than for those with fish to catch. The *Thames Water Authority* (New River Head Laboratories, 177 Rosebery Avenue, EC1; 01-837 3300) can be helpful. Their trout fisheries are at *Barn Elms Reservoir*, Merthyr Terrace, SW13 (01-748 3423) and it is to the *TWA* that information and inquiries about pollution should be addressed.

Best Fishing: *Canbury Gardens*, Kingston.
Worst Fishing: *Haydens Road Effluent*.

Fishmongers

Fishmongers tend to come in shoals. There are several around the old Billingsgate Market, and in Kingston Market, and two excellent fishmongers in Camden Town. One of these is *Steve Hatt* (88 Essex Road, N1; 01-226 3963). He will sell you live lobsters, oysters, eels and salmon from the River Tay. He smokes his own – haddock, trout and mackerel that is – and behind his counter he keeps a box of fishheads and fishy unmentionables for sleek and pampered cats.

R. Rowe and Sons (243 Camden High Street, NW1; 01-485 4676 and five other branches) stock over fifty varieties of fish. There ought to be a competition – haddock at fifty yards – between him and John Truman at *La Marée* (76 Sloane Avenue, SW3; 01-589 8067), who enjoys a challenge and stocks crab, lobster, langoustine, oysters, scallops, clams and dressed salmon. *Richard's Ltd* (11 Brewer Street, W1; 01-437 1358) could well have monk fish, octopi and sea urchins, raw prawns and fresh sardines as well as more plebeian fish. The assistants wear gumboots and will even sell you samphire. *Ashdown Ltd* in Leadenhall Market, EC3 (01-626 0178) has salt water tanks in its basements, so nobody's fish is fresher. On Sunday mornings *Bob White* (1 Kennington Lane, SE11; 01-735 1931) sells shellfish of all kinds, but it would be sacrilege to go to anyone but *Tubby Isaacs* (Goulston Street, E1) for jellied eels. The present Tubby is brother-in-law of the original Tubby.

On Friday mornings the fishcart from Grimsby anchors at *Flask Walk*, Hampstead, while the displays in *Harrods Food Hall* are scaly creations of great glory, and change daily.

Kingston-upon-Thames' splendid market is typical of many country towns – it's a fine market place too. The market is renowned for its fresh fish; but also in Kingston is *Jarvis*, fishmongers in Coombe Road. Customers travel 10 or 15 miles to buy *Jarvis's* fish and game, so that the queues can be long, particularly on Good Friday morning. But beware of the ever-vigilant traffic warden!

Also strongly recommended: *R. E. Wright & Sons* (10a Warwick Way, SW1; 01-834 7702) where the Minister of Agriculture and Fish gets his; *J. Mist & Sons* (254 Battersea Park Road, SW11; 01-228 6784), who smoke their own cod and haddock; *Talby's* (263 Camden High Street, NW1; 01-485 5000) sells splendid salmon trout in season; *Treadwell's* (94 Chippenham Road, W9; 01-286 9267); *J. F. Blagden* (64 Paddington Street, W1; 01-935 8321) and – notably – *Portch Brothers* (405 King's Road, Chiswick, SW10; 01-352 4464 and Upper Richmond Road West, SW14) are all deeply committed to matters fishy. The best smoked salmon in London comes from *Barnett's* of Frying Pan Alley, E1. But at *S. Baron* (Assembly Passage, Stepney, E1) you can buy smoked salmon in 'cocktail piles' at £1.15 per half pound.

Best Fishmonger: *Richard's.*
Worst Fishmonger: *Anywhere that stocks tins of peaches.*

Fish Restaurants

When the success of this book has made me rich (see under Clairvoyants), I shall have the following lunch twice a week: grilled Dover Sole served with the newest of Jersey potatoes and branch spinach followed by a generous portion of fresh raspberries and wild strawberries with coffee from Higgins and a Bendick's bittermint – but only one. Old-fashioned fish restaurants at which you can order just such a sole are numerous (though Dover Soles no longer come from Dover).

There is the *Wheeler's* chain of restaurants, now taken over by the Kennedy Brookes empire, and being extended and updated. The founder of *Wheeler's* was Bernard Walsh, whose father was a cockle and whelk salesman in Whitstable, where the oysters come from. The Old Compton Street premises were bought as a sorting house for the oysters he sold to the London Hotels. During the thirties young men and women party-goers would look in and request oysters to mend their hangovers. Bernard opened a bar to accommodate them. Then came the war and rationing from which oysters were excluded. *Wheeler's* flourished where other restaurants floundered. More recently the formula began to seem a little too predictable, as Pierre Martin brought haute cuisine standards to the cooking of fish and opened *Le Suquet, La Croisette* and *Le Quai St Pierre*. So now there are 10 Wheeler's branches as follows:

Wheeler's Log (once just the Log) 1-5 West Street, WC2; 01-836 4751.
Antoine's 40 Charlotte Street, W1; 01-636 2817.
Braganza 56 Frith Street, W1; 01-437 5412.
Wheeler's 19 Old Compton Street, W1; 01-437 2706.
Wheeler's 117/120 Kendal Street, W1; 01-724 4637.
Wheeler's 12A Duke of York Street, SW1; 01-930 2460.
Wheeler's Chelsea, 33c King's Road, SW3; 01-730 3023.
Wheeler's Blackheath 16-18A Montpelier Vale, SE3; 01-318 9273.
Wheeler's City 19-21 Great Tower Street, EC3; 01-626 3685/6, and
Wheeler's Highgate 6-7 South Grove, N6; 01-341 5270.

Since *Wheeler's* use oysters from their own beds, they certainly ought to be fresh, and, with a less extensive menu in the new branches, standards should be improving scale by gill.

Manzi's (1-2 Leicester Street, WC2; 01-437 4864) is reasonably cheap and particularly cheerful. A correspondent wrote gratefully: 'Their sole was everything you said it was. People in Canada would kill for fish this good. I also enjoyed high quality grilled tomato and fried potatoes as an accompaniment. Service was brisk and correct. The joke about Plonk de Plonk does not apply to Manzi's house white.'

Sweeting's (39 Queen Victoria Street, EC4; 01-248 3062) is about as close as you can get to a Victorian fish restaurant, although it is actually 150 years old. There are four bars, one serving sandwiches, the others oysters and traditional English fish dishes with spotted dick* or jam roly-poly for afters.

Bentley's (11-15 Swallow Street, W1; 01-734 4756) is another old-established joint (why *are* fish restaurants so long-lived? Orchestra conductors and psychiatrists are too, so maybe they eat a lot of fish) having been founded by a barrow-boy some 70 years ago. It

---

*Overseas visitors: don't worry.

still has its long oyster-bar upstairs and excellent turbot. The only recent innovation is the basement wine-bar. Beware of confusing this restaurant with *Bill Bentley's*, also a fish restaurant with branches in EC2, NW1 and SW3, and also pretty good.

As for *Sheekey's*, (29 St Martin's Court, WC2; 01-836 4118) well, that claims to be the oldest fish restaurant of all. So it may be. It is a lively old-fashioned restaurant, particularly after a show. We enjoyed artichokes stuffed with mushrooms as a starter, but my sole was more like a tiddler, there was too much salt in the hollandaise, and they refused to let me have two half portions of new and hash brown potatoes instead of a single portion of either. Rotters. In this category too I should mention *Geale's* and the *Sea Shell*, which I have described under Fish and Chips. Also the Kosher fish restaurant, *Grahame's* (38 Poland Street, W1; 01-437 0975). In this context Kosher means extra large portions and of course no shell-fish. Moving up-market brings me to the French Fish Restaurants of the *Le Suquet* group, including *Le Suquet* itself (104 Draycott Avenue, SW3; 01-581 1785), *La Croisette* (168 Ifield Road, SW10; 01-589 5774 next to *La Marée*, the fishmonger who supplies it). All are excellent, though they tend rather to Fulham chic; the last-named being my favourite. Order the Plateau de Fruits de Mer at any of them.

Whether you prefer these to the old-style fish restaurants above depends upon whether you think fish needs all the trimmings. It's my view that if the fish itself is fresh, it doesn't.

Four curiosities. *The Café Fish* (39 Panton Street, W1; 01-930 3999 and I won't give it its pompous full name) the first wine bar/brasserie, specialising in fish. The cover charge includes limited starters, salad and bread, so that fish (poached, grilled, fried, sautéed in butter, or baked) may be served as soon as it's cooked. A fine cheeseboard, nourishing puds and wine listed according to the grapes – which is like choosing your friends according to their family tree.

The O'Lavangate (99-103 Fulham Road, SW3; 01-581 8100) is a Portuguese fish restaurant, smart and expensive where those who have tasted the prawns piri-piri (in a burningly hot tomato sauce) or the turbot in Neuilly Prat don't soon forget them. The same family, the Costas, also run *Fogareiro*, improbably situated in Finchley (16 Hendon Lane, N3; 01-346 0315). Here you will please Mrs C. best by ordering the extraordinary fish-soup, but the piri-piri prawns set Finchley alight too. Does Mrs Thatcher dine there and could the prawns be behind her monetarist policies?

A Michelin Star has been awarded to *Tiger Lee* (251 Old Brompton Road, SW7; 01-370 2323/5970), and they don't give these away. It's expensive (£62 for a bottle of 1970 Dom Perignon) and serious about its Cantonese style fish – notably lobster. But I shall play safer and nominate . . .

Best Fish Restaurant: *Sweeting's.*

Florists

Should you see an aged crone with a basket of flowers on her arm shouting 'Vilets, luvly vilets!' in Covent Garden, she will be filming for American TV. But despite the market itself moving south of the river some good florists remain. *Albert's* (1 Betterton Street, WC2; 01-240 0450) and *Ellen Keeley* (4 Shorts Gardens, WC2; 01-836 2375) are two; the latter used to make barrows for the bummarees too.

Constance Spry (74 Marylebone Lane, W1; 01-499 7201) runs a school for flower arrangers at 53 Marylebone Lane; the shop is an excellent advertisement for the school. *Felton's* (5 Cheapside, EC2; 01-236 7261 and two branches), *Moyses Stevens* (Lansdowne House, Berkeley Square, W1; 01-493 8171) and *Flower Power* (94 Holland Park Avenue, W11; 01-229 8788) are all excellent but not cheap. Indeed flowers in the centre of London can't – and shouldn't – be cheap. A dozen orchids from *Moyses Stevens* will set you back £30 with an additional £3.50 for special delivery. The *Piccadilly Flower Company* (Old Compton Street, W1) is a beautiful flower shop, but rather too grand for its street, while the small flower shop in the entrance of *Heal's* (Tottenham Court Road, W1) is enchantingly pretty, just like the one Catharine Deneuve worked in in *Les Parapluies de Cherbourg.*

My favourite flower seller is the gentleman who sits outside the Spanish Embassy in Belgrave Square and has done so, year in, year out, for as long as I can recall. Franco, Juan Carlos, the Socialists, he has seen them come and seen them go to the scent of roses and jonquils in the spring.

Best Florist: *The one in Heal's.*
Worst Florists: *Those who set up their stalls at the approaches to hospitals and cemeteries.* Who about to bury a relative will hassle over a bunch of chrysanths? Be warned.

P.S. If you love flowers don't miss when you next visit Kew Gardens, the *Marianne North Gallery* (see under Art Galleries).

Football

There is never and never has been any trouble at *Charlton* football ground (The Valley), which is ironic since *Charlton*, unable to afford a ground of their own any longer, has taken a half share in Crystal Palace's ground. But *Charlton* is not a football team to inspire strong passions of any kind; not so *Millwall* and its bootboys; nor *Chelsea* whose Stamford Bridge fans are too superior for scarves and favours; button-down shirts and designer sweaters are more typical. But the suavity of the outfits is misleading; the racial taunting of black players by *Chelsea* fans is contemptible and alarming. Not much of that sort of thing down the road at Craven Cottage, the home of *Fulham*. *Tottenham's* fans in the west stand are a rough and ready lot. Maybe the obvious skills of their Argentine players have encouraged them to be broadminded. *West Ham's* ground (Upton Park) is in the centre of the Sikh community and the National Front maintain a strong presence at home matches. But the fan's have some moral sensitivity; they don't boo their own black players, only visiting black players. Probably the worst club in and around London is *Luton* – at least to judge by the state of the ground. The football is rather good. There have been occasions recently when half of Luton's team was composed of black players, Brian Stein, Ricky Hill and Nwajobi are powerful players for *Luton*; they are all black.

Best Club: *Queen's Park Rangers*.
Worst Club: *Millwall*.

P.S. Did I leave out *Arsenal?* Surely not. (Myself, I'm a *Darlington* supporter.)

Foot Scrapers

The wittiest foot scraper may be found outside the Foreign and Commonwealth Office in *Downing Street*. I'm sure there is a great deal of protocol as to who uses the thing and who brings the mud in from St James's Park. This scraper is in wrought iron, although most of them are cast. There are other interesting scrapers at *28 Meadway*, NW11 (a street full of interesting survivals) where a horse stands on on top of the actual scraper, at *30 Chester Street*, SW1 (like a pair of squatting toads), and at *36A Elvaston Place*, SW7 (hemispheric, double-ended with bulging finials). Outside the other *St Paul's* (The Ridgeway, NW7) you can scrape your feet on dolphins' tails and at *12 Blenheim Road*, NW8 on dragons' wings. But the best, which appears to be quite ancient, has a white face mask a bit like a silver hallmark above the scraper. Its expression is of someone who has seen it all and yet somehow survived. Wipe your feet on that! It is at . . .

Best Foot Scraper: *2 Cheyne Row,* SW3.

Fountains and Drinking Fountains

A winter's afternoon in Regent's Park. I trot southwards along the Broad Walk. To my right, securely (I trust) behind the railings of the London Zoo, wolves prowl. No roads, no houses are visible. Traffic hums, but distantly. A savage place, as mystic and enchanted as e're beneath a waning moon was haunted by a woman wailing for her demon lover. As they say. And then, most improbably, as I breast the rise, there is a hideous tent-shaped structure, some sixteen feet high, made out of crumbling granite and discouraging marble. It is known as the *Parsee Fountain.* Once it contained a water-clock, but time stopped in Regent's Park and the clock was removed. There remain extruding from the granite four rusting spouts for drinking water, but nothing flows through them. About the edifice stone lions prowl. On the northern side is a small cameo head of Queen Victoria, of whom you will have heard. On the southern side, the head of Sir Cowasjeen Jehangir, a Parsee from Bombay about whom I can tell you little – I could have told you more about his Parsee compatriot, Sir Jamsetjee Jeejeebhoy (1783-1859) who amassed two million pounds in the Bombay markets before he was forty and became a philanthropist and a baronet. This is the strangest fountain in London, a city whose climate is ill-suited to hurling gouts of water into the sky. Bravely at the *Barbican* they try it, and very fine it looks when the sunlight irradiates the spray. But generally the emphasis is less on how much water can be hoisted than on the allegorical and architectural possibilities of fountains.

· Most popular are mermaids and mermen, dolphins, naked ladies emptying flasks, naked boys, and, since the last war and Reg Butler, abstract designs of a watery nature. But one can also find a girl with a greyhound, elegantly contained within twisting bronze branches in *Green Park*, a boy with a frog in a begonia garden (*Queen Mary's Gardens*, Regent's Park) and a woman with a fish (*Cambridge Heath Road*).

You will have noticed that *Regent's Park* is rich territory for fountaineers. This is thanks to the artist and generous patron of the arts, Sigismund Christian Hubert Goetze (1866-1939), who lived in Grove House, a Georgian villa designed by Decimus Burton and the only such villa to survive in the park in its original form. Goetze has his own memorial fountain in the large pond in *Queen Mary's Gardens*. Here a merman blows water through a shell watched admiringly by naked acolytes who themselves are regularly doused by large and obliging fish. The splashing of this fountain (one of the few in London that seems always to be playing) is one of the most joyful features of these lovely gardens.

A similar fountain in a very different setting is the large Poseidon group in *George Yard* in the City. Within a basin tiled to resemble seaweed, a merman and a mermaid (modelled by Sir Charles Wheeler upon his glamorous second wife) appear to be taking snapshots of Poseidon (actually they are holding up shells through which water flows – or *ought* to flow). The Poseidon figure has massive calves like green watermelons and stands impressively tall, though the group has little of the eccentric charm of the Goetze memorial. The best thing about this fountain is that it enhances an otherwise barren modern courtyard.

Behind the *Royal Exchange* is a delightful depiction of Motherhood. A mother feeds one baby at her breast and looks lovingly at a second. The eminent figure of George Peabody watches her surreptitiously from across the courtyard. A few yards to the south is the first of the naked-women-emptying-jugs statues. In this one (the Cattle Trough Association Jubilee Fountain) the lady is guarded from stock-jobbers and the like by four fearsome lions, and in *Sloane Square*, Venus, who was paid for by the Royal Academy of Arts, kneels on a remarkably large sculpted urn to empty her jug. Around the urn King Charles II, sitting on his hat, plucks fruit from a tree while Nell Gwynn, hiding behind a fan, permits a coy nipple to escape her corsage. Nell is watched by a swan and a mature winged Cupid with two darts, and King Charles's spaniel chases a hart. Under the urn's rim the legend reads: 'Sweet Thames Run Softly Till I End My Song', an unacknowledged quotation from Edmund Spenser. Another kneeling girl emptying her jug is in *Guildford Place* opposite the former foundling hospital, whose choir was trained by Handel and one of whose most energetic patrons was Hogarth.

Appropriately the (draped) Woman of Samaria on *Clapham Common*, who offers a drink of water to an old crutched gentleman, was the gift of the United Kingdom Temperance and Provident Institution. This handsome lady, somewhat resembling Virginia McKenna, is set on rather too high a plinth. Nonetheless she dignifies the north east corner of the common, which could do with a touch of dignity, and you may drink from her too, whatever your age, and whether you are provident and temperate or not.

The two fountains in *Trafalgar Square* are not the originals, which were given to the City of Ottawa, but Portland Stone replacements. You should be there in the morning as Big Ben strikes ten to see them to best advantage. As the jets attain power, it's like watching a marquee go up. But despite the claims of all these fountains, important and artistic as they may be, and the historic fountain in *Fountains Court*, Middle Temple, my favourite is and always will be the charming little stone fountain – a simple modest spout amidst a dozen even modester – arising from a mossy and weather-worn basin in the centre of *Little Cloisters* in the precincts of Westminster Abbey. These cloisters, restored after the war, formed part of the ancient monks' infirmary, and no sweeter place to recuperate can possibly be imagined. Despite being within one of the most famous tourist spots in one of the busiest capitals in the world, the *Little Cloisters* remain a haven for weary souls. Don't please all go at once.

The first Metropolitan Drinking Fountain was squirted at the public in 1859. It may be seen outside the *Church of the Holy Sepulchre*, Holborn Viaduct. 'Replace the cup', it demands of guilty and innocent alike.

The one at *Spaniards End*, NW3 is reminiscent of the Pierian spring at Delphi, which Keats suggested you should drink deep of if you needed inspiration. (It did less for me than for Keats.) Outside *Queen Mary College*, Mile End Road, is a miniature temple, so grand that it seems a waste merely to drink water there, and the drinking fountains in *Birdcage Walk*, SW1, are embellished with what appear to be nude gardeners. Delightful is the drinking fountain in *Victoria Tower Gardens* upon which are carved in relief three leaping dolphins, but then I have a thing about dolphins. (See also under Horse Troughs.)

Oh, and the best drinking fountain for dogs is in *Kensington Gardens*, near the junction of the Broad Walk and Kensington Road. A charming but nondescript puppy, haunches and tail up, ears pricked, is begging for a ball or a stick to be thrown. Cunningly he has been sited just beyond the sign reading 'Dogs must be kept on a leash in this area'.

Best Fountain: *Little Cloisters*, Westminster Abbey.
Worst Fountain: *Parsee Fountain*, Regent's Park.
Best Drinking Fountain: *Victoria Tower Gardens*.
Worst Drinking Fountain: *Deptford Playground*, Watson Street, SE8.

Frames and Framing

There is, and has been for some time, a small-scale piece of chicanery practised on the British public. Antique dealers buy up old picture frames (they come cheap in job lots at auction), touch them up with a bit of papier maché and some gold paint, and fill them with mirror glass before selling them as antique mirrors. The glass looks modern and unbevelled, but people are still taken in by it. It's an excellent idea to buy up old frames in this way and to use them for your own pictures.

Framing services vary. *H. J. Spiller* (37 Beak Street, W1; 01-437 4661/7084) has the largest collection of authentic antique frames in the world. *Robert Sielle* (21 St Alban's Grove, W8; 01-937 4957) will provide a frame from his large studio to complement any picture you may bring him. He has made frames for Buckingham Palace, the White House, the Tate and will do it for you. He is also a skilled picture restorer.

A more modest operator is Terry Stocks of *Stocks* (174 Clerkenwell Road, EC1; 01-278 6209 not weekends) but he will collect and deliver and do the work in a day, if it's vital. Even speedier is *Frame Express* (1 Queen's Road, SW19; 01-879 3366 and 376 King's Road, SW3; 01-351 5975) with a while-you-wait service initiated by two recent business graduates with a loan from the government. At *Vortex Galleries* (139-141 Stoke Newington Church Street, N16; 01-254 6516) a framing service is only a part of it. There's an art gallery, a wholefood café and second-hand books. *Swallow Art Suppliers* (100-108 Battersea Rise, SW11; 01-228 0314) will either frame you or sell you everything you need to frame yourself. At *Fix-a-Frame* (280 Old Brompton Road, SW5; 01-370 4189) the staff provide you with the bare essentials and you do the framing at a workbench. They are closed Sundays and Mondays, but what more satisfying way could there be of spending a rainy Tuesday?

Also recommended: *Evans The Frame*, 71 Regents Park Road, NW1; (01-722 2009).

Best Frames: *H. J. Spiller*.

Free Entertainment

London can be free. By joining a squat, you need not pay rent, rates, nor hotel bills. You may eat free by cadging from market traders at the end of the day or by pocketing a hotel key and returning to eat meals there (but I would not recommend you doing anything so disreputable). It is also possible to eat free at press conferences (see under Canteens) or big exhibitions such as the *Ideal Home* – take a paper bag. Use skips to furnish your flat, or have an arrangement at the municipal dumps; it's surprising what you can find there if you have transport. To look respectable have your hair cut free as a model for one of the hairdressing schools, such as *Vidal Sassoon* or *Crimpers*.

Cultural activities may be enjoyed by starting your own magazine and informing the press officers of the various theatres, cinemas and publishers accordingly (printed letter headings help). You will then receive free tickets and review copies of books, which you can sell after reviewing. You might even become a press baron. God help you.

It is always possible by mingling with the crowds outside a London theatre to get in free to see the second half of a London play, and, by turning up at a pop venue at 3 p.m. on the day the band is scheduled to appear, you should be able to walk in and listen to them balancing their sound. Ice-skaters have to practise before the big competitions; one can usually sneak into the rinks and watch. There are free exhibitions of art, free 'platform' plays and recitals at the *National Theatre* and the *Barbican*, while at the *Commonwealth Institute* in Holland Park, there are free showings of films and free exhibitions, often of exceptional interest. Also free film shows at the *British Museum* (01-636 1555) the *Museum of Mankind* (01-437 2224) and the *Tate* (01-821 1313). Along the *Bayswater Road* and in *Piccadilly* at weekends, there are free art exhibitions but be warned if you are tempted to buy, for the 'artists' are often merely agents for unscrupulous wholesalers. Anyway, the commercial art galleries are always free. Try *Cork Street* for the best of modern art, and *Bond Street*.

Music, and particularly organ recitals, are commonly held at London churches (phone the *Guildhall*, 01-606 3030 for details); *Southwark Cathedral* has an excellent programme of lunchtime music, for instance, though contributions to the organ fund would be welcome.

At the *Piazza* in Covent Garden – a huge success – and on the Portico of the *Inigo Jones Actors' Church* there, street performances of all kinds are given, including Punch and Judy shows. The best time to watch these splendid gypsies is Saturday afternoons (see also Buskers).

Viewing at auctions is a favourite activity of mine, but it doesn't always turn out free. Read the *Telegraph* on Mondays or the *Antiques Trade Gazette* for details of upcoming sales.

The parks are free and in many of them there are free concerts of military music. A visit to the *Law Courts* is not only free but extremely instructive. Currently the liveliest entertainment may be pursued at the Probate Division (see Law Courts).

For those of a mechanical bent you can watch the planes taking off and landing at *Heathrow*. Those of us who live in West London would not consider that an afternoon well spent. The best place to watch from is the roof of the Terminal 2 Car Park. There's a children's playground on top of Queen's Buildings. On the last Sunday of every month there is a parade of custom cars from *Chelsea Bridge* along the King's Road, and *CND* marches are not only free, but may do some good, apart from enabling you to catch up on hits of the 60s. Obviously *Speakers' Corner* (Hyde Park at Marble Arch on Sundays) is free; it may change your life. So may the *Notting Hill Carnival!* I doubt whether a visit to the *Houses of Parliament* (01-219 4272) will. The *Stock Exchange* (01-588 2355) may. These tours are free too.

Most museums are still free, although special exhibitions may not be. A week at the *Victoria and Albert* would scarcely be enough to see all there is to be seen. Sir Roy Strong has imposed voluntary charges. I don't approve.

At the *BBC's Maida Vale Recording Studios* and at the *Paris Studio* in Lower Regent Street it is possible to enjoy quiz shows, comedies, concerts, poetry, and panel games in great comfort and entirely free. Write to the BBC Ticket Unit, BBC, London, W1A 4WW, or try Thames TV (01-387 9494), London Weekend (01-261 3434) or Channel 4 (01-631 4444).

The flowers in London are free, but the *Bluebell Wood* in Kew will cost 10p on top of your 25p admittance – a bargain in May. In February the crocuses around *Hyde Park Corner* are exceptional, so later in the year are the roses in *Regent's Park* and the azaleas in *Queen Isabella's Garden* (Richmond Park). Some like the *Changing of the Guard*; I am perfectly happy with them the way they are.

The *Lord Mayor's Show* is a grand day out, especially should the weather be kind. The floats are wonderfully inventive and the crowds and the police good-humoured. The best place from which to watch is Temple Gardens, if you know a lawyer who'll invite you in, but the Strand's OK.

The best free entertainment I ever enjoyed in London was pyrotechnical. The fireworks on the occasion of the last Royal Wedding were impressive but not a patch on those (by Le Maitre) at the tercentenary celebrations for Handel. These were so beautifully integrated with Handel's music in mood, in decibel-level, and in the choice of colours that it was clear someone very talented had been put in charge; we watched them across the Serpentine. Marvellous!

For further details get hold of *Free London*, which ironically costs 99p, from underground stations and tourist offices, or, from bookshops *London for Free* by Mary Peplow and Debra Shipley (Granada £1.95). The contents are preferable to the title.

French Restaurants

If I favour the *vieux jeu* as against the *nouvelle cuisine*, then it's because anyone – well almost anyone — can run a successful restaurant for a few weeks or months. I have tried many of these new places and liked them well enough, but it's the ones I cut my wisdom teeth on in the late fifties that I turn to with the greatest pleasure.

The first French restaurant I ever ventured into without a grown-up was *L'Epicure* (28 Frith Street, W1; 01-437 2829), and I continued to patronise it throughout the sixties and seventies. Often Harold Wilson was there, a clever man in affairs of food as in much else, for the service in this typical old Soho restaurant was always discreet, friendly and respectful. The food, often flambéed in front of you, was always what it purported to be: it was there I learned how to diane steak. *L'Epicure* has scarcely changed in thirty years. Soho grew squalid and then unsqualid but behind that naked lantern flame the 60s and 70s were cauterised. Then there was the *Chanterelle* (119 Old Brompton Road, SW7; 01-373 5522), where one was always made to feel important even if one wasn't. And the *Chanterelle* always *smelled* so good. It has changed ownership since those days, and is now run by Fergus Provan, whose cooking incorporates such ingredients as salsify, chestnuts, sorrel and sweetbreads. His salmon en croute is best. A set dinner at £9.50 which includes both coffee and dessert, in a restaurant of this class, is not to be sneezed at.

I used to be taken to *À l'Ecu de France* (111 Jermyn Street, SW1; 01-930 2837) by a friendly publisher in the days when publishers were friendly. It was always expensive but it used to be entirely dependable. The meat was succulent, the service was formal, and the food, it seemed, *mattered*. French restaurants in the grand style were few and far between in London; they still are. But it seems as though the *Ecu* has outlived its usefulness.

In the days of sexy Tory MPs and Lady Docker, the best of all French restaurants, I think, was *Daphne's* (112 Draycott Avenue, SW3; 01-589 4257). The tables were always a bit close together so that once, when my companion had spent the evening explaining to me that Laurence Olivier had been dreadfully over-the-top in *Othello*, we were rather stunned to be greeted by none other as he rose to leave from the next table. But Daphne elle-même, matronly and welcoming, has moved on to that great boîte in the sky and I hope she's serving them her mousse of smoked salmon with as much élan as she used to serve it to us. Today's speciality: Ambrosia.

Now of course *nouvelle cuisine* is a part of the language. It came, became fashionable, and was pushed aside at just the same time as structuralism with which it has plenty in common. People realise that if they were paying top whack for raw vegetables and meat, tiny portions of beautifully decorated pâtés with coulis of tomato and a mousse with kiwi fruit were not really value for money. Here then, regardless of fashion or price, are a few French restaurants (out of hundreds) that you just might enjoy to eat at.

Au Jardin des Gourmets (5 Greek Street, W1; 01-437 1816/4839). Established 1931. Very attractive, with attentive service, and a list of some of the best clarets available anywhere. On the wall a large oil of a one-eyed Biblical King with a dead chicken around his neck. Would it not put customers off chicken, I wondered. 'But we want to,' explained the Maître d', 'it's a cheap dish.'

Ma Cuisine (113 Walton Street, SW3; 01-584 7585). In this street of restaurants (and magistrates courts, alas) this one is the hottest ticket in town. Booking a table is like being elected to the Royal Society – worth it if you can. But the tables are too close together. Leave room for the mousse brulée. And fast for a day prior to your visit. An experience.

Au Bon Accueil. Heartily recommended for reliable French cooking without formality (27 Elystan Street, SW3; 01-589 3718).

La Tante Claire (68 Royal Hospital Road, SW3; 01-352 6045). One of the restaurants in London most seriously dedicated to the gastronomic arts. M. Koffman presides over the kitchen; Madame Koffman is front of house manager. Their way with scallops is unique. Very expensive and should be. Expanding into new premises. The set lunch at £12 seems too good to be true.

Au Provençal (295 Railton Road, SE24; 01-274 9163). Improbably situated at the entrance to Herne Hill Station, this imaginative and modestly priced restaurant coped remarkably well with my niece's 18th-birthday dinner and her effervescent friends. It maintains its standards impressively. Beware! No plastic money.

Lichfields (Lichfield Terrace, Sheen Road, Richmond, Surrey; 01-940 5236). My favourite place for the grand occasion. The chef, Stephen Bull, concentrates on a limited menu, but everything is supremely well cooked. The cheese gougères brought to you while you order melt in the mouth. Eat these and leave, pleading faintness.

La Poule Au Pot (231 Ebury Street, SW1; 01-730 7763). The producer of my first (and only) West End play used to manage this charming restaurant, which survives virtually unchanged after more than twenty years. Mustard imaginatively employed in the cooking. Friendly and welcoming, and supremely tactful in very trying circumstances.

The following recommendations were not included in *The Essential Guide to London*.

192 (192 Kensington Park Road, W11; 01-229 0482). Stylish and accomplished with a waitress called Mercedes. Very much in the *nouvelle cuisine* tradition.

Chez Nico (129 Queenstown Road, SW8; 01-720 6960). As a result of employing both the old and the new traditions and being talented and being south of the river, Nico Ladenis achieved his third Michelin star. Particularly good with such salads as 'pheasant salad au beurre de truffe'. Lunch better than dinner.

L'Escargot (48 Greek Street, W1; 01-437 2879). Since Ella Fitzgerald dines here, it has to be stylish. (But ignore the television people, who are noisy.) Elena, smiling and affectionate, welcomes you if you're lucky. Try to get placed in the painted room upstairs. (Downstairs is a brasserie.) Notable interest in wines.

Le Gavroche (43 Upper Brook Street, W1; 01-408 0881). An Albert Roux restaurant, and the Koh-i-noor in his crown, for it has the coveted triple award from Michelin. So keep it for a very special occasion (which it will be). New potatoes backed and slit and stuffed with caviare are merely 'nibbles' here. I intend to blow some of my Booker McConnell prize money there.

Hilaire (68 Old Brompton Road, SW7; 01-584 8993). Has been the subject of rave reviews in just about every restaurant column. Changes both lunch and dinner menu daily. The Chef was once an inspector for Egon Ronay; he's poacher turned gamekeeper; so far a successful transformation.

Interlude de Tabaillau (7/8 Bow Street, WC2; 01-379 6473). Despite crowded tables and volatile service the food – nouvellish – is sufficiently classy to earn inclusion. Wine included in a *prix fixée*. Useful for the Opera House, hence the name. Also for the police station.

M. Thompson (29 Kensington Park Road, W11; 01-727 9957). Very attractive and very French in an up-and-coming area of Notting Hill. The food was beautifully presented and tasted *almost* as good as it looked. The menu was small but fun, and I ordered a small portion of each of the puddings together on a plate.

Mijanou (143 Ebury Street, SW1; 01-730 4099). Quite formal, the food, which is intricate and rich, being served in a part of the owners' (Sonia and Neville Blech) house. A worthwhile addition.

Rue St Jacques (5 Charlotte Street, W1; 01-637 0222). Charlotte Street is increasingly devoted to food and wine. Commissioning editors find it sweetens the pill to say 'No' to producers in such chic surroundings. I thought that it had been a *little* over-praised. But try it for yourself – and let me know what you think.

Best French Restaurant: (for the grand occasion) *Le Gavroche*.
Best French Restaurant: (for the more intimate occasion) *La Poule Au Pot*.

Friezes

Since the *Elgin Marbles* in the British Museum are 'generally agreed to be the finest in the world' (*The New Penguin Guide to London*); and 'generally held to be the greatest ever executed' (*The Blue Guide to London*), it would be churlish and contrary of me to prefer any other friezes, so I won't; but the frieze on the pediment of *Liberty's* store, overlooking Regent Street, with its massive Britannia (1924), and Nash's flamboyant Wedgwoody frieze on the pediment at the top of *Cumberland House* in Regent's Park, are worth more than a cursory glance.

A notable high camp mosaic frieze of peacocks and cockatoos by Walter Crane in the Arab Hall of *Leighton House* (Holland Park Road, free admission) is not to be missed. The house with its delightfully secluded garden is a hymn to late Victorian culture. A curiosity is the frieze running along the *ABC Cinema* in Shaftesbury Avenue. Gladiators, actors, camels, bacchanalians, all in a sort of Eric Gill neo-Hellenic profusion; or confusion. They say that Eric Gill did his carvings on Broadcasting House up a ladder in a monk's robe without underpants. People *are* bitchy. A frieze on the *Dunlop* building in St James' Street where the lovely old theatre used to stand, features Shakespearean scenes.

I'm not sure whether it's a frieze or not, but the remarkable incised panels on what remains of the *Friern Manor Dairy*, Stroud Green, are charming, depicting the ancient and 'modern' styles of milk farming, grazing, milking, cooling, delivery and butter. Our late lamented poet laureate recommended that one should always look *above* the shop fronts in London; if you do so you will certainly discover many treasures – if you live long enough.

Best Frieze: *Elgin Marbles*.

Gambling Clubs

In this age of dogmatism and dole queues, the atmosphere of a gambling club seems anachronistic. Indeed almost all the big money men are Arabs, Africans, Americans and Japanese, and the clubs at which they play cater accordingly. American roulette has taken over from the French variety, which is altogether more sedate, and blackjack and punto banco are increasingly popular. Craps, which offers the gambler in search of a genuine even money chance the best opportunity (by betting 'Don't Come'), is not played in the posh places, being regarded as noisy and undignified. Sky Masterson played, you will recall, in a New York drain. But the most comprehensive change has been in the running of clubs. The Gaming Board inspectors have been responsible for such a tightening up of the regulations that it's as if the dice have to provide three referees before being thrown. Despite this, business is booming. The latest report from the Gaming Board reports an increase of £183 million in the 'drop', which is to say the money punted, in British casinos. Guess what the figure for 1984 was? £1,666 millions. Big, big money, and most of it gone beyond recall.

There has been a constant readjustment in the ownership of the big London clubs. Grand Metropolitan controls the Mayfair casinos, the *Ritz* and the *Casanova*, as well as four other clubs. Pleasurama, which bought out Trident Television which bought out the *Playboy Club*, was and is Grand Met's principal rival with seventeen provincial clubs and five casinos. London Clubs, formerly Mecca Sportsman, have the *Golden Nugget*, the *Sportsman, Palm Beach* and *Hilton* casinos. As you can see the competition is fierce.

I have a system which will defeat the heavy mob but I need to be fully capitalised. Any offers?

The Beaux Arts splendour of the *Ritz Casino* ('the last fling of a great age' – Betjeman) is all very well, but the handsomest house currently being gambled in is 20 Curzon Street, W1, the new *Crockford's Club*. Here is Horace Walpole writing about it in 1786: 'I was at Lady Macartney's last night. They have got a charming house in Curzon Street. It was Lord Carteret's and all antiqued and grotesqued by Adam, with an additional room in the court four score feet long, then dedicated to orgies, and now to books.' No orgies now, but a blackjack table with stakes from £100 to £1,000 and American roulette at up to £200 *en plein*. The club is in the same ownership as the *International*, Berkeley Square, and offers two bars, a French restaurant and a Chinese restaurant. Outside, the obsequious figure of Crockford, the hump-backed fishmonger from Temple Bar, invites you in. The gambling is conducted in English (which is naff), the croupiers are tactful and cheerful. *Aspinall's* still has considerable cachet, for John Aspinall has style. He ran the *Clermont Club* to subsidise his zoos, for he loves animals even more than gamblers.

Best casino: *Ritz*.

Garages

To understand why most garages are so disastrously bad, it is necessary to read *Zen and the Art of Motorcycle Maintenance* in which the problem is improbably set in its philosophical context. The author offers one useful hint. Any garage mechanic who works to music is likely to be less committed to his work than one who works in silence. Furthermore you should look at the condition of the tools scattered around (or hopefully *not* scattered around) the workshop. A more prosaic reason for the appalling standards of most British garages is that the Motor Agents' Association has persistently done so little to improve things, and that the motoring associations seem keener on selling life insurance and semi-literate magazines than in securing the health of their members' cars.

But to be positive. The following garages have done good work in the past, and so may be expected to continue to do good work in the future. *Carpoint* (69 Borough Road, SE1; 01-403 1314), *R. A. Creamer & Sons Ltd* (Drayton Mews, W8; 01-937 1275), *Daleham Garage* (19 Daleham Mews, NW3; 01-435 9136), *R. E. King* (1 Baynes Mews, NW3; 01-435 7096) (specifically for bodywork) and, more grandly, *Normand's* of Abbey Road, NW10 (01-965 7757). *Kennings* (12 Berkeley Square, W1; 01-499 3434 and branches) from whom I bought my last car, were straight and efficient, but I had a tough time with their insurance department and the guarantee did not live up to its promise. *Morris Stapleton Motors* of 4 Kendrick Place, SW1 (01-589 5259) have the prettiest showroom, for it is choc-full of the prettiest cars, Morgans, lined up in colourful array. *Motorists' World* in White Hart Lane, Twickenham is open twenty-four hours a day, and offers, besides spares, videos and refreshments.

For the rest it is well to anticipate the worst and avoid it by taking evening classes in car maintenance, or change to renting your cars. For repairs Renault and Volvo agents seem especially expensive. Attempting (successfully) to buy a second-hand Volvo estate from *Tamplins* in Twickenham it turned out that two salesmen had sold the same car to separate customers. The air turned blue.

On the street where I live is *Tiger Motors*, whose proprietor, Derek, takes a concerned interest in all of us. On cold winter mornings he will drop everything to jump-start our cars, and if any of us have to undertake at short notice a lengthy car journey, Derek *will not allow us* to leave without first checking our brakes. Furthermore a domestic crisis was avoided when he pumped up my daughter's space hopper. Less urgent repairs take longer. Just up the road on Richmond Hill, *Vineyard Motors* is conscientious and helpful.

Best Garage: *Tiger Motors*, Alexandra Road, East Twickenham.

Most improbable garage: 'The Chinese Garage' (*Park Langley Garage*, Wickham Road, Beckenham – built in pagoda-style).

Garden Centres

As a child, when I travelled west, either by car or by train on the Great Western Railway, the view I most looked forward to was *Waterford's Floral Mile*. The idea of *a mile* of flowers stimulated the mind of this would-be plutocrat. There were no such things as garden centres then. Plants came from nurseries, and seeds, gnomes and trellis work from Mr Chalk, the hardware man.

Now, in the age of the patio garden and the hatchback, we have garden centres. Of these the most celebrated is *The Clifton Nurseries*, which has expanded into three centres (Little Venice, 5a Clifton Villas, Warwick Avenue, W9; 01-286 9888; the Colonnades, Bishop's Bridge Road, W2; 01-402 9834 and 16 Russell Street, Covent Garden, WC2; 01-379 6878). There are many who swear by the firm, but others have complained to me that it is too expensive and that at the Little Venice branch 'they were amazingly rude on several visits'.

The Earl's Court Road is an improbable venue for a garden centre, but *Russell's* at No 80 (01-937 0481) is recommended and not just for koolabar cuttings; while the *Parkhill Garden Nursery*, 84 Parkhill Road, NW3 (01-485 5985) is as polite and helpful as others are – reportedly – rude. Both the *Croxted Road Garden Centre*, SE24 (01-674 4366) and *Cramphorn's* in Keston are a bit 'rich' (as they say in the markets); the latter is reported to have refused to change defective goods.

The cheapest places to buy plants and such are the street markets at *Columbia Road*, Bethnal Green (strongly recommended) and *East Street*, Walworth Road, SE17; also, predictably, the *New Covent Garden* flower market at Seven Dials, where the wholesalers will 'see you're all right'. The *Petersham Garden Centre* at Petersham Farm, 143

Petersham Road, Surrey (01-940 5230) is a delight. *Sutton's*, of course, is the place for seed (33 Catherine Street, WC2; 01-836 0619), just as *Garden Crafts* (158 New King's Road, SW6; 01-736 1615) is the place for garden statuary – some of their stock has to be seen to be believed. Well worth checking out is *Roots and Shoots* (Walnut Tree Walk, SE11; 01-587 1131 closed week-ends) a plant place run by young people with learning difficulties. Bedding and herbaceous plants, hanging baskets, filled or empty, herbs and such are sold at well under the going rates.

However, as a regular garden centre, *Syon Park*, Brentford (01-568 0134) is the place. You push a huge trolley around the spacious grounds which contain all you can reasonably expect, and pay at the check out with plastic money, if you're lucky enough to have any. You can combine your visit with a trip (I think it's the appropriate word) around the Butterfly House (see under Butterflies). But it's not particularly cheap.

Best Garden Centres: *Petersham* (for charm), *Syon Park* (for choice), *Columbia Road Market* (for value).

Gardens

God Almighty first planted a garden; and, indeed, it is the purest of human pleasures; it is the greatest refreshment to the spirits of man; without which buildings and palaces are but gross handy-works; and a man shall ever see that, when ages grow to civility and elegance, man comes to build stately sooner than to garden finely: as if gardening were the greater perfection.
– Francis Bacon

Kew is of course unique. The Royal Botanic Gardens were laid out in 1751 by William Chambers, tutor to the Prince of Wales, and fastidious author of the splendid *Treatise of Civil Architecture*. Dominating the gardens is the Palm House (Decimus Burton), a mere 362 feet long by 100 feet wide by 66 feet high at the centre. But dimensions can do no justice to the most beautiful glasshouse in existence (currently under restoration). Despite the claims of the Pagoda, the flagstaff on Victory Hill, the Bluebell Wood in early May and other vernal delights, *Kew Gardens* are not primarily frivolous. Many – possibly even most – of the 240,000 plants in existence are grown and studied at *Kew*, and since one tenth of these are under threat in our polluted world, one can appreciate the importance of the place. The Queen's Garden behind the Palace, an endearing replica of a 17th-century garden in which only 17th-century flowers are permitted to grow, the museums of botanical specimens, and the Temperate House, altogether less flamboyant than the Palm House but just as useful, are all to be visited. So are the pinetum, the herbarium in the library (over a million specimens), the azalea garden and many other delights. Open all the year round except Christmas Day and May Day, *Kew* charges adults 25p admittance, an extraordinary bargain.

Older than *Kew* by nearly a hundred years is the *Chelsea Physic Garden* contained within a triangle of less than four acres bounded by the Chelsea Embankment, the Royal Hospital Road and Swan Walk. 'Physic' in the sense of pertaining to things natural, for by the philosophy of Paracelsus, every plant in the world had curative properties if the right antidote could be brought into opposition with its contrasting ailment. So the garden, founded by and for the Worshipful Company of Apothecaries, once dominated by the four great cedars of Lebanon which were planted in 1673, contained as wide a variety of species as could be brought together, and under the ownership of the tubercular but munificent Dr Hans Sloane, it flourished. By 1795 specimens of over 3,700 varieties had been presented to the Royal Academy; Philip Miller, the greatest botanical horticulturalist of the age, had 'raised the reputation of the Chelsea Garden so much that it excells all the gardens of Europe' (Peter Collinson, a contemporary botanist).

Today the cedars have gone and the garden is no longer administered by the apothecaries, but it still flourishes. (Open Sundays and Wednesdays 2 p.m.-5 p.m. 01-352 5646.) From it cotton seeds were sent to the new colony of Georgia, and specimens were used as models at the Chelsea Porcelain factory just down the road. It sent Chinese bananas to Fiji and Samoa, tea to India and rubber to Brazil, and even in this century it has proved invaluable, for the Madagascan periwinkle has become invaluable in cancer research and Professor F. G. Gregory's work on photo-periodism and vernalisation has helped alleviate starvation throughout the world.

And the white marble statue of old Sloane looks benevolently out over the peaceful, ordered beds, the flowering shrubs, the heathers and rare trees, amongst which is the largest olive tree in Britain, and the finest example of a 'Willow Pattern Tree' (*Koelreuteria paniculata*). An amiable and secluded paradise, soon to be more available to the public. It should be added that the new curator, Donald Duncan, has radical plans which might even include the removal of Sloane to another part of the garden.

Conveniently close in the grounds of the Chelsea Royal Hospital is

Ranelagh Gardens, opened in 1742, and the scene of many wild parties, to the irritation of the patients in the hospital.

The *Royal Horticultural Society*, whose offices are at the Horticultural Hall, Vincent Square, SW1 (01-834 4333) is the regulating body for the annual Chelsea Flower Show each May at the Royal Hospital grounds. (The permanent gardens of the RHS are at Wisley, in Surrey.) Until you have displayed at Chelsea you are strictly second eleven.

Buckingham Palace possesses thirty-nine acres of generally 'natural' garden in the centre of London. If you have been to a garden party there you will not quickly forget the herbaceous border which is over 500 feet long, nor the imposing Waterloo Vase set amidst the shrubbery, nor the summerhouse. Over 100,000 crocuses have been planted and more than a hundred varieties of rhododendron. The list is almost endless.

It must not be inferred that these are the only memorable gardens in London. There is *Queen Mary's Gardens* in Regent's Park with its unforgettable roses; there are the formal sunken gardens of tulips and pleached limes in the grounds of *Kensington Palace*; and there are the gardens at *Hampton Court* – Dutch in influence thanks to William of Orange. These may be viewed through clairvoyees (ornamental grilles in brick piers) but there is something a bit *civic* about the Pond Garden, the Sunk Garden and the reproduction Knot Garden – too many lobelias and begonias amidst the fine old brick. The *Rembrandt Gardens* in Little Venice are an oasis amidst the concrete desert and *Richmond Terrace Gardens*, whose mysterious statuary and huge chestnut trees seem about to tumble into the Thames, are intriguing. In Richmond Park *Queen Isabella's Garden* is justly celebrated for its azaleas. A gorgeous place. The *Cutty Sark Gardens* in Greenwich and *Geffrye's Garden* in Shoreditch are full of charm, while the gardens attached to the gutted remains of *St Anne's*, Soho, *St Ethelburga-the-Virgin-Within-Bishopsgate* (see Churches), *St George's*, Mount Street (beautifully tended), the *Actors' Church* in Covent Garden, and *St John's*, Downshire Hill, NW3 are a few of the pleasantest church gardens in London.

And what about the gardens of *Lambeth Palace*, alight with daffodils? What about the *Inns of Court* (a wistaria and a fig tree flourish still in Lincoln's Inn) and *Victoria Embankment Gardens* with that sassy old camel? And what about the lamented *Beverley Nichols' Garden* (Sudbrook Cottage, Ham Common), which used to be open on Sundays in May to the public and was all that a cottage garden should be? He planted everything himself except the copper beech.

And what about all those private gardens, bird-bedecked,

deck-chaired and pleasuresome? For a list of private London gardens that can be visited contact *The National Gardens Scheme*, 57 Lower Belgrave Street, W10 (01-730 0359). Oh, and by the way, Covent Garden was originally *Convent* Garden – the garden of a convent.

Best Garden: *Chelsea Physic Garden.*
Worst Garden: *Chalcot Square Garden.*

Further reading: *The Gardener's London* by Dawn Macleod (Duckworth). *Gardens Open to the Public in England and Wales* (80p from booksellers or £1.10 from the National Gardens Scheme).

Gates

Amongst many wrought-iron gates the following are early 18th Century and splendid: *Old Abney House*, Church Street, Stoke Newington; *44 Vicarage Crescent*, Battersea; and the *Old Burial Grounds*, Dulwich Village. Better still though are the gates to the garden at *Burgh House*, Well Walk, NW3. The *Hobbs Gates* in memory of Jack Hobbs at the Oval and the *Grace Gate* at Lords in memory of the great doctor are of course splendid.

There is a fine pair of late 17th century gates which have been admiringly restored by the enlightened borough council of Enfield. What is curious about them (the gates not the borough council) is that they lead nowhere. Once they led to Gough Park, but the big house went, and the New River, which ran through the park, was taken away too. The fine original gates of the *Cremorne Pleasure Gardens* – last of these pleasure gardens to close – were removed to a brewery in Tetcott Road, Chelsea. Most breweries sport fine wrought-iron gates.

Magnificent iron gates by the great Frenchman, Jean Tijou, he of the Tijou Screen at Hampton Court, open upon the South Choir Aisle in *St Paul's*. There's not much to praise about *Buckingham Palace*, except maybe the mews, the gardens, the stamp collection, the welcome given to intruders . . . and the gates. These have agreeable cherubs on them, if you like cherubs, and were the gift of the Dominions in 1906, when we still had dominions.

The gates into *Queen Mary's Gardens* in Regent's Park, and those which open onto *Holland Park* from Kensington High Street are ornate to the point of vulgarity ('keep vulgarity for the bedroom', says a character in one of Joe Orton's plays) and I prefer the simple rusticity of the tottering gates which give into *Dulwich Park*. In fact, though it's a bit late in the day to admit it, I'm not sure I much care for wrought-iron gates at all. You may admire us, they seem to be saying, but we are here to *Keep You Out*. For this reason, but also because they're grand, I nominate as best in London the gates which lead nowhere.

The gateway into *Lambeth Palace* of russet Tudor brick is very pleasing.

Best gates: *Gough Park*, Enfield.
Worst gates: *Wormwood Scrubs Prison*.

German Food

My introduction to German food was accompanied by endless embarrassment. Staying in Essen in the modest home of a motor mechanic the family insisted on watching me eat a hot dinner while they and the tired bread-winner sat around picking at salad and covertly watching me, smiling whenever they caught my eye. Then in a stübe in Düsseldorf the noisy crowd of English people I was travelling with were banished to a private room because our crass behaviour put the stout citizens off their Königsberger Klops. Ah well, wasser unter den brücken, I suppose.

Not much choice in London. The *Cosmo* (5 Northways Parade, Finchley Road, NW3; 01-722 1398) is old-fashioned and authentic but less German perhaps than mittel-European. Recommended, particularly for breakfasts (q.v.). *Juggerhutte* (42 Queensway, W2; 01-229 7941) is cheap and cheerful, *Twin Brothers* (51 Church Street, W8; 01-937 4152) is friendly and consistent, but the best, improbably, is in Stoke Newington. Visit *Gerhard's* (124 Church Street, Stoke Newington, N16; 01-254 8860). It is intimate, which means, as I've said before, candle-lit, and decorated with Capodamonte, that most distasteful style of ceramics, but the food is excellent and wonderful value. You won't go wrong with the sauerbrauten. *Schmidt's* by the way, has long gone. Kaput.

Best German Restaurant: *Gerhard's*.

Ghosts

I am the ghost of Shadwell Stair.
Along the wharves by the water-house,

And through that dripping slaughter-house
I am the shadow that walks there.

from *Shadwell Stair* by Wilfred Owen (1893-1918)

I believe (though I can't prove it) that London is more cluttered with psychic phenomena than anywhere in the world. Many of these ghosts congregate around such places as Tyburn Hill, St James's Palace, the old London hospitals, Jack the Ripper country in the East End, and, of course, the Tower of London.

Most London theatres have their ghosts, notably the *Theatre Royal*, Drury Lane (the fourth theatre on the site), where a slim young man dressed in grey, with a white wig and carrying a tricorn hat occupies the first seat of the fourth row of the upper circle. Moving along the gangway at the back of the circle he disappears into the wall near the Royal Box. Unusually for a ghost, he only appears in daylight hours and his presence during rehearsals or at the start of a run augurs well for the success of the show.

The *British Museum* is haunted by a Priestess of the Temple of Amen-Ra, a malevolent spirit which drives dogs mad and, according to Thurston Hopkins, the ghost hunter, has been responsible for the deaths of at least thirteen people. The coffin lid which is supposed to exercise these fatal powers is Exhibit No 22542 and may be found in the second Egyptian Room, labelled: 'Mummy Cover from Thebes XXIst Dynasty, about 1050 BC. Presented by A. F. Wheeler 1889'.

Amongst numerous colourful ghosts in St James's Palace, the most picturesque is the ghost of *Sellis*, valet to The Duke of Cumberland. The Italian manservant sits up in bed, his throat cut from ear to ear. Before murdering his valet, the wicked Ernest had impregnated *Sellis's* daughter who killed herself from shame. Worst still, the phantasmal smell of the valet's blood infects the air. Another tumescent ghost haunts *Charlton House* (The Village, E7). This is old Sir William Longhorne (well-named) who still pursues nubile young women after some 300 years.

The *Tower of London*, where tortures and wallings-up and executions have taken place for a thousand years, contains many ghosts. The princes haunt the White Tower where they met their end. Headless women are almost commonplace while St Thomas Beckett, Henry Percy, Anne Boleyn, Sir Walter Raleigh, Guido Fawkes and a huge bear are just a few amongst many spectral celebrities. More intriguingly in 1817 a cylindrical tube containing a blue and white fluid attacked the wife of the Keeper of the Crown Jewels.

The Grey Lady of *St Thomas's*, an amiable middle-aged lady in grey uniform, appears in a sympathetic guise and Block 8 to those who are soon to die. She is only seen from mid-calf upwards, a detail attributed to the raising of the level of the floors when the hospital was rebuilt.

The nastiest ghost haunts, or haunted, since there have been no sightings for many years, *No 50 Berkeley Square*, now occupied by Maggs Brothers, antiquarian booksellers. Whether the ghost is a child who had been frightened to death, or a young girl who threw herself from the window to escape her lascivious uncle's advances, or merely a gang of counterfeiters pretending to be a ghost, is not clear, but the walls of the house are said to be 'saturated with electrical horror supernaturally fatal to body and mind'.

The *BBC* has a ghost in Langham Place, a limping butler with an empty tray, and at *Vine Street Police Station* there is a ghost of a police sergeant who committed suicide in one of the cells. There was a haunted jacket worn by actresses at the *Duke of York Theatre* which grew tighter and tighter the more it was worn, and a ghostly bus, driverless and without any visible conductor, which careered through *North Kensington*, forcing motorists off the road, but since the junction of St Marks Road and Cambridge Gardens was made safer, the ghost bus has apparently stayed in its garage – along with the 137.

The most improbable London ghost haunts *Pond Square*, Highgate. In March 1626 Francis Bacon, riding in his carriage through Highgate, ordered his coachman to stop by the pond and buy a chicken from a farm. This done, the coachman was instructed to kill, pluck and clean the bird, thereafter stuffing it with snow, more snow being packed tightly around it. This early experiment in refrigeration proved fatal not only to the bird but also to the 65-year-old scientist, who was overcome with excitement. It is not Bacon, however, who haunts *Pond Square*, but the bald chicken which flaps its wings and runs in frenzied circles.

In conclusion I feel obliged to mention the *Westminster Abbey* ghost, one Father Benedictus, a Benedictine monk. Tall, thin, sallow and contemptuous, he walks an inch above the ground between five and six in the evening, and talks in Elizabethan English. Not unlike his namesake.

For more ghosts see *Haunted London* by Peter Underwood (Harrap).

Best Ghost: *The Man in Grey*, the Theatre Royal, Drury Lane.
Worst Ghost: *The High Priestess of Amen-Ra*, British Museum.

Golf

A caddy at St Andrews named Lang Willie was teaching one of

the professors of the University the noble game. The professor was not a promising pupil. Willie fairly got out of patience and said to him: 'Ye see, Professor, as long as ye are learning thae lads at the College Latin and Greek it is easy work, but when ye come to play ye maun hae a heid!'

The Oxford Dictionary of Quotations

Picking up my clubs again manfully after some 15 years – it was a rare summer's evening and my Australian cost-controller was anxious for exercise – I found the strangest assortment of clubs, and unmentionables tucked away at the bottom of the bag (no putter), but we paid our £6 for a choice of two delightful public courses in Richmond Park (*Roehampton Golf Course*). What was both charming and symbolic was that the fairways were alive with thousands (I don't exaggerate) of baby rabbits. The course was flattish and not too hazardous. We played nine lovely holes.

But any *true* golfer – you will tell the true golfer by the awfulness of his or her trousers – will tell you that a golf course should either be a links with its bracing air, its sea vistas, its romantic associations – *Troon* is perfection – or a downs, with its springy turf, its heather, and its wide horizons. Park courses, even at their best (*Augusta National, Georgia*), are effeminate, and London courses, created on the clay of the London basin, tend to be dull, flat and soggy. There are fair courses around London; *Sunningdale*, *St George's Hill*, *Weybridge*, and *Wentworth* (très snob) to the south west; *Temple* to the west, breathtakingly beautiful especially in autumn and easy so long as you keep well to the right of the ninth fairway; *Moor Park* and *Sandy Lodge* to the north west. *Walton Heath* is high, wide, heathery and handsome. But the best of these is *St George's Hill*. The Scottish baronial clubhouse is no beauty, and the course is wretched if you can't carry the heather at the longholes, but for breath-taking, exhilarating loveliness at hole after hole, I doubt whether St George's Hill can be beaten. Woodpeckers, magpies and squirrels in abundance.

Within the Greater London area, *Highgate* is pleasant, and the *Royal Mid-Surrey* at Richmond, though flat, is on gravel as well as clay, and boasts partridges, pheasants, herons, swans and kestrels; birdies are not a problem here. Good salads too, but some of the members are rude.

Public courses are not necessarily inferior, but *Beckenham Place Park* is far too heavily golfed upon, with 88,000 green fees a year. Golf should not be like this; one should have space around one, room to brace one's shoulders and let fly. Read Patrick Hamilton's wonderful novel: *Hangover Square*. That says it better than I can.

Best Golf Course: (in or near London) *St George's Hill*.

Graffiti

See Wall Writings.

Greek Restaurants (including Turkish)

It was not really such a good idea after that gruesome first night to visit the *Cleopatra Taverna* (146-150 Notting Hill Gate, W11; 01-727 4046). Julie, our lovely première danseuse, was a regular there and before too long she and Gary, our lovely Home Secretary, were greeting the waiters like long-lost relatives and breaking plates as though they were going out of fashion. I *was* tired, but it was a mistake in an abandoned moment to hurl my ashtray onto the dance-floor . . . Another lively taverna is one of the originals, the *Anemos* (32-34 Charlotte Street, W1; 01-636 2289) which is all to do with dancing on the table, smashing your bouzouki over the head of Anthony Quinn, and throwing food. Try that sort of thing at *Beoty's* (which means 'Quality') (79 St Martin's Lane, WC2; 01-836 8768) and you will feel as if you're in a Bateman cartoon. *Beoty's* is very dignified with serious food; it is formal, and the waiters expect to be called 'Waiter'. The oddest Turkish restaurant in London is the *Gallipoli*, which stands in the courtyard of Bishopsgate Church (where Keats was baptised) looking like something dreamed up by a demented designer of cigarette advertisements. Once it was a Turkish bath, vintage 1895; today belly dancers wiggle and squirm as you tackle your Biryan Gallipoli. Quite an experience (01-588 1922). A much praised Turkish restaurant (indeed Capital Radio's restaurant of 1984) is *Topkapi* (25 Marylebone High Street, W1; 01-486 1872). Excellent food but too crowded for comfort.

Some of the best Greek food in London is to be sampled at the *White Tower* (1 Percy Street, W1; 01-636 8141), but it costs. Expect to pay £30 a head. The menu informs you that Aubergine Imam Bayaldi commemorates an Imam who ate so many aubergines that he bayalded. Nasty. At *Rodos* (59 St Giles High Street, WC2; 01-836 3177) you can enjoy a marvellous meze – 15 courses for £8.95.

Efe's Kebab House (80 Great Titchfield Street, W1; 01-636 1953) is great fun; substantial portions of succulent seftali kofte and

studio managers from Broadcasting House. When I visited *Efe's* there was a huge thunderstorm raging which helps to create camaraderie in a restaurant.

Bitter Lemons (98 Lillie Road, SW6; 01-381 1069) is still my favourite Greek Restaurant in London. On my last visit we were joined by the proprietor's large and friendly dog and later by his small and friendly daughter, who had come downstairs in her nightie. This is the sort of thing that tends to happen in Greek, Turkish and Cypriot restaurants. Oh, and the food's excellent.

My other recommendations are the *Salamis Taverna* (86 Hill Rise, Richmond; 01-940 7557), which has gods disporting themselves on the ceiling and a sensationally good Kleftiko (casserole of lamb); stylish *Daphne* (83 Bayham Street, NW1; 01-267 7322) – charming and with a roof garden – and, in the same management, *Lemonia* (154 Regent's Park Road, NW1; 01-586 7454), charming and with a conservatory; and *Kalamaras* (Mega) (76-78 Inverness Terrace, W2; 01-727 9122) and another restaurant of the same street *Kalamaras* (Micro) (No 66; 01-727 9122) which are informal, delightful and nourishing establishments – the former a touch posher than the latter. *Skorpios Taverna* (559 Finchley Road, NW3; 01-744 4179) is marvellous.

Demestica (white or red) is an excellent Greek plonk. Sea bass is the best Greek fish. And the *Greek Food Centre* (12 Inverness Street, NW1 – there's a coincidence! – 01-485 6544) is where to buy all middle-eastern comestibles. A splendid shop.

Best Greek Restaurant: *Bitter Lemons*.

Greengrocers

Between 1961 and 1971 the number of greengrocers in London declined by 27%. The statistic is remarkable, though no more remarkable than the fact that I carry it in my head, and sad. Perhaps the saddest loss was the *Compton Fruit Stores* in Old Compton Street. This was managed by Joe Lucas, his baldness concealed by a Basque beret. Joe, who had run a dance band at Maxim's, Juan-les-Pins, once delivered a customer's baby amongst the cauliflowers and peaches. One of the survivors is *Robert Bruce* (19 James Street, WC2; 01-240 0194), close by the site of the old Covent Garden fruit and vegetable market. The others have moved out, but *Bruce* seems to have flourished, and there is virtually nothing of a vegetable kind which you cannot get from him. Such delicacies as samphire, and the rarer kinds of dried mushroom are to him as everyday as sprouts, but he stocks your regular apples and oranges too. When I worked in Floral Street he would always sell off cheaply any perishables at the end of the day; he probably still does.

The most amusing places to buy fruit and vegetables are the street markets, and *Berwick Street Market* in particular. But if you get up early enough *Borough Market* in the shadow of Southwark Cathedral is the place. Two greengrocers within my immediate neighbourhood which I can unhesitatingly recommend are the splendid *Peter Childs* (8 Lichfield Terrace, Sheen Road, Richmond; 01-940 2934) and *A. C. Bush* (376 Richmond Road, Twickenham; 01-892 4042). The latter is not only an excellent supplier of whatever is in season and much that isn't, but he has been rash enough in the past to cash my cheques when things got desperate. The grocer may be a wicked man* but nobody could dislike a greengrocer; could they?

Best greengrocer: *Robert Bruce*.

Grocers

> * He keeps a lady in a cage,
>   Most cruelly all day,
>   And makes her count and calls her Miss
>   Until she fades away.
>   from *The Grocer* by G. K. Chesterton

See under Delicatessens.

Gunsmiths

> God save me from the Porkers
> God save me from their sons
> That ghastly younger brother
> who follows with the guns . . .
> from *Porkers* by Sir John Betjeman

No shortage of these, sadly. The choice of the best reduces to four, *Holland's, Purdey's, Evans*, and *Bland*.

Holland and Holland (13 Bruton Street, W1; 01-499 4411) take five years to make you a gun, and won't initially quote you a price. The firm endeavour to ensure that when you have your gun you won't discredit it. They engage to accouter you and to teach you to shoot straight – they own a rifle range a few miles out of town and it will simulate any conditions you may be likely to encounter on the moors.

James Purdey & Sons (57 South Audley Street, W1; 01-499 1801) have as distinguished a client list as *H. and H.*, and as secure an order book. A hammerless ejector game gun will set you back about £12,500, but people who patronise *Purdey's* are seldom short of the odd bob.

William Evans (67a St James's, SW1; 01-493 0415) is an old-established gun and rifle-makers which sells its own brand cartridges and everything else you might need to kill small birds and mammals.

Bland & Sons (21/22 New Row, WC2; 01-836 9122) have been selling guns since 1840.

Of course with any gun you need a licence. (And something to kill.)

Best Gunsmith: *James Purdey & Sons.*

Hairdressers

For me the idea of sitting passively in front of a mirror under bright lights is equivalent to the trauma of a Dorian Gray facing his aged portrait for the first time. What I need from a hairdresser is dim lights, discretion, and silence. Those unisex establishments that blast your ear-drums with their idea of music, gossip mischievously about their famous clients, offer you cups of coffee and then cut your hair into them, are to be avoided like herpes.

The poshest one for men is *George F. Trumper's* (9 Curzon Street, W1; 01-499 1850), as solid and tweedy as it sounds. A correspondent acknowledges its excellence and enjoyed an exquisite shave (£4) – 'Just what is required for weary jet lag. The gentleman to see for a shave is Mr Park'. *Truefitt and Hill* (23 Old Bond Street, W1; 01-493 2961) expect to shave several bridegrooms each week. Less traditional but recommended is *Joshua and Daniel Galvin* (69-71 Park Road, NW1; 01-724 2341), where, if Daniel gives you just a haircut you won't get away with it under £20, and you will probably be persuaded to have an avocado wax, or something equally exotic. For a short back and sides you need only pay £1.60 and it need only take ten minutes if you patronise one of the small Greek Cypriot establishments that abound in the Camden Town area of London, in Islington and in other inner suburbs. An excellent example is *George Papas's* establishment in Cowcross Street, EC1. Here you can even get a shave or a friction rub and a discreet packet of hum ha.

I enjoyed an excellent hair-cut at *Jim's* (7 Old Compton Street,

W1). Jim used to be at *Cyril Henry* (41 Old Compton Street, W1) but a hair transplant seems to have taken place. I hope Cyril hasn't gone for good – he was popular as an easy touch for a quid.

On the subject of women's hairdressers I cannot write with first-hand authority. But Fiona Byrne at the *Cut & Colour Salon* in Streatham (Streatleigh Parade, 12 Streatham High Road, SW16; 01-969 5151), won first prize in a nationwide contest, and, if you wish to be grand, *Leonard* (6 Upper Grosvenor Street, W1; 01-499 7409) is where to mingle with those celebrities who wish to be mingled with. *Vidal Sassoon* (60 South Molton Street, W1; 01-491 8848) you will already know about – and if you're male ask for Trevor – and *Hugh & Alan* (161 Ebury Street, SW1; 01-730 2196 and at the Hyde Park Hotel) are currently and deservedly in *Vogue* as well as in vogue. *Splinters* (27 Maddox Street, W1; 01-493 5169) is a large – it employs a staff of 40 – and smart establishment catering principally to clients who are black and female. Winston Isaacs, who runs it, is ambitious and influential.

A strong recommendation has come for *David and Joseph* (42 Berkeley Street, W1; 01-499 5470/3680). 'A friendly and relaxed atmosphere. Caters to the young and trendy as well as to the not so young, and to the very elegant.' You should ask Marc for the set and Gerda or Pat for the manicure.

Children's hair can be enjoyably cut at *Harrods* (of course) where there is a rocking-horse and plenty of books. It costs £5.50 for a shampoo, cut and blow dry. You need to book. For your child's very first haircut she/he gets a certificate and a lock of the hair in a plastic envelope as a memento. Ah! At the *Alan International School of Hairdressing* (about 17 branches) and at *Vidal Sassoon*, children are charged at a percentage of adult fees. Our children have their hair cut by Debbie, a visiting hairdresser, at home. It's cheap, fun and skilfully done.

Best Hairdresser (men): *Trumper's*.
Best Hairdresser (women): *David and Joseph*.
Best Hairdresser (children): *Harrods* (or Debbie).

Hamburgers

Although it should be a simple matter to serve a hamburger successfully it obviously ain't. There are more failures than successes. One reason is that most hamburger joints get their meat from a central supplier. Amongst the failures *Casey Jones, Huckleberry's,*

Wendyburgers, and *Wimpys* have been noted. At *Strikers* the service is slow and the hamburgers are too expensive to be enjoyable. At *Tramps* they are acceptable but the orange drinks taste of soap. *McDonald's* are quick and cheap but crowded and consequently tend to get grubby (evidence the Oxford Street branch between noon and 1.30 p.m.). Besides, on my last visit to a *McDonald's* (Wimbledon) they had run out of hats, badges and pencils, which was partly what the children had come for. All one wants is sesame seeds on the buns, a good selection of relishes, crisp salad, and meaty meat, but it's not that easy.

Garfunkel's (various branches) is pleasant enough. The hamburgers are a far better deal than the extensive help-yourself salad bar (q.v.) where everything tastes as though it's been left over from yesterday's party. *Rupert Street Junction* (7 Rupert Street, W1; 01-734 2097) is at least amusing – if you like sitting in railway carriages without a ticket – and the burgers at *Caesar's* (103-107 Waterloo Road, SE1; 01-928 5707) are surprisingly edible bearing in mind the awfulness of the decor. I mean, really. *Wolfe's* (34 Park Lane, W1; 01-499 6897 and 25 Basil Street, SW3; 01-589 8444) hamburgers are far better than average, and not expensive for their locations, while *Huby's* (159 Old Brompton Road, SW5; 01-373 1926) is another up-market glorified burger bar which is consistently OK. I've had good food and service at unsociable hours in *Maxwell's* (76 Heath Street, NW3; 01-794 5450 with two other branches), where you can sit outdoors. Desserts are good too. *Le Grand Café* (25 Battersea Rise, SW11; 01-228 7984) is extremely pretty with home-made soups, as well as hamburgers. But the monarch of them all is *Macarthur's* with branches at Sheen, Barnes and Turnham Green (opening a restaurant in Turnham Green is condemning yourself to a lifetime of bad jokes). Consistently over more than eight years *Macarthur's* have proved their hamburgers to be the best, their milk-shakes the thickest, their bills the most reasonable, their music the gentlest, and their tables the least crowded together. You also get an avalanche of peppermint eggs when you leave.

Best hamburgers: *Macarthur's* (Sheen branch).

Hampers

Although Fortnum's are famous for their hampers and most of the top stores will make you up a hamper for a special occasion, the place to order one from is *Hungry's* (37a Crawford Street, W1; 01-258 0376), a splendid sandwich bar which offered 88 different sandwich fillings at the last count. *Hungry's* will make up a hamper for you to your own specifications. *Paxton and Whitfield's* (see under Cheese) sell some great hampers of cheeses and biscuits and even include wine and meat at a pinch. And where to picnic? The bluebell woods at Pishill.

Best Hamper: *Hungry's*.

Hats

At *Lock and Co.* (6 St James's Street, SW1; 01-930 8874), which is at least 250 years old, the first bowler was created. It was called a Coke after William Coke, Gentleman, of Leicester, who wanted a sensible titfer for his gamekeepers. The material for the coke was supplied by Messrs Bowler. Since Lock's could refer at once to the head measurements of their regular customers the Earl of Rosebery used to stand in the doorway and shout 'Hat!' until they brought him one. Kaye Webb used to tell the story of a military gentleman who knelt down in church each Sunday with his top hat in front of his face. Why did he do it, a companion required to know. The reply was: 'I say "James Lock & Co., Hatters, 6 St James's Street, London, SW1" into it three times, then I know it's all right to get up!' Lock flourishes while the bowler is at risk. *Bates* (21a Jermyn Street, W1; 01-734 2722) also sounds like a hatter and, estimably, is. At *George Malyard* (137 Lavender Hill, SW11; 01-223 8292) they will make a hat to your specifications; they also sell that best of hats, the panama. For a fedora go to *Herbert Johnson* (13 Old Burlington Street, W1; 01-439 7397/8/9); they serve ladies hats in the basement. Toppers may be bought at any of the above, *Brown's* (23/27 South Molton Street, W1; 01-491 8733) or *Joseph* (6 Sloane Street, SW1; 01-235 2467) or hired from *Moss Bros* (Bedford Street, WC2; 01-240 4567 and 21 Lime Street, EC3; 01-626 4247).

The best variety of hats may be found at the unique *Laurence Corner* (126-130 Drummond Street, NW1; 01-388 6811) or *The Hat Shop* (58 Neal Street, WC2; 01-836 6718). The best hat for a man of style is the Panama, sensible, comfortable and chic.

Extrovert women buy their hats from *David Shilling* (44 Chiltern Street, W1; 01-935 8473), next to the *Radio Times*. Shilling, of course, is the milliner whose hats at Royal Ascot, as worn by his mother, do everything except frighten the horses. Such brave vulgarity can only be applauded; needless to say most of the hats on sale in Chiltern Street are somewhat less eccentric. But to be safely hatted a lady would probably go to *Simone Mirman* (9 Chesham Place, SW1; 01-235 2656). The best wearers of hats in London are still Lady Diana Cooper and George Melly.

Best Hat: *The Panama.*
Best Hatter: *Lock and Co.*
Best Milliner: *Simone Mirman.*

Herbs

There are some recommendations I cannot ignore and when I was told of a shop in London where you can buy frankincense and myrrh over the counter (for gold go to Hatton Garden), and which is served by 22 bus routes (3 of them night lines), 3 green lines, 3 expresses, 2 underground lines and 1 British Rail, I felt it would be ungrateful not to pass it on. 'What's more,' added my correspondent, 'they sell a sarsaparilla which has Afro/Caribbeans mewing like deprived seagulls all about Walworth Road during their annual holidays.' (Sarsaparilla may also be enjoyed by the glass at East Lane Market.) The shop is indeed a living legend. It is *G. Baldwin & Co* of 171/173 Walworth Road, SE17 (01-701 5550), and I cannot imagine how I lived 47 years (I wish I hadn't put that!) without it. All herbs are sold by the ounce and are listed from Agrimony (15p) to Yarrow (15p) and Yerba Mate (35p for 4 oz). Roots and barks include True and False Unicorn, Devil's Claw, Hemlock, Kava Kava, Polypody and many others. Culinary herbs include such varieties as tonquin beans and blade mace, powders include dragon's blood, musk crystals and holy thistle with gums, dried flowers, jars, tablets, essential oils and herbal extracts. Books are also sold, with *Potter's Cyclopoedia* (£8) and *The Herb Book* by John Lust the best introductions to this magical world of wormwood, witchhazel and wort.

There are, of course, other herbalists in London, including *Culpepper* (21 Bruton Street, W1; 01-499 2406 and 9 Flask Walk, NW3; 01-794 7263), *L'Herbier de Provence* (341 Fulham Road, SW10; 01-352 0012) – extremely pretty – and *Meadow Herbs Shop* (47 Moreton Street, SW1; 01-821 0094) but the choice has to be . . .

Best Herbalist: *G. Baldwin and Co.* (closed Mondays).
See also under Vets.

Hills

Some love to roll down Greenwich Hill,
   For this thing, and for that;
And some prefer sweet Marble Hill,
   Though sure 'tis somewhat flat!
Yet Marble Hill and Greenwich Hill,
   If Kitty Clive can tell,
From Strawberry Hill, from Strawberry Hill
   Will never bear the bell!

William Pulteney

Most London hills are 'somewhat flat'. *Corn-, Craven,* and *St Andrew's* are three examples. *Notting Hill* is really quite sharp as a view from the water tower will prove.

Primrose Hill rises to 206 feet above the Trinity high watermark of the Thames, and is a real hill. It used to be a forest filled with wolves and was originally called *Greenberry Hill,* supposedly from the names of three murderers. Green, Berry and Hill, executed there in 1678, but possibly innocent. Lurid murders also feature in *Muswell Hill* (350 feet high), which was once a place of pilgrimage for those with scrofula. The steepest may well be *Forest Hill,* and up it, in particular, *Canobie Road,* although *Nightingale Lane* which runs aslant *Richmond Hill,* is alarmingly steep for a short distance and *Highgate Hill* was steep enough to send a tramcar crashing fatally down in 1906. *Mill Hill* is by no means negligible. *Crooms Hill,* Greenwich, is rich in Georgian houses, with several earlier – Manor House (1697), the Presbytery (1630), and the Grange (No 52) with its summer-house are all seventeenth century, and desirable – not just to estate agents (q.v.). Almost as picturesque is *Forty Hill* in Enfield, at least if you can get off the main road. *Holly Hill* and *Golders Hill* deserve to be better known, but for charm and literary associations I shall not look further than *Downshire Hill,* NW3 where Keats lived. If you prefer C. Day Lewis to Keats, then you should prefer *Crooms Hill.*

The nastiest hill is either *Shooter's Hill* or *Denmark Hill* although it's not the fault of the hill. An old Army riddle: 'Where's the top of Shooter's Hill?' 'On the Barrack Field.' The explanation: gravel from the top of Shooter's Hill formed the surface of Woolwich parade ground.

Best hills: *Downshire Hill and Crooms Hill.*
Worst hills: *Denmark Hill and Shooter's Hill.*
Steepest hill: *Canobie Road,* SE23.

Homeless

> 'Without doubt London is the greatest city in the world to live in bar none. It can be the greatest place in the world if you come home and you've got a few pounds in your pocket. But when your money's gone, buddy, and you're on your Jack Jones it can be the loneliest bloody place . . .' Billy under the Hungerford Bridge.

If you are an eccentric millionaire with a desire to help those almost beyond helping, you will find them nightly dossing down under the arches at Charing Cross or the railway bridges along the embankment. The rootless and homeless are not always feckless; but many are hopeless. For relief organisations see under Hostels. The clinic which caters principally for the homeless is in *Great Chapel Street*, NW1. See again under Hostels.

Horse-Racing

See under Race Tracks.

Horses

The saddest horses are those which are bought and sold at *Southall Horse Fair*, which has been running every Wednesday for 295 years.

Most of the buyers are rag-and-bone men, and most of the horses are bound for the knacker's yard. The strongest horses are the dray-horses still employed by the old-established breweries. The most potent horses are those of the Royal Horse Artillery – see them charge around Wembley pulling their gun carriages at the Royal Show.

At *Deptford Playground* in Watson Street, SE8 is Bonny Bright Eyes, bridle long since gone, eyes blind, jutting under-lip, a survivor. A more cheerful sight is the blinkered dray above the door of *Ye Old Spotted Horse* in Putney High Street. There is a flying horse on a drainpipe in the *Inner Temple*, and the following brazen gentlemen are amongst those who ride horses for eternity through London: Prince Albert, Charles I, Richard I, George IV, St George, Edward VII, whose horse seems fractious, and Field Marshal Earl Roberts. Boadicea's fine pair strut and prance at *Westminster Bridge*, but for the real thing visit *Clapham Common* during the Greater London Horse Show.

Recommended riding stables:

(a) Smart

Civil Service Riding Club, c/o the Royal Mews (01-930 7232).
Ross Nye, 8 Bathurst Mews, W2 (01-262 3791).
Lilo Blum, 32 Grosvenor Crescent Mews, SW1 (01-235 6846).
Stag Lodge School of Equitation, Robin Hood Gate, Richmond Park, W14 (01-546 9863).
Snaresbrook Riding School, 67 Hollybush Hill, E11 (01-989 3256).

(b) Children, newcomers, nervous riders, those with handicaps

City Farm, 1 Cressfield Close, Grafton Road, NW5 (01-485 4585).
Willow Tree Riding Establishment, Ronver Road, SE12 (01-857 6438).
Lea Bridge Riding Centre, Myddelton House, Bulls Cross, Enfield, Middlesex (0992 717711).

For buying equine or equitative goods go to *Swaine, Adeney, Brigg & Sons* (185 Piccadilly, W1; 01-734 4277) for 'everything but the horse'.

Best live horses: *Royal Mews* (where else?).
Best dead horses: *Boadicea's*.

Horse Troughs

At the Cornhill end of the passage which runs behind the Royal Exchange a fountain commemorates in suitable fashion (a nude bronze girl inside a red granite base) the 1911 Jubilee of the Metropolitan Drinking Fountain and Horse Trough Association, whose portentous name may be found on horse troughs throughout London. But sadly there's no longer much call for horse troughs, and those who still operate by horse make their own arrangements. Some years ago the MDFAHTA gave all its troughs and fountains to the local authorities and its records to the London Museum – they now only operate abroad – and the Chairman, Mr Randall (Crayford 628062) was unable to direct me to any water troughs which still contain water. Flowers are what the local authorities fill them with, so flowers are what we must have. But many of the old troughs bear poignant witness to the tremendous work of the association. There's a typical trough in *Spencer Park*, SW18 and another, like a stone cot, at *Meadway*, NW11; *Albany Street*, NW1, has a fine example of a long double trough and you may have spotted others. My favourite, with delightfully intertwining wrought-iron griffins, stands outside the *Star and Garter Home* at the Richmond Gate entrance to Richmond Park. The one in *Chalk Farm Road*, NW1, is decrepit.

Best trough: *Richmond Gate.*

Hospitals

The newspapers constantly run stories about the closures or threats of closures of London hospitals. Recently the *Belgrave Children's Hospital* shut down. *St John's, Homerton, for Diseases of the Skin* (a wonderful hospital this), is under threat and many others. Three hundred jobs are to be lost at *Guy's*, a show-piece among hospitals. Nowhere, it seems, and no one is safe from the civil servants. But more cheerful stories may also be found. In Tower Hamlets the *Mildmay Mission Hospital*, which was phased out by the NHS, is back in business, privately, supported by donations, as a place where body and soul may both be administered to. The hospice movement which cares for the dying and makes an art of doing so – for too long the dying were regarded as unimportant, nor was it realised how much may be learned from their example – has become a force to be reckoned with.

Gossip about standards of hygiene in London hospitals culminated with a scandal involving the *Charing Cross Hospital*, whose kitchen was a theme park for cockroaches, ants, mice, thrushes and sparrows. Since hospitals are Crown property and immune from prosecution, there is not that much the Health Authority can do except complain. Nor is it easy for the sick to mount an effective campaign (doctors and nurses are usually too busy). A distressing vista. None of which detracts from the remarkable cheerfulness of most nurses in most London hospitals and the concerned care provided in most cases to most patients. Of more practical value is a list of hospitals with casualty departments, so in an emergency, try one of the following:

Charing Cross Hospital, Fulham Palace Road, W6 (01-748 2040) Hammersmith tube (but take your own sandwiches).
London Hospital, Whitechapel Road, E1 (01-247 5454) Whitechapel tube.
Middlesex Hospital, Mortimer Street, W1 (01-636 8333) Goodge Street tube.
Royal Free Hospital, Pond Street, NW3 (01-794 0500) Belsize Park, Belsize Park tube. (Cockroach problems here too.)
St Bartholomew's Hospital, West Smithfield, EC1 (01-600 9000) St Paul's and Farringdon tubes.

St Stephen's Hospital, 369 Fulham Road, SW10 (01-352 8161) Fulham Broadway tube/South Kensington tube then 14 bus.

St Thomas's Hospital, Lambeth Palace Road, SE1 (01-928 9292) Westminster and Waterloo tube.

University College Hospital, Gower Street, WC1 (01-387 9300) Warren Street tube.

Westminster Hospital, Ryle Street, Horseferry Road, SW1 (01-828 9811) Westminster tube/Victoria tube and 507 or 10 bus.

For hospital fanciers, the Coram's Fields/Brunswick Square area of Bloomsbury is where many may be visited. The *Hospital for Sick Children* in Great Ormond Street, situated here, was founded in 1852 and is the oldest of its kind. Nearby are the *London Homeopathic Hospital*, the *National Hospital for Nervous Diseases*, and the picturesque *Italian Hospital*.

Out-patients departments are extraordinary places for eavesdropping (and since the magazines are usually months out of date and appointments running late what else is there to do?) Here is a sample recorded by the great H. V. Morton:

> 'My sister 'ad the same pain as you've got. And she, poor thing, just faded away, she did. Worn down to a point, she was.'
>
> 'P'raps my case won't be so bad, let's hope.'
>
> 'I expect it's the same. Low down on the left side like a knife jabbing.' 'That's it.'
>
> 'It isn't my side; it's my leg.'
>
> 'Oh, I beg pardon. I thought you said habdomen.'

Best Hospital: *Great Ormond Street.*

Hostels

There are five recognised youth hostels in London, besides the YMs and the YWs. These are:

Carter Lane (36 Carter Lane, EC4; 01-236 4965) was once home and school for St Paul's choirboys. The vibrations of their singing still hang in the air. Usefully central.

Earl's Court (38 Bolton Gardens, SW5; 01-373 7083). A lively area for insomniacs and peripatetics. This hostel has direct access from Heathrow by Piccadilly Line underground to Earl's Court. Closed between 10 a.m. and 3 p.m.

Hampstead Heath (4 Wellgarth Road, NW11; 01-458 9054 and 7196). This former nursing college has a pleasant games room and something often frowned upon in youth hostels, a television.

Highgate (84 Highgate West Hill, N6; 01-340 1831). A Georgian house conveniently close to Kenwood and Keats House. This hostel is closed between 10 a.m. and 5 p.m.

Holland House (Holland Walk, W8; 01-937 0748). Incorporating part of a fine Jacobean pile (see Theatres – Open Air), Holland House is ideal if you wish to visit the Kensington Museum or the Commonwealth Institute.

If you don't qualify for youth hostels, you have problems. There are the *Church Army* hostels (HQ 01-903 3763) which charge a rate of between £4 and £5 a night, but permit no alcohol, no smoking, and lock the front doors at 11 p.m. Privacy scarcely exists.

Then there are camp sites, which will cost between £2.50 and £3 a night plus tent. These are:

Abbey Wood, Federation Road, Abbey Wood, SE2 (01-310 2233).

Hackney Camping, Millfields Road, Hackney Marshes, E5 (01-985 7656).

Lee Valley, Eastway Cycle Circuit, Temple Mills Lane, E15 (01-534 6085). April to September.

Pickett's Lock, Pickett's Lock Lane, N9 (01-803 4756).

Tent City, Old Oak Common Lane, W3 (01-743 5708).

The Centre Français, 29 The Boltons, SW10 (01-370 0606) and the *International Friendship League's*, Peace Haven, 3 Crestwick Road, Acton, W3; (01-992 0221) can both help with cheap (c. £4.50 per night) dormitory accommodation if you're youngish and not too choosy. For further advice contact the *London Hostels Association*, 54 Eccleston Square, SW1; (01-834 1545 or 01-828 3263 for bookings). There are relief organisations such as *Alone in London* (Euston Square, NW1; 01-387 5470), *Centrepoint* in Soho, a night shelter for the under-25s at *25 Oxford Street*, W1; the *Catholic Housing Aid Society* (189a Old Brompton Road, SW5; 01-373 4961) and *Stopover House* (65 Bell Green, Lewisham, SE26; 01-659 5060), but they are finding it hard to cope.

The best hostel for students is probably *Jerome House* (19 Harrington Gardens, SW7; 01-370 3145) but, if you can run to it, the best hostel in London has to be the *Albany* (between Piccadilly and Vigo Street) which was originally 'residential chambers for bachelor gentlemen'. Canning, Byron, Bulwer Lytton, Macaulay, Gladstone and Edward Heath were all residents at the Albany, and I almost was. Read

Peace in Piccadilly: The Story of the Albany by Sheila Birkenhead (1958) for the details.

Best Hostel: *Albany*.

Hotels

There have been several developments in the hotel business since I wrote the splendid predecessor to the present book. The *Stafford* (St James's Place, SW1) has been named Hotel of the Year for 1985, and a new kind of hotel with unusual characteristics has possibly set a trend for the future.

The *Stafford* is run by Terry Holmes, whose father was a porter at the Dorchester, and it has recently been bought for nine and a half million by Trafalgar House. I hope the change of ownership doesn't affect the particular quality of the Stafford – its niceness.

7 Down Street (7 Down Street, W1) is probably the smallest and certainly the most exclusive hotel in London. It has six suites, a bar and a restaurant to none of which the public is admitted. To use these facilities you have to become a member (£115 per annum currently); your reward? Privacy. The suites are the Shimiani, the Kalahari, the Brass Kettle, the Blue Suite, the Fu Shu Suite, and A. N. Other. Once you have become a member and reserved your suite, you may then use the varied services available to guests, such as Acupuncture, Jacuzzis, Adult Videos and almost anything else you can think of. It is not cheap.

Speaking of which, as, reluctantly, I have to do so often, the following are amongst the most expensive hotels in London: *Blake's* (22 Roland Gardens, SW7; 01-370 6701) which is highly fashionable and at which you can get porridge for breakfast; the *Berkeley* (Wilton Place, SW1; 01-235 6000); the *Sheraton Park Tower* (101 Knightsbridge, SW1; 01-235 8050), a handsome circular building which wrecks the proportions of all around it; the *Ritz* (Piccadilly, W1; 01-493 8181) with a handsome Louis Seize dining room in which Royal College of Music students perform on Sunday evenings; the *Inn on the Park* (Hamilton Place, W1; 01-499 0888), the *Hyde Park Hotel* (Knightsbridge, W1; 01-235 2000); the *Connaught* (Carlos Place, W1; 01-499 7070) which is discreet and snob-infested; *Grosvenor House* (Park Lane, W1; 01-499 6363); the *Churchill* (Portman Square, W1; 01-486 5800); *Brown's* (Dover Street, W1; 01-493 6020) which is not *quite* what it used to be, and the *Athenaeum* (116 Piccadilly, W1; 01-499

3464). At any of the above you should be reasonably content, particularly if somebody else is picking up the tab, but at £130 and more a night – often excluding breakfast – you should be made positively to glow. Of these top hotels (and others not mentioned) I would suggest you try *Blake's* first; then the *Athenaeum*, the *Berkeley* or the *Ritz*. But for full details refer to the *Good Hotels Guide* (Consumer Association/Hodder and Stoughton. Ed. Hilary Rubinstein £7.50).

The *Savoy* is for theatrical snobs, but it's architecturally fascinating too. Built by D'Oyly Carte some years after the theatre, it was Europe's first fire-proofed building. It had 'ascending rooms' (lifts), seventy bathrooms, and speaking tubes on every floor. Escoffier was the chef. Strauss led the orchestra, Pavlova danced in the cabaret. Sir Henry Irving, Sarah Bernhardt, and Elaine Stritch have all taken up residence there; Arnold Bennett based *Imperial Palace* on it. A remarkable institution. The Riverside Suite is the one to book when entertaining film stars discreetly.

William Claridge and James Brown were both butlers who became celebrated hoteliers, and both hotels have survived for well over a century. *Claridge's* is opulent, has a magnificent entrance hall, and caters for minor royalty; they have never permitted dancing or cabarets.

Of the six large hotels in Park Lane, the grandest is the *Dorchester*, now Arab-owned. The frontage on Park Lane is uninspired, and the food has been mediocre recently. Unless you book the Oliver Messel Suite which is not unlike Kew Gardens, I should suggest you try elsewhere. The *Basil Street Hotel* and the *Capital Hotel*, also in Basil Street, are a better bet than any of the Park Lane bunch, while the prettiest hotels in London are the creeper-lined *Brook Hotel* in Stamford Brook and *Durrant's* (George Street, W1; 01-935 8131). At Durrant's you will receive excellent personal service; it is well placed for the Wallace Collection.

The best valet service in town has always been at the *Connaught*. The *Sandringham Hotel* (3 Holford Road, NW3; 01-435 1569) is a pleasant modestly priced family hotel with notably large towels and breakfasts. The *Portobello* (22 Stanley Gradens, W11; 01-727 2777) is eccentric, chatty and fun. The restaurant is open 24 hours a day. Also recommended: the *Montcalm* (Gt Cumberland Place, W1; 01-402 4288) and amongst the cheaper ones the *Wilbraham* (1 Wilbraham Place, SW1; 01-730 8296) and the *Half Moon Hotel* (10 Earl's Court Square, SW5; 01-373 9956). The *Great Eastern Hotel*, Bishopsgate (the hotel for Liverpool Street Station travellers) has a magnificent dining room copied from the Palais Soubise in Paris.

The *Inverness Court Hotel* (1 Inverness Terrace, W2; 01-229 1444) was built by Edward VII for Lily Langtry and the bar of the hotel was once the Jersey Lily's private theatre. For a modest £80 or so you can even hire the Langtry bedroom suite with a four-poster and a sunken Roman bath.

I have had discouraging reports about the *Clarendon* (Montpelier Row, SW3), the *Mayfair Hotel*, the *Sheraton Skyline* near Heathrow, where a bottle of whisky ordered through room service set a friend back £38, the *Penta Hotel* in Cromwell Road, the Bloomsbury hotels in general and the Russell Square hotels in particular. The *Imperial* must be one of the ugliest post-war edifices in London.

A respectable bed and breakfast double room at less than £10 may still be found. The following are recommended. The *White House* (Mrs Mark), 242 Norwood Road, West Norwood, SE27; (01-670 3607): £9-£10; *London Budget Accommodation*, 169 Sutherland Avenue, W9; (01-289 0787): £9; *Mrs Miles*, 37 Brewster Gardens, W10; (01-969 7024): £6-£8; *Westpoint Hotel*, 170 Sussex Gardens, W2; (01-402 0281): £7.50; *Sass House*, 11 Craven Terrace, W2: £7.50; and *Londone Lodge*, 62 Lauderdale Mansion, Lauderdale Road, W9; (01-286 7067): £4.50.

Well, maybe not. These are 1984 prices, and I've not checked them since, so you need to add a bit on – but still, what value!

Best Hotel: *The Stafford* (expensive).
          Inverness Court (middle-range).
          Portobello (modest).
Worst Hotels: Those occupied by homeless people on DHSS bed and breakfast accounts. One such, the *Spencer Hotel*, in King's Cross, now compulsorily purchased, landed the owner in court on *43* public health offences. But all, or almost all, are dismal places.

Houses

(a) Big

I shall narrow the contestants down to five finalists, *Kenwood, Ham House, Fenton House, Queen's House*, Greenwich, and *Chiswick House*. I shall listen politely to those who press the claims of *Osterley Park* (very fine), *Winfield House*, the home of the American Ambassador in Regent's Park, *Leighton House* (see Friezes), *Apsley House* (on a traffic island and looking a lot less gloomy now it's been cleaned up), and the fine Adam houses, of which *Chandos House* (Cavendish Square) and the *Courtauld Institute*, Portman Square, have survived without being mauled. I should like to consider the amazing *Strawberry Hill*, and – but no, no, to the short list.

Kenwood House, a well-proportioned 18th-century mansion in Highgate (only just, it's almost Hampstead) is bigger but no better than many other houses of a similar period, but it is so beautifully renovated to its original Adam magnificence by the curator, John Jacobs, and it is so prettily situated, that it commands respect. So do the treasures of the Iveagh Bequest, which are housed there. Any house would look its best when it can display upon its wall a Rembrandt self-portrait and one of the finest Vermeers.

Ham House is Jacobean and magnificent. It was enlarged by the Duke and Duchess of Lauderdale in the 1670s; they were a flamboyant couple and ensured that only the finest craftsmen were employed to paint the ceilings, panel the walls and parquet the floors. Silver-mounted fire implements were the ultimate status symbols and, as with Kenwood, Ham has been wonderfully restored with much of the original furniture – including superb chairs – still in place. It is an annexe to the V and A. To arrive in style avoid the crowded Petersham Road, with some very fine Georgian houses along it, and take the ferry from Twickenham.

Fenton House in the Grove, Hampstead Heath, is almost as old as Ham House, and almost as magnificent. Where Ham House boasts a stone figure of Father Thames in its forecourt, Fenton House contains within its enclosed garden a statuette of a shepherdess being courted by a shepherd, who is shamefully unbuttoned. The house is notable too for its collection of musical instruments, pride of place going to a harpsichord played upon by Handel. Fenton House is not grandiose like the other houses in this section, but charming. The architect is not known – at least to me.

Queen's House, Greenwich. Designed by Inigo Jones (1573-1652) Queen's House is framed by Wren's Queen Mary and King William blocks, so that one gets a strange perspective on this symmetrical house, which appears as a retiring child hanging back between its two parents. Wonderfully preserved, it contains the haunted Tulip Staircase (not open to the public) where the Reverend Hardy and his wife took a photograph of one (perhaps two) ghosts. Canaletto painted the vista in 1755 from the north bank of the Thames, and it has scarcely changed in two and a quarter centuries.

Chiswick House. Now that it has been re-painted a rather surprising and improbable shade of duck egg blue, Chiswick House has emerged from genteel retirement like mutton dressed as lamb. Yet it is a Palladian villa of substantial reputation; it was built by the Earl of Burlington as a museum for his works of art and as a place to entertain friends in; so it has no bedrooms. The Inigo Jones gateway is there, of which Pope wrote:

> Oh gate, how cam'st thou here?
>> I was brought from Chelsea last year,
> Battered with wind and weather;
>> Inigo Jones put me together,
> Sir Hans Sloane
>> Let me alone,
> Burlington brought me here.

Another small Palladian villa, *Marble Hill House*, Twickenham, has also been renovated, and a determined effort has been made to furnish it according to the inventory made by the Countess of Suffolk for whom George II built the place in 1725, the same year in which Chiswick House was built. The curators at Marble Hill House are very kind, but, seriously considered, Chiswick House is finer.

It may be of incidental interest to record that there is in London the world's most expensive house. *Kenstead Hall*, Hampstead, changed hands in 1982 for £16,000,000.

Best big house: *Ham House.*
Worst big house: *Knightsbridge Barracks* (Sir Basil Spence).

(b) Small(ish) (see also under Cottages)
Those who argue that Nash was senile when he came to design *Buckingham Palace* in 1824 conveniently forget that in the following year he was responsible for the delightful houses known as *Park Villages East* and *West* (we have lost half of Park Village East but Park Village West survives). These, like the equally attractive houses on the *Bedford Park*, Chiswick estate – the first 'garden suburb', inspired by Jonathan T. Carr, cloth merchant, designed by E. W. Godwin and Norman Shaw in the 1870s – are all distinctive but complementary. Nash's designs were completed after his death by his pupil, James Pennethorne.

There are other such estates. The Georgian houses in *Bloomsbury*, the Victorian houses in *Primrose Hill*, *De Beauvoir Square* (neo-Jacobean with ornate Flemish gables), the back streets of *Chelsea*, miniature delights like *Hasker Street*, *Maunsel Street*, and the studios known as the *Italian Village* off the Fulham Road, all are agreeable to look at and happy to live in. *Holly Lodge Gardens*, off Highgate West Hill, is a sinister development of some eight or nine Gothic houses straight out of Hammer films. The stairs creak and mad axemen are a commonplace. Individual houses of distinction include *2 Harley Street*, *Kelmscott House* (William Morris's place in Hammersmith Mall), *Pond*

Cottage, Dulwich, Numbers *6* and *8 Rugby Street*, WC1, and the house which above all others I should like to live in, the *Wick*, at the top of Richmond Hill. Maybe the owner – it used to be Sir John Mills – is reading these plaintive words . . .

Best small(ish) house: The *Wick*.
Worst small houses: The *'Superloos'*, springing up throughout London.

Housing Estates

The old *Peabody* estates are rough enough (though considered enlightened in their day), but it's the high-rise estates of the early 60s which really bugger the residents up. We said so at the time but of course the architects never lived in them so nothing got changed. To give some idea of the number of high-rise dwellers still up in the sky, the figures suggest that 22,000 flats are in properties over 10 stories high; 122,000 in 5-9 storey blocks, and 388,000 in 3-4 storey apartments. A few high-rises are at least being demolished.

The worst estate is probably the notorious *Doddington Estate* (also known as Shoddington) in chi-chi North Battersea. 964 flats in 15 soulless blocks with muggings, vandalism and fires tiresomely commonplace. The local council spend £9,000 each week repairing the damage caused on the estate by hooligans. Or do you think that the *Golf Links Estate* in Southall is worse? There Asian families stay indoors to avoid attacks from skinheads. You don't need telling about the Broadwater Farm Estate in Tottenham, scene of recent riots.

By contrast there are tower-blocks which are regarded as highly desirable. Penthouse apartments in the prestigious *Barbican* development are bought and sold for more than £300,000. For that sort of money one could buy the very best of the houses in the *Stamford Brook* estate, where the enlightened disciples of Ruskin and William Morris erected a new Jerusalem; every house was, and is, different. Each is aesthetically pleasing in each tree-lined suburban avenue. Forget the Barbican.

Best Estate: *Stamford Brook*.
Worst Estate: *Broadwater Farm Estate*.
P.S. Of course if one takes 'estate' literally, then most of London was originally comprised of 'estates' built by speculators for their patrons.

Hungarian Food

Well, of course, there's the *Gay Hussar* (2 Greek Street, W1; 01-437 0973) and has been for as long as I can remember. Victor Sassie, the charming Hungarian who runs it, is 70 years old, but unflagging. As for the restaurant, publishers crush against authors: authors with trembling hands raise empty brandy glasses to pallid lips; beetroot everywhere, and soups made from all the wrong things – wild cherries, for example. The effect is irresistible and the food can be wonderful. *Mignon* (2 Queensway, W2; 01-229 0093) is also long-established, but no longer has a Hungarian chef, and it shows. The best food is the Wiener Rostbraten with cucumber salad, and you'll not go far wrong with Bikaver (Bulls Blood) to wash it down with. You get a piano accordionist and, whether you want it or not, a gypsy violinist throbbing at your ear.

Best Hungarian Food: the *Gay Hussar*.

Ice-Cream

Foubert's (162 Chiswick High Road, W4; 01-747 0210) has a genial ice-cream bar upstairs. The Coppa Strega chocolate is the one to go for. A year or two back I would cheerfully recommend *Fortnum's Fountain* (181 Piccadilly, W1; 01-734 4938) to all and sundry, but it's been re-decorated by Sir Basil Spence in mauve with lowered ceilings and tobacco plants, and the sorbets and coupes and ice-creams seem less appetising (see Tea Houses). The *Pasta Connection* (25/27 Elystan Street, SW3; 01-584 5248) is modest but pleasant, and the ices are excellent.

Marine Ices (8 Haverstock Hill, NW3; 01-485 8898) has been much enlarged and is now open seven days a week from 10.30 a.m. to 10.45 p.m. Their products are entirely without artificial additives, and their flavours include such provocative novelties as marsala, mango and walnut. Vesuvius, which is vanilla chocolate and marsala ice cream with crushed meringue, cherries and sponge soaked in marsala, is a memorable way of parting with £1.70. The *Gran Gelato* (Montpelier Place SW1) is a smart deco-style parlour. The owner, Max Rabino, supplies his own honey and brandy ice to the members of the Upper House in anticipation that it will rouse them from their lethargy. Nor should the claims of the *Regent Milk Bar* (362 Edgware Road, W2; 01-723 8669) be overlooked. Eaten amidst basic neon-lit 40s decor (green and yellow striped counter, chromium chairs) its gelati do something to redeem a glum area of London and its black coffee is splendid. *Dayville's* and *Baskin and Robbins* are on the retreat. The climate really doesn't justify so many specialist ice-cream sellers. For most people good old reliable *Walls* and *Lyons* in the freezer compartment of the sub post-office is quite good enough. (Choose the dark and golden or, failing that, the double choc or the rum and raisin.) *Marks and Spencer's* rum and raisin at £1.75 a litre is excellent.

The best sorbets in London are undoubtedly those at *La Maison des Sorbets* (140 Battersea Park Road, SW11; 01-720 8983/4) where Julian Tomkins, master sorbetier, pulps fruit from the nearby New Covent Garden Market into unforgettable confections and serves them in timbalines or a nougatine box of assorted and contrasting colours.

Best ice creams: *Marine Ices/La Maison des Sorbets*.
Worst ice creams: Those bought from vans outside tourist spots, especially Madame Tussaud's.

Indian Restaurants

Seating myself in a King's Cross tandoori restaurant the other night I sighed deeply ('Sighing is the Jewish Esperanto' – Bernard Kops) in blissful anticipation of a roghan josh and a bhindi bhaji. At which point a cockroach scuttled across the table cloth. I pointed it out to my waiter and he asked what a cockroach was. 'A sort of beetle,' I said, well aware that natural history has never been my bent. He seemed relieved. 'Oh,' he said, 'they get everywhere.' As I rushed for the door the heads of the other diners turned disapprovingly as though I had committed some solecism. If anything was going to cure my addiction for Indian food, that experience might have. It didn't.

In recent months the range and variety of Indian restaurants has strengthened to such an extent that one would need a whole book to deal adequately with what is already available.

The best is the *Bombay Brasserie* (Courtfields Close, Courtfield Road, SW7; 01-370 4040/01-373 6000). As soon as you enter what appears to be an Edwardian Club for ex-army officers, you find yourself in a cross between a setting for a Somerset Maugham film and the Palm House at Kew. A fresh fruit cocktail may be followed by Goan fish curry or Parsi Sali Boti (mutton with apricot), and rounded off with a fresh mint sorbet. I have been to few restaurants where everything combines thus to produce a sense of occasion. For an

Indian restaurant it is not cheap, but what sets it apart is that it is an Indian restaurant to which the best of the European tradition has contributed. Is this, as advertised, 'the authentic home-style taste of Bombay'? I doubt it. But it is delicious.

The *Last Days of the Raj* (22 Drury Lane, WC2; 01-836 1628) is a cooperative started with a grant from Camden Council and is reliably delicious if you can get a table and remain immune to the frosty welcome you may receive – but you can't expect the Bengali Workers' Action Group, who run it, to be obsequious. A shami kebab or a prawn purée followed by a meat thali or a murgh mus-alla and a frinee (ground rice with milk, pistachios, and flavoured with rosewater) will cost £11 a head inclusive, or a little more.

In the same management the *Red Fort* (77 Dean Street, W1; 01-437 2525/2410/2115) provides a highly sophisticated restaurant serving Moghul-food to ad men. The Chicken Jelfrezi is delicious but very hot; the basmati rice dull. Also the *Taste of India* (25 Catherine Street, WC2; 01-836 6591/2538) and the *Lal Quila* (117 Tottenham Court Road, W1; 01-387 4570/5332).

Another chain is the *Gaylord* restaurants with branches at 79 Mortimer Street, W1 (01-580 3615), at 16 Albemarle Street, W1 (01-629 9802), and in Manchester, Frankfurt, New Delhi, San Francisco and Hong Kong; the food is fresh and subtle, without breaking any rules. Lotus roots are recommended.

The Westbourne Grove curry houses are also strongly recom-mended. Notably: *Khan's* (Numbers 13/15; 01-727 5420) with its emphasis on Muglai dishes from the north of the sub-continent is preferable to the *Standard* (Numbers 21/23; 01-727 4818) which is quick, efficient, unglamorous, reliable and inexpensive. Go for the butter chicken. The *Diwana Bhel Poori House* (Number 50; 01-221 0721 with another branch at 121 Drummond Street, NW1; 01-387 5556) serves Gujerati vegeterian food, delicious and sustaining; try the Deluxe Dosa, a crispy savoury pancake, and the shrikhand (whipped cream with lemon and cardamom); it has no licence and is inexpensive; and the *Baba Bhel Poori House* (Number 118; 01-221 7502) with a similar vegetarian menu.

Many other recommendations, so the briefest details of the best of the rest (with a warning always to check the bill):

Agra, (135 Whitfield Street, W1; 01-387 4828). Tandoori specialities. A second generation restaurant, run by the founder's two daughters. *Bengal Lancer* (235 Kentish Town Road, NW5; 01-485 6688). An

Indian army setting, superb Tandoori food, and continuing justified popularity. The jeera (cumin) chicken and the murgh makhani are special.

Bombay Palace (50 Connaught Street, W2; 01-723 8855). Attractive and upmarket. The buffet at £7.95 includes six curries, rice, salads and raita.

Brilliant (72-74 Western Road, Southall; 01-574 1928). In the bustling bazaar that is now Southall, this is probably the best curry house. The furnishings are basic, the food delicious. Also in Southall, which has a fine town hall, the *Maharaja* (171-173 The Broadway, 01-574 4564), the *Moti Mahal* (94 The Broadway, 01-571 2620) and the *Roxy* – more properly called the *Safoo* and *Takhar* (114 The Green, 01-574 3476), should you fail to find a table at the Brilliant.

Chand Mahal (194 Mile End Road, E1; 01-790 0199). Intimate. Free spicy appetisers. Excellent king prawn korma.

Clifton (126 Brick Lane, E1; 01-247 2364). I was in trouble with a reader for not including a Brick Lane Indian restaurant. So this, complete with vast portions and opulently erotic murals is the one.

Diwan-e-Khas (110 Whitfield Street, W1; 01-388 1321). Where Channel 4 secretaries meet incognito Indian superstars, and what's good enough for them . . . Wonderfully hot mint sauce. Excellent fresh bhindi.

Diwan-I-Am (161 Whitfield Street, W1; 01-387 0293). Long-established, consistent, smart, with predominantly Asian clienteles.

Gurkhas Tandoori (23 Warren Street, W1; 01-388 1640). I was proud of discovering this one before the crowd. Since then, with the exception of one disastrous evening, it's been welcoming, intimate, and notable for hot Nepalese specialities.

Humara (Judd Street, St Pancras). But this one has not yet been discovered. For utterly crispy onion bhajis and tandoori chicken massala you can't go wrong. Wonderful value.

The India Club (143 Strand, WC2; 01-836 0650). A canteen for Indian students open to the public. Excellent value.

Maharani (77 Berwick Street, W1; 01-437 8658). Open till midnight, or early morning at week-ends, this is a better late-night bet than some of the more lackadaisical Chinese restaurants. Prawn and spinach curry with masala poppadoms a good choice.

Malabar (27 Uxbridge Street, W8; 01-727 8800). Highly popular, well-placed for the Notting Hill Gate, confident food. Try tandoori chicken-livers. Can get hectic.

Mandalay (100 Greenwich South Street, SE10; 01-691 0443). Only open 7 p.m. to 10 p.m. Thursday to Saturday. This may be (as claimed) the only Burmese restaurant in the country (so I'm cheating featuring it here; sorry). If you want to know what setaur, nun nun bin curry or hincho is, ring up and book; it's probably necessary. End with seaweed with coconut cream and fuluda.

Mandeer (21 Hanway Place, W1; 01-323 0660). A Gujerati vegetarian menu. Try katchoris (pulse samosas, sort of). Self-service at lunch in the Ravi Shankar Hall. Cheap, spiritual, exotic, devout.

Monty's Tandoori Restaurant (224 South Ealing Road, W5; 01-560 2619). The best in Ealing. *The Ealing Tandoori* (9 The Green, W5; 01-567 7606) is second best.

Perera Style Something Spicy Restaurant (112 St John's Hill, Battersea, SW11; 01-228 4412). Once again, not an *Indian* restaurant as such. The owner is Sri Lankan and the food comes from wherever, often vegetarian and usually intriguing. Coriander salad – lovely! Home-made ice-cream and over-priced wine. Pianist on Thursdays plays hot music.

Sabra's (263 High Road, NW10; 01-459 0340). Vegetarian Gujerati and Surati food with a wide range of delicacies. Regada patish is marvellous – I shan't tell you what it is, just have it. Excellent Indian sweets.

Trusha's (11-12 Dean Street, W1; 01-437 3559). Just the place for a light lunch. Sophisticated food and decor. Excellent service.

Viceroy of India (3-5 Glentworth Street, NW1; 01-486 3401). Up-market and excellent food from the north of the sub-continent, especially the vegetables, but not for the financially straitened. Quail tandoori, sag kamal kakani (spinach and lotus roots from Kashmir) – marvellous.

Best Indian Restaurant: *Bombay Brasserie.*
Worst Indian Restaurant: *The cockroach one.*

P.S. To stay up to date contact The *Curry Club* (P.O. Box 7, Haslemere, Surrey 0428 2452), for bhaji-lovers anonymous.

Italian Restaurants

(See also under Budget Restaurants, Pasta and Pizza)

Bertorelli's, *Bianchi's* and *San Frediano*, how many bowls of pasta, bottles of Barolo, oranges in caramel and zuppa inglese do those names recall?

Bertorelli's in Shepherd's Bush was where I used to eat with Peter Luke when we both worked on the BBC Wednesday Plays. Veal peperonata and a bottle of Verdicchio was what we ordered, and the wine always came marvellously chilled and cloudy with condensation. The service was motherly and the food nourishing. Then one day it was pulled down for a vast shopping complex which nobody much wanted. Bertorelli's Charlotte Street branch, where frankly the food was pretty terrible, is also gone (a sort of Franco-Italian brasserie/wine-bar has replaced it) and only a trendy branch in Covent Garden (44A Floral Street, WC2; 01-836 3969) remains. (The Bertorelli in Notting Hill is under different management, I believe.)

For years *Bianchi's* (21a Frith Street, W1; 01-437 5194) was run by Elena (Salvoni); indeed for many it was Elena. Then that tireless lady moved to L'Escargot across the road and it was thought that would be that; but *Bianchi's* has survived, and upstairs the same old journalists and writers bitch about their agents, while the publishers dine with their investment advisers at the *Gay Hussar* up the road. The food? Well, it's traditional London Italian. In an upstairs room Baird invented television. And now we go to Bianchi's to get away from it.

The *San Frediano* (62 Fulham Road, SW3; 01-584 8375) is the most recent of the three, and looks like what it is; a smart sixties trattoria; soups and pastas, liver and wild duck, an excellent house Chianti, all testify to the continuing success of this old favourite. Standards consistently high.

Leoni's Quo Vadis (26/29 Dean Street, W1; 01-437 4809/9585) is my fourth long-established Italian trattoria and unlike any other. In 1907 Leoni arrived in London to seek his fortune. In 1926 he opened his own restaurant in a house in Dean Street in which Karl Marx had lived (a library of Marx's research papers was found upstairs). As the years passed many members of Leoni's family joined him and the restaurant flourished. 'If they don't work', Leoni is supposed to have said, 'then they don't get no spaghetti!' As a centre of Bohemian London Jascha Heifetz used to dine there. One night he was looking for a piano-player to accompany him at a charity concert. 'Try Einstein, he's sitting over there,' said Leoni. Einstein agreed but at the concert the physicist failed to come in promptly after the cadenza. 'You don't keep time – you're late!' cried Heifetz. 'Ah well,' said Einstein, 'everything is relative . . .'

Leoni has been dead, oh, it must be 17 years but the atmosphere of the Quo Vadis survives. And the food tastes as good as it did when I visited it as a boy – my first Soho restaurant.

Some other recommendations:

Acquaviva (40 Goodge Street, W1; 01-636 4874/0430). Delightful, traditional and airy with a fine selection of daily specialities offered irresistibly on a trolley. Downstairs is more discreet.

Amalfi (31 Old Compton Street, W1; 01-437 7284). The quintessentially cheap and cheerful trattoria. Excellent pasta and cream cakes and gorgeous Gaggia coffee machine.

La Capannina (24 Romilly Street, W1; 01-937 2473). Old-established, friendly, crowded and delightful. Home-made pasta.

La Casalinga (64 St John's Wood High Street, NW8; 01-722 5959). Regular visits from a large and noisy section of my family have never given rise to a hint of impatience, no matter how curious our demands. The food is quickly served and extremely good, especially the starters which change daily.

Cecconi's (5A Burlington Gardens, W1; 01-434 1509). Fashionable, smart, expensive. Home-made pasta and self-made men. Wear a collar and tie. Take a credit card.

Covent Garden Pasta Bar (30 Henrietta Street, WC2; 01-836 8396). Recommended if you're short of time or money. Obviously the pastas are specialities, but the salads are good too.

Gianni's (Tottenham Street, W1). Slightly chaotic, but splendidly unpretentious in a tiny house with tiny tables and chairs. Good food, friendly.

Luigi's (15 Tavistock Street, WC2; 01-240 1795). Very much a theatrical haunt as you will see from the signed photographs. The tables are crushed together because this is a restaurant where everyone wants to eavesdrop. Hospitable, and they even welcomed my old dog. Food's O.K.

Mario and Franco Restaurants. Once the essence of chic, now firmly established as excellent middle-of-the-road Italian restaurants. There are nine of them, thus: *Terrazza* (19 Romilly Street, W1; 01-437 8991); *Don Luigi* (316 King's Road, SW3; 01-352 0025); *City Tiberius* (8-11 Lime Street, EC3; 01-623 3616); *The Club* (members only) (5 Halkin Arcade, West Halkin Street, SW1; 01-235 5532); *Villa Claudius* (10a The Broadway, SW1; 01-222 3338); *Terrazza-Est* (125 Chancery Lane, WC2; 01-242 2601/2); *Trattoo* (2 Abingdon Road, W8; 01-937 4468) and *Villa Augusta* (Bucklersbury, Queen Victoria Street, EC4; 01-248 0095).

Pasta Connection (25-27 Elystan Street, SW3; 01-584 5248). Authentic home-made pastas, ice-creams and sorbets. Waiters with small bottoms speaking Italian. Young clientele.

La Preferita (163 Lavender Hill, SW11; 01-223 1046). Good news for Wandsworthies. An excellent small Italian restaurant with all the usual features, good sea-food, and daily specials.

Rugantino (26 Romilly Street, W1; 01-437 5302). Franco, the manager, trained at the Savoy, and it shows. This small establishment is often crowded but the service is always courteous and the food excellent. Try the bresaola (cured beef with olive oil and lemon) and the zabaglione. Excellent coffee.

Santa Croce (112 Cheyne Walk, SW10; 01-352 7534). One sits at tables covered with lemon-yellow cloths in one of the prettiest restaurants in London. There was not enough salt in the spinach and I was pursued relentlessly with a giant pepperpot, but Santa Croce is charming.

The Spaghetti House (see phone book for branches) suffers sadly from their nasty piped music although the pasta itself is excellent and moderately priced. Casual to a fault. I have never eaten well at *Paradiso e Inferno* (389 Strand, WC2).

Topo Gigio (46 Brewer Street, W1; 01-734 5931). Named after Signor Wences' delightfully shy mouse which charmed television audiences A.D. (Ante Dallas). A friendly subterranean dive with excellent osso bucco and an extensive list of regional Italian wines.

Best Italian Restaurant: *Leoni's Quo Vadis.*

P.S. Try reading *The Best of Italian Cooking* (Angus and Robertson £3.50 paperback).

Japanese Food

Although I dislike eating raw fish in particular and Japanese food in general, I am prepared to concede that the Japanese have been around a great deal longer than I have and have achieved rather more culturally. That being so, the problem is to find a Japanese restaurant sympathetic to my shortcomings. I had heard that the *Ajimura* (51-53 Shelton Street, WC2; 01-240 0178) could be the answer, but it was not on the night I was there. The diner is given an illustrated recipe card to take away and study, but I ate nothing which tempted me to try to repeat the experience at home. The set lunch at £5 must be good value, unless it is horrid. Tends to get crowded. Speciality is sashimi, which is fillets of raw fish, alas.

The Azami (13 West Street, WC2; 01-240 0634). A combination of many things; sushi bar at which you sit and watch the sushi chef doing wonderful things with raw fish, seaweed and rice; night club; and karaoke bar. What is a karaoke? Why, a tape deck of course, and one which will accompany you with guitar, rhythm and full orchestra on almost anything you care to sing. Other karaoke bars in London include the *Cattleya* (West Street, W1) and the *Jun* (58-59 Great Marlborough Street, W1; 01-734 9420), but they are vastly popular in Japan and look like catching on here too. Other Japanese restaurants to try for the food alone:

Suntory (72-73 St James's Street, SW1; 01-409 0201) with branches in Paris and Milan. Hugely expensive, very stylish, specialising in sukiyaki, shabushabu and teppan-yaki, all of which are cooked in front of you. It should be emphasised that in a Japanese restaurant the *eating* of the food is almost incidental; the whole evening should be a spiritual, intellectual and aesthetic experience – like Hill Street Blues with a glass of Glenfiddich followed by a hot foam bath, and an hour or so with Muriel Spark.

The Hiroko of Kensington (Kensington Hilton, 179 Holland Park Avenue, W11; 01-603 5003) is quiet and pleasing and the chef provides small samples of Japanese delicacies with each set meal, so you can learn painlessly and not too expensively which dishes you prefer.

The Ikeda (30 Brook Street, W1; 01-629 2730). Very plain with bench seats and a respect for classical Japanese cuisine. Refreshingly unfussy.

Ikkyu (67 Tottenham Court Road, W1; 01-636 9280 – evenings only). Cheaper and more cheerful than most, *Ikkyu* offers yakitori for starters; these are Japanese kebabs at 60p per skewer. Then maybe a vegetable omelette and an elaborate mélange of fresh fruit. Delicious and only about £12 a head.

The Koto (75 Parkway, NW1; 01-482 2036) is as modest as a Japanese restaurant can permit itself to be. You need to climb a spiral staircase and remove your shoes before being admitted to the low room with sloping blinds, white walls and paper lanterns. It's all very restful (once you get there) and the menu is extensive and excellent. Try the tempura prawns, the chicken yakitori or the miso (soya bean) soup.

Best Japanese Restaurant: *The Suntory*.

P.S. Seaweeds imported from Japan and other Japanese delicacies such as sake, rice cakes and green tea may be ordered or purchased from *Sunwheel Mail Order*, 196 Old Street, EC1V 9BP (01-250 1708).

Jazz

The *Pizza on the Park* (11 Knightsbridge, SW1; 01-235 5550) and the *Pizza Express* (10 Dean Street, W1; 01-439 8722) are admirably committed to good cheap food and music. There is even a Pizza Express All-Star Jazz Band. Pizza Express concentrates on groups, P on the P on visiting musicians, often from overseas. But there is only one *Ronnie Scott's* (47 Frith Street, W1; 01-439 0747).

It was the crazed and scintillating Sonny Rollins; it was Blossom

Dearie with her smokey-sweet voice and immaculate technique; it was cherubic George Melly like an evil-minded putto; it was, above and beyond the rest, Roland Kirk RIP, blind and with a mouthful of saxophones, driving himself and his musicians to new heights of joy and new depths of pain; it was all these and more; it was Ronnie's, and still is. Ronnie's jokes ('My girl-friend is so dumb she thinks Moby Dick is a venereal disease') about the generous nature of the waitresses, about the misanthropy of the chef, get no better with the passing years – just more familiar, as do the faces of the regulars, Spike Milligan, Michael Phillips, David Spanier and Suzy Menkes, and those boring people who will keep tapping out rhythms with their knives and forks. The bouncer/maître d' is departed and we mourn him, the prices are high and we grumble about it, but at least Ronnie's has survived – just.

The *Bass Clef* (35 Coronet Street/1 Hoxton Square, N1; 01-729 2476/2440) has been open eighteen months. A wonderful debut. Big bands – well, quite big – and notable jazz as well as blues with the emphasis on contemporary sounds. There is a bar and restaurant and lunchtime sessions (usually free).

Other jazz venues in London include:

Archduke Wine Bar, (Under the Arches, South Bank, SE1; 01-928 9370) – only chamber jazz.
Beggar's Banquet Bistro (15 Harrington Gardens, SW7; 01-373 2303).
Brahms and Liszt (downstairs), 19 Russell Street, WC2; 01-240 3661). Mainly soloists.
Brentford Waterman's Arms Centre (40 High Street, Brentford, Middx; 01-568 1176) – free at Sunday lunchtime.
Bull's Head (Barnes Bridge, SW13; 01-876 5241).
Cricketers (Kennington Oval, SE11; 01-735 3059).
M and M Jazz Bar (Mary Magdalene Crypt, Munster Square, NW1; 01-240 2430).
Palookaville's (13a St James' Street, WC2; 01-240 5857).
The Restaurant (Dolphin Square, Chichester Road, SW1; 01-828 3207).
7 Dials Jazz Club (46 Earlham Street, WC2; 01-892 2443).
Tufnell Park Tavern (Tufnell Park Road, N7; 01-272 2078).
100 Club (100 Oxford Street, W1; 01-636 0933).

And don't forget to pick up a sheet of forthcoming events from Pizza on the Park or Pizza Express. Nor to refer to *City Limits* or *Time Out* for current gigs.

Best Jazz Clubs: *Ronnie Scott's* and *Bass Clef.*

Best Jazz Pub: *Bull's Head*.
Worst Jazz: Anywhere where they request 'When the saints . . .'
    Even worse if it's *not* requested and they still play it.
    See also under Pubs with Entertainment.

Kiosks/News Stands

According to New York folklore, when your first night is over you repair to Lindy's where you await the early editions in which you will read whether the butchers of Broadway have chopped your play into gobbets and fed it to the crows. Well, it wouldn't work here. Papers are only actually *sold* in Fleet Street on Saturday nights and Sunday mornings, but you can get them free by going into the newspaper office and asking. At King's Cross Station you can get the *Sun* before 10 p.m. (but not with the late evening racing results in it), or, as my correspondent wittily adds, 'If you want a newspaper, you can wait until 11 p.m. for the *Times* or midnight for the rest'.

When Londoners had a choice of evening papers the fun of it was whether the news vendor could guess right; were you a *Star*, or *News*, or *Standard* man? Now that there's a choice once more, the newsreaders are out of practice.

But some of the newspaper sellers still feel free to comment. According to a friend, the vendor at West Hampstead tube 'always smirks when you buy *Spare Rib*'. Leaving aside hotel lobbies, which don't count, the classy place to buy your paper is the small but charming kiosk next to Sotheby's in New Bond Street (you can even get the *Burlington Magazine* there!) or the Crown Passage bookstall in St James's. But there is also a kiosk in Kingsway with an awning and above it a signboard announcing that 'The Times, TES, TLS, THES on sale here'. Very classy.

The kiosk at South Ken tube is good, while the one at Bank tube is bad. In Leicester Square is a theatre kiosk, where you can buy half-price tickets for West End shows that have not sold out on the day of performance. This kiosk is reminiscent of the tent in which Oliver's Richard III passed such a troubled night before the battle of Bosworth Field. Almost as though he was waiting for the reviews in the first editions.

Best kiosk: *New Bond Street*.
Worst kiosk: *Piccadilly Circus*.

Kites

The new fashion is the Flexifoil, a stunt kite which is a long way removed from the friendly old box kites. Prices range from £37 for the novice's Skysail to £80 for the Super 10. But for smallish children something more amenable is more sensible. Fighter kites from £1.50, Mr T or Viking kites from £5, and beautiful bird kites from £9 would all be fine. So too would indestructible, wind-inflated, soft kites like the Supertube (£9). Chinese paper kites are fragile, though pretty. The kite season officially begins at Easter with the *Blackheath Kite Festival*, and along with *Parliament Hill*, *Primrose Hill* and *Hampstead Heath*, *Blackheath* is ideal. For the less ambitious *Kensington Gardens* or *Streatham Common* – but watch the trees. Besides the larger toy (q.v.) shops I can recommend three specialist kite shops:

(a) The Kite & Balloon Company (613 Garratt Lane, SW18; 01-947 8505) runs a kite hospital and also sells vast helium-filled balloons.

(b) Mitsukiku (90 Regent Street, W1; 01-437 5582).

(c) The Kite Store (69 Neal Street, WC2; 01-836 1666).

Best kite flying: *Parliament Hill*.
Worst kite flying: *Park Lane*.

Knitwear

Just a few among many of the new school of designers who have turned the cardi into high art:

Artwork (33 St Christopher's Place, W1; 01-486 4733). Glitzy and fun but pricy.

Colourways (112a Westbourne Grove, W2; 01-229 1432). Pastelly and flowery jumpers often with those delta-wing sleeves, useful for keeping sandwiches in.

Edina and Lena (141 King's Road, SW3; 01-352 1085). Variations on the Fair Isle and other animals.

Melinda Cross (60 Chiltern Street, W1; 01-486 7651). Only three of any design by Melinda Cross will ever be made, so you know you are in select company. Or you may order from your own designs. Also have a wide variety of mohairs and cashmeres. Expensive naturally. The original branch is at 1 Copenhagen Street, N1; 01-833 3929).

Tomlinson and Tomlinson (8 Hornton Street, W8; 01-937 5173). Not solicitors, as you might suppose, but designer knitwear. All the fave names; once it was chic to look like a Maoist peasant. Since the cultural revolution it's O.K. to dress like a Breton fisherman. I'm so glad.

Don't, of course, ignore charity shops and jumble sales (need I tell you?).

Korean Restaurants

First the refugees, then the restaurants. But Korean food needs no apology. It's based around beef with seven spices used in different combinations: garlic, ginger, spring onions, sesame seeds, sesame oil, black pepper and soya. Then there is the Gu-shul-pan, a compartmentalised lacquer box in which hors d'oeuvres are served. Seven Korean restaurants are listed in London of which five are under the same management. Possibly best to tempt your palate at the original, the *Arirang* (31-32 Poland Street, W1; 01-437 6633/9662). Soups, spare-ribs, rice, kim-chee, a very hot cabbage pickle and fruit are staples, but you will be offered courteous advice and should eat well. Set lunch is £3.50, so it won't cost too much to experiment.

When you feel ready tackle the more sophisticated and spacious *Korea House* (10 Lancashire Court, 122-123 New Bond Street, W1; 01-493 1340/491 4762). Romantic in a covered garden you will be served 'city food' here, including Bulgogi, barbecued beef, served at your table. Lobster if you give a day's notice, and, if you have a party of 100 Korean businessmen or extras from M.A.S.H., all can be accommodated.

Best Korean restaurant: *Korea House*.

Kosher Food

Having enjoyed an excellent salt-beef sandwich – the beef spread thick with lashings of mustard and the bread an authentic rye – at the inappropriately named *Continental Bar* (30 Charing Cross Road, WC2; 01-836 4233), I asked for a latke.

'Where's your membership card?' flashed back Gaby, from behind the counter. It is improbable that Gaby is one of the Chosen, and his bar prides itself, besides its salt beef, on falafel, shawarma and kebabs, none of which is traditional Jewish food. (In fact the Palestinians took

Israel to the UN for adopting falafel which belonged by rights to the Arabs.) But Gaby serves a falafel every bit as good as his salt beef on rye.

For a while the pivot of Soho Jewish life was Great Windmill Street. Jack Solomons had his boxing gym there, a Mecca for all professional boxers, and fans could often meet Dempsey and Tunney and the handsome Carpentier at Jack Solomon's. Then one would adjourn to *Isow's* kosher restaurant. It was Jack Isow who, when faced with anti-semitism at a restaurant outside London, bought the place. But, alas, Isow's has gone and although there are those who pray by *Reuben's* (20A Baker Street, W1; 01-935 5945 and 01-486 7079) – excellent soups – the doyen of kosher restaurants has to be *Bloom's* (90 Whitechapel High Street, E1; 01-247 6001). Morris Bloom opened his first restaurant in Brick Lane in 1920 and, his talents appreciated by immigrants nostalgic for gedempte meatballs and lockshen, for stuffed kishka and kneidlach, never looked back. Within ten years he had opened a kosher food factory, and in 1960 his son, Sidney, inaugurated a canning department so that Bloom's food, supervised by a rabbi and a religious adviser every day, may be eaten nationwide.

Now I shall take the liberty of quoting from a correspondent's report on Bloom's, for the writer is clearly a man of discernment:

'The advanced age of our waiter in no way diminished his energy or marketing ability. Please warn North American Jewish readers that Bloom's serves up kishka denuded of its *essential* derma covering. Also, the pickles are disappointingly sweetish in the gentile gherkin fashion. On the other hand, the salt beef was very tasty and the rye bread better than any I have had in Canada or the United States.'

Being adjacent to Petticoat Lane and the Whitechapel Art Gallery, *Bloom's* attracts many tourists. At the other branch (130 Golders Green Road, NW11; 01-455 1338) *Bloom's* predictable but hugely sustaining food is served to affluent suburban Jews. I have heard alarming reports recently about this restaurant.

The best kosher fish restaurant is *Grahame's Seafare* (38 Poland Street, W1; 01-437 3788), while *Harry Morgan's* (31 St John's Wood High Street, NW8; 01-722 1869) sometimes has the unusual habit of serving all the courses simultaneously, but the food is more elegant than *Bloom's*. Good value, big portions, but only seven tables, so book early. The food at *Harry Morgan's* has not been authorised by the Beth Din, so if you're fruhm, schlep elsewhere.

New York Jewish food, trendier and flashier than the British variety, is available at *The Widow Applebaum's* (amazing decor), 46 South Molton Street, W1 (01-629 4649) and *Poppy Joe's*, 176

Battersea Park Road, SW11 (01-627 4614) where the burgers and bagels and salt beef are excellent.

I've dealt with the *Cosmo* (5 Northways Parade, Finchley Road, NW3; 01-722 2627) under breakfasts. The Cosmo is Old Vienna, and recommended.   .

Finally in Hendon there's the *Kosherina* (sic!) 8 Sentinel Square, Brent Street, NW4; (01-202 9870). Not only Beth Din, Kashrus and Kedassia but vegetarian as well – except the fish curry. You cannot get more ideologically sound than that – and the food tastes O.K. too!

Best kosher restaurant: (for food) *Harry Morgan's*.
                                  (for fish) *Grahame's*.
                                  (for atmosphere) *Bloom's* E1.

Lavatories

Now here's a sad story. Derek Gillan lived for 20 years in a changing cubicle at the main gents in Waterloo Station. An ex-boot-black, he was paid £5 a week to keep the place spotless, which he did. The gents was everything to him. He had lost touch with his family and, as he commented wryly: 'I don't have many mates and I can't really invite them down here for an evening, so my social life is not very busy.' Well now, his facilities and his name have been replaced by those monstrous superloos, complete with piped music and concealed cameras.

Certain general rules may be followed when taken short in London. Department stores are a better bet than underground stations. Temple underground station is without loos at all; cinemas and theatres are grim, especially during the intermissions; London clubs have lavatories which are awe-inspiring in their magnificence. (Kipling remarked that whenever he went to the lavatory in the Athenaeum he expected to find a bishop on his back kicking his legs in the air like a black beetle.) Hotels are the safest option. *Durrant's* (George Street, W1) is the best for men with marble surfaces and Pears' soap (if you happen to be a man with marble surfaces).

The ladies' lavatory at *Paddington Station* used to house Tiddles, a fat cat much loved by the regulars, but here too the lavatories are being 'privatised'. Over the lavatory at *St Pancras* is 'GENTLEMEN' beautifully carved in Lombardic lettering; an architecturally distinguished loo. Other stations are less interesting, and *Richmond*,

Westminster and *King's Cross* are disgraceful.

The ladies at *Fortnums* oozes old-fashioned elegance, but *Selfridges'* ladies, which used to be elegant, is now just run-of-the-mill. The public lavatory in *Fleet Street* is for men only, and it's no use unaccompanied ladies seeking relief in El Vinos. The lavatories at the *National Film Theatre* are very limited, so whip your bladder over to the *National Theatre*.

Besides those mentioned above, I can recommend: *The Greenwich Pier* ladies (spotless), *Sydney Street*, Chelsea, the *Royal Academy*, the *RAC Club*, Beckenham High Street, *Harvey Nichols*, the *Law Courts*, *Queensway* (just opened, nice railings), *Harrods*, and the ladies' toilets in *Cambridge Gardens*, East Twickenham which have carpets and pictures on the walls. The *Anchor* pub on Bankside and the early Victorian *Union Jack* pub in Union Street have surviving outside urinals. I cannot recommend the *Aldwych Theatre*, Kingsland Road, E8, or Mortlake Green. Almost all London schools have vile lavatories. A constipated generation will surely result. What a false economy!

Wembley Stadium was singled out by Illtyd Harrington, ex-GLC chief: 'There are better hygiene arrangements in the bull ring at Pamploma,' he snorted.

There are now some 24 French-designed 'superloos' in *Westminster*. I tried one. For my 10p I had fifteen minutes of (supposed) privacy (one can imagine what these loos will principally be used for), hygienically cleaned pans and seats, a rather low bowl, which helps children and recalcitrant bowel movements, and a selection of Hawaiian guitar music which, if things are touch and go, would certainly militate against going! There are very few public lavatories in Belgravia.

Best lavatory: *Royal Box*, Covent Garden.
Worst lavatories: *Too numerous to specify*.

Learned Societies

La Collège de Pataphysique (President Alfred Jarry) exists for the study of improbable solutions, so do not expect to find it in the phone book. There are societies for the *Friends of Reptiles*, for the *Friends of Bulgaria* (if you can befriend Bulgaria you can befriend anything), for the *Industrious Poor*, for *Foreigners in Distress*, for the *Scientific Study of Anomalous Phenomena* (everything from marine monsters to metal bending) and for *Public Lighting Engineers*.

The *Knights of the Round Table* swear that every word of Malory's

Morte d'Arthur is literally true, while the most exclusive society in London has only two members, Jean Campbell, Beaverbrook's grand-daughter, and Andy Garnett. Neither has a navel.

Moving up the intellectual scale there exists an *Anarcho-Syndicalist Association* (I wonder how they elect their president), the portentous *Institute for Strategic Studies*, and the estimable *Linnaean Society* at Burlington House, to whom Darwin first read *The Origin of Species*. The *London Society for the Study of Religion* does excellent work, and the *Society of Genealogists* (37 Harrington Gardens, SW7; 01-373 7054) has the biggest selection of books on genealogy in the world, and is open to non-members during the daytime.

However there can be no doubt about the best and worst in this category:

Best Learned Society: *The Royal Society.*
Worst Learned Society: *The Society for the Conversion of the Jews.*

Lebanese Restaurants

The comparisons between Beirut and Babylon are hard to resist. Once both were cities devoted to pleasure, where the east met the west, and, after its destruction, Babylon may well have looked a lot like Beirut does today. But the tradition of Lebanese food, at least, survives, and in the Edgware Road of all places. There is *Zem Zem*, unlicensed and orthodox, at No. 458 (01-724 1183); *Aladdin*, excellent value, at No. 295 (01-723 9693); *Al Diwan* at Nos 61 to 69 (01-724 1161); *The Lebanese Restaurant*, chic and an authentic kitchen at No. 60 (01-262 9585) and *Maroush*, classy though surly, at No. 21 (01-723 0773). There is even a Lebanese take-away next door to the Maroush.

The essence of Lebanese food is the mezze, a series of dishes that can be taken separately or together and including most of the familiar elements of middle-eastern cookery, such as pitta bread, falafel, raita, humus, tabbulah, cream cheese, beans, aubergine purée, vine leaves, doner, kefta, shish and cous cous. Accompanied by salad and arak, the mezze should be your complete meal. It should take a long, long time and the conversation should at some point include Mohammed the Prophet and the metal futures market.

Probably the best Lebanese restaurant in London – the most expensive is certainly the *Omar Khayam* (117 Regent Street, W1; 01-437 3000) – is the *Fakhreldine* (85 Piccadilly, W1; 01-493 3424) with a splendid, double-glazed view over Green Park. The mezze is (are?) excellent and is (are?) followed by sticky sweets filled with honey and almonds, belly buttons, and other such delicacies. Expect to pay about £30 a head.

The *Olive Tree* (11 Wardour Street, W1; 01-734 0808) is simple and unpretentious offering two menus, one vegetarian, one carnivore. There's not much competition around Leicester Square, but this is quite a find.

Best Lebanese Restaurant: The *Fakhreldine*.

Libraries

The *Reading Room* of the British Museum is unique. If the quintessential dust of all the learned men and women who have studied there hangs in the air, it must also be the place most likely to impose inspiration on its students. But getting a reader's ticket is not easy, since you have to show that what you need is not readily available at the more plebeian libraries, and, once you have your ticket, getting the book or books you need is a lengthy and elaborate procedure. This is a library to be used when you are entering upon a prolonged course of study, but never casually.

The *London Library* (14 St James's Square, SW1; 01-930 7750) is a registered charity run by a committee of members of the library and dedicated to accumulating standard and authoritative works in the humanities. With over a million volumes, almost all of which are on free access, the annual membership fee of £60 (tax deductible and, if you genuinely can't pay, the Trust may be able to help) is truly a bargain. A grand and generous-hearted institution.

The *Colindale Newspaper Library* – actually a branch of the *British Library*, which is a part of the British Museum – contains the National Collection of Newspapers, provincial from 1700, London from 1800. It is not easy to find, and once found, is profoundly eccentric. The book of rules states: 'Persons under 21 years of age are not normally admitted. In the interest of the preservation of the collections admission is not granted for the purpose of researching into football match results and horse and greyhound racing, or for competing for prizes.' Other conditions make it something of an obstacle race before you can actually sit down in front of the research material you are after, and no sooner have you done so than at the early hour of 4.45 p.m. a warning bell is rung and the newspapers are cleared from the room. Nonetheless it is a priceless establishment, and the only one of its kind in the country.

After my last guide was published I received a letter from a librarian at the *Limehouse Area Library*, which puts me in something of a moral dilemma. The safest thing to do is to quote direct: 'Perhaps the library I work in could be included in a future edition. You see we have *two* copies of *all* your novels, housed in our special fiction collection (part of the Joint Fiction Reserve Scheme which operates in Inner London Public Libraries). You might or might not know about this useful co-operation scheme whereby libraries acquire novels by authors within certain letters of the alphabet.' It would surely be ungrateful if I were not to mention the Limehouse Library – there, I've done it again! – particularly since the library also houses an extensive collection of French and German Literature, which is extremely hard to come by. I know. I've tried.

I would also like to say a word about those oases of peace and tranquillity, the local archive libraries. I recently spent some days in several of them and was treated with great courtesy and kindness, notably at the *Marylebone* and *Bethnal Green Libraries*; only in Victoria was the mood shattered when I was forbidden to bring take-away coffee into the library. I tried charm but it didn't work. A particularly well-run example of a local archive is the *John Harvard Library* in Borough High Street.

Other useful and agreeable libraries in London include the *Keats Library* at Keats Grove, NW3, where a particular effort is made to engage the imagination of children; *Dr Williams Theological Library*, Gordon Square, WC1; the *Fulham Public Library*, which a writer friend claims to have 'the best research facilities in the world'; the *Westminster Reference Library*, St Martin's Street, WC2, with a first-rate collection of books on art, cinema and the theatre; the *Financial Times Library;* the *Swiss Cottage Library* (airy and pleasant to work in), and *Sutton Central Library*, St Christopher's Way, Sutton, Surrey, where there is a coffee bar, a story-telling pit for children, study carrels with typewriters to hire, an exhibition area, and even, if you're lucky, a tame author to bait. A curiosity is the *Marx Memorial Library* (37a Clerkenwell Green, EC1) with the Lenin Room in which he edited *Iskra*. The room has been kept just as it is. My working conditions are worse than Lenin's.

Among the less successful libraries in London one has to include *Streatham Public Library*, the *Bishopsgate Institute*, and *Richmond*, which is not peaceful, and where you get charged for the stamp on a letter reminding you that your book is overdue *even after that book has been returned*. I mean, really . . .

Best Library: *The London Library.*

Lights

See under Street Lights.

Lions and Eagles

London is a-prowl with sculpted lions. The bronze ones in Trafalgar Square, designed by Landseer and erected around *Nelson's Column* as an afterthought in 1868, are 20 feet long and 11 feet high; splendid creatures, except that their paws are those of cats, not lions. Fine stone lions guard the Lion Gates at *Hampton Court, Syon Park* and *Kew*. The haughtiest lion preens itself hugely at the *British Museum*. The fiercest lion is rampant on the wall of *White Lion Street*, N1 with his date (1714), and the most bewildered lion stares out at a noisy world from *19 Durand Gardens*, SW9. The royallest of lions wears one crown and clutches another on the top of *Palace Gate* at the entrance to Kensington Gardens. At *Eltham Palace* there's a stone lion (paws missing) with what looks like a Scotsman's tammy on its head but I expect it's meant to be a crown. There are lions with unicorns all over the place. Easily the finest graces the *King's Arms* pub in Newcomen Street, SE1. Dated 1760 this used to be attached to the south gate of London Bridge. Another fine stone lion (by Coade, and rescued from the old Lion Brewery) guards *County Hall*. Stucco lions prowl moodily around the roofs and gables of terraced houses in *Parson's Green*, hundreds of them, and there is even a composition lion called Flora to be found on Flora's lawn at *Syon Park*. It was made by the props department at Shepperton Studios. *St Peter's Square* Hammersmith, boasts quite a variety of lions and eagles as well as a sad church designed by a bridge builder. The greatest London eagle, however, must be the bald American one which spreads its wings to a span of 35 feet on the roof of the *American Embassy*. Made from gilded aluminium, its head is turned the opposite way to the official American eagle, as though turning a blind eye to all those intended immigrants who sidle up to the immigration officers looking as though they've got ice-picks in their back-packs.

Other fine eagles sit atop the gatepost of *Oakfield Park School*, SE21, hover over *Counter Court*, Southwark, brood outside the *Pheasantry* (152 King's Road, SW3), prepare for take-off from the top of the *RAF Monument* (Victoria Embankment) and glare disapprovingly from *118 Clapham Common West Side*, SW11. A lion with eagle's wings supports the frieze of the *De Vere Hotel*, De Vere Gardens, W8 and another plays with a ball on the *Holborn Viaduct*.

Best Lions: *Trafalgar Square* (but not their paws!)
Best Lion and Unicorn: *King's Arms*, Newcomen Street.
Best Eagle: *US Embassy*.

P.S. for further information see *Lion Hunting in London* by Fran Mannheim.

Litter Bins

The best litter bin in London is a huge squatting toad with an open mouth in *Battersea Park*. Children cannot resist feeding it with rubbish. The Lewisham shopping precinct has other litter-beasts besides toads.

Very horrid are the yellow plastic litter bins in *Trafalgar Square* and now spreading ominously elsewhere. But the worst litter bin in London is a big round pebble-dash thing in *St Botolph Street*, EC3. It's not so much the thing itself as where it is. Which recalls to mind the story told me by the poet P. J. Kavanagh, who was paying a sentimental visit to Dove Cottage, home of Wordsworth in the Lake District. He was standing in awe in the poetic bedroom, when the curator crept up behind him and startled him out of his mellifluous reverie with the words: 'Sobers is out!'

Best litter bin: *Battersea Park*.
Worst litter bin: *St Botolph Street*.

London Clubs

The clubs of St James's are older and more distinguished than the clubs of Pall Mall, and the oldest club in St James's is *White's Club* (37 St James's Street), which evolved in 1693 from a coffee house of the same name. It was a hotbed of the Tory establishment (unless that is a contradiction in terms), with its principal rivals being *Brooks & Boodles*. Also *Almack's* which was unusual in that it was a club for both sexes in which the women nominated and voted for the men and vice versa, and *Crockfords*, founded by the fishmonger from Temple Bar, and a club where an entire generation of English lords were removed from their patrimony. The men's clubs in St James's survived where the livelier 'hells' did not and those who go to a London club in search of 'a good time' these days will have to settle for billiards or bridge or the latest from the Hong Kong exchange.

Of all the clubs which became politically influential, the most celebrated is the *Carlton*, founded in 1832 in Carlton House Terrace by a committee including the Duke of Wellington. Within a year the *Carlton*, which was also the official Tory headquarters, had 500 members. In 1835 it moved to Pall Mall and in 1940 after two bombs struck the building while the Cabinet were at dinner inside it moved again to St James's. There is a potent saying that 'it's easier to get into the House of Commons from the Carlton than into the Carlton from the House of Commons'.

The *Reform Club*, at 104 Pall Mall, is best known as the setting for Phileas Fogg's wager that he would travel round the world in 80 days – both Fogg and the wager are, sadly, fictional, although the Reform played host, like the *Savile*, to numerous Victorian literary figures. The agreeable design is by Charles Barry, who also designed the *Travellers' Club* and the House of Commons, but in this case he took the Palazzo Farnese in Rome as the inspiration for what he called his 'creative imitation'. The Reform always had a high gastronomic reputation (although Lamb Chops Reform are a sad disappointment) and the first chef was Alexis Soyer who wrote numerous cookery books and organised soup kitchens for the starving Irish during the Famine and the first field-kitchen in the Crimea at Scutari. The political bias of the club created the emergent Liberal party. To be a member it is necessary to acknowledge and affirm the Reform Act of 1832.

The reputation of the *Savile* was literary (Robert Louis Stevenson was a prominent, though noisy, member) and academic; hence it was the target of snobbish attacks. A member of the *Guards Club* was asked his reaction to playing host to the *Savile*. 'They were quite decent little fellows. No trouble. Make their own trousers, of course.'

I find the institution of London clubs faintly absurd, although they keep a lot of eccentrics off the streets and the reading stands provided for solitary diners are a delight. The *Garrick*, with its famous staircase, has a unique collection of theatrical mementoes, and is rich in leading men banging on about Frank Benson and Binkie.

Whatever your views on the morality of such places, they perform several useful functions. Visiting Americans who have reciprocal rights with Clubs in New York and Chicago stay at the *Oxford and Cambridge* or the *St James's* in much greater comfort than in even the best hotel, and architecturally they add considerable dignity to the London scene, with the *Athenaeum* and the *United Service Club* ('The Senior') providing an elevated framework to Waterloo Place. So far as members are concerned bishops and Fellows of the Royal Society join the *Athenaeum*, actors and publishers the *Garrick*, diplomats, politicians, and spies join *Brooks'* the *Travellers'*, *Boodles* or *White's*.

The *RAC* has the best facilities including a splendid swimming pool, the *Turf Club* the most dukes, the *Carlton* the top Tories, and the *Junior Carlton* the ones who would like to be top Tories.

According to the late Ian Fleming, at *White's* the members 'gassed too much ' so he lunched at *Boodle's* because he 'liked dull clubs'. *Brooks's* he described as 'like a duke's house – with the duke lying dead upstairs'.

For women the *University Women's Club*, formed in 1883, provided 'facilities for intercourse' for university-educated women. It also provided lavatories which were not readily available for women at the end of the last century. This club, which has been in Audley Square since 1921, still flourishes, and just as well, since almost all the men's clubs, with the notable exception of the *Army and Navy*, are inimical to women; the worst in this respect is the *Naval and Military*, otherwise known as the In and Out, whose marvellous entrance in Piccadilly is for men only.

All in all most traditional London clubs provide dull food, better wine, boring company, a smoky atmosphere, and seats it is almost impossible to rise from after marmalade sponge. But they do provide cheap accommodation (once you're a member), excellent cellars of wine, telex machines, and sometimes squash courts and swimming pools.

Arnold Bennett, who was extremely clubbable, put it even better than I have. Here are club members in a typical smoking-room:

'The atmosphere of the place has put . . . them into a sort of exquisite coma. Their physical desires are assuaged, and they know by proof that they are in charge of the most perfectly organised mechanism of comfort that was ever devised.'

A newcomer on the London scene is the *Groucho Club* at 45 Dean Street (01-439 4685) named after Groucho who, you will remember, did not wish to join any club that would have him as a member. Membership is £150 p.a. but about to be increased, food is excellent, and most of the members are media-folk, particularly publishers, vying to show off their most eminent guests. ('Raise you!' they mutter as they pass.)

I'm a member of BAFTA (195 Piccadilly, W1; 01-137 1635), excellent for snacks, meeting friends and seeing screenings of new films pre-release, and old classics.

Best London Club: *The Garrick.*

See also Gambling Clubs.

Magistrates' Courts

The most enlightened courts in London at present – although much depends upon who is sitting – are *Marylebone, Hampstead* and *Bow Street*. The most severe are *Highgate, Highbury Corner* and *South Western*. *Highgate* refuses 46% of legal aid applications; *Hampstead* 6%. I got costs against the police at *Marlborough Street*, was discharged from *Greenwich*, where my evidence confused everybody present, myself included, at the end of a tiring week, and was treated very civilly at Petty Sessions in *Walton Street*. Mr Mark Romer, sitting at *Clerkenwell*, recently gaoled a man for seven days for whispering in court, which seems excessive.

The *Marylebone* court has a reputation to bely its modest architecture ('insignificant Italianate' says Pevsner) and successive stipendiaries have been noted for their wit and wisdom. Mr Plowden in the twenties, a man whose sayings frequently delighted the readers of the periodical press, Mr Romain in the sixties and seventies, and now the handsome Mr Fanner have upheld and enhanced the tradition. A slightly sourer note is inscribed in the public pews of No. 2 court. 'Don't fuck old Bill', says the anonymous author, 'you'll walk sideways.'

Best magistrates' court: *Marylebone*.

Mews

But should it be mewses? To mew was to moult. A mew was the cage in which a hawk or a falcon was confined while mewing, and, since the Royal Stables were where the Royal Mewing Falcons were kept, so they became the *Royal Mews*. From which you will gather that 'mewses' is as ridiculous as 'geeses'. However . . . (Admittance to the *Royal Mews* Wednesdays and Thursdays 2-4 p.m.)

Originally the Royal Stables were situated where the National Gallery now is, but when John Nash remodelled Buckingham House into Buckingham Palace (1824-26) he kept his happiest inspiration – many would say his *only* inspiration so far as that building is concerned – for the *Mews*. The architecture curves as generously as a horse's rump, but horses are only a part of what is on show there, for you may also see the state coaches and carriages, the landaus used at Royal Ascot, and horsey tackle given to the royals by the rulers of Turkey and Libya and Mexico; by Nikita Kruschev and the Maharajah of Jaipur.

Most mews are to be found in Kensington, Marylebone, and Belgravia; in those residential areas of London in which people who were rich enough to have grooms and stables lived. A fine example is *Hyde Park Gardens Mews*, for here, tucked discreetly behind the magnificence of Hyde Park Gardens, you have mews cottages which complement the big houses perfectly. But I doubt if any grooms live in them today. While charming, these cottages bear all the signs of decadence: modern bulls' eyes in the glass bows; over-varnished stripped pine doors, and reproduction Staffordshire spaniels in the windows.

Not only is a mews address a considerable expense. There are obvious disadvantages. Despite the yellow lines (why did the authorities have to choose such a hideous shade?) mews are fair game for illegal parkers, who are likely to get away with it. Even if you are a resident, negotiating your car into a mews is difficult, particularly so if the entrance is arched, as it often is. The struts of the arches bear witness to those who just didn't make it. Incidentally, the arch over the entrance to *Albert Mews* has a plaster representation of the Prince Consort's handsome head. Since the war many of the mews have become little more than garage space. *Queens Gate Palace Mews* is a mass of little men doing clever things to snazzy cars. And, should you venture into the labyrinth of *Queen's Gate Palace Mews* – one of London's most extensive – you will find several of the snazziest cars in London for sale at Coy's. And living in a mews one must accustom oneself to the *backs* of things. *Blackburne's Mews* is wrecked by the backside of the American Embassy – not a pretty sight, while *Chilworth Mews*, which displays some pleasant creepers, and *Eastbourne Mews* are wrecked by the unsmiling backs of large anonymous slabs of office.

Despite all this the *small scale* of a mews, the feeling of living in a community within a village within a city, must give mews-dwellers a feeling of security, especially if the mews is single-ended. For a double-ended mews means a busy mews. A disastrous example is *Edwards Mews* behind Selfridges, little but skips and cars and angry faces behind wheels. But a closed mews, such as *Hollywood Mews*, off Hollywood Road, Fulham, is more like a tiny Mediterranean village square than a part of London. In *Hollywood Mews* the cottages are identical, though painted in contrasting shades of blue, grey and puce. Each has a balcony – what a setting for a midsummer production of *Romeo and Juliet* – and in the middle of the yard are three trees, a hawthorn and two which may be sycamores. I hunted for others as charming and found *Clabon Mews, Elizabeth Mews, Belsize Park Mews*, and *Chelsea Mews*, which have much to recommend them.

183

Kynance Mews is bounded on the north, not by a slab of office, but by a pleasant church with an inspiring spire (Christ Church 1851). In the yard of the church is the Pooh Corner Montessori School, with a wooden shed marked 'Eeyore's House'. Cobbled and narrow with dustbin problems, *Kynance Mews* may have seen better days. Certainly I spotted next to an empty window box a plaque reading: 'Kensington Society 1967 Window Box Award'. *Conduit Mews*, in which a successful attempt has obviously been made by the residents to achieve individuality within an harmonious whole boasts one house (Numbers 27/28) which is a kind of vertical, or hanging, garden. Plants climb, creep and dangle out of every orifice, grow out of pots and barrels and painted lavatory pans in a madness of contrasting greens. Messages abound too. Here is an example:

> The Gardener's Prayer.
> Great God of little things
> Look upon our labours
> Make our little gardens
> A little better than our neighbour's.

One prayer at least which was answered.

Best mews: *Hollywood Mews.*
Worst mews: *Edwards Mews and Winsland Mews.*

Mexican Food

There is some confusion at the flamboyant *Texas Lone Star Saloon* (154 Gloucester Road, SW7; 01-370 5625) as to whether it is a Texan or Mexican establishment, and frankly does it matter? This Tex/Mex place is so deeply committed to cheering everyone up – country music, pre-recorded tapes by the ubiquitous Tim Rice, gun-toting cowboys on the TV – that one may not notice that the food is really rather good in a macho way – spare ribs, chilli, frankfurters and T-bone steaks. It's no place to take your Red Indian friends. A second branch at 117 Queensway, W2 (01-727 2980) has recently opened, an indisputable advertisement for the success of the first.

At the *Café Pacifico* (Langley Street, Covent Garden, WC2; 01-379 7728), which is cheerful, clean, noisy and a bit silly, the menu is genuinely Mexican, which is to say that almost every dish consists of corn, beans and chilli contained in pancakes of differing shapes and sizes. Four of us ate sopa de elote (sweetcorn soup), quesadilla, quesada, enchillado el burrito (I don't think it was mule) which, with coffee, an almost undrinkable sangria, and wine to take the taste away, came to £30, or £7.50 a head. Cocktails are also served and the atmosphere is described accurately as 'Cantina'. From Sundays to Wednesdays tamales are served, and pretty nasty they are too.

Although there is no restaurant in London called The Cockroach, there is one called the Cockroach in Spanish: *La Cucaracha* (12 Greek Street, W1; 01-734 2253) is elegantly up-market. Although Mancha Manteles de Cerdo ('The Pork that Stains the Tablecloth') was 'off' when I last visited, there were many authentic Mexican alternatives. The most authentic was Mole Poblano de Guajolote, turkey in chocolate and chilli sauce, which is the national dish of Mexico, and the reason why the Mexicans never could shoot straight. The extremely hot appetiser makes the Dos Equis (imported beer) almost essential, and, if only the tortillas had been crisper and the guitar player in tune, I could have recommended it.

Finally a word of praise for an informal (you relieve yourself in the bathroom), quirkish and delightful Brazilian restaurant, *Paulo's*, (30 Greyhound Road, W6; 01-385 9264), open Mondays to Saturdays, evenings only. Oh and read, if you're interested, *The Book of Latin American Cooking* by Elizabeth Lambert Ortiz.

Best Mexican food: *Café Pacifico*.

Milestones

Why do so many milestones feature Hounslow and Uxbridge (not places that one often wants to visit)? And what is the significance of the mysterious stone on *Haverstock Hill*, outside No. 79, which reads: '4 Miles From The Post Office 45° North'? I'm fond of milestones with pointing fingers such as the one at *No 1 Kensington Gore*. Here the fingers appear to be pointing at one another. There is a fine carved obelisk on *Richmond Bridge* marking the spot where tolls used to be exacted. It bears highly informative legends on three of its sides and on the east facet it says: 'The First Stone of this Bridge was Laid 23 August 1774 and Finished December 1777'. It's more like reading a novel than a milestone. Another obelisk, the fine one in the grounds of the *Imperial War Museum*, has mileage around its base, thus: 'One Mile CCCL Feet From Fleet Street'. More succinct is the one in front of the *Old Grammar School*, Dulwich: 'V Miles from the Standard, Cornhill'.

The handsomest milestone is the one in *Harmsworth Park*, SE7. In fine bold script (the same as is used in the corners of penny reds) it says: 'One Mile From Palace Yard Westminster Hall', and there's no arguing with that. Sadly most milestones removed during the war, were never replaced.

Best milestone: *Harmsworth Park*.

Model Boats

Whitestone Pond, *Hampstead*, on a fine spring Sunday is the place for model boats. Here it was that Shelley used to sail paper boats for Leigh Hunt's children. A flag pole nearby marks the highest point of Hampstead Heath (440 feet) which may be why the model boats sail so bravely there. Easily second best is the Round Pond at *Blackheath*, followed by the Round Pond, *Kensington Gardens* (not so windy, but classy Harrods boats), and the pond at *Clapham Common*.

Best for model boats: *Whitestone Pond*.
Worst for model boats: *The Quaggy*, Lewisham.

Modern and Commercial Buildings

Most modern London buildings appal by their dreariness rather than by their spitefulness. It's the mean, cheese-paring style of office block, the disheartening greyness of the high-rise accommodation that makes the shoulders droop and the spirits wilt. *State House* (corner of Red Lion Street and High Holborn) is an example. Under the name of the architects on the foundation stone graffiti artists write: 'Ought to be ashamed of themselves'. Consider too the Department of the Environment, *2 Marsham Street*, SW1, which should be setting us all such a good example; the *Shell Centre*, SE1; the *Inn on the Park*; the dreadful *Sunley House* in the Upper Richmond Road by Putney High Street; the *Polytechnic of Central London* in Marylebone Road ('architectural Marxism', I've heard it called); almost any of the commercial buildings along the North Circular Road. Then they have the gall (Trafalgar House do) to pull down the *Firestone Building* – one of the very few amusing commercial buildings in West London.

The new *Lloyds* building in Leadenhall Street, EC3 has been the subject of much criticism. Designed by Richard Rogers, the co-architect of the brilliant Pompidou Centre in Paris, this vastly expensive (£157,000,000) pile, already known as the Oil Refinery, has been described by R.I.B.A. as bringing to high technology 'an element of baroque, a richness, and a popular touch'. I concur. And while having doubts as to whether it is tactfully sited, one can quite see that Lloyds wouldn't want to move their staff, say, to Worksop. The curious thing about contemporary London buildings is that it takes a while before *anyone* knows whether they're good. Here are some that, for me at least, pass the test.

There's the headquarters of the *Hogg Robinson Group* (9 Crutched Friars, EC3) which is composed of gold or bronze reflecting mirror glass and is very beautiful. *Wool House* in Carlton House Terrace, SW1 is tactfully deferential to the adjacent Pall Mall clubs. The *Natural History Museum* extension is far more agreeable than the Islamic Centre opposite, while the extension to the *Covent Garden Opera House* is such a brilliant pastiche that it's almost impossible to tell where the old ends and the new begins. The *Daily Express Building* in Fleet Street is an art deco gem, and the interior details are splendid; running your hands along the banisters may be enough to restore your fading virility. The *Michelin Building* (Brompton Road, SW7) is a well-known treasure – though ominously deserted at the moment – by François Espinasse (1905). It features the exterior tile panels by Gilardoni Fils et Cie of Paris which record with wit and charm the early history of motoring. The *Michelin Building* may be at risk; the *Battersea Power Station* (Sir Giles Gilbert Scott, 1929-35 completed 1944-46) certainly is. Wandsworth Council has plans to use it for waste disposal. Huh. The *HMSO* building in Seven Dials is energetic in blue and silver, while the new *Covent Garden Market* next door is imaginative but ugly. Both have an engaging Lego flavour to them.

The *Economist Plaza*, set a little back from St James's Street and designed by Alison and Peter Smithson in 1966 is a success and on the other side of the street at *No 66* are offices belonging to Credit Suisse in futuristic rocket launcher style of granite, grey steel and curved glass (by Tripos). Distorted in the windows, which complement the traditional bow-windows of the St James's club, is a reflection of the eighteenth century.

With some buildings it's almost impossible to separate the architecture from the symbolism. *Centrepoint* (St Giles' Circus), designed in 1965 by Richard Seifert & Partners, seemed not unsuccessful until the scandal of its continued emptiness while the homeless lived in railway waiting rooms, soured us to its merits. Latterly it is used to house both the young homeless and the Confederation of British Industries; the symbolism continues to intrigue. Also designed by Seifert is the *NatWest* Building in Threadneedle Street, EC2. At over 600 feet this is the tallest building in Britain, but what's the use of that when only NatWest executives and possibly their friends and fancy women are allowed to go to the top?

On a more domestic level the house which Michael Hopkins built for himself in *Downshire Hill*, NW3 from steel and glass and determination for less than £20,000 is a triumphant example of the new complementing the old. In *Blackheath*, 10 Blackheath Park is a house of a great beauty designed by Leslie Bilsby of Span. It consists of three conjoined pentagons in stone and black glass with steps and a ramp inviting you up to the front door.

The best estates are *Crown Reach*, the new Wates development in Grosvenor Road, SW1 (next to Vauxhall Bridge); it is four houses and fifty-six apartments which advance and recede in witty perspective around the central lift shaft. *Brooklands Park*, Blackheath is pretty good too. The worst is the four-tower-block development at the corner of Adelaide Road and Fellows Road which casts a derisive shadow over the vast acreage of residential north London. But see also the entry on Housing Estates.

Best modern building: *66 St James's Street.*
Worst modern building: *Polytechnic of Central London.* Also *56/67 Portland Place* (see under Architecture).

I recommend: *Modern Buildings in London* by Ian Nairn (London Transport).

Most Confusing Street

John Street becomes *Doughty Street* becomes *Mecklenburgh Street* becomes *Mecklenburgh Square* all within 500 yards. Within half a mile *Southampton Place* becomes *Russell Square* becomes *Woburn Place* becomes *Tavistock Square* becomes *Upper Woburn Place* becomes *Eversholt Street*. The Belsize Park area of Hampstead would even confuse a code-breaker, and there are motorists weeping in the gutter at their failure to circumnavigate the *Chipstone Street/Bolsover Street/Warburton Street* patch to the south of the *Euston Road*.

As for the house numbers in *Holland Park Avenue* it would take the patience of a water-diviner to sort them out.

The least confusing street? *The Inner Circle, Regent's Park.*

Murals

The *Town House Studio* in Goldhawk Road has a witty trompe l'oeil mural which makes it appear other than it is. Magritte in the Goldhawk Road is not to be sneezed at. There are fine murals by

Archibald Zieger at *Toynbee Hall* in Commercial Street, but they are often hidden by a curtain and you may have to ask a friendly social worker to let you see them. In *Tottenham Street*, W1, facing Tottenham Court Road and Heal's, there is a massive mural; all human life is there. It's awfully ugly. Most adventure playgrounds have murals which make up in enthusiasm what they lack in sophistication.

A mural 75 foot long by more than 12 foot high overlooking *Dexter Square*, Brixton, displays London's black community in 'situations of conflict against racism, but with a positive outcome envisaged'. Not an easy commission for the artists, Gavin Jantjes and Tom Joseph.

There has been a row in Brixton about another proposed new mural by Christine Thomas (who also painted the one in *Elspeth Road*, Battersea). It was planned to enhance the limited attractions of *Strathbone Street*, but now some residents fear that it may lower house prices. Gulley Jimpson, would you were living at this hour . . .

See also Friezes and Tiles.

Best Mural: *Toynbee Hall*.

Museums

Recommended:

Apsley House, Piccadilly, W1, restored, for its Wellingtonia, for the Waterloo Gallery, 90 feet long, for the Waterloo Vase, and for many fine pictures. Here the survivors of Waterloo met for an anniversary dinner each year until Wellington himself was called to the great parade ground in the sky. Also called the Wellington Museum.

Bethlehem Royal Hospital, Monk's Orchard Road, Beckenham Kent. (Admission by appointment.) An exhibition incorporating many pictures of, and by, the 'poor lunatics'.

The British Museum for its Print Room, its Elgin Marbles, its ghosts, its books, its mummies, its antiquities and much much more. Wear stout shoes.

The Courtauld Institute Galleries, Woburn Square (don't go to the Institute itself in Portman Square by mistake, as I did) for its superb Impressionist and Post Impressionist pictures. My sister is right to be disappointed by Lautrec's *Bar at the Folies Bergère*.

David Percival Foundation of Chinese Art (53 Golden Square, WC1; 01-387 3903, open Mon, Tues, Sat). The best in the country for oriental ceramics. Ethereal shapes, textures and patterns.

Dickens' House (48 Doughty Street, WC1). Run by fanatics, so allow plenty of time to argue the toss. In this house Charles' daughter died in his arms, as a result of which Little Nell had to die too.

Doctor Johnson's House (17 Gough Square, EC4). A curious amalgam of memorabilia of the great Doctor. In the garrett he composed his dictionary.

The Geffrye Museum (Kingsland Road, Shoreditch) for its furnished rooms, each representing a period of British history. Best period: the thirties (Herbert Wilcox, Melville Gideon, the Co-optimists, ah!).

The Geological Museum, South Kensington, for its astonishing range of minerals and fossils, of precious and ornamental stones, its wonderful reference library, and its piece of moonrock, brought back on Apollo 16 and thought to be nearly four million years old.

Ham House, Ham, Surrey, for its beautifully restored rooms (it dates from 1670) and its lovely furniture. Polo at week-ends in the summer. See the Lely portrait of the Lauderdales. It would be respectful, since this was once *their* house.

The Horniman Museum, Forest Hill, for its participatory events for children. Apart from its remarkable clock it has little of significance in its permanent collection except stuffed animals, mummies and masks. But ideal for a leisurely week-end stroll with the family.

The Kew Bridge Pumping Station, Green Dragon Lane, Brentford, for its five giant beam engines, which demonstrate the majesty of machinery. Lovingly restored by amateur well-wishers.

The London Dungeon for their showmanship. You may not care to see hangings, drawings and quarterings, boilings to death, amputations, devil worship, human sacrifice, leprosy and syphilis (get all that at home), but you have to admire the panache with which it is presented. It's usually the boys who faint.

The London Planetarium for its Zeiss star projector. Its astronomical programmes are inspirational, and its laser lights concerts remarkable. *Madame Tussauds*, to which it is linked, is too well known to require a description.

The London Toy and Model Museum, 1 Craven Hill, Bayswater, is a delightful private museum specialising in model train sets, cars, soldiers, meccano and dolls. Also Peter Bull's collection of teddy bears. Informal.

The Museum of Childhood, Bethnal Green. The branch of the V and A, saved from imminent closure by Paul Channon, is charmingly cheerful. It is over-crowded with a collection valued at nine millions, but doesn't feel over-crowded. The dolls' houses are terrific.

The Museum of Mankind, Burlington Street, for its anthropological exhibits. This is a particularly well-maintained museum with an unusual care for detail. They even spray the exhibits daily with the authentic odour.

The Natural History Museum for its exuberant architectural façade, and its fifty million exhibits including souvenirs from Captain Cook, Captain Scott and Charles Darwin. Dinosaurs and whales, scorpions and tarantulas. Essential but overheated.

The National Maritime Museum and Library, Romney Road, Greenwich, for its comprehensive collection of nautical antiques, and don't miss the Barge House. Nor the planetarium. On this site young Raleigh took off his cloak, and flung it into a puddle in front of the Queen. Later he discovered the potato.

Patrick Cook's Bakelite Museum (by telephone appointment only on 01-691 2240). A unique display of the products of the inventor Dr Leo Baekeland; in Greenwich. Extraordinary.

Sir John Soane's Museum, 13 Lincoln's Inn Fields, WC2. The house and museum of a small country builder, who made good. After his wife's death in 1815 and being disappointed in his two sons, he turned to collecting. Besides the stunning Hogarths (*The Election* and *The Rake's Progress*), the Sarcophagus of Seti I in alabaster with hieroglyphics is an astonishing relic. Open Tuesdays and Thursdays; free admission; charming and knowledgeable assistants.

The Victoria and Albert for its superb collections of glass and ceramics, and general Victoriana. Its identification service (01-589 6371 for details) is extremely useful, although wisely the V and A won't value items brought in. The size and scope of the museum ('fine and applied arts of all countries and periods') is so immense that several visits are called for. It is to the museum's credit that occasional exhibitions reflect contemporary life. A new restaurant is about to open in the basement of the Henry Cole Wing (Exhibition Road entrance) and can only be an improvement on the old one.

Vintage Wireless Museum (23 Rosendale Road, SE21; 01-670 3667). Gerald Wells, whose private collection this is, is an enthusiast and has 20,000 valves to prove it. Some visitors unroll their sleeping-bags in his living-room.

The Wallace Collection, Manchester Square, for its completeness. The majority of the treasures were collected by the third and fourth Marquesses of Hertford and are lodged where they belong in Hertford House, so it doesn't seem like a museum. Wonderful French furniture and European pictures, many of which are familiar old friends.

But I can't recommend *The Black Museum*, New Scotland Yard, Victoria Street, SW1. This is unlike the London Dungeon, for these exhibits are not reconstructions. Death masks, murder weapons, victims' remains and other stomach-churning trouvailles make it no place for the faint of heart.

Best Museum: The *British Museum*.
Worst Museum: The *Black Museum*.

For further information refer to *Museums and Galleries in London*, edited by Malcolm Rogers, which lists some 160 museums. Essential really.

Music Halls

On my 18th birthday I went to see Max Miller on what must have been his final tour. He looked as old and tired as the nudes who shared the bill with him, but wore more rouge than they did. If this was music hall it deserved to die.

Most of what passes for music hall in London today is geared more to tourists than to aficionados and attempts to revive the camaraderie of the real thing are as hollow as those dude ranches in Arizona where they re-enact great shoot-outs of the past with blank bullets.

Recent television compilations have suggested that, with a few exceptions, the standard of all but the greatest acts was, to today's taste, unremarkable. The environment was everything and that cannot be reproduced.

The tourists choose between the Abadaba Company at *The Pindar of Wakefield* (3-8 Gray's Inn Road, WC1; 01-837 7769) and the *Players' Theatre*, once Gatti's Music Hall, under the arches at Charing Cross (01-839 5080). The Players has been going the longest and its performers are more experienced in such matters as soubrette singing, but the Abadaba remains relentlessly cheerful. Note that it only gives performances from Thursdays to Saturdays inclusive. Neither of these two companies is cheap.

Numerous pubs offer old time music of various kinds while the *Prince of Wales* (73 Dalling Road, W6; 01-748 1236) can seat 300 people in its upstairs lounge where Black and White Minstrel shows may be seen at weekends. A few of the London Borough Councils organise music hall evenings for what they choose to call their senior citizens. On these occasions the performers are often as venerable as the audience, but everyone seems happy enough. The *Lewisham Town Hall* is a regular venue. A unique survival is *Hoxton Hall*, which used to be known as Clark and Macdonald's Music Hall. If anyone wished to revive the art here is the perfect venue.

Ah, but Collins burnt down, the old Met was redeveloped, and the Empire became a cinema. I actually *saw* Albert Chevalier (at a Butlins!) perform and Elsie and Doris Waters were wonderful, but the very best was Lily Morris singing, 'Don't Have Any More, Mrs Moore'.

Best music hall: *Players' Theatre.*

Night Clubs

Here is a sad extract from an otherwise happy tourist: 'We tried the *New Twilight* – Charing Cross Road, not realising that "clubs" in London are not "clubs" as we know them. £100 buys you one bottle of champagne and the company of two women who won't take "NO" for an answer. My friend and I departed quickly leaving our "friends" in that dingy den of deprivation!' The moral: be explicit to the cabbie, say 'disco', not 'club'.

You cannot be too careful. Talking to a girl who had been a hostess at one of the traditional London clubs (see list below), I was told that most of the girls will go home with the customers and will charge £200-£300 a night. Even at that rate there is no shortage of customers. Since this money is on top of the official wage and undeclared, a robust girl can expect to clear up to £2,000 a week tax-free.

Most of the 'night-clubs' in London change hands regularly as much to avoid VAT and Health Inspectors as unsatisfied customers. Here are a few which have survived and should survive for a while yet – as long as there are lonely and wealthy mugs in town:

The Boulogne (27 Gerrard Street, W1; 01-837 3815). Edwardian type of plush in deepest Chinatown. Twice nightly cabaret. Fancy food. Middle-range prices. Long established (1852 they claim).

Champers International (5a Stratford Place, W1; 01-629 6312). Champagne for £50 a bottle (De Lahaye). A minimum of £25 hostess fee to have a girl sit with you (more, I imagine, to be left alone). Dinner at £25 and breakfast at £15. The girls wear underwear. The decor is gilt mirrors, bronze alloy chandeliers and Napoleonic reproductions. Old Sinatra movies are shown on the video screen. Closed Sundays. The club 'bubbles with an intimate glamour which is both new and exciting'. In other words, *tacky*.

Churchill Suite (52 Piccadilly, W1; 01-408 0226). Here champagne (unspecified) is a mere £20 a bottle and there is an 'erotic' cabaret every thirty minutes – how can they keep it up that long? Closed

Fridays, Saturdays and Sundays. Admission £6. Food and hostess extra.

Director's Lodge (13 Masons Yard (off Duke Street) St James's, SW1; 01-839 6109). The mixture as before. Closed Saturdays and Sundays.

The Gaslight (4 Duke of York Street, SW1; 01-930 1684). Hostesses in Regency corsets, a topless bar, striptease, live musicians (well . . .) and a clientele of wide-eyed hicks from the sticks. An established part of the London scene. Grim though.

L'Hirondelle (Swallow Street (off Regent Street), W1; 01-734 6666). Two bands and twice-nightly floorshows 'starring the fabulous L'Hirondelle dancers and topless showgirls'. About £75 for two. Surprisingly small; ambitious food and expensive cellar 'of incomparable distinction'.

The Pinstripe Club (21 Beak Street, W1; 01-437 5143). Here the ambiance is Victorian (as opposed to Edwardian – nice distinction), with topless maids. Victoria would not have been amused.

Saddle Room (123 Cromwell Road, SW7; 01-370 1203). Must have fared better when the air terminal was still open. The usual trimmings, but why go to Cromwell Road for them? A touch more strait-laced than the others.

Stork Club (99 Regent Street, W1; 01-734 3686). Unusual in that it prides itself on its 'stunning lighting effects', though they're not a patch on what you'll get at many discos (q.v.). Food marginally cheaper here and no membership charge. 'London's total nightclub scene' – more an admission than a boast.

Quite probably if you give the name of any of the above to your taxi-driver, he will try to persuade you that he knows somewhere better – better for him, that is. Which is why most of the clubs provide 'courtesy cabs' or 'complimentary chauffeur-driven limousines'. Occasionally tempers get frayed and bombs get left in Soho clubs, but they seldom go off.

Really the only night club I can recommend is *Annabel's* (44 Berkeley Square, W1; 01-629 3558). It does have a touch of style, exclusivity and discretion. But, once again, it's not cheap.

Best Night Club: *Annabel's*.

See also Discos, Gambling Clubs, Strip-tease, Prostitutes, etc.

Non-Smokers

For those who cannot abide eating in an atmosphere of cigarette smoke, ASH has published a book giving the names of 69 eating and drinking establishments where smokers are not admitted. Send 25p and an SAE, or drop in at ASH, 27/35 Mortimer Street, W1 (01-637 9843).

Obelisks

The obelisk was originally the Egyptian sun-worshipping symbol and stood for eternal life. Which makes the black *Katyn Memorial* obelisk in Gunnersbury Cemetery all the more poignant. This was erected in memory of 14,500 Polish prisoners of war who disappeared in 1940. Other cemeteries contain fine obelisks, particularly that to Sir Richard Mayne in *Kensal Green*, and the example erected by the Society of Friends in the *Great Northern Cemetery*, Brunswick Park.

Cleopatra's Needle, which dates from 1450 BC, was first erected in Heliopolis where it was one of a pair. It finally reached London in 1878 after being twice abandoned in the Bay of Biscay. The 186 tons of pink granite were cleaned in 1979 with money donated by a kindly Arab who preferred to remain anonymous. But it is so badly sited on the Embankment that few Londoners notice it. It has nothing to do with Cleopatra.

On the site of Wildcroft Manor on *Putney Heath* is an obelisk with this interesting inscription: 'The Right Hon John Sawbridge, Esq., Lord Mayor of London, laid the foundation stone of this pillar 110 years after the fire of London on the anniversary of that dreadful event and in memory of an invention for securing buildings against fire.' The invention was fireproofing by laying metal sheets between double flooring. To prove the efficacy of the invention by David Hartley, George III lunched with his royal entourage in an upper room of Fireproof House on Putney Heath while a bonfire blazed merrily on the ground floor.

Near the Imperial War Museum is the *Brass Crosby Obelisk*. Crosby (1725-1793) was a friend of Wilkes and a staunch libertarian; his monument is beautifully proportioned as befits such a rational man, and has a milestone (q.v.) carved into its base.

Best obelisk: *Brass Crosby*.

Oculists

What you need to do is get a test from an ophthalmic optician who will then prescribe a lens suitable to your needs. Next you visit one of the branches of *Special Eyes* (try 25 Central Mall South, Riverdale Centre, Lewisham SE13; 01-318 3134; they will give you the details of other London branches) and they will charge you £11.50 from their vast stock of lenses while you choose a free frame from their vast stock of frames. (If you want a designer frame this may cost a pound or two). Fitting the lens to the frame will take them just a moment and – this is the good news if, like me, you regularly sit on your spectacles – any frames broken within a year will be replaced. A good deal.

Best Oculist: *Special Eyes.*

P.S. The Glass House, opposite Victoria Station, has launched a campaign to collect 15,000 pairs of glasses to be distributed to African charities. Donate your old spectacles to The Glass House, Underwoods stores, John Menzies at Paddington or Euston, or W. H. Smith at Victoria, Waterloo or Liverpool Street.

Open-Air Food

No point eating in the open air if you find yourself sitting on a pavement with carbon monoxide infiltrating your watercress soup. And no point either if the open air is more crowded and insanitary than an air-conditioned basement. As a general rule, if the weather is set fair go to a deli (q.v.) and buy a picnic to eat in a park (q.v.) or square (q.v.). So these recommendations are strictly limited to those places where the atmosphere is horticultural and the air fresh.

Problems at the *Barbican* where, having selected our food and paid for it, Chloe and I carried it off to eat by the sparkling fountains. Then Chloe dropped her apple in the water . . .

Brinkley's (47 Hollywood Road, SW10; 01-351 1683). French food tending to nouvelle which is served in an Edwardian dining room or a charming garden. Not cheap. No riff-raff. Nice puds.
The Cherry Orchard (241 Globe Road, E2; 01-980 6678). Impossible to leave this Bethnal Green café without being physically and spiritually improved. It's run by the Buddhists. It's vegetarian. It's wholesome. They serve spring water. The garden is peaceful. And it's cheap.
Henry J. Bean's Bar and Grill (195/197 King's Road, SW3; 01-352 9255). American food with fried potato skins (yum), burgers,

cheesecake, pecan pie, that sort of thing. But – and this is the point – a very large garden with a special children's playground (for special children). Useful.

Old Rangoon (201 Castelnau, SW13; 01-741 9655). What was once a pub there is now a fast food restaurant specialising in spicy, vaguely Indian dishes. You can also buy (£4.50) a picnic hamper to eat in the landscaped gardens (floodlit at night). 'East is east and west is west and never the twain shall meet' contended Kipling, but the Old Rangoon was not open in Kipling's day.

Le Routier (Camden Lock, NW1; 01-485 0360). Although crowded at times, and not at all like a French lorry driver's caff, Le Routier has an urban charm amidst the trendy market and the old canal. Food's good and connections can be made.

Wilfrid Sailing Barge (Victoria Embankment, WC2; 01-379 5496). A converted sailing barge. Below decks is for posh food, but excellent cold snacks may be taken on deck.

Best open-air eating: *The Cherry Orchard.*

Opera

The revival of the English National Opera has neatly balanced the decline of *Covent Garden*. The *Coliseum* is London's largest house with 2,380 seats. David Poutney, director of productions, and Mark Elder, music director have ensured that operas are not only sung in English, but in an English accessible to the predominantly young audiences attracted to the ENO. Acoustics are excellent. The appreciation index is noticeably high (few doze off, even during Wagner) and seats are moderately priced (300 at £3.50 for every performance). Having said which there is no substitute for grand opera in a grand opera house, and they don't come much grander than *Covent Garden*. Elijah Moshinsky's production of *Samson*, for instance, with Domingo and Agnes Baltsa under the direction of Sir Colin Davis attained a pitch of emotion which can rarely be experienced elsewhere. And when you consider that by queuing at the Floral Street Box Office on the day of the performance you can buy a seat in the Slips, where the sound is as good as anywhere in the house, for just the price of a couple of pints of beer, you realise just how privileged opera-lovers in London are. Except when the orchestra goes on strike.

Kent Opera which tours the south east and sometimes makes it to *Sadler's Wells* (a bad house to play in) concentrates on small-scale productions with great musical sophistication. Visits to London by the *Welsh National Opera* have been more successful than those by the *Scottish Opera*, though both should be tasted. The WNO play at the Dominion, Tottenham Court Road, which is normally host to rock stars.

Productions by *Opera Bouffe* at the French Institute and by the Singers Company should be sought out, but there is more imagination in most modern musicals, especially when Hal Prince is involved, than in most modern opera productions.

Attending *A Masked Ball* not long ago at the *Sydney Opera House* (name dropper!) I was impressed by an innovation sponsored by American Express. Above the stage an electronic system translated simultaneously the libretto into English. You could read it or ignore it. Are there plans to introduce something similar here?

Best Opera: *Covent Garden* (at its best).
English National Opera: (consistently good).

Orchestras

A contrite apology. In *The Essential Guide to London* I made no mention of the *Philharmonia Orchestra*, the world's most recorded orchestra, according to my correspondent who honourably admits that 'I *am* a vested interest'. He also argues that the Philharmonia is 'currently the most popular London orchestra by attendance figures . . . and consequently has the best bank balance!' Well, there's no arguing with that.

I was also remiss in making no mention of the remarkable *London Sinfonietta*, who have done so very much to popularise twentieth century music and who know best under Michael Viner, their enterprising musical director, and David Atherton, their energetic conductor, how to play it. They are flexible and play the right notes – even in those pieces when it doesn't matter.

The *Royal Philharmonic Orchestra* is also surviving, thanks in part to the astonishing and deplorable success of its *Hooked on Classics* recordings, the first album of which sold more than six million copies. Can six million people be wrong? You bet your sweet bippy they can. Was the RPO ill-advised therefore to undertake such a cynical project? Emphatically no. On New Year's Day 1983 it played its hits at the Orange Bowl American Football Final in Miami Beach, an event which was beamed to a breathless world by satellite. And now this policy of living in the real world has been extended to the appointment of André Previn, star of stage, screen and TV commercial, to be its musical director.

The *London Symphony Orchestra*, installed at the Barbican but still rather quarrelsome, is also an extrovert organisation and plays that way. (*Pops in Space* is their bid for the big time.) Although Abbado is principal conductor, the orchestra is dependent on the Davis clan, Sir Colin and Andrew conducting and Michael the exemplary leader.

The *London Philharmonic Orchestra* has played under six principal conductors, Beecham, of course, and Van Beinum, Boult, bless him, Pritchard, Haitink and Solti. It's a sign of the times that to the LPO's regular sponsors have been added three new names, Mars Bars, McDonald's Restaurants and Prudential Assurance. But there is no evidence that the orchestra's increased dependence on commercial sponsorship has affected its high artistic standards or its programming. Don't miss it when the LPO tackles Mahler.

The *BBC Symphony Orchestra* is the mainstay of the Proms, and always strong in its woodwind section. If none of these orchestras ever quite attains the nobility of, say, the *Berlin Philharmonic* at its best, they are all musicianly and committed.

Amongst the smaller groups, the *Academy of St Martin-in-the-Fields* is outstanding, and the *Italian String Quartet* among the best in the world (the *Lindsay Quartet* is a promising foursome of younger players), which is more than can be said for the *London Mozart Players* or the *Dagenham Girl Pipers*.

Best Orchestra: *Depends on who is conducting*.

Organs

The best classical organ is the one in the *Festival Hall*. The *Albert Hall* instrument is still the original one and has been well-described as 'the second coming in Panavision'. It has 9,999 pipes, is excellent for French music, and may soon wear out the way old organs do. The Father Willis organ which will figure in the rebuilt *Alexandra Palace* should be worth the wait. The organ in *Southwark Cathedral* is given a canter in public on Mondays at lunchtime. It too is rather special, being the finest achievement of the great T. C. Lewis, and the only Lewis organ which remains to us in anything like its original condition. (Donations for essential work on the console to the Organ Appeal, 9A St Thomas Street, SE1.) A decorative gem is the Renatus Harris Organ in the Church of *St Sepulchre Without Newgate*. Both Wesleys certainly played it, and Handel and Mendelssohn probably did. It was built in 1667 and carries Charles II's monogram. Even more spectacular is the *Whitehall Organ,* removed to St James's, Piccadilly. For playing on, the new organ at *St Paul's Girls' School* is strongly recommended.

A fine collection of organs, including the only self-playing Wurlitzer in Europe, may be enjoyed (and played) at the *National Musical Museum* (368 High Street, Brentford, Middx; 01-560 8108). Also there is a grand selection of pianos and over 30,000 music rolls. Open Sats and Suns 2-5 p.m. April-October.

The best cinema organ used to be at the *Granada*, Tooting, but now it's eyes down for a full house. Autres temps, autres moeurs . . .

Best organ: the *Festival Hall*.

Owls

The only city-dwelling owls are the tawny ones, although these have been spotted as near the City Centre as Bloomsbury and South Kensington. Fiona Bateman is organising an Owl Prowl with the view of encouraging owls back to London and building up a dossier on those already here. So should you meet an owl tell it to contact Fiona at *London Wildlife Trust*, 1 Thorpe Close, W10 5XL (01-968 5368), or to phone the Owl phone line (01-670 6080).

It is never easy to buy owls from antique dealers. They are considered lucky and it's profitable to have one in the shop. Not so with peacocks – disastrous!

See also Birds, and Street Lights.

Best Owl: *Tawny* (no competition).

Oysters

We eat ten million oysters a year in Britain.

Sweeting's, Sheekey's, and *Wheeler's* branches in Old Compton Street, Duke of York Street and Frith Street all have specialised oyster bars. *Wheeler's* have their own oyster-beds in West Mersea, Essex. For details see under Fish Restaurants. Green's Champagne and Oyster Bar (35/36 Duke Street, SW1; 01-930 1383/1376) is for oysters, champagne – well, it's obvious – and the great British pudding. *Bentley's* (11-15 Swallow Street, W1; 01-734 4756) is traditional. *Rudland and Stubbs* (35/37 Greenhill Rents, Cowcross Street, EC1; 01-253 0148) is basic, old-fashioned and good. A correspondent writes on the subject of *Motcomb's* Wine Bar (26 Motcomb Street, SW1; 01-235 6382): 'The Colchester oysters were matchless, although so costly that I am embarrassed to repeat the price . . . all the young ladies looked like Princess Diana.'

Best Oysters: *Bentley's.*

Palaces

The story of London palaces should begin: 'Once upon a time . . .' Once upon a time in the 15th century Humphrey, Duke of Gloucester, built a palace on the banks of the Thames at Greenwich, and called it Placentia. Hither it was that Katherine of Aragon went to recover from marital disharmony, and here she was replaced by the young Anne Boleyn, and here it was that the King courted her. On the site stands Greenwich Naval College. Once upon a time *Winchester Palace* on Bankside was the home of the Bishops of Winchester. Now little remains beyond a rose window. The *Crystal Palace* is just a football team and a memory, the *Kennington Palace* is just a plaque on the wall; all that remains of *Whitehall Palace* is the (marvellous) Banqueting House, and all that remains of the *Palace of Sheen* (renamed Richmond Palace by Henry VII, the Earl of Richmond) is the gateway and a quantity of bricks, but that still leaves at least seven palaces more or less complete (or eight if you count *Greenwich*) viz *Kensington, Fulham, Lambeth, Westminster, Buckingham, St James's* and *Hampton Court.*

I am not alone in finding *Buckingham Palace* displeasing; everyone always has. Poor old John Nash. It could not have been easy working for George IV, and, after the king's death, the design was taken away from Nash and given to Edward Blore, although his work too was substantially altered in 1913 by Sir Aston Webb. The rudest commentator was von Raumer:

'For my part I would not live in it rent-free; I should vex myself all day long with the fantastic mixture of every style of architecture and decoration – the absence of all pure taste – the total want of feeling of measure and proportion. The grand apartments of the principal story are adorned with pillars; but what kind of pillars? Partly red, like raw sausages; partly blue, like starch – bad imitations of marbles which nobody ever saw, standing upon blocks, which art rejects, to support nobody knows what . . .' and so on.

Each of the others has something to recommend it. *Lambeth Palace* has been the London home of the Archbishops of Canterbury since

1197. Most of the buildings are of the 15th and 16th centuries, though the chapel and crypt are older. The Great Hall houses a famous ecclesiastical library (q.v.). Then there are the fig trees and a wonderful hammerbeam roof. *Kensington Palace* has its ornate Cupola Room, decorated by Kent, and the state bedroom, in which Victoria passed so much of her lonely childhood (her toys and the cradle she slept in are on view). *Fulham Palace*, where the bishops of London bishopped, has a pleasant public garden in what once was the moat, but it is becoming an embarrassment to the local authority. *St James's Palace* was originally an asylum for 'Maidens that were lepers living chastely and honestly in divine service', and although Charles II, James II, Queen Mary and Queen Anne were all born here, all preferred to live at *Whitehall Palace*, burned down in 1698. *St James's Palace* has a wonderful musical tradition, counting Tallis, Byrd, Orlando Gibbons, Purcell, Boyce and Sullivan amongst its choristers and organists. It also has a splendid clock tower. The *Palace of Westminster* has the cheapest beer in London, and *Hampton Court*, well *Hampton Court* apart from the maze and the gardens and the orangery and the tennis courts and the wrought iron and the letter box has chimneys like sticks of liquorice as created by a paranoid schizophrenic.

Just a mention of *Eltham Palace*, now the headquarters of the Institute of Army Education. Just off the A2 London to Rochester road it has a splendid chestnut hammerbeam roof (restored), and a moat with a medieval bridge across it, and a wonderful old brick wall.

Best palace: *Lambeth*.
Worst palace: *Buckingham*.

P.S. Read *Private Palaces of London* by E. B. Chancellor (1908).

Parking Meters

Now the parking meters picket and pick the Georgian locks and invisible
Meters tall as the yellowing trees docket and dock our history,
Though Charles James Fox unconcerned in a bath towel sits on his arse in Bloomsbury Square
While plane tree leaves flop gently down and lodge in his sculptured hair.

from *October in Bloomsbury* by Louis Macneice (1907-1963)

I have just been clamped and it is not pleasant. Expensive (£55), time consuming, and humiliating. Nonetheless it is effective and conditions in the West End, and particularly in those areas, such as Bond Street, in which the clamp patrols operate, have improved. In the first two years of the clamping operation 86,000 motorists were clamped. In response to the clamps a Mr Michael Green started the Car Clamp Recovery Club. If you're clamped, a team of motorcyclists pay your unclamping fee, then wait by the car to contact you as soon as it's unclamped. The cost to members of the Club is £25 per year plus £5 whenever they use the service.

If you wish to buy your own personal clamp, a Mr Ted Raine sells the Autoclamp for £86.25 inc VAT (Sadly I can't give you his address because I don't have it). Useful to avoid your car being stolen. Useful, I suppose, to avoid being clamped, because I doubt whether even the most resolute clamper would double-clamp.

In meter areas there are various devices which have proved successful in the battle against fines. The rottenest of these is the removal of a ticket from a nearby car and the putting of it on *your* car's windscreen. Notices such as 'Wife Having Baby – Sorry' or 'Delivering Double Bass to Chief Constable' are often treated with the contempt they deserve by the wardens, who are known in Paris, incidentally, as the Periwinkles, from the distinctive colour of their uniforms. The friendliest London periwinkle is the smiling lady in *Long Acre* who used to operate outside Harvey's Auction Rooms before they removed to Neal Street. It was always a pleasure doing business with her. There used to be a dead ringer for Marilyn Monroe operating in *Hammersmith Broadway* where they could keep an eye on her from the upstairs window of the Hammersmith Police Station. Where is she now? An equally pretty periwinkle operates at the *South Ken* end of the *Old Brompton Road*, but she has no humanity in her deep-frozen heart. If you do get ticketed it is unwise to pay the fine at once. A high percentage of parking tickets get permanently gummed up in the bureaucratic works.

By the way, 1985 was the 25th anniversary of the London meter maids.

You are most likely to get away with it in *St John's Wood, Finsbury Circus*, and *Rugby Street*, WC1. The riskiest areas are *Lincoln's Inn Fields, Pelham Street, Richmond Green, Essex Street* (disastrous), *Bond Street* (horrific), *Mayfair*, and *Doughty Street*, WC1, where Dickens lived. Here hoards of traffic wardens duck out of sight whenever they see a motorist likely to park illegally; what ensues thereafter makes the Alamo seem like coffee-time at the Mothers' Union.

Best parking meters: (least attended) *St John's Wood*.
Worst parking meters: (most attended) *Essex Street*, WC2.

203

Parks

If you call *Epping Forest* a park, then at 5,600 acres it is easily the largest in the Greater London area. Thereafter in diminishing dimensions we find *Richmond Park* (2469 acres), *Wimbledon* and *Putney Commons* (1178 acres), and *Hampstead Heath*, including *Kenwood* and *Parliament Hill Fields* (800 acres). The smallest are *Highgate Woods* (70 acres), *Green Park* (53 acres) and *Waterlow Park* (26 acres), but there are also the tiddlers such as the *David Copperfield Gardens*, New Kent Road, *Bethnal Green Gardens, Cannizaro Park*, Wimbledon, *Kelsey Park*, Beckenham, and so on. In mid-summer London from the air appears to be one big park.

It is more difficult to think of areas without parks than of parks themselves.

First the sad ones. It's hard to find anything encouraging about *Finsbury Park, Shepherd's Bush Green, Shoreditch Park, Brockwell Park* (OK for tobogganning), the *Rookery*, Streatham Common – a pretty name though – or *Gunnersbury Park*. One walks sadly in them head lowered to avoid the turds; this is no way to be in parks.

But then consider the glories of *Regent's Park*, which originally contained 'wooded glades and lairs of wild beasts, deer, both red and fallow, wild bulls and boars'. Study the roses, the water, the bandstand, and the general air of privilege and power.

Hyde Park was once Henry VIII's deerpark, then a popular race-course, a duelling ground, the site for the Great Exhibition, and a training ground for demagogues. It has a bird sanctuary and some fine statues. *Kensington Gardens* which adjoins it is best bib and tucker – *Green Park* and *Hyde Park* are more suitable for courting in. *Holland Park* is to do with a hill and the remains of a fine house and an open-air theatre and a fine avenue of trees. *St James's Park* has herons and mallards and guards being changed and diplomats taking the air. James I had camels (an unusual gift from the King of Spain) grazing there. As with the rather boring *Green Park*, there's too much walking through it and not enough lounging around in it.

People are possessive about the smaller parks. *Waterlow Park* (29 acres) is delightful. There's a lake set amidst woods, and concerts, flowers, tennis courts, and a bowling green. Refreshments are served in the splendid *Lauderdale Park*. *Pymmes Park* (53 acres), Edmonton, is marvellously rustic (another lake) especially when you consider how adjacent it is to the horrid North Circular. Edmonton is a literate suburb. John Gilpin's Bell Inn is there, Charles and Mary Lamb are buried in the parish churchyard, and lived in – wait for it!

– Lamb's Cottage, while in Church Street Keats served his apprenticeship to a local surgeon. Keats had just finished his student days at Guy's and must have enjoyed the fresh air. *Clissold Park* (55 acres), Stoke Newington, is equally charming. A correspondent expresses it more vividly: 'This park is clean (or was when I lived there), spacious, and has a nice clientele, mainly yer trendy Highbury-ites.' My own local park is *Marble Hill*, Twickenham, with a historic tree (q.v.) and squirrels and birds that eat from your hand. *South Park*, Fulham, is used and loved by all Fulhamites, who are engaged in fighting the threats of the Hammersmith bureaucrats as I type these words. *Greenwich Park* has everything to recommend it, the spectacular view over the river to the City, but Greenwich residents often prefer the lesser known *Cutty Sark Gardens*, where concerts and children's shows add to the gaiety of the nation. *Golders Hill Park* is also very much for the residents, with tennis courts, excellent refreshments, a secluded garden and deer, though nothing like as prolific as the deer in the magnificent *Richmond Park*. *Battersea Park* belongs too much to some of the people – the violent ones – and consequently too little to the others. Which is a shame because it has a fine history. It was laid out by Sir James Pennethorne, Nash's pupil, and boasts such features as a 16 acre lake, a flower garden, a children's zoo, and much else, especially for children. It is the site for the annual Easter Parade, for the Royal Tournament march past, and provides concerts at the Pavilion in North Carriage Drive. It is also the first park to take dog dirt seriously. Brown cardboard scoops are issued free by the Council to dog-owners with a special red bin for what is in the scoops.

But I have no hesitation in nominating *Regent's Park* as the finest in London. Indeed on a fine summer's day I can imagine no nicer place in the world than *Regent's Park*, and on a murky February evening during the Friday rush hour I can imagine few places more dispiriting than *Shepherd's Bush Green*.

Best Park: *Regent's Park*.
Worst Park: *Shoreditch Park* (*Shepherd's Bush Green* being too small to qualify).

For details of entertainments in the Royal Parks in the summer telephone: 01-212 3434; for entertainments in the other parks try: 01-633 1707. For a full review read Hunter Davies's book, *A Walk Round London's Parks*, or *The Royal Parks of London* by Richard Church (1956).

Pasta

To enjoy pasta's flavour to the full you should properly eat it 'al burro' (served with just butter and black pepper) accompanied by a bottle of classic Chianti and a crisp green salad. The most inventive variations on this delicious staple may be enjoyed at the following, who, I believe, only serve home-made pasta:

Antipasto e Pasta (511 Battersea Park Road, SW11; 01-223 9765). Gleaming and cheerful with fresh flowers and waiters on and at the tables. Friendly, but slipshod.

Beccofino (100 Draycott Avenue, SW3; 01-584 3600). Cool and attractive middle-range Italian restaurant.

La Bersaghiera (372 King's Road, SW3; 01-352 5993). Very King's Road, very popular, very good.

La Botte (266 Watford Way, NW4; 01-203 4533). Splendid, informal, modest place.

La Capannina (24 Romilly Street, W1; 01-437 2743) is old-established, jolly, crowded and unfashionable. The pasta is superb.

Flavio's (1A Langton Street, SW10; 01-352 7414/7517). Intimate, classy and pricey.

Pasta Fino (27 Frith Street, W1; 01-439 8900). Innovative and the best. Wonderful brown and rainbow spaghetti, a wide choice of sauces with regional specialities. Prices moderate. Take away available.

Pasta Pasta see under Take Away.

Pastificio (various suburban branches at Ealing, Windsor, Wimbledon, Epsom, Kingston and Sutton). Berni Inns go Latin. Specialities include Fettuccine and Lasagne. Better than you might expect. Inexpensive.

Pasta Underground (46 Camden High Street, NW1; 01-482 0410). A pink basement with other dishes besides pasta.

San Martino (103 Walton Street, SW3; 01-589 3833/1356). Spaghetti San Martino (cooked in a paper bag with shellfish, garlic, parsley and pepper) was invented by Alfredo, who passed on his secrets to Giancarlo, his second-in-command. But all the food is excellent with glorious wine from Montepulciano. ('Noble', the Tuscans call it; so it is.) Goldfish in the ladies' lavatory (q.v.).

Solopasta (26 Liverpool Road, N1; 01-350 7648). Limited choice of pasta, but all recommended. So is the garlic bread. Cheap.

La Tartaruga (212 West End Lane, NW6; 01-431 2891). Authentic, 'typical', with as much as you can eat of the pasta of the day for £2.50. (Closed Sundays and Mondays.)

Trattoria Cappuccetto (17 Moor Street, W1; 01-437 2527). Start with Tortelloni Alberto and see if you've room for anything else. Moderately priced and charming.

Valentino's (147 Green Lanes, N13; 01-889 1847). Fettucine alla panna is the speciality, but choose in confidence. Include the house wine and the garlic bread.

Not included are the following – details under Italian Restaurants: *Amalfi, Covent Garden Pasta Bar, Pasta Connection* and the *Spaghetti House* branches.

Pasta on the Hill (3/5 Hill Road, W8; 01-938 1830) and *Pasta on the Piazza* (39 King Street, WC2; 01-240 2939) include pasta amongst other items on a long menu. Attractive in a rather cocktaily way.

To buy your pasta for home-cooking, there are several excellent places in Fulham and Chelsea, but I would recommend the old-timers: *Lina Stores, O Bellusci, La Ciocciara, Gazzano's* and *Terroni's* (details of all under Delicatessens/Grocers).

Best Pasta Restaurant: *La Capannina.*

Peacocks

There are peacocks at the *Belvedere Restaurant* (which also incorporates *The Fisherman's Wharf* restaurant), Holland Park, W8; (01-602 1238). They are arrogantly tame and live on steak, strawberries and dry-roasted nuts. A stuffed peacock guards the banisters at Leighton House. More plebeian peacocks (three of them) strut about the garden of the *Prince of Wales* pub (37 Fortune Green Road, NW6; 01-435 0653), and lounge around the animal enclosure in Clissold Park, N4. There are white peacocks in the enclosure at *Golders Hill Park*. The peacocks at *Chessington* and *London* zoos are less willing to display their tails than those at *Whipsnade*. If you want to buy a peacock, *Palmers* (33-37 Parkway, NW1; 01-485 5163) is your best bet; *Harrods* used to be able to help you. I expect there are peacocks at the *Peacock Club*, 225 Streatham High Road, SW16 (01-769 3300), but I haven't yet visited it.

I can't recommend best or worst peacocks. They are volatile creatures, and by the time you read this they may be quite altered.

Antique dealers regard peacocks as unlucky, and don't care to stock them. Owls (q.v.) on the other hand bring great good fortune.

Pens and Pen Nibs

> They come as a boon and a blessing to men
> The Pickwick, the Owl and the Waverley Pen.

Thus runs the centrepiece in what is one of the most remarkable window displays in London – at *Philip Poole & Co. Ltd* (182 Drury Lane, WC2; 01-405 7097). Prominently on view is a display of William Mitchell pen nibs against a stained glass catafalque – the whole a bit like a miniature Wurlitzer organ. The window, lit flickeringly at night by gas, is an unforgettable monument to The Pen. Mr Poole, known I expect as His Nibs, has a stock running into millions and many of the nibs have marvellous names such as the Figaro, the Times, the Empress, the Flying Dutchman, and others. Some are shaped like a human hand or the Eiffel Tower. The best buy must be the Time Is Money pen which 'may be left in the ink-pot' and does not 'flood, choke, splutter or need shaking'. Despite the obvious claims of the admirable *Wheatsheaf Art Shop* (76-78 Neal Street, WC2; 01-836 7186/01-379 7215), you would be callous indeed not to patronise . . .

Best pen shop: *Philip Poole & Co. Ltd.*

Perfumes

Two hugely traditional parfumiers with impressively contemporary outlooks are *Floris* and *Penhaligon's*.

Floris (89 Jermyn Street, SW1; 01-930 2885). Closed Saturdays, Sundays. Has been parfumier to the Court of St James's since 1730. Here you will be tempted to buy English essences (red rose, honeysuckle, lily of the valley, stephanotis and so, idyllically, on), with a few special preparations for men (lime, the rather mysterious 'Number 89', and the even more mysterious 'Special Number 127'). A seventh generation shop, where your change, should you bother about such petty matters, is handed to you on a velvet cushion.

Penhaligon's (55 Burlington Arcade, W1; 01-629 1416), with branches at 20a Brook Street, W1 and 44 Wellington Street, WC2). William Penhaligon was Baker to Queen Victoria's court and *Penhaligons* still use the recipes from William's own notebook. An interesting collection of antique scent bottles and dressing-table furnishings is also on display.

And one less traditional parfumier: *Les Senteurs* (227 Ebury Street,

SW1; 01-730 2322) which is the exclusive stocking for Anmick Gouval's range. This includes Heure Exquise, 'a stunning rose and iris with only the faintest sandalwood base to make it warm and sensuous'. They also stock Eau de Monsieur (Mister's Water) which is crisp and woody and based, I'm relieved to discover, on bergamot and cedar-wood.

Best Perfumes: *Floris.*

Pets

No sooner do fish pass my threshold than they give a little sigh and turn their toes to the stars. We no longer want them in the house, although we do have two dogs, two hamsters, a guinea pig, and many silverfish. But for those who do a visit to *Palmer's Animal Fair*, or *King Fisheries* is called for.

Palmer's (33-37 Parkway, NW1; 01-485 5163) is an exotic pet shop, where you may find, between the talking parrot and the red-kneed bird-eating spider, your required fish. If you don't, *Animal Fair* (17 Abingdon Road, W8; 01-937 0011) may be relied upon to be helpful with puppies, kittens and white mice as well as tropical fish. But the specialists are *King Fisheries* (Tropical and Marine Fish) of Beckenham. This is a fascinating place with healthy fish and knowledgeable staff; furthermore they will buy back at half price any fish which you buy from them and with whom you don't hit it off. But if you're not snobbish about where your pets come from visit *Battersea Dogs' Home* (see Dogs) or phone the *Cats' Protection League* (see Cats). Or buy *Exchange and Mart* which has an extensive Animals Section.

Best Pet Shop: *Palmer's.*

Pillar Boxes

> The pillar box is big and red,
> Its mouth is open wide,
> It wears a tammy on its head,
> It must be dark inside!
>
> Rose Fyldeman.

The redness of its pillar boxes and telephone booths was the best thing which the GPO had to offer a weary world, and it was crass beyond belief when the newly formed British Telecom (what can you expect from a body with a name like that?) decided to paint its booths yellow. Fortunately they have not yet got around to pillar boxes.

My favourite pillar box is built into the ancient walls of *Hampton Court Palace*. I like to feel that Cardinal Wolsey used it to pop a card in the post to Henry but I don't suppose he did.

All pillar box designs have been successful although none has quite come up to the octagonal Victorian pillar box, a fine example of which may be seen on the corner of Bedford Road and The Orchard in *Bedford Park*, Chiswick. Even the Royal monograms are a pleasure to look at.

Eccentricities abound. In *St Paul's Churchyard* is a double box reminiscent of those conjurors' cupboards in which spangled ladies disappear and reappear, and there is a handsome Victorian one set into the old brickwork of *3 Hampstead Lane*, N6. But almost every pillar box is a happy marriage between the arts and the sciences. If only they cleared them more often.

Best pillar box: *Hampton Court Palace*.

P.S. It may be worth remarking that old telephone booths retail at a cool £200. Why? Because they make ideal shower booths.

Pipes etc

> Give a man a pipe he can smoke
> Give a man a book he can read,
> And his home is filled with a calm delight
> Though the room be poor indeed.

Alfred Dunhill

The meerschaum is so called from its likeness to petrified sea-foam ('*l'écume de mer*'), and in the old days as a captain in the Guards you would have had a young subaltern smoke one in for you. Now you visit *Astley's* (109 Jermyn Street, SW1; 01-930 1687) for antique meerschaums which don't need to be run in. *Smokes* (24 Upper Street, N1; 01-226 0266) specialise in tobaccos, cigars and imported cigarettes, but for lovers of the Turkish, *Sullivan Powell* (34 Burlington Arcade, W1; 01-629 0433) is the place. Snuff boxes may be elegantly purchased from *Eric Graus* (125 New Bond Street, W1; 01-629 6680), or from *S. J. Phillips* (139 New Bond Street, W1; 01-629 6261) where the directors' lunches served in the basement are a great comfort to the afflicted soul. *T. H. Gilbert* (11 Gray's-in-the-Mews, Davies Street, W1; 01-408 0028) has nice pipes, but knows how to charge for them.

Nathan's Pipe Shop (60 Hill Rise, Richmond, Surrey; 01-940 2404) is a little like a pipe shop in a Beatrix Potter book – very pretty. At *Alfred Dunhill* (30 Duke Street, St James's, SW1; 01-499 9566) you are in the presence of the experts, but can see your money go up in smoke too. *Desmond Sautter's Pipe Shop* (91 Piccadilly, W1; 01-499 4319 and three branches) will actually repair pipes; to a pipe-smoker that is really something. *Astley's* also repair them but charge more.

A correspondent, who has been a pipe-smoker for more than a quarter of a century and is therefore a man of discernment and integrity writes as follows: 'The most interesting pipe shop in London is that of *S. W. Sims* in Junction Road, N19. He is one of the few remaining pipe-makers in England, and the old man who runs this marvellous musty shop with his sister could well invite you into his sanctuary once you have established yourself as a regular customer. There he makes the most superb pipes for all the big firms like Bewlays, Comoy etc, who promptly charge four times as much as he does when they shove their own insignia on to the stems.'

Best Pipe Shop: *S. W. Sims.*

Pizzas

The numerous pizza chains, of which the most popular is the *Pizza Hut* (various branches), and *Pizzaland* (various branches) and the *Deep Pan Pizza Company* (various branches), provide pretty horrible food at reasonable prices. The food is bound to be horrible because the thick and substantial base and crust of their pizzas sits on the stomach like the concrete pile of a motorway. The imaginative variety of the fillings becomes irrelevant, though the deep toppings (contradiction in terms) help somewhat.

The *Pizza Express* chain (see under Jazz), which has branches in Coptic Street, WC1; Dean Street, W1; and Knightsbridge, SW1; (01-636 3232, 01-437 9595, and 01-235 5550 respectively) serve pizzas which are significantly better than average, though it's the atmosphere and the music you go for, not the food.

Now three specialists:

Pizzeria Amalfi (107 Southampton Row, WC1; 01-636 5811). Uncomfortably close to a branch of *Pizzaland* (see above), one might think. The interesting feature is the Calzone – a folded pizza, or Italian pancake.
Pizza The Action (678 Fulham Road, SW6; 01-736 2716). Attractive, and juicy pizzas.

Pizzeria Castello (5 Walworth Road, SE7; 01-703 2556). Wittily named after the Elephant and Castle. A correspondent, bubbling with enthusiasm, tells me that the pizzas there are 'the best in the world'. He adds 'Norman Fowler and the Mandarins from the DHSS across the road eat there, although I am not sure if this constitutes a recommendation. Queuing is mandatory, even if you book. Since spending over £5 a head is difficult, it could also qualify as a budget restaurant.'

See also Italian Restaurants.

Best Pizzas: *Pizzeria Castello*.

Poetry

My friend, Alan Jackson, believes that poetry should be made illegal, and that all poets who persist in writing the stuff should be sent to prison where at least they would be fed and housed and encouraged to suffer, thus deepening and enlarging the scope of their poetry.

In the meantime there are occasional poetry competitions – the biggest being those run by the Cheltenham Festival and the Arvon Foundation.

Poets may be hired from the *London Poetry Secretariat* (25 Tavistock Place, WC1; 01-388 2211). Fees range from £40 upwards, depending upon the poet's rating in the charts and whether they have won either of the above competitions. The best meld is one established poet and one young hungry one.

The *National Sound Archive* at the British Institute of Recorded Sound (29 Exhibition Road, SW7; 01-589 6603) holds one of the largest collections of recorded literature in the world, including Brecht giving evidence to the Un-American Activities Committee, Tennyson reciting *The Charge of the Light Brigade*, and the only recording of Sylvia Plath – just three of the treasures. Also available in record shops are spoken word recordings by Argo, Caedmon, Listen (especially Stevie Smith) and Stream, who produced a recording of Basil Bunting reading his superb *Briggflats*.

The *Poetry Society and Centre* (21 Earl's Court Square, SW5; 01-373 7861) has useful facilities for poets and a 'critical service' which will analyse your poem for a fee. Try sending them a little-known work by Andrew Marvell, appending your name to it, and . . .

The *Arts Council Library* (9 Long Acre, WC2; 01-379 6597) is well worth an afternoon and the *Association of Little Presses* (262 Randolph Avenue, W9; 01-824 8565) can give you all the information that you need about magazines which publish poetry, and have produced an excellent guide: *Getting your Poetry Published* (20p excluding postage). But avoid publishers who require a fee to publish your verses.

Poet's Corner in Westminster Abbey is where poets who have been mocked and starved during their lifetimes are honoured in perpetuity. In the South Transept it includes Wordsworth in a dressing gown and Dr Johnson splendidly sculpted by Nollekens. Said Johnson of this bust: 'I think my friend, Joe Nollekens, can chop out a head with any of them'.

An engaging anthology of London poetry is: *London between the Lines* compiled by John Bishop and Virginia Broadbent. (Simon Publications 1973).

Of the venues where poetry is regularly read and appreciated try *Riverside Studios*, Crisp Road, W6 (01-748 3354), the *Waterman's Arms*, 40 High Street, Brentford, Middlesex and the *Arts Centres* (q.v.). At the *Waterman's Arms* there is a writer-in-residence, Robert Rankin, who organises such things and might discuss your poems.

Pubs include the *New Royal Oak*, 120 Whitechapel Road, E1 (01-533 1638), the *Chestnut Tree*, Lea Bridge Road, E17 (10-527 8750) and the *White Swan*, New Row, WC2; (01-340 6224).

The following is a list of the more active poets' workshops in the London area. A list of local workshops and writers' groups is available in your local public library.

It is advisable to telephone the organisers of these before turning up.

(a) North London
Black Writers Workshop (Jenake Arts, 49 Balls Pond Road, N1; 01-249 6062). 3 p.m. Sundays, led by Adziko Simba.
Mill Lane Group (62 Mill Lane, NW6). Weekly on Fridays at 7.30. Telephone 01-624 8603 in the evenings.
Pentameters Theatre (above the Three Horseshoes, Heath Street, NW3, 01-435 6757).
Thurlow Road Poetry Workshop (20 Thurlow Road, NW2; 01-435 6806). 6.30 Wednesdays.

(b) East London
The Clinker (Crown and Castle, 600 Kingsland Road, E8; 01-249 2510). Poets, musicians and film-makers.
Stratford Poets (at the Tom Allen Centre, Grove Crescent Road, E15; 01-504 6306/586 5832). Mondays at 8 p.m.
Basement Writers (Basement, Old Town Hall, Cable Street, E1). Tuesdays at 8 p.m.
Ignition Poets (155 Hassett Road, E9; 01-985 6882). Tuesdays.

(c) South London
Poetry South East London (90 Mycenae Road, SE3; 01-852 9704). Thursdays fortnightly 8 p.m.
Writers Workshop (Clapham Community Centre, St Anne's Hall, Venn Street, SW4; 01-622 2042). Wednesdays at 7.30 p.m.

(d) West London
Richmond Writers' Circle (Richmond Adult Colleges, Parkshot, Richmond, Surrey; 01-994 0842). Wednesdays, 8 p.m.

Polish Food

I only know of three Polish restaurants in London and I can only pronounce one of them. The two, which I shall do my best to spell, at least, are *Lowiczanka* – upstairs at 238/246 King's Street, W6 (01-741 3225) and *Ognisko Polskie*, 55 Exhibition Road, SW7 (01-589 4670). The first is a branch of the Polish Social and Cultural Centre; the second a club for expatriate Poles – though open to all. At both you will be well fed and looked after and will stagger into the sunlight, because Polish food, which includes plenty of beef and rice and cabbage and buckwheat, is certainly substantial.

The third is *Daquise*, 20 Thurloe Street, SW7 (01-589 6117), about as near to the atmosphere of a pre-war café in Warsaw as you are likely to find west of Berlin. Chess is played. As to why so many Poles live in a square bounded by Hammersmith, Olympia, South Kensington and Fulham I await an answer from a Polish reader. They certainly enrich the lives of others living there, as I once did.

Additionally there is *555* (555 Battersea Park Road, SW11 (01-228 7011/5643) which is sort of Polish/Slavic and cooked by a most genial Irish woman called Vera; it is usually crowded and no wonder. Strongly recommended by (among others) an osteopath. So there.

Best Polish Food: (sort of) *555*.

Ponds

Attentive readers will already have noticed references to ponds under such disparate entries as Model Boats and Parks. Here I shall just deal with ponds qua ponds. As the purpose of a pond – well, it has no purpose, except as William Allingham (1828-1889) expressed it:

Four ducks on a pond,
A grass-bank beyond,
A blue sky of spring,
White clouds on the wing:
What a little thing
To remember for years –
To remember with tears!

So there is the *Princess of Wales Pond*, which I *have* mentioned elsewhere, but which, standing where it does on bleak Blackheath, helps to give a human dimension to the scene. And there is *Peter Pan's Pond*, which used to be called Southend Pond before Peter and Wendy and Tinkerbell entered the collective subconscious (with dire results, I suspect, but that's another story and another book). Well, this is the Pond where you turn off the main road, Catford to Bromley, for Beckenham. It's not just a pond, more a feature, so local people will direct you via it with some pride. And then on Wimbledon Common there is *Queen's Mere*, near the windmill and best approached from it. *Queen's Mere*, a rather sinister man-made hollow with misleading acoustics. *King's Mere*, not too far away, is natural, and more like a lake than a pond, with swans on it, and the ghostly ripples of ghostly duellists who stood square on to their opponents and shot crooked.

Carshalton Ponds are highly decorative with magnificent trees and stockbrokers all around but I believe they are not really ponds at all, but bits of the River (q.v.) Wandle, so I shan't count them.

Oh by the way, should you have a pond which is giving you trouble, a new company called *The Pondlife Company*, formed by Philip Andover, a biologist, and Jane Carey, a zoologist, is in Upper Norwood. Their business is to build and stock freshwater ponds, and very successfully they are doing it.

Best Pond: *King's Mere*, Wimbledon Common.

Post Offices

The *Dulwich Post Office* sells knitting patterns and knicker elastic along with the latest commemoratives. *Kew's* post office in the station precinct is like a little brick gazebo, bright blue with a red letter box.

Lisson Grove Post Office is well sited. It is opposite the Actors' Labour Exchange and Phillips' Marylebone auction rooms. On Friday mornings there is a lot of action in Lisson Grove. The post office itself is minute and crowded with notices about colorado beetle and such adorning walls. It conjures up an age when London still consisted of village communities, when people went to the post office for a gossip. The Ugandan Asians who run so many of the suburban post offices are competent, kind-hearted and industrious, but they are not yet very good at gossip.

But in terms of quaintness, you have to rate *Parkfield Stores*, on the corner of Upper Richmond Road, SW15 and Parkfields. From the road all that is visible is a delicatessen (q.v.) and rather a good one, but at the rear of the store is a Post Office Counter, and all that goes with it. Highly countrified.

The *Trafalgar Square* branch office (22-28 William IV Street, WC2 – alongside St Martin-in-the-Fields) is open from 8 a.m. to 8 p.m. on weekdays and from 10 a.m. to 5 p.m. on Sundays for telephone, telegraph business, and the sale of stamps. The *Chief Post Office* is in King Edward Street and has a 150-feet counter. It also contains the National Postal Museum (see under Stamps) and is opposite the Postal Headquarters Building. Adjacent too is the statue to Rowland Hill, responsible for the whole thing, and the Postman's Park. Beneath the post office is the Post Office Railway, which runs between Whitechapel and Paddington by a circuitous route. It conveys 40,000 mailbags a day at 35 mph, which is a lot of letters per foot per second.

Best post office: *Lisson Grove.*

P.S. Now the GPO has been privatised, and the red is turning sickly yellow, one trembles in one's shoes at the probable fate of tiny sub-post offices throughout London.

Prostitutes

Men are all right so long as they are regularly despunked. If they're not getting their oats, they're bloody pests.

Cynthia Payne

Nearly 2,000 women a year are convicted of prostitution (a 'common prostitute' can be picked up for loitering or soliciting after three cautions), but the Street Offences (or kerb-crawling) bill is so hard to administer that few men in search of their oats will get arrested and even fewer charged. The law is absurd in any case. It permits prostitution but not if there are two or more girls in the room, in which case it's a brothel, nor if the prostitute's husband or boyfriend takes the money (pimping) nor if the girl or boy solicits openly on the street.

A spanking parlour is only illegal if more than one person is operating it, and so on.

Prostitutes have been back on the London street in force, particularly since the Yorkshire Ripper terrified so many girls into coming south. And still they come, though now they are known as Thatcher's Girls, because they claim that it is unemployment forcing them to it.

Many prostitutes work through advertisements for 'escorts' in men's magazines. But the classiest pros operate from smart hotels; sit in the lobby or at the bar and if they think you can afford them they will approach you. Recent British Rail concessions have made it profitable for parties of prostitutes to come up to town from South Wales at excursion rates. There must be a television play in that! The saddest girls operate from 'walk-ups' (small upstairs flats usually in *Soho*). If you press the bell saying 'Linda – Model with Large Chest' you will find yourself negotiating with the 'maid' before you meet Linda by which time it may well be too late. 'Clippies' who take your money and give nothing in return, operate from *Soho* streets, in particular *Peter Street, Meard Street, Bateman Street, Greek Street, Archer Street*, and *Great Windmill Street*. A better class of prostitute (i.e. more expensive) may be observed in *Bourdon Street* and in the area contained within *Curzon Street, Half Moon Street, Piccadilly* and *Park Lane*. But as a general rule *Soho* is where you get clipped, *Mayfair* is where you get laid, and the suburbs along the trunk roads used by the truck drivers are where you get VD. Or worse. The *King's Cross* area has been cleared, and many of the kids now operate around the railway stations. Some of them are main-lining. It's tragic. Women in search of toy-boys used to have some success at *Fortnum's Fountain*, which has been disastrously 'done up'. I don't suppose Les Boys are still there now. Maybe the small ads in *Playgirl* . . .?

A hint: If you must pay the girl or boy in advance, tear the note/notes in half. Give him/her half and promise the other half after you've been despunked. This ensures good faith on both sides.

See also under Brothels and Night Clubs.

Protection Agencies

Over and above the usual firms, such as *Chubb's Security* (69 St James's Street) housed in a fine old building with barley sugar-twist pillars to the shop windows revealing hideous office furniture within, which you will readily find in the yellow pages, there is a new agency called *Krayleigh & Co.* in Cleveland Way, just off the Mile End Road. If the Kray Twins, Ronnie and Reggie, who are behind the venture (and bars for a while yet) cannot protect you, who can? You have no recourse but to look under Gunsmiths (q.v.)

A robot security man called PROWLER (Programmable Robot Observer with Logical Enemy Response) has been developed and two have been sold for £250,000 each. It can kill an intruder *without* a direct command from a human being. If you are fascinated by this whole area subscribe to Security Letter, 166E 96th Street, New York 10128 which will bring you up to date.

Publishers

Odd and alarming things have been happening within the London publishing business. As merger has followed merger and the dust clears it becomes apparent that 50% of British publishing is now in the hands of just eight companies. The biggest three, being the *Pearson Longman* group, the *Octopus Heinemann* group, and the *Collins* group are responsible for about a third of all turnover. The effect of this trend will be to reduce an author's options and therefore, in due course, his/her royalties. It seems (and is) a long time ago that my first publisher paid me a modest advance on my first novel and then had me to dinner regularly to read him the chapters I had written. In comparison with which the ranks of editors I once saw in a New York sky-scraper was a traumatic moment. 'But what do they all *do?*' I asked. But secretly I knew. They *rewrote*. Not a word against publishers however will I put in this book. They are wonderful people, truly patient, generous to a fault, and inevitably punctual with their payments. The only question is which is the *most* wonderful, the *most* patient, the *most* generous, the *most* punctual, and to that question there can be but a single answer . . .

Best London Publisher: *Sphere*.

Pubs

For a full survey of this subject see the *London Pub Guide* compiled by Judy Allen (Robert Nicholson Publications). Or telephone the *Pub Information Centre* (01-222 3232) for up-to-date news.

First the licensing laws. These allow drinking in pubs between 11 a.m. and 3 p.m. and between 5.30 p.m. and 11 p.m., but in the City of

London the evening drinking hours are usually between 5 p.m. and 8 p.m. On Sundays one may drink in pubs between noon and 2 p.m. and between 7 p.m. and 10.30 p.m. There are exceptions and, where food is served, drink may accompany a meal. It is quite possible that these hours will soon be changed and an early experiment has permitted drinking in pubs along the Old Kent Road until 2 a.m. The experiment has not been an official one, but has been brought about by a logical application of the regular extension system by determined landlords. The result, which points up the absurdity of the present system, may bring about its demise.

In 1831 there was a pub in London to every 168 people; in 1931 there was a pub to every 535 people, and now it is a pub to every 600 people. A hundred years ago every town had its own brewery, a different bitter in each village. It was a matter of local pride. There were 16,000 breweries in Britain. Now there are 130.

I shall divide pubs into the following categories:

(a) Real ale pubs
(b) Riverside pubs
(c) Pubs with entertainment
(d) Gay pubs
(e) Straight pubs
(f) Pub food

(a) Real Ale pubs

The Campaign for Real Ale (CAMRA) has been astonishingly successful. Not only has it promoted the re-introduction of real ales even in pubs tied to the big breweries, but it has started running its own pubs. One such is *The Nag's Head* (79-81 Heath Street, NW3; 01-435 4108) and here you can pamper yourself with exotic brews like Brakespeare's Bitter, Green King Abbott Ale, Wadsworth 6X, Gale's HSB, Sam Smith's Old Brewery Bitter, Ruddles' Country and Simon's Tower Bridge Bitter. The *Windsor Castle* (The Walk, Church Lane, N2; 01-883 5763) stocks fifteen real ales on a rota of seven pumps; there's also a large walled garden for the children. The *Hole in the Wall*, 5 Mepham Street, SE1 (01-928 6196) has eight real ales in stock, including Godson's. Try ordering Red Barrel in this fanatical place and you'll end up in a barrel. The *Wall* and the *Hole* are adjacent to Waterloo Station.

The *Crown* (24 Aberdeen Place, NW8; 01-289 1102) has six real ales, a ghost, and live entertainment, while at the *Worcester Arms* (89 George Street, W1; 01-935 6040) there is a guest 'beer of the month'. The *Man in the Moon* (392 King's Road, SW3; 01-352 5075) is a theatrical pub with beautifully engraved glass for the actors to look at themselves in, and five real ales. Another fantasy in glass, with real ale to boot (nine varieties) is the enchantingly Victorian *Princess Louise* (208-209 High Holborn, WC1; 01-405 8816). The *Lamb* (94 Lamb's Conduit Street, WC1; 01-405 0713) is a Bloomsbury Young's pub with gorgeously engraved glass snob screens and sepia fin de siècle celebrities on the wall. The *Sun Inn* (63 Lamb's Conduit Street, WC1; 01-405 8278), just down the road from the *Lamb*, has vast cellars awash with real ale – seventy varieties, some say, but no one has lived to tell the tale – and twenty varieties on tap. This is what a tourist told me: 'The pub is unpretentious in the best sense of the word. The day I was there I found no CAMRA shrillness whatever. I do remember an elderly English gentleman in the corner earnestly explaining the origin of stout to his interlocutor, but he was very quiet about it. The rustic snacks such as pasties were well made. I learned to my cost that Owd Roger ale is not intended for multiple unit consumption, but I can hardly blame you for that.' The *Bricklayer's Arms* (63 Charlotte Road, EC2; 01-739 5245) has twenty-one real ales and beer-drinking contests as well as Morris Dancing, which often comes to much the same thing. One cautionary word. A kind of Real Ale fascism infects some of these pubs, and trendy snobbism can drive out the regulars.

Best real ale pub: *The Bricklayer's Arms.*

(b) Riverside pubs

It would be contempt of Parliament to call the *House of Commons* a riverside pub, but the cheapest beer in London is served on the terrace, and the licensing laws don't apply. So get yourself elected. The *London Apprentice* in Isleworth (62 Church Street; 01-560 6136) is the pub at which the young apprentices to the London Guilds would celebrate their holidays. Under its pretty Italianate ceiling you can drink Watneys beer, and in the restaurant upstairs you can eat duck, but the best thing to do is drink on the terrace and watch the barges; opening times are irregular. The *White Swan* on the river at Twickenham and the *Rose of York* on the river at Richmond (Preston Road) are both splendid old pubs with excellent food.

For riverside pub-crawling Strand on the Green and Hammersmith Mall offer plenty of ports of call. My favourite at Strand is now the *City Barge*, 27 Strand on the Green, (01-994 2143) so called because the Lord Mayor's barge used to moor here. Coming up to its 500th anniversary, which makes it 50 years older than the *Bull's Head* next door, where Cromwell was nearly caught by the pursuing royalists, and about 400 years older than the *Bell and Crown* (72 Strand-on-the-Green; 01-994 4161). Obviously you have to pub crawl along the towpath and make your choice.

It's the same plethora of pubs at Hammersmith Mall, where of the four it would be just plain ornery not to choose the *Dove Inn* (19 Upper Mall; 01-748 5405). It is also known as *The Doves* – it is not easy to count doves after a pub crawl. *The Dove* is not quite on the river, which the neighbouring *Old Ship* (25 Upper Mall, 01-748 2593) is, but it is nearly 300 years old, has a fructiferous vine and is where James Thompson allegedly wrote Rule Britannia. Now a bit too jolly. Also along the Mall you will find the *Blue Anchor* (18 Lower Mall, 01-748 5774) which has a most unusual eight-pump antique pewter bar.

Also recommended: *The Grapes*, 76 Narrow Street, E14 (01-987 4396) with an extensive view of the river as well as oysters in season; Dickens called it 'a narrow lopsided wooden jumble of corpulent windows . . . with a crazy wooden veranda impending over the river'. Talking of which *The Dickens Inn*, St Katherine's Way, E1 (01-488 1226), a converted docks warehouse, rather modern and touristy but serving a useful choice of food and Ruddles, and exuding optimism; *The Anchor*, Bankside SE1 (01-407 1577) for Mrs Thrale's steak and kidney pudding and a first edition of Johnson's dictionary (Boswell and Johnson drank there); also three restaurants, the obligatory minstrels' gallery, real ale (Courage), an outside urinal of the old-fashioned type and a terrace overlooking the Thames.

The Prospect of Whitby (57 Wapping Wall, E1; 01-481 1095) is noisy and raucous; tourists are unwisely encouraged to sing. It was best in the days of Queenie Watts, but it's too loud for me.

It's true that pubs are usually recommended on quaint and historical grounds. For an entirely up-to-date pub which won't leave you feeling your historical education was inadequate, visit *Dogget's Coat and Badge* at Blackfriars Bridge (01-633 9057). Wonderful views of the city, delicious food, and their own special brew – Thomas Tipple's.

Best Riverside pub: *London Apprentice.*

(c) Pubs with entertainment
(See also Discos, Jazz, Theatre (Fringe)). A selection:

The Bull's Head (Lonsdale Road, Barnes, SW13; 01-876 5241). A remarkable history of providing excellent modern jazz on the banks of the Thames. (See above.)
Crown (24 Aberdeen Place, NW8; 01-289 1102). Always known as Crockers Folly. Crocker intended it as Marylebone's Station Hotel, but they moved the station without telling him. Grand Victorian fittings: real ale, and nightly varied entertainment. Spacious.
The Half Moon (93 Lower Richmond Road, SW15; 01-788 2387). A

rough-and-ready sort of place which specialises in bands and artists from the 60s and 70s. The customers are walk-ons from Woodstock, but the night Roy Harper played was unforgettable.

The Hare and Hounds (181 Upper Street, N1; 01-326 2992). Calls itself a honky tonk. Country music and rhythm and blues. Fun.

The King's Head (4 Fulham High Street, SW6; 01-736 1413). Pub rock with dancing Thursdays to Sundays. Admission charge varies with artist. Lively.

The Maple Leaf (41 Maiden Lane, WC2) is for visiting Canadians who may drink Molson's and eat hugely. On Monday evenings and at lunchtimes on Saturdays full length videos of Canadian ice-hockey matches are shown.

Old Queen's Head (113 Stockwell Road, SW9; 01-734 4904). Rock till eleven, then two hours of jazz almost every evening. A West Indian landlord and a great future. Inexpensive.

The Red Lion (318 The High Street, Brentford, Middlesex; 01-560 6181). Contemporary rock every night of the week. No bikes and no leather.

The Ruskin Arms (386 High Street North, Manor Park, E12; 01-472 0377). Loud rock, but not on Tuesdays or Wednesdays. The manager is a boxer and keeps the customers sweet, no matter how heavy the music. What would Ruskin have thought?

Should all this pall try *The Gilbert and Sullivan* (23 Wellington Street, WC2; 01-836 6930) and listen to G & S on the juke box. Or take in *The Pindar of Wakefield* (see under Music Halls).

Of course in the old days pubs really *did* provide entertainment. This is a description of the *Coal Hole* (91 The Strand), which still has the notorious Wolf Parlour in which 'meetings were no more than debauched drinking sessions with argument, song and copulation with prostitutes and actresses'. And to think that the last time I visited the Coal Hole I could not even get served.

Best Pub with entertainment: *The Bull's Head*.

(d) Gay pubs

This is a volatile and fast-moving scene. To be where it's at is an art. There are certain pivotal places. *Gay's The Word* bookshop (66 Marchmont Street, WC1; 01-278 7654) is one, the *London Lesbian and Gay Centre* is another (69 Cowcross Street, EC1; 01-608 1471); the *Hackney Women's Centre* (27 Hackney Grove, E8) is a third. *Gay Switchboard* (01-837 7324) is essential for information and advice with *Lesbian Line* (01-251 6911) and *London Friend* (01-359 7371) for gay women and men respectively. Now to tide you over a short list of predominantly gay recommendable pubs.

North London

The Bell (259 Pentonville Road, N1). Mostly young drinkers. Crowded.

Euston Tavern (73 Euston Road, NW1; 01-387 4566). Predominantly male. Young. Live Music.

The Entertainer (72 Balls Pond Road, N1; used to be the Greyhound). Excellent entertainment. Very camp.

The Fallen Angel (65 Graham Street, N1). Vegetarian, mixed gay, relaxed.

King William IV (77 High Street, NW3; 01-435 5747). Very Hampstead. Predominantly male. Up-market.

The Laurel Tree (113 Bayham Street, NW1). Small and intimate. Gentle atmopshere.

New Black Cap (171 Camden High Street, NW1; 01-485 1742). Mixed gay. Drag acts.

The Pied Bull (1 Liverpool Road, N1). Lesbian.

East London

The Alternative (34 Redchurch Street, E2). Mainly lesbian. Men welcome as 'guests'. Music on Wednesdays.

The Hop-Picker (483 Hackney Road, E2). Exclusively women.

London Apprentice (333 Old Street, EC1). Still where the action is. A tough leather and denim cruise bar.

South London

The Cricketers (317 Battersea Park Road, SW1; 01-622 9060). Gay and straight. Viv Spanton is a unique landlady. Girls on Tuesdays. Drag acts other nights.

The Elephant and Castle (2 South Lambeth Place, SW8; 01-735 1001). Drag shows every evening in the saloon bar. Scruffy but with excellent drag acts from time to time.

Market Tavern (Market Towers, 1 Nine Elms Lane, SW8; 01-622 5655). Mixed and friendly.

Ship and Whale (2 Gulliver Street, SE16; 01-237 3305). Male, with electronic games and a floodlit (spoilsport!) garden.

Union Tavern (146 Camberwell New Road, SE5; 01-735 3605). Predominantly male and a touch theatrical.

West London

Bolton's (216 Old Brompton Road, SW5; 01-373 8244). Victorian pub. Predominantly male.

Campion (1 Wellington Terrace, W11; 01-229 5056). Large bar with snuggery for snuggers. Predominantly male, predominantly local.

The Chepstow (39 Chepstow Place, W2; 01-229 1708). Straight but welcomes gays.
Coleherne (261 Old Brompton Road, SW5; 01-373 5881). Predominantly male with a grandfather clock. Old established.
Imperial (3 The Square, High Street, Richmond; 01-940 1477). Victorian gas-light. Predominantly male.

Central London
Ship and Shovel (Craven Passage, WC2; 01-930 7670). Real ale and a nautical theme. Predominantly male. The best bacon and kidney rolls this side of Tel Aviv.

Best Gay Pub: *The Fallen Angel*.

(e) Straight pubs
This list is for those who believe that London pubs are being over-run by CAMRA fascists, punk rockers, and gay libbers, and just long for some peace and quiet.

Blackfriar (147 Queen Victoria Street, EC4; 01-236 5650). A louche hymn to art nouveau; the 'side-chapel' is unforgettable in the way that peritonitis is unforgettable. If you don't go, you'll never know. Charrington Bass, Wetherell, Director's Bitter.
The Blue Posts (8 Bennet Street, SW1; 01-493 3350). Friendly, genteel, traditional and just behind the Ritz. The paintings are for sale. Shame about the video games. Raven Taverns.
The Brewery Tap (69 Wandsworth High Street, SW18; 01-870 2894). Attached to Young's Brewery, so see under Breweries.
The French House (once the York Minster) (49 Dean Street, W1; 01-437 2799). The centre for the Free French during the war, and the centre for the Soho Set after the war. Dylan Thomas, Francis Bacon, Colin MacInnes, and Brendan Behan all appreciated its qualities, but it doesn't welcome tourists. Walls decorated with French vaudeville stars, boxers and cyclists. No pint mugs available. Shorts, champagne and wine encouraged. Watneys.
Lamb and Flag (33 Rose Street, WC2; 01-836 4108). Run by an author, ex-farmer and wine merchant, this pub was once known as The Bucket of Blood. Agents for the Duchess of Portsmouth, who fancied herself libelled, made an attempt here on Dryden's life. There used to be bare-knuckle boxing in the upstairs room, now often used for poetry (q.v.). Dryden Night is December 19th, and Burns Night is also celebrated. Sadly it lost its stucco façade a few years ago. Strong real ale, excellent food. Courage. Pretty.
Pontefract Castle (Wigmore Street, W1; 01-486 3551). The most

interesting feature of this interesting pub is that it serves in the Balcony Bar twenty varieties of malt whisky; obviously several visits are called for.

Queen's Elm (24 Fulham Road, SW3; 01-352 9157). A Bohemian pub which has always been popular with writers. In the upstairs room the successful Public Lending Right campaign was masterminded by such stalwarts as Brigid Brophy and Maureen Duffy. Courage. (What else?)

The Railway Telegraph (112 Stanstead Road, SE23). Darts, inexpensive beer competently served and a landlord who cares, more than compensate for the unspectacular view of the South Circular.

Red Lion (2 Duke of York Street, SW1; 01-930 2030). Not to be confused with the other *Red Lion* in Crown Passage just a couple of hops away. Your reception here may be surly (mine was) but there's no denying the ravishing glitter of the engraved mirrors, each bearing a different British flower. It's not unlike drinking on an old-fashioned merry-go-round. Ind Coope. Crowded.

Rose of York (Petersham Road, Richmond; 01-940 0626). One of the prettiest pubs in one of the prettiest settings (Ham Common). A carvery on Sundays, and Samuel Smith beer. Classy.

The Star Tavern (6 Belgrave Mews West, SW1; 01-235 3019). Very friendly with brass and blazing fires in winter. The publican is genial, the food is excellent and there are pictures of dogs.

Still and Star (1 Little Somerset Street, E1; 01-488 3761). In the middle of Jack the Ripper land which may account for the welcoming atmosphere inside, the S and S is run by a lady Freeman of the City of London. Charrington and IPA.

The Gunmaker's Arms (Eyre Street Hill, EC1) is a charming curiosity on a miniature scale. Natural to feel 'tight' here.

The Opera Tavern opposite Drury Lane in Catherine Street, is also small, highly ornate and atmospheric. A delight. Ind Coope.

I am not enamoured of any of the following: *Windsor Castle*, Campden Hill Road, W8 (despite the tortoise); *The Hour Glass* (Brompton Road, SW1); *Cockney Pride* (Jermyn Street, SW1); *The Norbury*, (Norbury SW16); the *Bricklayer's Arms* (Beckenham, SW7); *The Tournament* (Old Brompton Road, SW7).

Best straight pub: *Lamb and Flag*.

(f) Pub food

If you can get to the *Coach and Horses* (29 Greek Street, W1; 01-437 5920), which is the Private Eye pub, early enough, you will be served by a little old West Indian lady-chef, who is indestructible. She does bangers and mash the way they ought to be done, and similar delicacies. The proprietor, Norman Balen, is a dead ringer for Walter Matthau, which is only of interest, I suppose, to the two parties concerned. He was cross at being mentioned in *The Essential Guide to London*, but I can't imagine why. He's often cross and throws those he considers boring bodily out of his pub.

Other recommendations:

Simpson's Tavern (Ball Court Passage, 38½ Cornhill, EC3; 01-626 9985) for a stewed cheese speciality; *Ladbroke Arms* (54 Ladbroke Road, W11) for an excellent carvery; *Queen's Head* (13 Brook Green, W6; 01-603 2696) for their fresh home-made buffet; *Ye Olde Cheshire Cheese* (145 Fleet Street, EC4; 01-353 6170) for game puddings (from October); the *Grenadier* (18 Wilton Row, SW1; 01-235 3074) for good, if expensive, English food; *The Ship* (41 Jew's Row, SW18) for its Lancashire hot pot and bubble-and-squeak; *The Old Spotted Dog* (212 Upton Lane, E7) for basics at the bar and better in the restaurant; the *Bunch of Grapes* (207 Brompton Road, SW3; 01-589 4944), a pretty pub with lip-smacking food; the *Fox and Anchor* (Charterhouse Street, EC1; 01-253 4838) for home-made soups, the biggest mixed grills in London and breakfasts; the *Grafton Arms* (72 Grafton Way, W1; 01-837 7923) for Scottish food; the *Warwick Castle* (6 Warwick Place, W9; 01-286 6868) for shepherd's pie; the *Cutty Sark* (Lassell Street, SE10; 01-858 3146) for whitebait; the *Samuel Pepys* (Brooks Wharf, Upper Thames Street; 01-248 3048 for the restaurant) for game pie and spotted dick; the *Wattenden Arms* (Old Lodge Lane, Kenley) for fresh crab salad; the *Dover Castle* (43 Weymouth Mews, W1; 01-636 9248) where children are welcome.

Book in advance at those pubs which accept bookings. If not, arrive before 1 p.m. and, if there is a 'today's special', have it! It is less likely to have been recently defrosted.

The idea of executive businessmen eating 'Ploughman's Lunch' has always seemed absurd, but now that 'Executive Ploughman's Lunch' has been noted on a pub menu (in Maidenhead), the mind boggles.

Best Pub Food: *The Fox and Anchor* (also under Breakfasts).

P.S. A pleasant book is *Victorian Pubs* by Mark Giraud (1975).

Pub Signs

England's leading pub sign artist is George Mackenney. In an extraordinary career spanning 30 years or more he has painted almost

6,000 signs. If you want to know what George looks like, the sign at *The World's End* (459 King's Road, SW10) is a self-portrait of the artist rather older than in real life as Father Time. Another of his finest boards is *The Chelsea Potter* (119 King's Road, SW3). But my favourite of those which I have identified as being by George is the staid, unshowy, but entirely satisfactory *Builder's Arms*, in St Paul's Road, N1. The builder in question is a brickie, but perhaps when the sign was commissioned it was thought that there were already quite enough Bricklayer's Arms in London. Anyway there he is with brick and trowel, his body much lived in, the same shape as Nye Bevan's, the forearms massive, the head behind its moustache and underneath its flat cap owing nothing to anyone. He is neither proud of his calling nor ashamed of it. He just goes on adding brick to brick, the way most of us have to, whatever kinds of bricks we deal in.

A couple of others:

The Blind Beggar, a pub notorious in the past for murder and mayhem, has a fine sign overhanging the Mile End Road, Stepney. It shows the eponymous beggar accompanied by a rather stout young lady who has him by the arm. Is she his wife, his daughter, his fancy woman? Is she helping him, robbing him, or interviewing him for market research? We have no way of knowing. *The Hog in the Pound*, 28 South Molton Street, W1, is a prime (sic) example of what posh art dealers call genre art. It shows two pig's trotters hanging over the fence, considering the world and all its follies from their superior position. The sign itself is rectangular with hemispheric extensions at either end. It's not a thing of beauty, but it's original and well-conceived, with graphics in a sort of Wild West script.

Best Pub Sign: *The Builder's Arms.*

P.S. A good game for children on a car journey. Give them one point for each leg (human, heraldic or animal) visible on pub signs. This game is capable of many sophistications but you'll have to devise them for yourself.

Queues

Queue fanciers most appreciate *meaningless* queues. The one that forms at 9.15 a.m. at *Waterloo Station* (Waterloo Road exit) consists of docile anonymous humanoids in mackintoshes. Fifteen minutes later and they've gone, whisked away like Pinocchio and his friends to a fate too appalling to contemplate. The *Victoria Station* taxi queue is not as long, but neither is it so ephemeral. It's always there, yet any of those waiting in it would only have to walk a few yards in almost any direction to find a cab without much delay. The queue for the *Queen's Gallery* alongside Buckingham Palace is a dreary one because a draughtier spot it would be hard to find. At least the impressive *Madame Tussaud's* queue has some shelter, a delightful iron canopy with hanging lights like grapefruit though once they get inside what awaits them is another even longer queue. The *Hard Rock Café* queue is mystifying. I can only suppose that some sort of inverse snobbery is at work here; i.e. this is an important queue to be seen in, who needs to find a table anyway, definitely passé to sit down, don't you agree?

The most magnificent queue, and quite the longest, is the one which forms each June in the leafy suburb of Earlsfield. This, of course, is the queue for Wimbledon tickets and now those killjoys on the Wimbledon Committee have decided to phase out queuing. As it is, the only seats to be queued for have restricted viewing. What are those bureaucrats playing at? Don't they know that Britain only got where it is today by queuing?

Honestly!

Best Queue: *Waterloo Station* (Cross-refer: Bottlenecks).

Racecourses (around London)

Ally Pally was the only genuine London race track and now it's gone and we mourn its passing. Known disrespectfully as the Frying Pan (from its shape) it was primitive. Once I remember the starter barricading himself in his shed after being stoned by the crowd; the favourite had been left many lengths at the start, which was in front of what passed for a grandstand. There on summer evenings we'd plunge on ageing Doctor Blimber, the ugliest horse in racing, and sometimes he'd win.

Of the courses adjacent to London, *Kempton Park* is like an old whore who's run to seed, and *Epsom* is even worse. The trek from the stand to the paddock is exhausting, the crowds on Derby Day cannot be coped with, and the whole place reeks of dilapidation. But it's exciting to back a fast short-runner there over the quickest five furlongs in racing.

Sandown has lost much of its charisma since the new stand was built, but visibility is good, crowds are well contained, and the joints in the Saddle and Tack Room are delicious, though the waitresses have all been lobotomised. Last time I visited *Sandown* my friend Karen had a forecast up at 280/1. They had to send for an official to check the winnings. One has to like a track like that, although why the unsaddling enclosure is so far removed from the grandstand is a mystery.

The Royal Meeting at *Ascot* offers the best racing, the priciest women and the most valuable horses, but I am not impressed by a Royal Enclosure which admits me. Though fields are small, the jumping meeting in the spring is to be preferred. A Monday evening meeting at *Windsor* can be a pleasure, though finding the winner of a 23-horse selling handicap there poses problems to test an Einstein (the draw is not as significant as it used to be); but it's informal and amiable. Travel a little further, and you'll discover the delights of *Fontwell*, pleasanter by far than nearby *Goodwood*.

The best tipster used to be Robin Goodfellow of the *Daily Mail* (Arthur Salter) who went through the card on three successive days – a unique 18-horse accumulator. Garry Owen of the *Daily Record* has the best recent record.

Best Racecourse: *Sandown.*
Worst Racecourse: *Epsom.*

Railway Lines

The first passenger line in the South of England was the London to Greenwich, and a remarkable achievement it was, a large part of its length being constructed on arches with a road (some of which survives) at the base of the struts. These arches then became ideal for small enterprises – wheelwrights, blacksmiths, totters and what you have you. Nowadays many of them are occupied by respray merchants and men who grind crankshafts and deal in defective greyhounds.

Both for reasons of sentiment and convenience the *Broad Street Line* (now known as the *North London Line*) is the best in London. Hampstead to Richmond in twenty minutes during the rush hour is not to be sneezed at. It runs three times an hour from Richmond to Broad Street and back through gardens hung with washing. Children still wave at Broad Street trains as they pass, and the graffiti tend to be richer in sexual imagery than on the more populated lines. For as long as I can remember the line has been under threat of permanent closure, but we shall fight on. But Broad Street Station has gone.

The *Drain* (*Waterloo and City Line* running between Waterloo and the Bank) is a law unto itself. Moving walkways and a single ticket price are just a part of its old-fashioned charm. The *Bakerloo Line* beyond

Queen's Park is hair-raising. Like as not you'll end up (sic) at Watford Junction.

Best line: *Broad Street.*
Worst line: *Southern Region to Blackheath and beyond.*
P.S. Full details in *London's Railways* by Edwin Course (1962).

Railway Stations

See under Stations.

Records/Tapes

A selection:

(a) General

HMV (363 Oxford Street, W1; 01-629 1240) is the daddy of them all, and claims to be the largest record store in Europe. Their stock (on three floors) is certainly comprehensive, but the assistants lack the enthusiasm of those in smaller emporia. You can get steel needles for 78s here.

Beggar's Banquet (8 Hogarth Road, SW1; 01-370 6175) specialises in independent labels and has its own. Second-hand and trade-in facilities. Branches throughout west London.

Record and Tape Exchange (38 Notting Hill Gate, W11; 01-727 3539 and three branches). The claim is that everything brought in for exchange will be accepted at prices from 1p to £2.50. All the shops are open every day of the year 10 a.m. to 8 p.m. Wholesale discounts for dealers. Rarities upstairs at the Notting Hill branch. Obviously the place to go at 7.50 p.m. on Christmas Eve when you've got no money to buy presents, just a few old discs.

(b) Classical

Caruso and Company (35 New Oxfrod Street, WC1; 01-379 5839). Opera including imports. Australian titles. Contemporary music.

Covent Garden Records (84 Charing Cross Road, W1; 01-379 7635). Compact disc centre with ten booths for listening in. The two marmalade cats, Figaro and Aida, in the branch at 20 James Street, WC2 (01-379 7674) are not for sale.

Farringdon Records (42 Cheapside, EC2 and 28 Holborn Viaduct, EC1 (01-248 2816). Worthwhile special offers.

Harold Moores Records (2 Great Marlborough Street, W1; 01-437 1576). Excellent advice and assistance.

Music Discount Centre (97-99 Dean Street, W1; 29 Rathbone Place, W1; 437 Strand, WC2; inside Coutts). Branches specialise in second-hand compact discs and tapes (Rathbone Place sells nothing else).

Orchesography (10 Cecil Court, WC2; 01-836 2314). Cut-price, deletions and special offers, mainly in the classical range.

(c) Opera
Collector's Corner (62 New Oxford Street, W1; 01-580 6155). New and second-hand opera recordings – especially rarities. And see Classical above.

(d) Jazz
Dobell's (21 Tower Street, W1; 01-240 1354). Historic, though now removed from the long-established Charing Cross Road premises. Excellent for early jazz and blues.

Mole Jazz (374 Gray's Inn Road, WC1; 01-278 8623). The home of Mole Jazz records, the first to convert to compact discs. Strong on European and avant garde.

Ray's Jazz Shop (180 Shaftesbury Avenue, W1; 01-240 3969). Includes a fine collection of jazz 78s and a library of jazz books.

Rhythm Records (281 Camden High Street, NW1; 01-267 0123). Includes rock and punk, reggae and salsa as well as jazz. Second hand record-exchange included.

(e) Musicals
Due to a change in management That's Entertainment is now called *Dress Circle*. It is still at 43 The Market, Covent Garden, WC2; 01-240 2227, but it has opened a new branch in Monmouth Street (57/59 Monmouth Street, WC2) where, besides tapes, records and videos of musicals, you can buy sheet-music, posters and theatrical memorabilia, with occasional exhibitions. Also: 58 Dean Street, W1 (01-437 4500).

(f) African Music
Stem's African Record Centre (116 Whitfield Street, W1; 01-387 5550). Everything from Africa down to the latest fashion *Cadence* from the Antilles.

(g) Latin Music
Hitman Records (2 Lexington Street, W1; 01-437 8708).

(h) Gospel
Miracle Music (4 Acre Lane, SW2; 01-274 1027).

(i) Country
Record Corner (27 Bedford Hill, SW12; 01-673 6130). For independent

black American labels, as well as the mainstream of country music. (Jerry Lee Lewis gets worse and worse.)

(j) Reggae
Daddy Cool (84 Dean Street, W1; 01-437 3535). Vast stock.

Dub Vendor (274 Lavender Hill, SW11; 01-223 3757). For imported Jamaican labels.

Greensleeves (44 Uxbridge Road, W12; 01-749 3277). Long-established and popular with its own (unlikely) label.

Orbitone Records (2A Station Road, N10; 01-965 8292). Rhythm and blues as well as reggae. Robert, the owner and promoter of the Orbitone label, is an expert in calypso.

(k) Folk
Collett's Folk Department (Basement, 131 Charing Cross Road, W1; 01-734 0782). Authentic, ideological, ethnic . . . and fun.

Kay's Irish Music Shop (161 Arlington Road, NW1; 01-485 4880). Instruments as well as music. A marvellous selection of heart-breaking republican songs: 'My only son was shot in Dublin' and the like.

(l) Soul
Bluebird Records (155/157 Church Street, W2; 01-723 9090). One shop for hip-hop, another for more traditional fare. Also has its own label.

Grove Records (52 Greek Street, W1; 01-430 8231). Wonderful stock. Deserved reputation.

Record Shack (12 Berwick Street, W1; 01-437 3655). Throbbing disco, hip-hop, and punk, as well as old-fashioned soul.

(m) Rock 'n' Roll
Plastic Passion (2 Blenheim Crescent, W11; 01-229 5424). Head-bands, flower-power, and Maharashi music.

Rock On (3 Kentish Town Road, NW5). The brain child of Ted Carroll of Ace Records.

Rocks Off (36 Hanway Street, W1; 01-580 8898). Includes in its stocks some rarities from the late 50s.

Rough Trade (130 Talbot Road, W2; 01-229 8541). Specialises in 70s rock and rockabilly.

Sea of Tunes (3 Buck Street, NW1; 01-482 1784). Including second-hand and re-issues of rock classics.

Spinning Disc (54 Chiswick High Road, W6; 01-994 4606). Elvis experts and traditional rock 'n' roll.

(n) Women's Music
Sisterwrite (190 Upper Street, N1; 01-226 9782). The emphasis is

folksy; the US labels are Redwood and Olivia; the records from an expanding department within this feminist bookshop. But what to do about the hole in the middle?

Repairs

See under Emergency Services.

Restaurants

See under Nationality (i.e. Danish), the meal (i.e. Breakfasts, Tea-houses, All-Night Eating) the type of food (i.e. Hamburgers, Pasta etc), the price (i.e. Budget Restaurants) or the Category (i.e. Pub Food, Wine Bars etc).

Rip-Offs

The most expensive are the £100-a-bottle-of-champagne night-clubs (q.v.); the most fraudulent are the artists who claim to be selling their own work when what you end up with is a shoddy reproduction. There is a ticket machine at London Bridge which according to an illuminated sign at the top will give change for a £1 coin but according to a smaller sign at the bottom won't. As for the chocolate machines on tube stations, they are a law unto themselves. What I do know is that, although they have often stolen my money, they have never given me free chocolate. Then there are the three-card tricksters. A group of these men came to court recently and they were sent to prison – the first time such a punishment has been used. These card-sharps make huge fortunes out of gullible tourists by sleight of hand, although the mugs ask for it by participating. A cover charge is a rip-off if it doesn't bring a cover (i.e. a cloth, napkins, bread and butter and even water), and the buyer's premium charged by auctioneers is a con. So are those shops which are never without a 'sale'.

Ice-cream van proprietors, street photographers, minicab drivers and such are frequently rip-off merchants, though not always – and the new telephones are shocking rip-offs. They frequently don't work, although the card-operated ones always do. A plot to make everyone get cards.

But on balance (see Free Entertainment) you have to be

astonishingly innocent or astonishly stupid (or both) to get less out of London than you gain.

Rivers/Streams

London is a city of lost rivers, and one which has been refound. The lost rivers are reflected in street names. There used to be a river which descended from Kilburn (the *Kil Bourne*) via Westbourne Grove (*West Bourne*) to Bayswater (*Baynard's Water*) and Knightsbridge (the bridge over which two knights fought in armed combat) to Sloane Square – if you look up from the tube station you can see the conduit which carried it underground at this point – after which it was dammed to make the Serpentine before entering the Thames.

Then there was the *Ty Bourne* which flowed from the heights of Hampstead, via Hyde Park (Tyburn Hill), Stratford Place (the *Street Ford*), to Green Park, where it created the Bason, a valuable reservoir. The *Fleet* descended from the Vale of Health via King's Cross (it wisely went underground for part of its passage here) to where it met the *Hol Bourne* (Holborn), and the two rivers continued jointly via Ludgate Circus and, of course, Fleet Street, into the *Thames*. Remarkably the Holborn Viaduct still has the look of a bridge over a river, although the *Hol Bourne* was never much of a river. What was once the insalubrious *Fleet Ditch* is now a perfectly sanitary sewer, although no longer visible to city workers crossing the viaduct. Also in the City was the *Walbrook*, and in south London such poetically named streams as the *Falcon Brook*, the *Neckinger*, and the *Tygris*. The *Wandle*, rising in Carshalton Ponds, is still a familiar feature of the Wandsworth area. It runs along Garratt Lane and once had 20 water mills upon it.

Wandle water, which Pope referred to as 'blue transparent Vandalis' was thought highly desirable. No wonder when you realise that London drank water from the Thames into which was discharged in 1828 the effluent from 129 sewers as well as gas-houses, dye-factories and the like. Thames Water today scored high marks when tested against the 'natural' waters currently on the market.

The *New River* was man-made by Sir Hugh Myddelton's engineers, who brought the water a distance of thirty-eight miles from Chadwell Springs in Hertfordshire. The water flowed for the first time on September 29th, 1613, and the New River Company still exists (30 Myddelton Square, EC1; 01-837 2105). Although straightened in the 19th century, it was still permitted to meander, as a river should, through the meadows of Enfield. Equally picturesque for much of its length is the late poet laureate's favourite river, the gentle *Brent*, which undulates through Hanwell, swallows up golfballs in Brent Lodge Park, passes under the Wharncliffe Railway Viaduct – Queen Victoria used to instruct the driver to slow down here while she enjoyed the view – and the horrific Uxbridge Road. On a recent reconnaissance I am happy to report that I found clumps of willowherb, was stung by nettles, and stared at by a man with a wheelbarrow. Exploring the *Brent* is rewarding, and useful hints may be picked up at the Grange Museum of Local History on a traffic island in the inappropriately named Blackbird Hill.

As for the *Thames*, what a success story this continues to be! It is clean, it is fresh and yet still, along the eel-filled Twickenham stretch, untamed. As Rupert Brooke put it:

> One may not doubt that, somehow, good
> Shall come of water and of mud . . .

As for the *Quaggy*, it is hard to believe that not so very long ago it gurgled along the village green at Lewisham Triangle, and along with its tributary, the *Ravensbourne*, sparkled like beaten silver in the sunlight. Now it is choked with abandoned supermarket trolleys, unwanted prams and babies, and other unmentionables; not a subject to dwell on.

Best River: *Thames*.
Best Stream: *Brent*.
Worst Stream: *Quaggy*.

An excellent companion is *The Lost Rivers of London* by N. J. Barton (1962).

Roadsweepers

The most notable London roadsweeper is *Floyd Whitby*, the singing roadsweeper of Ilford. One day Louise Newman (19) saw him sweep, sweep, sweeping, and gave him a cup of tea. 'Sweeping is OK', said Floyd, 'as long as no one talks to you. My big mistake was getting promoted to foreman.' Now he and Louise have released a single called *Minute by Minute* and Floyd runs a club in Tufnell Park called Poverty Point.

Roadsweepers used to be called crossing-sweepers, and it was an independent trade. One chose one's crossing, and saw people across, and picked up a good living in tips. Some sweepers used also to beg – Mayhew talked to a 'negro crossing-sweeper, who had lost both his legs'. And many were juveniles. This according to a 15-year-old who talked to Mayhew was how it used to be done. He worked in a party of six.

'We do it this way: if I was to see two gentlemen coming, I should cry out, "Two Toffs!" and then they are mine, and my mate is bound not to follow them; for if he did he would get a hiding from the whole lot of us. If we both cry out together, then we share. If it's a lady and a gentleman, then we cries "A toff and a doll!" Sometimes we are caught out in this way. Perhaps it is a lady and a gentleman and a child; and if I was to see them, and only say, "A toff and a doll", and leave out the child, then my mate can add the child; and as he is right and I wrong, then it's his party.' And so on for many marvellous pages.

Really everyone ought to read *Mayhew's London*.

Roofs/Chimneys

One could not ignore the claims of the *Battersea Power Station* chimneys (Gilbert Scott 1934) even if one wanted to. Beside them most other London chimneys shrink into insignificance, as Hemingway's did when he looked at Scott Fitzgerald's in the rive gauche lavatory. Or was it the other way round?

Each of the three stacks rise to 340 feet; the complete triptych is a massive symbol of controlled power. H. J. Massingham found the right phrase when he described Battersea Power Station as The Cathedral of the Electrons. I must put in a word for the crooked chimneys of *44-52 Waterloo Gardens*, E2 and of *2 Flask Cottages*, NW3. Curiously patterned pots, as on the *Hampton Court* chimneys, were much imitated, notably on *The Lodge*, Waterloo Park, N6, where a row of six such chimneys look like sticks of rocks.

Harrods roof is an amazing sight; you feel you ought not to be looking at it, as you might feel you ought not to be looking down a duchess's cleavage. *St Pancras* roof is, of course, pure Gothic Disneyland. Then there is the roof of Nash's *Cumberland Terrace* at the east end of Regent's Park. The statues seem designed to stand in silhouette against the dawn. Glance too at the roof of the *Royal Geographical Society* (corner of Kensington Gore and Exhibition Road), at the *Bishop of Southwark's house* in Tooting Bec Gardens, at the *Ritz Hotel*, at the houses in *Welbeck Street*. The *Great Hall of Lambeth Palace* has a marvellous seventy-feet-high hammerbeam roof. *Eltham Palace* has a fine one too, but it's been restored.

Best roof: *Great Hall, Lambeth Palace.*

Best chimneys: *Battersea Power Station.*
Worst chimneys: *The flats in Peabody Avenue*, SW1.

Rugby Football

'The Club' – *Blackheath Rugby Football Club* to the uninitiated – was founded in 1862 and is therefore the oldest Rugby Football Club in England; it plays on the Rectory Field.

But despite the claims of Blackheath, and despite that there are those who would lie down and die for the *Harlequins* or the *Barbarians*, there is really no question but that *Twickenham's* the place. Actually the headquarters of rugby is in *Whitton* (next to All Hallows, a Wren city church re-erected in a leafy suburb). The turf drains effectively so that seldom if ever do matches have to be abandoned. The only problem is visibility. In mid-December when the Varsity Match is played, during what Ivor Brown calls 'the dull droop of a short mid-winter afternoon', and the sun sinks low behind the huge western stand and the mist rises then the figures on the field acquire the reality of crowds during the showing of a D. W. Griffith film on a badly adjusted portable television set when Concorde is flying low overhead. The England/Wales match in January is always likely to be fogged out, but England/Scotland in March is worth waiting for, as are the Middlesex Sevens in May. The vast new video screen aids visibility at the expense of atmosphere.

Best rugby: *Twickenham.*

Salad Bars

Self-service salad bars are the gastronomic equivalent of striptease (q.v.). That is to say they encourage you to heap your plate (because it's not value for money if you don't), then leave you feeling quite unsatisfied as though you haven't had a meal at all. But I'll go through the motions . . .

All these offer self-service salads:

Garfunkel's (Upper Regent Street, W1; 01-629 1870) and branches throughout the West End. 45 different ingredients. A small plateful costs £2.95, a large plateful £3.85. Everything is kept frozen far too long under lights which are too bright and when you finally get to taste your selections it's an anti-climax. Smoked mackerel is good; artichoke hearts are stringy.

Justin de Blank (54 Duke Street, W1; 01-629 3174). One of the best selections and at £1.90 for a small plate and £3.80 for a large one, good value.

Pappagallis Pizzas Inc (7-9 Swallow Street, W1; 01-734 5182). Only 20 items to choose from but they include the improbable, such as alfalfa sprouts, mung beans and sunflower seeds. Hum. On a more positive note a good selection of cocktails and Marine ices. Salad starters £1.85, main course £3.75. Six dressings.

Spatz (Hill House, Shoe Lane, EC4; 01-583 2441). Only open at lunch for figure-conscious business folk, this burger, salad and cocktail restaurant is efficent and air-conditioned.

Surprise (12 Great Marlborough Street, W1; 01-434 2666). One of the first London restaurants to incorporate a self-service salad, it is still just about the best, though certainly not the cheapest.

Note too that self-service salads are included in all Berni Inn steak and carvery bars, and make a sensible starter to a perfectly good steak or joint. There is also an excellent salad bar in the basement of Habitat in the Tottenham Court Road.

Imaginative take-away salads from *Food For Thought* (31 Neal Street, WC2; 01-836 0239) at £1 a portion.

Best salads: *Surprise*.

Sandwiches

A recipe I picked up in Australia recently for something called a Celebration Sandwich: 'De-crust thinly, cut bread in triangles. Spread with butter, place a fresh oyster on one piece, cover with the other which has been spread with caviar. Press edges to hide oyster. Serve with chilled champers to celebrate Coolangatta's centenary year.'

I shall never be satisfied with the familiar British Railbar cheese and tomato again.

For the ethnically minded a salt-beef sandwich at *Bloom's* (see under Kosher Restaurants) or an open-decker at the *Danish Coffee Room* (see under Danish Restaurants) should satisfy, otherwise:

Hungry's (37a Crawford Street, W1; 01-258 0376) which I have already praised under Hampers is dragging the sandwich into the high-tech world, although the jokey titles are distinctly sixties. So you can try 'prawns, avocado, corn and sultanas marinated in rum with lettuce and mayonnaise' if you're feeling brave. All the sandwiches from Hungry's may be delivered anywhere in W1 (free if the order is worth £10 or more).

At *Jules Bar* (85 Jermyn Street, SW1; 01-930 4700) which I recall as a 'gimme one more for the road' sort of place, changes have been under way, and distinctly classy sandwiches (minute steak or smoked salmon at £4.95) are available in distinctly classy surroundings.

Two other sandwich delivery places are *Swift's* (Unit 5, 38 Mount Pleasant, WC1; 01-833 1795) which serves the City and North London. Their most intriguing invention is mackerel pâté and asparagus with bacon and avocado a tasty second. 'Platter delivery' costs £5.50 extra but they will also deliver wine.

Finally *Zak's* (32-34 Goodge Street, W1; 01-580 1857) a white-tiled Valhalla with hanging baskets of greenery and Saatchi secretaries. A blackboard on the pavement outside advertises for temporary and permanent staff so it looks as though *Zak's* is here to stay. Sandwiches are pretty good and there is wholewheat pizza for figure-conscious Italians.

A friendly New York publisher – would there were more of them – writes: 'Just before I left London I had a most memorable meal at Heathrow. A smoked salmon sandwich, made with whole wheat bread. Cut into quarters and decorated with a bit of watercress and a radish. All served on a plate and tied down in cellophane. Cost: One pound and 35 pence. I had two – and was reaching for a third when we were all ordered to proceed at once to Gate 15 and to board our aircraft immediately. I realize now that this little feast would be well worth missing a plane for.'

Best sandwiches: *Swift's.*

Sauna/Massage Parlours

Your actual Finnish sauna is unforgettable. As we chugged along the lake in our paddle-steamer naiad children ran along the bank waving freshly plucked birch twigs at us. These, when we moored, we purchased; and taking them into the small wooden hut which housed the sauna and stripping off we switched our backs with them, not hard but just hard enough to allow the sap to seep out and with it the quintessence of birch.

Then, scented and sweating, we raced from the hut and leapt into the frigid lake, after which we wrapped ourselves in our warmest clothes and huddled in rugs around the bonfire on which the freshly caught sprats sizzled in melted butter. As dusk crept like velvet across the sky the Finnish women began to keen snatches of old songs, while the younger members of the party spoke wonderingly about Life and Destiny and Whether Or Not To Go Off Into The Woods Together.

It's a long way from that cis-Arctic night to a massage-parlour near King's Cross, and I shall not recommend anything so squalid, although for those determined to plumb the depths you will find details of many such places in *What's On & Where to Go In London* (weekly 50p at most newagents). The only sauna I shall recommend here is the *Finland House Club*, 56 Haymarket, SW1; 01-839 5400), which is authentic, though metropolitan. The saunas at the *Great Park* and *Cavendish Court Hotels* are perfectly respectable (as indeed are most hotel saunas in London).

Best Sauna: *Finland House Club.*

Schools

This is serious business. All I can do is pass on recommendations for six state and seven private schools, about which I have heard or at which I have observed only good. I should welcome more comments, especially about schools in tougher areas of the capital.

State
Fitzjohn's Primary, 83 Fitzjohn's Avenue, NW3; 01-435 9797.
Fleet Primary, Agincourt Road, NW3; 01-485 2028.
Fox School, Kensington Place, W8; 01-727 7637.
John Ruskin Primary School, John Ruskin Street, SE5; 01-703 5800.
Pimlico School (comprehensive), Lupus Street, SW1; 01-828 0881.
White Lion Street Free School, 57 White Lion Street, N1; 01-837 6379.

Private
Arnold House, 3 Loudoun Road, NW8; 01-286 1100.
The Hall School, Crossfield Road, NW3; 01-722 1700.
Ibstock Place School (Froebel Demonstration School), Clarence Lane, Roehampton, SW15 5PY; 01-876 9991.
The Mall School, Hampton Road, Twickenham, Middlesex; 01-977 2523.
St Paul's Boys' School, Lonsdale Road, SW13; 01-748 9162.
St Paul's Girls' School, Brook Green, W6; 01-603 2288.
Westminster School, Dean's Yard, SW1; (various numbers).

Secrets

If you ask a taxi-driver to take you to the headquarters of MI6 or to Overseas Intelligence and Espionage, he will drop you off at *Century House*, 100 Westminster Bridge Road. The address for Agent Recruiting and Diplomat Monitoring is *60 Vauxhall Bridge Road*, for Recruiting Interviews is *3, Carlton Gardens*, St James's, and for Training is *296/302 Borough High Street*. MI5 Headquarters is in *Curzon Street* around the corner from the Director of Army Recruiting (*Lansdown House*, Berkeley Square, W1). And close to the U.S. Embassy in Grosvenor Square you will find the Headquarters of US Naval Forces in Europe (*7 North Audley Street*, W1) just a stone's throw ('People who live in bugged houses . . .') away from the Counter Spy Shop (*62 South Audley Street*, W1; 01-408 0287). The UK Government's Defence Sales Organisation is at *Stuart House*, 23/25 Soho Square. The Director General in charge of Weapons Electronics Systems is in *Castlewood House* and the Director General of Strategic Electronics Systems is in *Prospect House*, both in Oxford Street. The Supreme Council of the Freemasons may be found at *10 Duke Street*, St James's SW1.

The Director of Air Contracts on behalf of the RAF, who deals in Nimrods, Sea Harriers and Tornados, is at *1/13 St Giles High Street*, WC2 (the mysterious building mentioned in *The Essential Guide to London*). A company with offices in *Betterton Street*, Covent Garden produces a riot control van, the metal of which can be electrified at the touch of a button. This was to have been exported to Chile, except that, after considerable press comment, an export licence was refused. Meanwhile the SAS Group of Companies was manufacturing electric prods also intended to be used by the Chile Police. The CIA is among the Service Reserve Offices attached to the US Embassy named in the Diplomatic List.

To save time I should add that all of the above information was gleaned from the Civil Service List, the Civil Service Yearbook 1984, the Street Directory, *Phonetappers and the Security State* by Duncan Campbell (published by the *New Statesman*), *British Intelligence and Covert Action* (ditto), *The Brotherhood* by Stephen Knight, a book on Northern Ireland by Roger Faligot (who knows the title?), *HighTime: the Shocking Life and Times of Howard Marks* by David Leigh, *Dirty Work* Vols 1 & 2 by Agee and Woolf, the *Guardian* and the *Observer*. It was monitored for me by Len Still who believes, as I do, that the fewer secrets we have the better for all concerned. Ronnie Stoneman, please copy.

Best kept secret: *Lord Lucan.*

Sewers

The problems of sewermen have been swept underground. Many London sewers are 4 ft high and some no more than 3 ft. It's best to walk backwards, with the flow of the water, to beware of gas leaks, and not to touch the walls for fear of 'Rat's Disease'. Here is one sewerman, Tony Murphy, recorded by Kaye Webb. He had broken his light: 'I kept whistling and singing to myself, but when I stopped I cound hear the bunnies (rats) squeaking away, it really put the wind up me!' And Bill Blackburn: 'The smell is much worse when it comes above ground. Down there, we're so used to it we hardly notice – I always tell the wife it gives me an appetite! Of course, it's nicer when we're under the perfume factory.' Quotations from *Looking at London* by Ronald Searle and Kaye Webb (*News Chronicle* 1953).

With 1,500 miles of sewers under London who knows what treasures may be down there? The classiest is the *Tyburn Sewer* which runs from Hampstead under the American Ambassador's house in Regent's Park, under Buckingham Palace, Wellington Barracks, New Scotland Yard and The Treasury and into the Thames at Westminster. Because of its upper-crust route it contains the highest density of bunnies in the whole of the system.

For further details read *London Under London* by Richard Trench (sic!) and Ellis Hillman (John Murray £14.95) or *London Beneath the Pavement* by Michael Harrison (1971).

Sex Shops

According to the Williams Report the statistics for sex crimes in Britain have remained remarkably stable since we became 'permissive' – not that London, compared with most European capitals, is 'permissive' at all. The Williams Committee suggested that such outlets as sex shops do serve a valuable social function, but the squalor of these places is endlessly disheartening. The coin-in-the-slot movie shows are gloomy beyond belief and the cubicles smell like monkey houses. Avoid them.

So far as the shops themselves are concerned numbers have been considerably reduced and a strange compromise reached which insists that so long as no more than 5% of its stock is 'hard-core' a shop will not be interfered with. Only three chains of shops are worth

242

mentioning (many of the Soho shops come and go like thieves in the night).

Ann Summers (Marble Arch, W1 and branches) specialises in *equipment*. That is to say things to put into places and things to tie things up with and things to pop into things to make things happen. The atmosphere of the shops is bright and breezy, not unlike a millinery store, but the objects themselves are terrifying to behold.

Janus Books (Old Compton Street, W1 and branches). Janus specialises in magazines, films and tapes which concern themselves with spanking. Why people should want to look at pictures of people spanking and being spanked is another of life's mysteries (like the plastic milk carton and the intelligence of the dolphin). But if you want spanking without the pain, go to *Janus*. Why Janus? Because the god turned the other cheek perhaps . . .

Private Shops (numerous branches throughout the suburbs and elsewhere). The fastest growing sex-shop operation with the main emphasis on video-hire and magazines. Overpriced, even at sale time, which is most of the time.

To recommend any shop in this list would imply that they have anything truly erotic to sell, which they seldom have. Beware of anything shrink-wrapped. Demand to see some footage of any film or video before buying. Most tourists face a sad disappointment when they return to the solitude of their hotel room. Still, as Woody Allen memorably said, masturbation is having sex with someone you love.

Best sex shop: *Whatever turns you on.*

.   .   .

Ships

Deptford was the home of ship-building since Henry VIII selected it as the site of the Royal Dockyard. Thereafter those sea-faring men who did not come from Devon were Deptford-born. From 1437 to 1882 the Pett family were shipwrights, architects, and officers in and of the navy. A master-builder in the dockyards in the time of Pepys was Jonas Shish. Here is John Evelyn writing about him in 1680: 'I was at the funeral of old Mr Shish, master shipwright of his Majesty's yard here, an honest and remarkable man, and his death a public loss, for his excelleent success in building ships (tho' altogether illiterate), and for breeding up so many of his children to be able artists. I held up the pall with three knights, who did him that honour, and he was worthy of it. It was the custom of this good man to rise in the night, and to pray kneeling in his own coffin, which he had lying by him many years.'

The Cutty Sark, a tea-clipper of the 1860s, preserved in dry docks at King William Walk, Greenwich, was built to the highest specifications and is one of the most beautiful ships ever created. Her collection of figureheads is worth a study. Nearby too is Sir Francis Chichester's Gipsy Moth IV, looking frail. Other fine ships include the cruiser, HMS Belfast, commissioned in 1939. She it was which opened the bombardment of the Normandy Coast on D Day, and she may be seen at Symon's Wharf, Wine Lane, Toolley Street, SE1.

The Tate and Lyle Sugar Ship, moored at Woolwich, is a beauty. Captain Scott's Discovery, presently in St Katherine's Docks Ships Museum, is fascinating, and other fine maritime survivals may be seen there and at the National Maritime Museum in Greenwich.

Best ship: The Cutty Sark.

Shirts

If one demands to have one's shirts made to measure, a great luxury, then Harvie & Hudson (77 Jermyn Street SW1; 01-930 3949), classic shirt makers, or Hilditch & Key, almost next door at 73 Jermyn Street (01-930 5336), or Turnbull & Asser at 71/72 Jermyn Street (01-930 0502), gently trendy, may be relied upon to pamper and flatter and cosset. As a general rule any establishment in Jermyn Street whose name includes an ampersand will be All Right.

For a bespoke shirt visit John Langford (23 Woodfield Road, W9; 01-289 0066) or the elegant Deborah & Clare (14b Beauchamp Place, SW3; 01-584 0641) or the Sale Shop (2 St Barnabas Street, SW1; 01-730 5913 and 5 Park Walk, SW10) whose traditional shirts are sold at better than traditional prices. Ted Lapidus (164 New Bond Street, W1; 01-629 2323) has such beautiful clothes that he can afford to be surly. Also recommended are Crolla and Paul Smith (see also under Tailors).

Best shirts: Turnbull & Asser.
Worst shirts: Nylon ones which cling.

Shoe Shops

In shoes more than anything else – except possibly life insurance and coffins – you get what you pay for. If you buy your shoes at the

Oxford Street chain stores or their high street branches, you won't of course, get originals, nor shoes in half sizes. *Lilley and Skinner's* (various branches) do specialise in smaller or larger than average feet, so give them a try. But even smaller (sizes 13-3 for women) and larger (women's sizes 8-11) feet can be accommodated at *Sally Small* (71 York Street, W1; 01-723 5321) who will send shoes on approval and at *Crispin's* (5 Chiltern Street, W1; 01-935 7984) and also caters for narrow feet (AA & AAA). Women who are able to pay for original shoes should visit *Manolo Blahnik* (49-51 Old Church Street, SW3; 01-352 8622) who makes the most beautiful shoes in London. Très glam (as they used to say in bad American musicals) are the shoes there and at *Santini e Dominici* – well, the name hardly suggests slipper socks, does it? – at 14 and 16 South Molton Street, W1 (01-629 9617). But for classic women's shoes try either *H. & M. Rayne Ltd* (57 Brompton Road, SW3; 01-589 5560 and branches) or *Charles Jourdan* (39 Brompton Road, SW3; 01-581 3333). Since the two shops are adjacent it's possible to test your purchases by walking from one to the other. At *Blackman's Shoe Shop* (28 Cheshire Street, E2; 01-739 3902) it is still possible to buy the classic English shoe for £15.

Men with small feet (from size 5) are catered for at *William Timpson* (424 Brixton Road, SW9; 01-274 4735 and branches) and handmade, handsewn shoes may be ordered from *H. Maxwell & Co Ltd* (11 Savile Row, W1; 01-734 9714). According to John Taylor, who ought to know, the best shoemaker in London is *G. J. Cleverley*, who made shoes for Valentino in *Blood and Sand*. Does he still make shoes? Ring him up (01-530 4797) and ask. Awkward feet are fitted and difficult repairs undertaken at *Gohill's Footwear* (246 Camden High Street, NW1; 01-485 9195), but for fine Italian shoes in traditional or flamboyant colours, *Rossetti* (177 New Bond Street, W1; 01-491 7066) is the place. Then of course there's *Kickers* (331 King's Road, SW3; 01-352 7541), whose boots are cheerful and durable . . .

If I were rich, which I shall be if you buy enough copies of this book, I should get my shoes at *Lobb's* (9 St James's Street, SW1; 01-930 3664), which, besides being one of the handsomest shops in London (not original though) and having cut shoes for Queen Victoria, makes a wooden last for each customer's foot and cuts and sews each piece of leather by hand. They do everything except milk the cow. Allow six months.

For children's shoes you should go to *Johnson's* (37-39 King's Parade, Twickenham, Middlesex; 01-892 9012, and branches in west London). Nothing is too much trouble for them and time seems limitless even for sneakers. High fashion children's shoes come from *Instep* (118 New Oxford Street, WC1; 01-637 7594). Continuous cartoons are played and the shoes are on specially low stands. The *Children's Foot Health Register* (84-88 Great Eastern Street, EC2; 01-739 2071) will help with all queries.

See also Cobblers.

Best shoes: (women) *Manolo Blahnik*.
Best shoes: (men) *Blackman's*.
Best shoes: (children's) *Johnson's*.

Shop Fronts

The most famous shop front in London is *James Smith and Sons*, 53 New Oxford Street, WC1 (01-836 4731). With wrought-iron above and sensationally good Gothic lettering everywhere, it seems churlish not to buy an umbrella (q.v.) or a shooting stick. Architecturally the most interesting is a Huguenot (c 1757) shop front with a fine double bow-window at *56 Artillery Lane*, Stepney (next to E. Patson and Son, scale makers) but *Berry Bros & Rudd* in St James's, that street of excellent shop fronts, is perfect 18th century. Nothing is more charming than *Woburn Walk* in Bloomsbury, where in 1822 Thomas Cubitt created a small shopping precinct, which has fortunately been preserved. For restrained good taste I recommend *Purdey & Son*, the gunsmiths (q.v.) in South Audley Street, W1, while *Gucci* in Bond Street and *Andrew Grima* in Jermyn Street are brilliant modern designs. I don't know which is more vulgar, *Denisa* (with a coronet over the D), the *Lady Newborough*, who spreads over several shop fronts in White Horse Street, W1, or *Jones* in Beauchamp Place, whose name is proclaimed in a kind of cable-knit script on a red marbled ground. At *46 South Molton Street*, a street of restrained opulence, *The Widow Applebaum's* is London's trendiest New York/Jewish restaurant and presents a façade of such exuberant crudity that one can only warm to it.

Other recommendations: *Penhaligons*, parfumiers of Covent Garden; *John Martin*, wine merchants of Eastcheap; *J. Wippell and Company*, haberdashers of Tufton Street, W1; and the minuscule but delightful headquarters of *Twinings*, tea merchants, in the Strand.

Quite the worst is *McDonald's* with their hideous logo. The trouble is there are so many branches; quite takes the appetite away. And *Kentucky Fried Chicken* is not much better. *Conduit Office Supplies* present a hardboard fascia to Conduit Street, which is lowering for Mayfair. Oh dear.

Best shop front: *Berry Bros & Rudd*, St James's.
Worst shop front: *McDonald's Hamburgers*.

Shopping Arcade

On the site of the old Lyons Corner House in Coventry Street just off Piccadilly Circus, stands the *Trocadero Arcade* – 'you've never been anywhere like it in your life'. It contains the most improbable selection of goods and services, living up to its slogan. There's the Guinness Book of Records Show, the modern equivalent of a freak show, although the freaks are only simulated and sponsored by a brewery, a gallery of holograms, Flex, a trendy Italian tailor and fashion-monger, several rather gloomy eating places, a disheartened fountain, and a cavernous bookshop with many books about royals and pop-stars. Not, on the whole, a place I would want to spend much time in.

See also Arcades.

Best shopping arcade: *Burlington Arcade*.
Worst shopping arcade: *Trocadero*.

Shove Halfpenny

The shove halfpenny championships of the world are held at the *Heroes of Alma Pub* (11 Alma Square, NW8; 01-286 3195). It should be added that this is emphatically not a spectator sport, and as yet the tobacco firms have not moved in as sponsors.

The Old Nun's Head (15 Nunhead Green, SE15; 01-639 1745) runs several teams of shovers, and at the *Rose and Crown* (47 Colombo Street, SE1; 01-928 4285), a lively family pub, halfpennies are shoved with great élan.

Signposts

Pleasantly old-fashioned signposts, some with pointing fingers, can be found in and around *Dulwich Village* and in the *Brent* area of north west London. The most poignant signpost is the one at *Streatham Vale*, SW16. It combines two signs on a single post. One says 'Lonesome Depot', the other 'South London Crematorium'. In *Hoe Street*, E17, there is a large and fierce sign reading: 'HALT Beware of Pedestrians'. It's as bad as being told to beware of low flying aircraft or, in France, of beetroots. The coyest sign is in the *Bayswater Road* – No 123 – where it announces: 'Decency Forbids – Lavatory Opposite'.

The best signpost in London – well in the world really – is the one which announces the Prime Meridian of the World (Latitude 51°28′ 38″ North, Longitude 0°00′00″); this, of course, is at the *Royal Observatory* in Greenwich. But the Meridian may be abolished.

The most ineffective signpost in London is the one in *Trafalgar Square* which announces that the west side of the square is open only to buses and taxis. Hardly anyone sees it, and many of those who do fail to understand it.

Best signpost: *The Prime Meridian*, Greenwich.

Skating

For a country which continues to produce such fine skaters, there are surprisingly few rinks. In London I can recommend the *Richmond* rink (Clevedon Road, East Twickenham; 01-892 3646), *Queens* (Queensway, W1; 01-229 0172), the *Sobell Leisure Centre* (Hornsey Road, N7; 01-607 1632) and *Streatham* (386 Streatham High Road, SW16; 01-769 7861), though this can get rowdy.

Old-fashioned it may be, but *Richmond* still has the best reputation. It produced John Curry and John Curry produced all the rest. In the Woolwich churchyard is a memorial to the boys who drowned in the Bowater Pond when tempted onto the ice by bigger boys throwing coins onto it.

Best rink: *Richmond*.

Snacks

See under All-Night Eating, Budget Restaurants, Fish and Chips, Take-Away Food, Tea Houses etc.

Softball

It's a gentle game for expatriate Americans, and it's getting a hold on

248

the Brits. Every Sunday in *Hyde Park* a team called the Hypsicos play. Originally the Hypsicos were those Americans involved in film-making in the days when London was the cheapest place for Americans to make films. And still they play, though some are now a little senior. There's a regular tournament called the Slick Willies Softball Tournament held at the *Eastway Sports Centre* in Hackney.

Best softball: *Hyde Park.*

Solicitors

Amongst the best:

Ashurst, Morris, Crisp & Co. (7 Throgmorton Ave, EC2; 01-283 1070).
Dawson & Co. (2 New Square, WC2; 01-404 5941).
Charles Doughty (civilised divorces) (20 Essex Street, WC2; 01-836 8400).
Harbottle & Lewis (theatrical) (34 South Molton Street, W1; 01-629 9871).
Hicks, Arnold, Rose, Johnson (6 Exchange Court, WC2; 01-836 4234).
Kennedy, Ponsonby & Prideaux (46 Cannon Street, EC4; 01-248 4741).
Lovell, White & King (21 Holborn Viaduct, EC1; 01-236 6011).
Rubinstein Callingham (literary) (6 Raymond Buildings, Gray's Inn, WC1; 01-242 8408).

To name the worst would undoubtedly lead to litigation. But I would win.

Squares

There is a popular misconception that *Bedford Square* is the last complete Georgian Square in London. Well, it isn't. It is the last complete early Georgian Square in London, but the unheralded and unsung *Myddleton Square* in Finsbury is uniform and complete and dates from the early 19th century. Other little-known delights from that period include *Cleaver Square*, SE1, and *Cloudesley Square*, N1 (church by Barry); while off the Commercial Road in Stepney, *Albert Gardens* is a regular three-sided square of early 19th century houses, unpretentious and charming. Indeed there are plenty of good old squares to choose from, as the actress said looking down from the gallery of the House of Commons.

Initially the squares were built by aristocrats and their agents, latterly by speculators who sometimes were, shamefully, aristocrats. The earliest (*Bloomsbury Square* and *St James's Square*) were planned before the Great Fire (1666) but most of the square-building took place in the century after the ashes stopped smouldering. The names of the speculators, Bond and Clarges, Frith and Neale, Panton and others, are familiar to us from street names. Nicholas Barbon, who laid out £200,000 in building costs but economised by standardising the designs, was for a time the most successful, but he was a hard bargainer and when he died I'm sorry to say that his will stipulated that none of his enormous debts should be paid. Typical Barbon houses may be studied in Bedford Row.

Sadly much of what the 19th century put up, the 20th century speculators pulled down. Whatever happened to *Portman, Tolmer, Grosvenor, Sloane, Tavistock, Berkeley* or *Audley Squares?* In *Union Square* the square-bashers left half of the square intact to display most eloquently the mess they had made of the other half. Occasionally the squares were unpleasant from the start, and *Milner Square* is very strange. In the words of the great Sir John Summerson: 'It is possible to visit *Milner Square* many times and still not be absolutely certain that you have seen it anywhere but in an unhappy dream.'

For myself I like *Lincoln's Inn Fields* and *Old Palace Yard*, Westminster, hugely, but they are not what one means by a London square. While *Golden Yard*, Hampstead (tiny, Elizabeth Goudge-ish), *Percy Circus, Fitzroy Square* and *Smith Square* (Headquarters of the Conservative party and a dignified setting for the prettiest concert hall (q.v.) in London), deserve to be mentioned, my choice will be *Manchester Square* (1776-1788) because, although dominated by Hertford House, the home of the Wallace Collection, and otherwise little regarded by the architectural historians, it is green and pleasant, and less disturbed by traffic fumes than many of the grander squares. Runners-up include *Dorset Square, Bedford Square* (inevitably), *St James's Square* (very fine, excellent to park in, with an enchanting vista of the Haymarket Theatre), *Mecklenburgh Square* (J. Kay, 1812), *Kensington Square, Lonsdale Square* and *Paulton's Square*.

On the subject of *Kensington Square*, where my Granny lived, this is where John Stuart Mill's maid used Carlyle's only copy of the manuscript of his *History of the French Revolution* – a massive work – to light the fire. It is also expensively and upwardly mobile.

Disasters, besides those mentioned above, include *Leicester Square* – no matter what they do to it, it remains squalid and acid rain eats away at the faces of the statues – and *Finsbury Circus. A History of London Squares* by E. B. Chancellor was published in 1907.

Best London Square: *Manchester Square.*
Worst London Square: *Leicester Square.*

Squash Clubs

Squash clubs have been poking up all over London as this excellent game gains popularity. I used to play at the *Griffin Club* in Shepherd's Bush Road when Jonah Barrington was just a nipper up from Cornwall and keeping himself, I seem to recall, by working as an artists' model. The real trouble with most squash clubs is the heartiness of their members (and their uncanny aptitude for getting my best serves back). The best club – besides the *RAC* in Pall Mall, and *Queen's Club* (for those posh venues squash is only a minor part of their activities) – is *Putney Squash Rackets Club* (84 Upper Richmond Road, SW15; 01-870 7086), which enjoys some of the warmest courts on bitter winter mornings and the friendliest bar staff.

Best squash club: *Putney.*

Stamps

The cutest stamp shop must be the one on Waterloo Station with this endearingly candid notice: 'My entire stock is in the window'. Other candid notices explain why the shop is open so infrequently: 'I live 40 miles from London and with the train service so unreliable . . .', invite one *not* to ask for change for telephones, and so on. The owner is honest and at great pains to point out the flaw, wrinkles and missing gum of the really very handsome classic stamps he sells at such moderate prices. At *Phil's Stamp Shop* (370 Upper Richmond Road, SW14; 01-876 5132) I have always received a very fair hearing: I say 'hearing' advisedly, for it is very unusual for a stamp shop actually to want to buy stamps from a customer, although Phil actually does sometimes. I do hope his health improves.

Most London stamp shops are in and near the Strand, clustering around the formidable *Stanley Gibbons*, like poor relatives around a famous man. At *Stanley Gibbons* one expert on Rhodesia told me that my £5 Rhodesian stamp of 1903 was a real treasure and that the last one they had like it had been sold privately for £900, but at the end of the week his colleague dismissed the 'treasure' to me as an 'obvious fake'. Try to sell stamps at the *Strand Stamp Centre* opposite *Stanley Gibbons*, and they look at you much as if you'd asked whether Edward VIII should abdicate over Mrs Simpson. The conglomerate of collectors opposite the Embankment tube station and under the arches at Charing Cross are more accommodating. One Saturday I took a stall there and sold my entire stock for £2,100 cash.

It can be most frustrating. I invited *Robson Lowe's* comments on a hand-stamp from the first Paris Commune. They had never seen anything like it, they said, and photocopied it, sending the original to their agent in Paris. He had never seen anything like it either, and *Robson Lowe* (50 Pall Mall, SW1; 01-839 4034) concluded that its very uniqueness rendered it, so far as they could tell, valueless. The politest of all brush-offs came from *Argyll Etkin Ltd* (recently moved to 48 Conduit Street, off New Bond Street, W1; 01-437 7800). There, ever so charmingly, they begin by saying, 'You're going to hate us after we've told you our view of your stamps . . .' But the last time they said that I sold the same stamps by public auction for £470. *Argyll Etkin* have just sold a collection of early American stamps and postal history for the staggering sum of £11,000,000.

Phillips (17 Blenheim Street, W1; 01-629 6602) auction stamps most Thursdays. *Harmer's, Christie's, Sotheby's* and *Stanley Gibbons* more infrequently. *City of London Auctions* (27 King Street, the Strand, London WC2; 01-240 8459), hold fortnightly lunchtime sales, which are principally for City businessmen. They are extremely jolly affairs, but the auctioneers like to be paid in cash. A recent innovation is to sell off unsold lots, sight unseen, at half the estimate.

The *National Philatelic Society* is at 1 Whitehall Place, SW1 (01-839 1987) and the *Royal Philatelic Society*, unparalleled for solemn elegance, is at 41 Devonshire Place, W1 (01-935 7332). A certificate of authentication from the RPS is as eagerly sought after as a safe conduct out of hell, but their consultations are very slow. One of the finest stamp collections in the country is the Stamp Room at *Buckingham Palace*. No problem about getting in to see that. Just shin up a drainpipe . . .

The *National Postal Museum* is upstairs from the Central Post Office (King Edward Street, EC1). The museum is empty. But closer inspection reveals hundreds of handles on the walls. Pull on one and out comes a sample of the other most important stamp collection in the world. The original was a gift by Reginald Phillips in 1965, but it has been much extended since.

The *Penny Black* public house (Tentor House, Moorfields, Moorgate, EC2; 01-628 3675) is a philatelists' pub and has a large exhibition of photostats from the GPO Museum, while the *Mayflower* pub in Rotherhithe Street, SE16, is the only pub in the world licensed to sell postage stamps.

Best stamp dealer: *The GPO*.

Stationers

> From a Donald MacGill comic postcard:
> Customer to Nubile Assistant in Newsagent's Shop: 'Do you keep stationery?'
> Nubile Assistant: 'No, I wriggle about a bit sometimes.'

At *Pen to Paper* (11 Long Acre, WC2; 01-379 6560) I bought 500 sheets of good quality weave – A4 in a tasteful shade of mauve – and set about trying to find a printers or stationers who would print my name and address at the top of it in a type of my choosing. The price quoted by commercial printers was close on £50. Obviously too extravagent. *W. H. Smith* said they *would* have done it, and quoted a sensible price, only it was the firm's policy never to print on somebody else's paper. In the end I was reduced to having a rubber stamp made (£8). A bit non-U, déclassé, arriviste and naff.

Despite strong recommendations for *Scribner's* (29 St James Street, WC2; 01-240 7640) with contemporary importations from France and the USA, *Smythson* (54 New Bond Street, W1; 01-629 8558), *Chisholm's* (four branches), where you can buy the Filofax system, without which governments fall and worlds collide, and the *Walton Street Stationery Co.* (97 Walton Street, SW3; 01-589 0777), which is so seductive that it almost makes you want to pay bills, the verdict lies between *Paperchase* (213 Tottenham Court Road, W1; 01-580 8496 and a Fulham Road branch), to be avoided at Christmas, and *Lamley and Co.* (5 Exhibition Road, SW7; 01-589 1276), a somewhat haphazard stationer and bookseller, whose leisurely concern for the customer is welcome. I want to say a few more words about the Filofax system, because there is now a competitor in the rather cheaper Microfile Executive, retailing at £28.50 – where Filofax starts at £35 and rises to £300 for the lizard-skin model. And although *Chisholm's* was the original London stockists, *Just Facts* in Covent Garden Market is now also able to sell Filofax. Microfile is available at *Gill Wing* (194-195 Upper Street, N1; 01-359 7697).

The best specialist paper retailers is *Falkiner's Fine Papers* (117

Long Acre, WC2; 01-379 6245) with a range of over 1,000 papers and such accessories as gold leaf and calligraphy supplies.

Best stationer: *Lamley and Co.*

P.S. Would it not be agreeable if you could buy stamps wherever you buy envelopes and postcards?

Stations

> Aug 3, 1856 – We went to meet Papa this evening at King's Cross Station, waited half an hour in dimness and desolation, till ring a ring a ring, up go the lamps, a hundred people start out of the earth, in climbs the train with its two yellow eyes fuming along the line, out pour the passengers and we were just getting frightened, when yes there he is. And so thank God for bringing him home again.
>
> – Anne Thackeray Ritchie.

At the official opening of Giles Gilbert Scott's *St Pancras Station* the architect collapsed in tears, muttering – for those close enough to hear: 'It is too beautiful!'

Now indeed the beauty of *St Pancras* has emerged for all to see with the removal of a century's grime and dust from its red bricks. Not that the front of the station – what we usually refer to as the station – is in fact the station. The station is the curved iron magnificence under which the trains used to puff and pant and hoot – now they merely sigh. But really *St Pancras* does us proud.

One fine London station currently under threat of closure is *Marylebone*, and *Broad Street* has been demolished.

Marylebone was the last of the Metropolitan termini to be erected. Sir Edward William Watkin conceived it as an essential link between the industrial midlands, the south coast, and the continent, but the struggle to persuade local VIPs and the MCC that the station was desirable cost Sir Edward so much that he had to employ a jobbing engineer for the actual building. The simplicity of what resulted is charming. In *England, their England* A. G. Macdonell described Marylebone as a place where 'porters go on tiptoe, where the barrows are rubber-tyred and the trains sidle mysteriously in and out with only the faintest of toots on their whistles, so as not to disturb the signalmen'.

Marylebone still is peaceful. There are padded chairs in the ladies waiting room – even though the seats have been slashed. The concourse has been aesthetically ruined by numerous yellow litter-bins (q.v.).

Broad Street, terminus of the old North London Railway and the North London Line from Richmond, was opened in 1866. It had in recent years acquired a poignant derelict charm.

Victoria is the busiest station in Britain. Between 1902 and 1908 no less than two million pounds was spent on rebuilding and enlarging it. The platforms are each more than a quarter of a mile long, and the station can accommodate 18 trains, but only 24 passengers can sit down on the paltry seats provided by British Rail in the whole of the concourse. The Brighton line, of course, was immortalized by Oscar Wilde.

Victoria boasts a sock shop, a fruit and flower shop, a heel bar, a hairdressing salon, a tourist information centre and plenty of bars and buffets. You can buy a burger at Casey's until 2 a.m.

Charing Cross, Paddington, Cannon Street, London Bridge and *Waterloo* all have their fan clubs. But there is little doubt about the worst London station. *Liverpool Street* is a slum, the Bowery of the transport system. No bars or buffets are attached to Eastern Regions trains – if anyone can help it, and trains are cancelled with gleeful enthusiasm. A very sad case.

Best station: *St Pancras*.
Worst station: *Liverpool Street*.

See also Railway Lines and Underground Stations. And read *London's Termini* by A. A. Jackson (David and Charles).

Statues/Sculptures

Queen Victoria's
statue is
the work of her
daughter Beatrice.
The shape's all wrong,
And the crown don't fit,
but – bless her old heart!
She was proud of it – Humbert Wolfe (1885-1940)

There are nine statues of *Queen Victoria* in London and five of *Shakespeare* – a most undistinguished selection for our greatest poet and playwright. Until recently there were two statues of *Pocahontas*. One of them, opposite Cassell's in Red Lion Square, was naked and would have turned the head of a less susceptible man than Captain Smith. But the rotters took it away.

On the subject of nakedness, Canova's *Napoleon* in Apsley House is nine feet tall in white marble and naked except for his marshal's baton and victorious fillet. Outside on Hyde Park Corner and on an even grander scale is Sir Richard Westmacott's 30 feet high nude of *Achilles* (1882), cast from French 24-pounders captured at Salamanca, Vittoria, Toulouse and Waterloo. The statue was subscribed for by the gentlewomen of England in honour of the Iron Duke. They were more than a little alarmed when they saw what their money had got them. Even Achilles' fig-leaf (he is not really Achilles, but the sculptor had to call him something) was scarcely enough to pacify their beating hearts. It may be that some of the gentlemen of England found him provocative too, for his fig-leaf was chipped off in 1871 and 1961, the present one having survived for over twenty years.

The matter of size is interesting. One wouldn't wish for *Karl Marx's* stupendous head in Highgate Cemetary (by Laurence Bradshaw) to be an inch less than its terriffic four times life-size, but gigantism has its dangers. The recent *Mountbatten* statue (by Franta Belsky), which looks across Horseguards Parade to the Admiralty, is 9 foot high on a 5 foot plinth; a fair likeness of the ageing Admiral of the Fleet with a jaunty quiff of hair and a vast pair of naval binoculars. *Montgomery* (Oscar Nemon), though dwarfed by the hideous Ministry of Defence, is 14 foot high, a bronze of the colour and texture of a chocolate birthday cake. He in turn dwarfs William Macmillan's more interesting statue of *Sir Walter Raleigh*, but the old general is set far enough upstage of the poet/colonist to keep the perspective orderly. Macmillan (1887-1977) was one of the most distinguished of London's sculptors with *George VI, Beatty, Trenchard, Alcock and Brown*, and *Rolls and Royce* to his credit, as well as a most intriguingly sculpted lightning conductor at the Kensington and Chelsea Town Hall.

Also at Hyde Park Corner is *King David*, representing the artillery; he is said to have a most fetching bottom, and since the traffic passes close by, numerous accidents are caused to and by drivers of a certain persuasion. *Sir Arthur Sullivan* has a naked lady weeping at his ankles – successful composers get these – together with a mis-spelled quotation from *The Yeomen of the Guard*, but the most erotic nude statue in London is *La Déliverance* by Emile Guillaume. It may be seen at the junction of Finchley Road and the North Circular. A naked girl, symbolising the emotions felt by the allies at the conclusion of the battle of the Marne (1914), stands on tip-toe on a globe with a sword upraised. Someone with a sense of humour chose Lloyd George to do the unveiling.

Many of London's finest statues are grouped together in Victoria Embankment Gardens, Leicester Square and Waterloo Place. In the first named, besides *Sir Arthur Sullivan*, you may find a charming memorial by Major Cecil Brown to the *Camel Corps* (1920). It's a camel, and there's another camel at the foot of the *Albert Memorial*. Also a fine bronze of *Robert Burns* sitting on a tree trunk and composing poetry (Sir John Steel), and statues to an advocate of temperance, the founder of the Sunday Schools, and others. A wall fountain to *Henry Fawcett* (no pun intended, one supposes), the blind statesman, refreshes.

Leicester Square, once a duelling ground and now a pedestrian precinct, offers statues of *Shakespeare, Reynolds, Hogarth* and *John Hunter*, the founder of modern surgery; also a sentimental figure of *Charlie Chaplin* by John Doubleday (1981), and a most inadequate memorial to *Sir Isaac Newton*.

In Waterloo Place, besides the National Memorial to Edward VII and various military men, *Captain Scott* may be observed sculpted by his wife in Antarctic kit (he wears it; I doubt whether his wife when she sculpted him did), and *Florence Nightingale* next to her friend and victim, *Sidney Herbert*. A less formal *Florence Nightingale* is on the North Terrace of St Thomas's Hospital. She wears a cap and frilled cuffs and carries a lamp, but she is only a replica, for the original was stolen by thieves. Also at Thomas's a delightful bronze of *Edward VI*, 'a most excellent prince of exemplary piety, and wisdom above his years. The glory of his reign and most magnificent founder of this hospital'. Another king well served by his sculptor is *Charles I*. Hidden during the Civil War, the statue of him which now stands at the top of Whitehall is simple, dignified and venerable. The best likeness I know is the bust of *Queen Mary* – regal determination, arrogant charm – by W. Reid Dick in the National Portrait Gallery.

Other fine likenesses to have been spotted include Belsky's *Admiral Cunningham* (the north side of Trafalgar Square alongside the first world war admiral, *Beatty* – handsome and doesn't he know it – and *Jellicoe*) and *David Livingstone* (by Huxley-Jones), just around the corner from *Sir Ernest Shackleton* in a niche on the Royal Geographical Society, Exhibition Road. *Livingstone* – what a good name for a sculptor's model! – is leaning on a stick, carrying a book with a coat over his arm, dressing on the left; he has tightened his belt and wears a cloth shielding the back of his neck from sunburn and mosquitoes. His is the sort of stare that says: 'And what have *you* discovered?'

But it is when the sculptor attempts considerably more than a close likeness that the fun begins. The first *Baron Baden-Powell of Gillwell OM*, outside the house that bears his name, is an ambivalent memorial by Donald Potter. Considerably larger than life, his large, bald head bears a vacant expression and a rather sickly smile, his shrunken shoulders seeming to suggest that perhaps none of the effort was worthwhile, not when you look around you at what became of the Empire.

In Kensington Gardens may be found two of London's most loved statues, *Physical Energy* by G. F. Watts (1906) and *Peter Pan* by George Frampton. The *Peter Pan* tableau, which derives from Barrie's *The Little White Bird*, which he set in Kensington Gardens, includes mice and rabbits and fairies and such, and has been polished smooth by generations of posh children playing on it. The actress Nina Boucicault modelled for Peter. Just along the road at Bowater House, the main entrance to the Park, is a group which is circumvented by a vast tonnage of traffic every day. This is Epstein's work; some know it as *Pan*, others as *The Family of Man*. A mother and father, two children and an excited dog, are permanently frozen as they run towards the trees. Close on their heels and playing his pipes is the untrustworthy figure of Pan (not Peter).

London contains several *boys on dolphins*, easily the most attractive being the one by David Wynne on the corner of Victoria Embankment and Oakley Street. The boy is airborne but keeps hold of the dolphin's fin with the tips of his fingers. David Wynne was also responsible for a *girl on a dolphin* (in front of the Tower Hotel, St Katharine's Way), and the grandiose figure of *Guy the Gorilla* at London Zoo, the same Guy who died in 1978 at the age of 32 and is still mourned.

The oldest statues in London are the marble sculptures found in the *Temple of Mithras*, Walbrook, and presently to be seen in the London Museum. *King Alfred* in handsome Trinity Church Square, SE1 (formerly in Westminster Hall) is thought to date back to the 14th century. He looks wise but worried, perhaps because nobody is sure whether he is King Alfred.

The best statue of *Churchill* (Ivor Roberts-Jones 1973) is in Parliament Square. Impressive and business-like, this *Churchill* is striding off the plinth as though he cannot wait to get back into the debating chamber and at the throats of the mining MPs. Together with *Freud* (near the Swiss Cottage Library), *Gandhi* (in Tavistock Square), and *Sir Thomas More* (handsomely represented on the

Embankment outside Chelsea Old Church) he has not been diminished by his statue.

St Thomas à Becket, set amongst orange and yellow roses like purifying flames in St Paul's Churchyard, is depicted, gaunt and tortured as he falls backward, protecting his eyes either from his assassins or from the dazzle of eternity. The sculptor, Edward Bainbridge Copnall (1903-1973) also deserves our gratitude for his figures on the RIBA building in Portland Place and for his marble relief of *Laurence Olivier* and *Vivien Leigh* as Caesar and Cleopatra (in King Street where the St James's Theatre, in which they played those roles, once stood – see Friezes).

An extraordinary bronze by B. Kubica, depicting *Chopin* and donated by the people of Poland was erected 'through the initiative of Professor Stefania Nekrasz' in a tiny ivy-girt garden to the east of the Festival Hall. The face appears eaten away, crushed by rock strata or rushes or heavy drapes or standing corn, an artist striving to be heard amidst the concrete cacophany of the South Bank.

Although I'm fond of Barbara Hepworth's *Winged Victory* excitingly placed on the wall of John Lewis's at Oxford Circus, and of the charming lady shoppers outside Jeeves in Pont Street (black cement by Derek Holmes/Kate McGill) who are obviously hell-bent on a cup of tea and a Kunzle cake in Harrods, the award must rest between Henry Moore's *Draped Seated Woman* on the Stafford Estate, Jamaica Road, SE1 and Epstein's bronze *Madonna and Child* (inspired, I believe, by Michelangelo) on what was once the Convent of the Holy Child, Cavendish Square, W1. This piece he called his 'passport to eternity', but both Moore and the Epstein are deeply serious and unforgettable. For an expert analysis see *London Statues* by Arthur Byron (Constable).

Best Statues: *Sir Thomas More* by L. Cubitt Bevis; *Draped Seated Woman* by Henry Moore; *Madonna and Child* by Jacob Epstein.

Most inadequate statues: *Sir Isaac Newton; Dr Johnson* (behind St Clement Dane's).

Worst modern statue; *Field-Marshal Earl Haig.* The horse's legs are improperly synchronised; Haig is in uniform but without a hat; and the old rogue doesn't deserve a statue anyway.

P.S. A delightful letter points my attention to a statue in Pimlico Park which was raised in honour of the first man ever killed by a railway train, *William Huskisson*. He is draped in a sort of toga because the sculptor felt that this was the only way to display the human form. (See also Umbrellas).

259

Steaks

Not at all easy to get a decent steak in London. A survival of the old-style steak houses is the *London Steak House*, 96 Dulwich Village, SE21 (01-693 6880) and *Berni Inns* (various branches) are still beavering away. I can strongly recommend *Rowley's*, 113 Jermyn Street, SW1 (01-930 2707), and *Sexton Blake's*, 38 Panton Street, SW1 (01-930 8042). *Simply Steaks* 66 Heath Street, NW3 (01-794 6775) do at least specialise in what we are talking about, and do it well. *Simply Steaks* is open till midnight.

But the best steaks are served at *Chez Gerard*, 8 Charlotte Street, W1 (01-636 4975). They are charcoaly and come with a massive plate of pomme frites – much nicer than common or garden chips – and one of those pleasant salads with bits of bacon in it. The hollandaise sauce has come in for criticism, but not from me. Service is cursory, and the plates are almost as thick as the steaks. Not a subtle place.

Best steaks: *Chez Gerard.*

Steps/Staircases

The grandeur of the steps leading to the *Albert Memorial* (designed by Sir Gilbert Scott for £120,000 which Albert would have considered excessive) represents the optimism of an age which could afford to be expensive. The *Duke of York Steps* which descend from Waterloo Place to the Mall and St James's Park are much loved. They form a matching set with the Duke of York's Column (Benjamin Wyatt, 1833) – steps should lead to something high – which marks the site of Carlton House, built by John Nash between 1827 and 1832 for Crockford, the fishmonger turned bookmaker who wished to put Buckingham Palace in the shade, and did. From these steps one has a fine view over the park to Big Ben, the House of Commons and numerous high-rise blocks, and having climbed the steps, one can enjoy the statues before relaxing for a refreshing cup of tea at the Ceylon Tea Centre in Lower Regent Street. I'm also delighted by *Holly Bush Steps*, which descend into Heath Street from Holly Bush Hill in Hampstead. They are charming, but the steps leading up to *St Bride's Institute*, just off Fleet Street, are gloomily impressive. Best for sitting on are the steps at the *National Gallery* and the *Tate* (but the Metropolitan Museum steps in New York are the very best for sitting on).

Dirty, windy and bleak are the steps at *Bromley South Shopping Precinct*. Even worse are the steps at most multi-storey carparks. Disastrous are the steps up to the *Monument*. Restful are the front steps at *The Sanctuary*, adjoining the Westminster Abbey Bookshop. Mr Thorne who works in the building writes: 'We like to think that throughout the world, there are many posteriors that abode their hour or two and went their way.'

There are fine staircases everywhere in London. The *Tulip Staircase* at Queen's House, Greenwich; Wyatt and Barry's Grand Staircase at *Lancaster House*, St James's which uses the full height of the building; the magnificent Cromwellian staircase in the finest oak at *Cromwell House*, Highgate; the staircase of exceptional splendour at *44 Berkeley Square*; the fine iron staircase (c 1700) at *37 Stepney Green*. The elliptical staircase (1810) in *7 Albemarle Street*; the painted staircase (1720) of *8 Clifford Street*, W1, and the fine mid 18th-century staircase in the *Skinners' Hall* (8 Dowgate Hill, EC4); represent everything that staircases are about. An unusual open-air staircase is the one in the Italian manner starting up the side of the threatened *Broad Street Station*. I could continue. But space requires me to choose . . .

Best staircase: *Cromwell House*, Highgate.
Best steps: *Waterloo Place*.

Stores

There is a rumour, possibly apocryphal, that there is a lady living just two blocks from *Harrods* to whom a single small carton of yoghurt is delivered every morning – free of delivery charge, of course. Certainly *Harrods* (motto: 'Omnia, Omnibus, Ubique' – 'All things to all people everywhere') is the best place for changing unwanted Christmas presents and they will even take back sales goods, which very few other stores will. One can even haggle at *Harrods* and then demand a further reduction by paying cash. If you have an account at *Harrods*, you are permitted to reserve sale goods on the day before the sales open to the public. I have found it a useful rule of thumb to patronise sales only at high class stores since the substantial discounts offered on classic goods constitute real bargains, while rubbish remains rubbish no matter how cheap it may have been. A recent *Harrods* advertisement suggests the unique quality of the place rather well – 'Who will send a box of Kippers to Texas? Where can you get your software, your hardware, and your underwear? Where can you leave your husband in the Green Man and Rover in the dog-house? Where can you sip a Singapore Sling, choose a Chinese carpet and pamper a Persian Blue? Where can you get the family jewels valued while you wait, have them insured and buy the silver polish? Who else makes so little fuss about giving a banking service on Saturdays (and up till 5 p.m. during the week)? Where can you have your suit, your kitchen and your birthday cake made to measure? Where can you have your face painted, your father photographed and your great grandmother traced? Where can you book your perm, your seat at the Proms and your flight to Palermo? Where can you buy a gold-plated TV and an orchid for your wife and have them both gift-wrapped? Where?'

But it needs to be added that, excepting the food hall, the goods at *Harrods* are displayed in a thoroughly uninspired and old-fashioned manner.

Of course, *Harrods* is not the only London store. *Liberty's* in Regent Street is splendid for walking through and – inevitably – getting lost in. The only vulgar goods I have ever seen in *Liberty's* were those leather rhinos. Their silks, of course, and wallpapers are wonderful. *John Lewis* and the various stores linked to the partnership pride themselves on never being knowingly undersold; they are strongest in textiles and furnishing fabrics. *Harvey Nichols* are old-fashioned but courteous, while *Fortnum and Mason's*, whose salesmen wear tailcoats, is not so much a shop, more a trip to the moon on gossamer wings. Having given up half its space to *Habitat*, *Heal's* is a skeletal shadow of its former glory – though the restaurant is grand. At *Marks and Spencers* the clothes are slightly old fashioned, as they have to be when such huge quantities are involved, but they are excellent value. There is never any unpleasantness about taking unsatisfactory purchases back; if you are unprincipled you can get cash back for goods which you have purchased by cheque; a useful standby in times of crisis. Once when I had wrecked a corkscrew trying to decork a bottle of wine bought at M & S, they gave me a replacement bottle of wine and a pound to buy a new corkscrew with. They don't take credit cards at Marks and Sparks, but have issued their own. *Woolworth's* is not to be derided. The counters loaded with sticky sweets are not an inspiring sight on Monday mornings, but for goods such as watering cans, giant boxes of matches, light bulbs etc. you can travel a lot further and pay a lot more.

Probably the best of the old-fashioned family stores is *Barber's* (417 North End Road, SW6; 01-385 6666) a splendid place in Fulham particularly for Christmas presents.

I have also heard good reports of *Ely's*, 16 St George Road,

Wimbledon, SW19 (01-946 9191) (for courtesy) and *Bentall's* (Wood Street, Kingston-upon-Thames; 01-546 1001) whose courtesy I have experienced at first hand. Both of these suburban stores excel in storage and removals. In Oxford Street *The Pantheon* is the exception, because for most of its length Oxford Street is a shopping disaster area. But *Selfridges* (Oxford Street, W1; 01-629 1234) has at last found itself a role and is altogether more cheerful these days. Miss Selfridge and the kosher food department are splendid.

Of all the stores which London has lost I mourn *Whiteley's* most; without it the Queensway and Westbourne Grove area lacks dignity and seriousness of purpose.

Best store: *Harrods*.

Street Lights

Many of the early gas-holders are magnificent. Look for example, at the bold lamps guarded by winged dragons, on *Holborn Viaduct*. Almost anything may hold or guard a lamp. Serpents do it (*1 Wimpole Street*, W1; *193 Euston Road*, NW1; *23 Queen's Square*, Isleworth), winged mermen do it (*15 Harrington Road*, SW7). Atlas does it on holiday from carrying the world (*18 Finsbury Square*, EC2), a Viking ship does it (the *Norwegian Church*, Albion Street, SE16), and even an owl does it sleepily and slyly (the *Bank of England*).

Most impressive are the ironwork lamp-holders (c 1750-1760) by Isaac Ware outside *44 Berkeley Square*; most dignified are those along the north face of *Drury Lane Theatre* (the only original section remaining); most delightful are the cluster of converted gas lamps opposite the *Garrick Theatre*. Covent Garden is the area for hunters of old gas-lamp holders; there are several in *St Martin's Court*, WC2. London bridges are particularly well lit. From the frivolous clusters on *Putney Bridge* to the outrageous nautical nonsenses on *Lambeth Bridge*, from the solemn dignity of *Westminster Bridge* and *Tower Bridge* to the cheerful silliness of the lights on *Hammersmith Bridge*, all enhance their function.

After the advent of electricity designers of street lamps were able to direct the light source downwards, but greater freedom did not necessarily mean that their designs were more imaginative. I seem to have seen the celebrated four-sided lantern in the *Strand* with 'Savoy Theatre' engraved on the glass in countless films of the forties and fifties. If Edgar Lustgarten didn't stand in front of it to deliver homilies he ought to have done. In *Carting Lane* alongside the Savoy is another famous street lamp. Lit by gas, it is never extinguished. Nor is the flame outside *L'Epicure* (see French Restaurants).

The most elaborate of all and probably the most loved are those lamp standards along the *Thames Embankment*. Sir Joseph Bazalgette gave us twisting dolphins above lion masks along the *Victoria Embankment*; the *Chelsea Embankment* is even more elaborate with children clambering up the lions and fish bearing torches to light the lamps. In *Trafalgar Square*, close to Admiralty Arch, the lamp standards are encrusted with fat putti amidst a wild cluster of animal and marine life. But I think that despite the claims of these and of the fine lamps which illuminate the Nash terraces, the best street lights in London are those in *Lincoln's Inn Fields*. Have a look at them.

Best street lights: *Lincoln's Inn Fields*.
Worst street lights: *Cromwell Road Extension*. Though the lighting in Jermyn Street is an opportunity sadly wasted.

Street Markets

Petticoat Lane, alias Middlesex Street, alias Hogs Lane, used to be the boundary between the City of London and the County of Middlesex. Once it was monopolised by the Irish; then the Jews took it over, proudly proclaiming: 'We are perhaps the sons of dealers in old clothes, but we are the grandsons of prophets'. Their philosophy was that to sell something you have to someone who wants it is not business, but to sell something you don't have to someone who doesn't want it, that is business. Now it has been handed over to the Arabs, whose new mosque shines out across Whitechapel Road like a good deed in a naughty world. According to Henry Mayhew who conducted his survey into the London working classes a century or so ago, there was one significant detail about the Petticoat Lane market: 'Everything is at the veriest minimum of price. The bottle of lemonade which is elsewhere a penny is here a halfpenny.' And Walter Besant in *All Sorts and Conditions of Men* described it thus: 'Here are displayed all kinds of things; bits of second-hand furniture, such as the head of a wooden bed . . . skates sold cheap in summer, tight clothing in winter; workmen's tools of every kind . . . books, boots, shoes . . . cutlery, hats and caps; rat-traps and mouse-traps and bird-cages; flowers and seeds; skillets . . . bloaters and haddocks . . .'

As everyone must know *Petticoat Lane* these days is more for tourists than for bargain hunters; not many antiques there, except the jokes told by the stall-holders. And keep your hands in your pockets. They used to say that you could walk through Petticoat Lane, and see your own handkerchief for sale on a stall by the time you got to the end. But V. S. Pritchett tells how at the old dog market in Bethnal Green you could buy back your own beloved airedale painted black and offered as a retriever! While on the subject, the continuing market in lost and stolen animals, often kept in degrading conditions, at *Club Row*, E2, on Sunday mornings, is an outrage. So is *Southall Market*, the only weekly horse market in Britain. Most of the horses sold there (and many of them have been stolen) are bound for butchers' shops in France and Belgium.

For fruit, vegetables and junk, *Whitechapel* is good, but *Hoe Street Market*, Walthamstow, E17, is better; there's a mile of it. And *Borough Market*, next to Southwark Cathedral, is best. *Brick Lane*, E1, early on a Sunday morning is over-rated, although it's lively enough and almost the only place to go for plastic flowers. *Brixton* is excellent, especially for cut-price reggae music. For antiques, *Bermondsey Market* (the *New Caledonian*, on Fridays) is among the cheapest, but you need to get there exceptionally early (about 4.30 a.m. in summer) and you'll not make it without private transport. Take a torch too or you'll regret it. *Portobello* (Saturdays) has a quarter of a million customers through its market; specialists can usually find their stall somewhere – and don't ignore the covered arcades, where most of the better quality items are to be found. I sold a Japanese print there for £25 that I couldn't get 25p for in my shop. *Cutler Street* (just off Petticoat Lane, Fridays to Sundays) is for silver, coins, medals and stamps; *Farringdon Road* (weekends and Saturdays, lunch-time) is for books, but only about six stalls survive and it is a shadow of past glories. *Columbia Road Market* (Bethnal Green, Sunday mornings) is superb for gardeners, but they don't sell tools; these you should get at *Leather Lane* near the City (Monday to Friday 11 a.m.-3 p.m.) or at *Franklin's Camberwell Market* (159/161 Camberwell Road, SE5 – closed Mondays) where Reuben Reubens, collector of banjos and dealer in toys may be found.

Camden Passage, Islington, is for good quality antiques with prices to match. Better value on Wednesdays (from 7.30 a.m.) than on Saturdays (from 9 a.m.). But there are still several amiable junky stalls. *Camden Lock* is too trendy for my taste, but it's useful if you want to discover the lastest collecting craze (currently old linen). I used to have a stall at *Streatham Market* (not a street market because it's in a church hall next to the bus station) on Thursday mornings (7 a.m. to 1 p.m.). It's principally for dealers, but the public can do well – they used to make a killing at my stall.

Best street market: (for vegetables) *Borough.*
    (for antiques): *Bermondsey.*
    (for fun): *Petticoat Lane.*
Worst street market: *Club Row.*

Street Names

The street names of the City of London give a vivid picture –
sometimes all too vivid – of what life must have been like in medieval
London. Under Henry I's laws a 'street' had to be wide enough for
two loaded carts to pass each other and for sixteen armed knights to
ride abreast; a 'lane' had to be wide enough for a cask of wine to be
rolled along it transversely with a man on either side – staggering
probably.

Some of the more colourful names have not survived. There used to
be a Gropecuntlane in St Pancras, and *Sherborne Lane*, EC4, used to be
Shitebourne or Shiteburgh Lane, the place where the privy was to be
found. *Pudding Lane*, where the Great Fire started, is not named after a
homely pud, but after the bowels and entrails which the butchers of
Eastcheap would cast into the Thames. (A Cheap, by the way, was a
market.) *Addle Street*, EC2 derives from the Old English adela,
meaning stinking urine or manure, while *Stinking Lane* was renamed
King Edward Street in 1843. Could this have been the unamused
Victoria's doing? Even the familiar *Houndsditch* was the trench into
which dead dogs were thrown. But the trade is not entirely one way.
Spital Street, E1, is a diminution of Hospital Street.

A study of London street names is endlessly fascinating. *Old Jewry*,
EC2 was the area in which the Jews used to live before their expulsion
in 1290. *Jewry Street*, EC3, used to be known as Poor Jewry – the
change, it seems, was a conscious one! *Crutched Friars*, EC3, meant
originally the friars of the Holy Cross, for 'Crutch' or 'crouch' in
Middle English meant 'cross', and *Bevis Marks*, EC3, which sounds so
aristocratic, derives from a simple mistake, an 'R' being misread for
a 'V', the name meaning the boundaries (marks) of the bury (abbey).
Threadneedle Street, EC2, derives not from an inn sign nor from the arms
of the needlemakers' company, but from the children's game of
threadneedle, an early form of oranges and lemons. As for *Turnagain
Lane*, that merely means a cul-de-sac. Much of the charm of the City of
London would be lost if we were not constantly reminded of an earlier

city in such street names as *Distaff Lane, Beer Lane, Bread Street, Milk Street, Ironmonger Lane, Honey Lane, Sugar Baker's Court, Old Fish Street* and *Wood Street*. These need no explanation.

Moving beyond the square mile of the City of London, there are some delightful groups of names. In the Borough, for instance, we are deep in Dickens country, so we find *Pickwick Street, Marshalsea Road, Sawyer Street, Quilp Street, Dorrit Street, Weller Street, Doyce Street, Copperfield Street,* etc. These are some of the streets which Dickens used to tramp nightly in search of inspiration.

Down in the Surrey Docks things become romantic and practical with *Dock Head, Muscovy Street, Cathay Street, Pickle Herring Street* and *Shad Thames,* while in Dulwich a whole area is named after that local benefactor, Edward Alleyn, and his thespian colleagues. The Alleyn/Dulwich Connection is an interesting one. By letters patent, licence was granted in 1619 to Edward Alleyn to found a college in Dulwich, to endure for ever, and to consist of a master, a warden, four fellows, six poor brethren, six poor sisters and twelve poor scholars. There was also the stipulation that the master and warden were to be of Alleyn's blood, or to share his name and be unmarried.

The streets around Charing Cross used once to spell out in acrostic: 'George Villiers, Duke of Buckingham', but, alas, *Duke Street* is gone and *Of Alley* has changed its name.

Here at random are a few of my other favourites: *Perkin's Rents, Bleeding Heart Yard, Edith Grove, Haunch of Venison Yard, Straightmouth, de Crespigny Park, Frying Pan Alley, Crooked Usage,* and *Tranquil Vale,* Blackheath (anything but).

And some of the worst: *Coldbath Square,* EC1, *Glamis Way,* Northolt, *Industry Terrace,* SW9, *Tweezer's Alley, Little Plucketts Way,* Buckhurst Hill, *Freke Road, Ogle Street, Organ Lane, Thermopylae Gate,* E14, *Balls Pond Road* and *Quex Road.*

A delightful correspondent suggests: *Agamemnon Road,* NW6, *Ave Maria Lane,* EC4, *Beasley's Ait Lane,* Sunbury, and *Bellestaines Pleasaunce,* E4 as interesting additions and *Airfix Court:* 'a street of model homes perhaps'. And he had only looked through the Geographia A-Z as far as B!

An excellent read is: *Street Names of the City of London* by Eilert Ekwall (OUP 1965).

Best Street Name: *Bleeding Heart Yard.*
Worst Street Name: *Coldbath Square.*

Streets

In spring the best street in London is *Vicarage Gate*, Kensington. The blossom is overwhelming in its pinkness. In autumn it's *Maida Avenue*, Little Venice. *Doughty Street* in Bloomsbury is not just an architectural delight – south of Guilford Street it is intact almost exactly as it was in 1790, except for the traffic wardens – but full of happy memories. The publisher of my early novels had his offices there and threw parties in his back garden. That's the thing about streets, they swarm with ghosts. *Pont Street*, SW1 for instance, which is amusing – those tall, red, fin de siècle monsters which Osbert Lancaster calls 'Pont Street Dutch', that fine austere St Columba's Church of Scotland (Sir Edward Maufe 1950-1955) – is haunted by ghosts who want to show you a good time; and the liveliest of them all, Nell Gwynne.

Streets which tell of the past . . . *Battersea High Street*, which, despite everything, has still the atmosphere of a village street. *Marylebone Lane*, once a muddy path to Marylebone Parish Church is still in no hurry to get anywhere very much. *Old Compton Street*, swarming with cheerful women and the ghosts of Huguenots, Italians, Jews, Irish . . . *Borough High Street* where you can almost hear the sound of stage coaches setting off for Dover or Canterbury or Sittingbourne, and *Arlington Street* where matters of state were debated until dawn. Horace Walpole lived at No 5, Charles James Fox at No 4, and it was here that Lady Nelson walked out on her less than admirable admiral. As for *St James's*, well, it's raucous with ghosts; highwaymen, radicals, courtiers, clubmen, Wellington and Crockford, Rosebery and Ude.

Streets in which one has been happy . . . *Crooms Hill*, Greenwich, *Frognal*, NW3, *Lamb's Conduit Street*, WC1 and the adjacent *Rugby Street*, WC2, *Keats Grove*, the erratically meandering *Marylebone Lane*, *Marylebone High Street*, *Percy Street*, *Gainsborough Gardens* and *Riverside* at Twickenham: it's partly because of the street that one was happy. It is natural to feel a touch of excitement in what remains of *Regent Street*, and a touch of alarm in *Pall Mall*. There's hardly a dull street in Westminster amidst all those Anns and Peters and Pyes. *Lord North Street* is exceptional. And *Beauchamp Place*, SW3 is so frivolous it's irresistible. The best street in Chelsea is the secluded *Margaretta Terrace*, SW3. This is a street which shines out like a good deed in a naughty world. *Maunsel Street*, SW1, is best in Pimlico. *Melbury Road* in Holland Park, where many pre-Raphaelites lived, is full of good things. *Tavistock Terrace*, N19, is another charming street; exceptionally pretty.

But then what can one say in favour of *Oxford Street?* Or *Tottenham Court Road?* Well, in *Tottenham Court Road* there used to be a very fine farmhouse with 70 acres of 'extraordinary good pastures and meadow, with all conveniences proper for a cowman . . . and dung ready to lay in'. And in the same road Richard Brothers, alias 'The Prophet' once met the Devil, 'walking leisurely'.

They've changed the name of *Rillington Place*, where Christie did his women in, but the East Enders are rather proud of Jack the Ripper and the alleys in which he did his messy work. And what about *Beech Street?* Where's *Beech Street?* Why, it's only the principal thoroughfare to the Barbican Centre, and look at it! Graffiti ('LEB Dry Riser Inlet'), debris and a tunnel of such hideosity that Dante should have set his motto over this hell-hole.

Best Streets:
Clarges Street, W1 (for architecture).
Church Row, NW3 (for elegance).
Godfrey Street, Melbury Road and *Margaretta Terrace*, SW3 (for charm).
Old Compton Street, W1 (for interest).
Beauchamp Place, SW3 (for frivolity).
Worst Street: *Beech Street*, EC2.

P.S. I recommend *The Streets of London Through the Centuries* by Thomas Burke (1949).

Striptease

> After a time you can get very tired of chicken
> (Though they'll never believe that, back on the farm).
>
> from *Striptease* by Gavin Ewart (b 1916)

So there I was in the cause of your research sitting through the rather predictable acts that make up the bill at *Sunset Strip* (30 Dean Street, W1; 01-437 4842) when something *most* unusual came on dressed in a turban and jungle cotton robe. With sophisticated echo effects she proceeded to recite the whole of 'Jabberwocky' poking an inattentive middle-aged man with a long bamboo pole to jerk him to attention. Then, when the poem was over, she fixed us all with a school-marmish look and inquired severely: 'Now does anybody know who wrote that?' This stripper, Karen, has spent six years in clubs and pubs trying to create a dialoogue between punter and stripper. Brave girl.

There are only a few genuine striptease shows left in London. The oldest established is *The Carnival Strip Club* (12 Old Compton Street, W1; 01-437 8337) which recently celebrated its quarter-

269

century. There *Rusty de Bono* sits at the entrance taking the punter's money, his pekinese beside him for company and/or protection. From time to time as I chatted to Rusty, the girls emerged from their dressing rooms to put their bets on the horses at Goodwood, which Rusty was watching on his portable TV. The show itself was basic, even by the modest standards of fringe theatre. The set consisted of a large mirror stashed on the floor and a kitchen chair. There was a colour-wheel and an ultra-violet strip for the lighting; one electric fan (working) for the audience; a second one (static) for the girls. There is no more poignant proof of the contention that the English take their pleasures sadly than the Carnival Strip Club.

Raymond's Revuebar (6 Walker's Court, W1; 01-734 1593) is very plush, very vulgar, very successful. It specialises in glossy continental acts and is quite carefully staged. There are cheap rates for OAPs (should we be encouraging them?) and for members of the armed forces. Shows are at 7 p.m., 9 p.m. and 11 p.m. Monday to Saturday. Some years ago I saw there a stripper called Rita Himalaya. Raymond has expanded his operations to include *La Vie en Rose* (Great Windmill Street, W1; 01-437 6312) where he presents his Razzle Dazzle Burlesque Show (9 p.m. and 11 p.m. nightly) which 'takes to unprecedented limits what is sexually permitted on the London stage!' But of course the emphasis is wrong. It's not how far you go but how interesting the journey is . . .

The *Doll's House* (4 Carlisle Street, W1; 01-734 8396) was the first strip-club to be licensed by the GLC. In the basement, which is rudimentary, the girls strip (£4). Upstairs in the Tolouse Lautrec room, you may have a drink with them.

There are also lunchtime strip-shows at a few London pubs, notably the *Golden Lion*, Fulham (57 Fulham High Street, SW6; 01-736 3139). Here the strippers are housewives earning a bit of pin-money and the show is altogether jollier and more earthy.

The nasty new fashion for Nude Encounter Studios, Bed Shows and Peep Shows should be discouraged. But there is a *Peep Show* (28 Wardour Street, W1) which is owned and operated by women. They are very cheerful about it, probably because if they are to be exploited they might as well exploit themselves.

Best stripper: *Karen from The Sunset Strip*.

Sundials

Of London's numerous sundials I shall mention just three. In *Ruskin*

Park a sundial marks the site of the house in which Mendelssohn, who taught Queen Victoria the piano, lived. On the southern face of *St Mary The Virgin*, Putney (down by the river) is a glorious sundial with the pertinent inscription: 'Time and Tide Stay for No One'. The church, raped by vandals a few years ago, has been lovingly restored and is ancient. The other sundial is the one which graces the quadrangle of *Morden College*, Blackheath, founded as a refuge for decayed merchants. It is a glorious sundial and insists 'Sic Umbra Sic Vita' (Thus Shadows, thus Life). It was constructed in 1725 'for keeping the clock right which often goes wrong'.

Best Sundial: *Morden College.*

Supermarkets

London's largest superstore (it's a little old fashioned to refer to them as supermarkets) is *Tesco's* on the North Circular at Neasden. 65,000 square feet, 11,000 customers a day, a 70 foot sign to remind motorists to stop, parking for 1,100 cars and 47 check-outs. The stock is comprehensive. The North Circular is where the biggest superstores now congregate. The reasoning is that they are convenient for shoppers in the centre of London and in the suburbs. Another nearby superstore is *Waitrose* at Brent Cross which opened in 1976 and contains cellular outposts of several high street stores. Near Hanger Lane and still on the North Circular is *World of Leather*, and near Staples Corner is *Leatherland*; you pay your money (a lot for leather) and take your choice. At Staples Corner itself is *Queensway* (carpets and beds) and *B and Q*, a do-it-yourself and furniture centre. In Park Royal, just off the North Circular is a huge *ASDA* (50,000 sq foot) and *Texas Homecare* (for households, DIY, furniture and tiles). Obviously if you have to furnish and enjoy a house and kitchen in a hurry the North Circular should feature in your plans. *World of Leather, Leatherland, B and Q* and *Queensway* are all open on Sundays.

For everyday goods, loo-paper, food, lemonade and vegetables the neighbourhood supermarket is a great convenience for those without too much time to shop around.

What I ask for is that the supermarket stocks everything I want at prices I can pay without an endless queue; the staff should be helpful, the trolleys should be steerable, and the car park should be within easy reach. What I do not ask for is 'Ave Maria' played on an electric organ and piped to all parts of the store through crackling loudspeakers.

The most helpful assistants are to be found at *Marks & Spencer's*, whose convenience foods are almost as good and almost as cheap as the real thing. There too you can buy a small selection of English cheeses packed together as a single item and their cheap and cheerful wines are just that. Also recommended: Chinese chicken, sausages, pies, croissants and scones.

Waitrose has the most comprehensive stock, with everything that a nuclear family could possibly need for its housekeeping requirements. The presentation of the food is wholesome and the best branches are at East Sheen, Finchley Road and Brent Cross.

At *Sainsbury's* in Vauxhall the aisles are too narrow, at *Sainsbury's* in Muswell Hill I am told that 'you can't get out' (can that be true?). *Sainsbury's* stock the best brown sugar and soft margarine in town and give good value for money and helpful service.

The best thing about *International Stores* is that you can buy your food with a Barclaycard if you are lucky enough to have a Barclaycard, but shopping there can be confusing and discouraging. *Safeway*, being American run, is strong on ethnic goods and health foods, while *Tesco's* is, on average, the cheapest of the major London supermarket chains. The Wandsworth branch has not been well reported on, but *Tesco's* seldom disappoints. I have no good reports of *Bags*, in Kentish Town Road, of *Shepherd's* in Chiswick High Road or of the various *Europa* branches. My chief grouse, however, is that having spent £15 for a week of groceries you are everywhere expected to pay for a carrier bag, and only rarely can you get your purchases delivered.

Cheon Leen (4-10 Tower Street, WC2; 01-836 3478) presents all the wonders of the Orient available in wirebaskets.

Best supermarket: *Waitrose*, Brent Cross.

Surprises

Once travelling on the top of a West End bus, I heard an English lady identifying to her American friend various tourist attractions. Pointing to the National Gallery she announced that it was Buckingham Palace. Pointing to Eros she announced that he was Nelson, and the Knightsbridge Barracks she identified as the Horse Guards Parade. Enigmatic and unexplained, this incident was just one of many surprises daily to be experienced in London. Here are some more:

There is a *Tudor House* in Petersham much admired by those casual passers-by who see its twisted chimneys from the 65 and 73 buses. Yet it appears in no antique maps of the locality. Why not? Because it was removed just a few years ago brick by brick from Kent.

The biggest room in the world is 340 feet long and may be found in *Lloyds*. The biggest black cat in the world may be seen at *Catford Shopping Centre Precinct*, while a giant watch hangs like a symbol from an early Bergman film above a watchmaker's in *Southampton Row*. In *Lancaster House* (Stable Yard, St James's Street) there is a Great Gallery, over 120 feet long, and the best painted ceilings in London, including one by Veronese. (Open Sats, Suns and Bank Holidays 2 p.m.-6 p.m.)

The *Gothic Castle* in Green Lanes, Stoke Newington, contains no princes or princesses, merely a pumping station.

From the grandiose to the miniature: there is a model of *St Paul's Cathedral* on the struts of Vauxhall Bridge along with other miniature symbols of the arts, and *No 49 Strand-on-the-Green* has a front door large enough only to admit midgets.

It is always worth looking up when walking along London streets. From the M3 flyover near Teddington you can see on the roof of *Job's Dairy* a series of brown and white cows grazing placidly in silhouette. There are flamingos in the roof garden above *Derry's*. And high up on the *Royal Exchange* you will see a model grasshopper, the symbol of the Gresham Family.

Numbers 23 and 24 Leinster Gardens, Bayswater, are not houses at all, merely a dummy façade concealing the extension of the Metropolitan Railway from Edgware to Westminster (1868). In *Battersea Park* is a peace Pagoda as a memorial to Hiroshima victims. Next to it a cherry tree has been planted. Finally when all else fails (even *Feminist Tarot Readings* – phone Marlene at 01-226 8451 and *Lesbians Against Pit Closures*) do not forget to visit the squirrel-racing at *Kenwood*. This unique event is held annually; the preliminary heats are on 31st February, the all-English championship is on 1st April. See you there.

See also Secrets and Unusual Shops.

Swedish Food

There are three restaurants I can surely recommend, although I cannot understand why everyone has gone so batty for gravad lax (also known as gravlax) which is not unlike eating foam rubber underlay – or have I just been unlucky?

Armstrong's (182 Lavender Hill, SW11; 01-228 2660) is a pink restaurant (paradoxically in Lavender Hill) where you can order Jannsen's Temptation, but beware of the anchovies. *Anna's* (249

Upper Richmond Road, SW15; 01-876 4456) is not to be confused with *Anna's Place* (90 Mildmay Park, N1; 01-249 9379). The first is the equivalent of a Swedish country house, and, as in a Swedish country house children, babies, and animals are all welcome. The food is delicious. The second is set in an Islington terrace which by no stretch of the imagination can be mistaken for Sweden. Again delicious Swedish food, but with reference to France and nouvellish developments in gastronomy. These are three excellent restaurants and it would not be fair to single one out as the best.

Swimming

The *Serpentine* in Hyde Park has been swum in every day of the year for as long as anyone can remember. The Serpentine Swimming Club make a feature of breaking the ice with their heads, so hardy are they. It would account for a lot. It's remarkable really, the Serpentine. You can swim for a quarter of a mile. You can feel secure that the water is clean (samples are tested by the Department of the Environment every day) and it's chlorinated by underwater pipes. There's even a bit of discreet nudity when the weather relents.

If you like skinny-dipping, try *Kenwood* or *Highgate Pond* (men only) or the *Ladies' Pool* on Hampstead Heath (women only). *Lordship Lane*, N17 is agreeable for open-air swimmers; also *Parliament Hill Fields*.

Swiss Cottage Pool (Winchester Road, NW3; 01-278 4444) is clean and big and well attended, but there is a danger of chlorine inhalation. The new *YMCA* in Tottenham Court Road has a fine pool, and you are likely to make new friends there. It also has rock climbing facilities in its magnificent gym. The *Crystal Palace Sports Centre*, (Ledrington Road, SE19; 01-778 0131) has a sophisticated modern pool to championship standards, but membership and entrance are expensive. The *White City Pool* (Bloemfontein Road, W12; 01-743 3401) has its own wave machine and tropical plants. Here and at the *Elephant and Castle Leisure Centre* (Elephant and Castle, SE1; 01-582 5505) there are gently sloping bottoms so that children and non-swimmers feel as secure as when they're on the beach. The *Kensington Baths* (Walmer Road, W11) are also ideal for children and *Richmond Pool* (Chertsey Road, Richmond) is now celebrated for its Waterslide (see under Children). The *Kingfisher* at Kingston is a new 'super leisure pool' about which I have heard very favourable reports, but you'll need to join. Ditto the *Putney Pool* in the Upper Richmond Road.

Porchester Baths at the top of Queensway are splendidly period. If you can afford to, try the pool at the *RAC Club* (89 Pall Mall, SW1; 01-930 2345) or the even more exclusive one in the *Berkeley Hotel* (Wilton Place, SW1; 01-235 6000) – not advised unless you can boast an overall tan. At the *Holiday Inn* (17 Sloane Street, SW1; 01-235 4377) you can eat a leisurely roast Sunday lunch (£8.50 inclusive) while your children disport themselves in the pool in front of you. All *Holiday Inn* hotels have pools.

Sadly I cannot speak so highly of *Kentish Town*, *Wandsworth* (mucky), *Whitechapel*, the *Brockwell Park Lido, Chelsea, Camberwell*, or *Forest Hill* pools, although I suspect that my friend who says of the last-named: 'Frogs and cockroaches abound' is exaggerating.

Best swimming: (open air) *Serpentine*.
Best swimming: (indoor) *Richmond Watersplash*.

Synagogues

The oldest and most beautiful synagogue in London is the *Spanish and Portuguese Synagogue* in Dukes Place, Bevis Marks. Rebuilt after the Great Fire, it survived the Blitz, and is still in use, though only on high days and holidays. During run-of-the-mill days it remains locked up and access is only gained by prior arrangement. The design is similar to many Wren churches, and the wood was carved by the same craftsmen. The next oldest synagogue in London, the *German Synagogue* (James Spiller 1788-1790) was comprehensively bombed by Hitler; a tragic loss. But of course a synagogue is more than bricks and stones; essentially it is a community of ten men or more, and an ark, and the Law and the Prophets, and one person to bake a strudel, and lots of people to claim that they have a better recipe.

The *Liberal Jewish Synagogue* (28 St John's Wood, NW8; 01-286 5181) is not to be confused with the *St John's Wood Synagogue* in Grove End Road, NW8, which is small, intimate and orthodox. The *LJS* has a large and fashionable congregation who come to shul three times a year, and when they need to be confirmed, married or buried. It has an excellent choir and two rabbis, John Rayner, sonorous and dignified, and David Goldberg, witty and worldly-wise, whose sermons are always pertinent. It was the first Liberal synagogue in London. The *LJS* is to be redeveloped (the ceiling is falling down) and will include in its new plans – if I have anything to do with it – a telescope in the roof and a microscope, since we must learn to find the pattern of existence both in the immensity of space and the minutiae of the cell.

The *West London Synagogue* (33 Seymour Place, W1; 01-723 4444), has a fine preacher and excellent pastoral rabbi in Hugo Gryn. The *Westminster Synagogue* (Kent House, Rutland Gardens, SW7; 01-584 3953) is the building in which the young Queen Victoria received the momentous news that she was to become Queen of England, and is the most expensive synagogue in the country. Members are expected to pay £500 a year or more, with no guarantee of life after death, but, since the Rabbi, Albert Friedlander, is a theologian of parts, they should at least receive the best advice that money can buy. No riff raff get in and there are beautiful old (Jacobean?) seats in the ante-room. The *Marble Arch United Synagogue* is sometimes referred to as the Banqueting Suite with a Synagogue attached – the *King David Suite* being the one referred to.

The *New West End Synagogue* (10 St Petersburgh Place, W2; 01-229 2631) is an Ashkenazi establishment which has lost something of its former glory. Former rabbis included Ephie Levine and Louis Jacobs. Ephie enjoyed the best that life had to offer. When offered thanks after conducting a wedding or funeral, he would say: 'Don't thank me now; thank me by post'. Louis Jacobs was and is a fine, contentious scholar and preacher, whose appointment the United Synagogue refused to endorse.

Shorter reports: *Greatorex Street*, E1, contains a survivor of the old East End synagogues; here something of the old hemische atmosphere lingers. The East End Jews moved to Cricklewood (the synagogue is in *Walm Lane*) then on to Finchley. The *Finchley Synagogue* (Kinloss Gardens, N3; 01-346 8551) is – how shall I put this tactfully – architecturally uninspired. There is a golf club attached. The friendliest synagogue is the *North Western Reform* (Alyth Gardens, NW11).

The most civilised United congregation is to be found at the *Hampstead Synagogue* (1 Dennington Park Road, NW6; 01-435 1518); the congregation at the *Edgware United Synagogue* however, under their powerfully rhetorical Irish Rabbi Bernstein, supported Begin in his worst excesses. One has to admire the courage of the congregation at the *Kingston Liberal Synagogue* (Rushett Road, Long Ditton, Surrey; 01-977 4640) which literally built its synagogue around it. The *South London Synagogue* (Prentis Road, SW16; 01-769 4787) is distinguished both by its choir and by its rabbi – in this case a lady rabbi (one has abbesses but not rabesses) who is also an SDP PPC (if you follow me) and whose energy and cheerfulness are infectious.

Best synagogue: (architecturally) *Bevis Marks*.

Tailors

> The House itself began to fall
> It tottered, shuddering to and fro.
> Then crashed into the street below,
> Which happened to be Savile Row.

The important thing to bear in mind is that, as confirmed by tests recorded in *Which* Magazine, Savile Row suits really *do* survive the exigencies of modern living better than less aristocratic suits. In 1960 there were some 60 or so Savile Row tailors; in the mid-seventies 25; today, well, six or seven. Prices for a two-piece made-to-measure suit at a top tailor now run around the £800 mark.

Here are a few of the best tailors in and around Savile Row:

Anderson & Sheppard (30 Savile Row, W1; 01-734 1420/1960) eschew stuffing; their clothes are therefore of an exceptional softness and durability. The head cutter has categorically stated that if a customer doesn't find the soft draped silhouette appealing he must go elsewhere. The shop opens at 8.30 a.m. so that customers can have a fitting on their way to work. No man-made fabrics.

Benson & Clegg (9 Piccadilly Arcade, SW1; 01-491 1456). David Clegg is the son of a Lancashire cutter and inherited the business from his father. Swift, no-nonsense fittings, wonderfully traditional suits.

Helman (10 Savile Row, W1; 01-629 2949). Two brothers, Harry and Burt who learnt their business from their Jewish tailor/father in Lodz, in pre-war Poland. 'The first thing to go in our business,' says Harry sadly, 'will be hand-made buttonholes.'

Douglas Hayward (95 Mount Street, W1; 01-499 5574). Social acceptability is measured by the number of ex-directory numbers in your 'phone book, whether your bookmaker calls you by your first name, and whether you have your suits made by *Douglas Hayward*.

Hawes and Curtis (22 Burlington Gdns, W1; 01-493 3803) dress the male members of the Royal Family. Also shirt-makers and hosiers.

H. Huntsman & Son (22 Savile Row, W1; 01-734 7441) cut their suits square on the shoulder. The nabob himself – Colin Hammick – may cut your suit, but you will have to join a waiting list. Huntsman has bunches from the five main English cloth houses, but specialises in heavier fabrics. Meticulous.

Kilgour, French & Stanbury (33a Dover Street, W1; 01-629 5074) made Fred Astaire's tails for *Top Hat*. The shop tends to specialise in Ambassadors, and retains a tailor in New York for minor alterations.

But none of these tailors, howsoever grand, can measure up to the great *Harry Poole*, the first tailor to open in Savile Row. He it was who when the Prince of Wales at the turn of the century dared to complain about one of his suits, took some chalk from his pocket, drew white marks all over the Prince's jacket, barked out: 'Bring it in for alterations!' and marched off.

I can also recommend for ready-made as well as for made-to-measure, *Jaeger's* (204-206 Regent Street, W1; 01-734 8211); *Crolla* (35 Dover Street, W1; 01-629 5931) with a fine selection of shirts; *Paul Smith* (44 Floral Street, WC2; 01-379 7133); *Webster Brothers* (56 Cornhill, EC3; 01-626 5838) – also shirts and *Nutters* (35a Savile Row, W1; 01-437 6850).

The best range of ready-made suits come from *Simon Ackermann; Chester Barrie* suits are available at *Austin Reed* branches.

For repairs and alterations, *Stitch in Time* on Waterloo Station (01-928 5593) undertakes men's and women's tailoring repairs to be collected the same day, while the gentleman at *365 Worple Street*, Whitton, Middlesex charged me a mere £4.75 for repairs to a silk Paris suit by Ted Lapidus, which I bought for a tenner at an antiques fair, and completed an excellent job in three days. *Altar Ahmed* of the 5-Star Cleaners (339 Upper Street, N1) will also undertake any repairs, and will clean anything graciously and expeditiously.

Best tailor: *H. Huntsman & Sons Ltd.*

Take Away

It is now possible to fool just about all the people all the time. Quite apart from Butchers (q.v.), who prepare their meat to gourmet standards, there are an increasing number of delicatessens, where home-cooked and frozen food is available for the overworked hostess or inept bachelor. Here are four of the best:

Acquired Tastes (9 Battersea Rise, SW11; 01-223 9942), is open until 9.30 p.m. seven days a week. Renowned for their pâtés and terrines – most of them are made locally – they do an excellent line in Mushrooms à la Grecque, and have an exceptional counter of some 50 cheeses, all of them fresh. Also a wide choice of teas, wine, herbs etc.

Big Mamma.(70 Lupus Street, SW1; 01-834 1471). A huge pot of lasagne and a fine selection of salads (95p for a generous portion of Niçoise) distinguish this life-enhancing establishment from similar delis. Hot dishes (or at least they will be hot when you heat them) include Chicken Chasseur (£1.25 for a portion which would cost three or four times as much in a restaurant).

Joanna's (between Lots Road and Cheyne Walk, SW6). A miniature shop stuffed full of croissants, baguettes, spicy sausage rolls, home-made chocolate chip cookies, fresh fruit, sorbets and such. A freezer is crammed with supper-dishes in foil. But the assistants ought not to smoke in a shop such as this.

For a fresh take-away pasta go to *Pasta Pasta* (52 Pimlico Road, SW1; 01-730 1435). The pasta is made daily in the basement (£1.20-£1.60 per lb) and a selection of classic sauces (£2.50 per lb) is also available. Or *Pasta Fino* (see under Pasta).

Best Take-Away: *Acquired Tastes*.

See also Fish and Chips, Delicatessens, Butchers, Sandwiches etc.

Talent Shows

I have told you about the karaoke bars (see Japanese restaurants), and if you visit the *Cattleya* Bar in West Street, WC2 or the *Jun* in Great Marlborough Street, W1, you will have an opportunity to sing your heart out to a real live paying audience. You pay too, of course.

But talent contests are something else. Here are a few venues:

The Hop Poles Variety House. Every Tuesday. Phone 01-363 0381 for details. No groups. A promise of 'recording work if good enough'.

The Giraffe (45 Penton Place, SE17; 01-735 2088). 'Semi-finals and finals will be judged by theatrical agents, big money.'

The Gloucester, Every Tuesday. 01-858 2666 for details.

The Horn of Plenty. Every Wednesday. 01-981 0620 for details.

Sutton Arms, Caledonian Road, N1. Every Tuesday. All acts except bands. Mr P. Scott on 01-278 9911 or 01-677 1335 for details.

And of course there's always the *Comedy Store* (28 Leicester Square, WC2; 01-839 6655) (see under Cabaret) at which self-proclaimed comedians can test their material against an audience out for blood.

Best Talent Show: *The House of Commons*.

Taxis and Taxi-Ranks

Consider: to be a taxi-driver you have to pass an examination tougher than any comparable test anywhere in the world. You are self-employed, but unlike other self employed people you are not able to set your own tariffs. There are no fewer than six Acts on the Statute Book dealing with London cabs. When you decide finally to buy your own cab it will set you back £12,000 with an additional £3,000 for HP, VAT etc.

The London taxi is designed as a taxi and not as a car. Regulations require that there should be seating for five adults, with enough headroom for a man to keep his top hat on, and that the privacy of the passengers be protected at all times. This means that the driver's rear view mirror must not be angled so that he can see what is going on in the back of the cab. A taxi is also required to have a narrow turning circle. As Nubar Gulbenkian who owned one put it: 'It can turn on a sixpence – whatever that may be.' The passenger has pullywag loops to hang on to, control of heat and light, ashtrays and a tinted rear window. I am old-fashioned enough slightly to resent the advertisements on the tip-up seats, but they can hardly be said to scream at you. It is also remarkable how rarely a taxi breaks down.

The best ranks to find taxis are outside the Law Courts in the *Strand; Sloane Square; Hanover Square*; and *Cadogan Gardens*, where the Squire Bancroft shelter has miraculously survived. The worst ranks are in *Leicester Square, Charing Cross, King's Cross* and *Euston Stations*.

And always bear in mind that if several of you are making a London journey it will probably save money to take a taxi now that public transport is expensive. And that a cabbie will receive a commission from hotels and night clubs to whom he introduces guests.

See also under Queues.

Tea

When Dr Johnson paid his visits to Mrs Thrale at Streatham it is recorded that he sometimes drank as many as twenty-five cups of tea in rapid succession. His tipple was a mild bohea, and the cups he drank it out of would be the tiny ones without handles after the Chinese manner. (Incidentally tea is cheaper to buy now than when it was first imported.) Other celebrated tea-fanciers include Lord Petersham, who had *pekoe, souchong, congou* and *gunpowder* in his caddies, and Edmund Waller, who was told by a Jesuit who had been to China that the boiling water should remain on the leaves 'while you say the Miserere Psalm very leisurely', thus ensuring that 'the spiritual part of the tea' was not wasted. In those days, of course, you blended your own in the bowls provided in the caddies. These days

Britons drink more tea than America and the rest of Europe together. In London 20 million cups a day.

All of which is a preamble, for I had intended to tell you about the firm of *R. Twining & Co* who have been selling tea in London since 1706. They are indeed the oldest ratepayers in Westminster. And the old firm is still where it has always been, in a tiny shop in the Strand opposite the Law Courts and underneath those familiar sculpted Chinamen. It's still the same family there, and it would be disloyal surely to recommend that you went anywhere else for your tea. Sam Twining drinks *English Breakfast* blend for breakfast, a *Darjeeling* with his lunch, an aromatic *Lapsang Souchong* for tea or, if the weather is chilly, a *Russian Caravan*. Other interesting teas include *Assam*, which is potent and requires milk; *Jasmine*, which is perfect with Chinese food, *Keemun* for those who dislike too much tannin, and *Ceylon* as a relaxative.

You should always – according to Twinings – use fresh cold water and only boil it once. Never hurry the tea along, whether you use bags or loose tea. Double the brew for iced tea and add crushed ice, lemon, and fresh mint; Darjeeling and Lapsang are suggested for this refreshing drink.

You can buy your tea at the auctions every Monday morning, or at *Twinings*, or *Whittard's Tea Emporium* (111 Fulham Road, SW3; 01-589 4261) offering some 80 varieties from a modest household blend (£2.28 per lb) to the intriguing *Formosa Oolong* (£14.80 per lb) which includes the tiny flowers and stalks with the leaves. You may also for a few pence buy a sample of any of the teas. Whittard's also offers seven Tisanes, which are excellent for curing headaches, nervousness and indigestion. Giles Hilton, who manages Whittard's, sells coffee, honey and chocolates along with tea in this delightful shop, in which the staff wear brown dustcoats.

The *Ceylon Tea Centre* (22 Regent Street, SW1; 01-930 8632) and the *Indian Tea Centre* (343 Oxford Street, W1; 01-499 1975) permit you – encourage you – to taste your tea in congenial surroundings before committing yourself to buying the leaf.

Best tea: *R. Twining & Co.*
Best cuppa: *Ceylon Tea Centre.*

P.S. I bet you didn't know that Widow Twankee was named after a brand of China tea.

Tea Houses/Cream Cakes

For people whose religion is cakes, Old Compton Street is Mecca.

Patisserie Valerie (No 44; 01-437 3466) and *Amalfi* (No 31) are experts, while just round the corner at 28 Greek Street, W1 (01-437 6007) is *Maison Bertaux*. *Valerie's* is wonderful for croissants and éclairs, *Bertaux* for mille feuilles and *Amalfi* accompanies your cakes with revitalising Gaggia Cappucino coffee, sprinkled with chocolate grains.

Many armies are engaged in the battle of the cream cakes. There are those who swear by *Maison Sagne* (105 Marylebone High Street, W1; 01-935 6240); a true Viennese flavour distinguishes it, and, if the sachertorte or the almond pastries don't blow your mind, the mural certainly will. In competition with *Sagne* is *Gloriette* (7 St John's Wood High Street, NW8; 01-732 1039 and various branches) a highly professional patisserie; *Louis* (32 Heath Street, NW3; 01-435 9908 and 12 New College Parade, NW3; 01-722 8100), where you can almost always find a table free; and *Maison Bouquillon* (41-45 Moscow Road, W2; 01-727 4897 and 28 Westbourne Grove, W2; 01-229 2107). At either branch of *Maison Bouquillon* you can sink your teeth into a tarte aux fraises de bois, for the merest taste of which I would have the children of my best friend shipped to a white slaver in Buenos Aires. They also do an excellent line in made-to-order birthday cakes. But there is better . . . *Pechon's Restaurant and Tea-rooms* (127 Queensway, W2; 01-229 0746) has a selection of over 100 cakes; scope here I should have thought for a sponsored charity event. Most of them are memorable. Tea at the *Ritz* is for those suffering a crisis of confidence, but remember to wear a tie; until recently it was the only meal the *Ritz* provided which was satisfactory. Tea-dances – £13.50 for a substantial four-course tea – are a return to the days when men in spats rumbaed with their wives. If you can bear ravishing fashion models with legs like fork-lift trucks swanning around you (most of their energy is taken up with fluttering those massive eye-lashes) then *Fortnum's* is the place. At least it *was* the place. Sir Basil Spence's redecoration seems to have pleased nobody and there have been several *thousand* complaints from regulars. Striped mauve upholstery, lowered ceilings and nasty chandeliers did the damage. It really is beastly. On Fridays and Sundays (3.30-6.30) at the Palm Court in the *Waldorf* (Aldwych, WC2; 01-836 2400) there are thés dansants (£6.95) to an elegant quartet, but for the true sophisticate the *ABC* in Euston Road cries out to be visited. If it isn't full of Bulgarian spies being 'turned' by Smiley's People, then it ought to be.

While recognising that *Richoux* (41a South Audley Street, W1; 01-629 5228 – my typewriter gave me South Awfly Street which is rather good) has claims to be considered among the greats, the best cake in London, or anywhere in the world, is the original *Maid-of-Honour*, as served at the café of that name (288 Kew Road, Kew, Surrey: 01-940 2752) in a fine Georgian terrace opposite the gardens. A mélange of almonds, pastry, honey and eggs, it is the sort of confection for which saints would cast down their golden crowns around the glassy sea. An astonishing survival for both the cake (which may be taken home and heated for five minutes in a moderate oven before eating) and the café are of ancient renown. It also serves chocolates and other superior delicacies of a pastrified nature.

A little further west is the *Peg Woffington Cottage* (167 High Street, Teddington; 01-977 5796) where fine teas are served at week-ends (lunches throughout the week). Peg, a close friend of David Garrick's, was an Irish actress who specialised in 'breeches' parts. In Dublin they would sing of

> That excellent Peg!
> Who showed such a leg
> When lately she dressed in men's clothes,
> A creature uncommon
> Who's both man and woman,
> And the chief of the belles and the beaux!

There is a stone to Peg in St Mary's Teddington; but the tea-room, leafy and enchanting, is as cheerful a memorial as anyone could wish.

A few more recommendations:

Primrose Patisserie, 136 Regent's Park Road, NW1 (01-722 7848).
Hampstead Patisserie, 9 South End Road, NW3 (01-435 9563).
Perry's Bakery and Haminados Patisserie, 151 Earl's Court Road, SW5 (01-370 4825). Tiny and Bulgarian.
Patisserie Parisienne, 2A Phillimore Gardens, W8 (01-938 1890).

For children's birthday cakes you should either read Jane Asher's book of instructions on how to do it yourself, or telephone Cairisty Burnet on 01-221 8621. If you can afford her (a minimum of £25) she will construct a delicious and hugely rich cake to your own design, or one suggested by her. A zebra-skin map of Africa and a white grand piano wedding cake posed no problems.

Best Tea-house: *Maison Bouquillon.*
Best Cake: *The Original Maid-of-Honour.*
Worst Cake: *Anything with coconut and a glacé cherry on top.*

Telephones

It is a mystery that since the launch of British Telecom on the Stock Exchange as a public company a conspiracy seems to have taken place to ensure that the public don't get to use the telephones. At least why else is it that all the coin-operated 'phones in London seem to be out of order while the beastly card 'phones are all working? Nor is there any indication from outside the box whether it takes coins or cards. Maybe an explanation will be given if you visit the *Telecom Technology Showcase* (Baynard House, 135 Queen Victoria Street, EC4; 01-248 7444 – 10 a.m.-4.30 p.m. Mondays to Thursdays free). Vintage phones and the latest developments are all there.

The most antique telephone would seem to be the one in the *Hertford* pub (Shepherd's Market, W1) in which the telephone is contained within the Duke of Cumberland's converted sedan chair. Interesting telephones may be bought from *The Telephone Box* (339 Fulham Road, SW10; 01-352 4574) or from the *Bell Marketing Telephone Shop* (364 Fulham Road, SW10; 01-351 7111).

Best telephone: *Hertford pub*.

Tennis

The most delightful place to play tennis in London must be the court which adjoins *St Botolph, Bishopsgate* (be warned: there are three St Botolphs within a few hundred square yards). Keys may be obtained from the verger.

London is better supplied with open air and indoor courts than it has been for some time. A new indoor club, the *Vanderbilt* at Shepherd's Bush has recently been opened by Charles J. Swallow, an ex-schoolmaster who coached the Harrow School rackets team. The Vanderbilt is for those who take tennis seriously. There are five courts, a limited membership of 500, an entrance fee of £400 and an annual subscription of the same amount. There is a physiotherapist and Shirley Brasher, mother of the beautiful Kate, as one of the coaches. Shirley was good but Angela Buxton was better. An ex-Wimbledon champion she now runs the *Angela Buxton Centre* (16 Winnington Road, N2; 01-455 6216 for information) which is both club (2 all-weather acrylic surface courts and 2 artificial grass courts) and school. Angela's record as a coach is as impressive as her record at Wimbledon. She was rather surprised when playing recently at *David Lloyd's Slazenger Racket Club* in Slough to be told to bugger off the courts (the language was even richer) by young Mr Lloyd after a mix-up over bookings. There have been other incidents.

So far as tennis players are concerned the finest facilities may be enjoyed at *Queen's Club* (Palliser Road, W14; 01-385 3421). Not only do they have eight varieties of surface to reproduce the conditions experienced anywhere in the world, as well as squash, real tennis, rackets and ping-pong, but they also have the distinction of having expelled John McEnroe from membership after his foul-mouthed rudeness to a senior member playing there. When the news of the brat's expulsion was announced spontaneous applause broke out throughout the club. (I might add that I was an admirer of McEnroe's, despite his loutishness, but his moony-eyed sentimentalism where Tatum O'Neal was concerned was more than I could stomach.)

If *Queen's* is the best for tennis, *Hurlingham Club* (01-736 8411) on the river bank at Fulham (see under Croquet) has the most social atmosphere. Swimming and polo and croquet and dinner dances and tiddly fornication under the hydrangeas create a louche old-worlde charm that is hard to resist. If, as a solid *New Statesman* subscriber, you do resist it, then the best public courts are at York Gate in *Regent's Park*, in *Battersea Park*, and in *Parliament Hill Fields*. The courts in *Waterlow Park* are fair and the courts in *Golders Hill Park* are being resurfaced; they needed it!

A word of recommendation for Mark Cox's indoor club in *Wimbledon* and a suggestion that you have a fiver on Lendl and Barbara Potter for Wimbledon 1986.

Best tennis club: *Queen's.*
Best public court: York Gate, *Regent's Park.*
Best private court: *Centre Court, Wimbledon.*
Best equipment: *Lillywhite's.*
Best coaching: *Angela Buxton.*
Best British player: *There isn't one.*

Theatres (Fringe)

Hard to keep up with them. Increasingly plays are being performed in pubs, galleries, drill halls, cafés and tents, and it is obviously wiser to refer to the weekly listings magazines for the latest on the new venues. The latest development, logical enough, is a company (*Acme Acting* 01-278 5893) which will perform plays in your own home. The cost is about £75, and the onus is therefore on you to organise a full house. I wonder whether there are different plays for different rooms: *Miss Julie* for the kitchen, *The Man Who Came To Dinner* for the dining room, and *Peter Pan* for the bedroom.

The best I can do for you in these pages is direct you to a few of the fringe theatres which have been and are likely to remain in business for a while.

The most enterprising currently is the *Almeida* under its remarkable artistic director, Pierre Audi. Dave Lovett, Chief Technician and cycling fanatic and Nigel Hinds, Programme Coordinator, together with the rest of the team, seem untiring in their efforts to exploit the possibilities of 'fringe' to the full. The annual four week music festival is bold and adventurous. Who else cares sufficiently about contemporary music to dedicate so much time and energy to it? But other festivals have followed. Under-employed talent from the RSC, the most innovative work from the provinces, and foreign dance troupes have all been welcomed to the *Almeida* in recent months. It has two great advantages over most of its rivals however. An excellent wine-bar (q.v.) next door and, equally adjacent, the offices of *Time Out* magazine.

Other fringe theatres?

The King's Head, (15 Upper Street, N1; 01-226 1916) is claustrophobic and loud with the clatter of cutlery as rather hectic meals are served before the performances begin. The productions are usually more satisfying than the food and can be memorable; in the adjoining pub the bar staff still insist on dealing in pounds, shillings and pence.

The Riverside Studios (Crisp Road, W6; 01-748 3354), once BBC rehearsal rooms, have been under constant threat of closure, but their adventurous policy of playing host to avant-garde dancers, musicians and theatre companies has given exposure to some of the most brilliant international talents. Public rows culminating in the loss of an excellent director have put the theatre even more at risk.

Almost as vulnerable is the *Lyric* (King Street, W6; 01-741 2311), which boasts within its brutalist shell a gem of a Victorian proscenium theatre and a versatile studio. But it receives no Arts Council funding and may not survive, although productions of usually contemporary plays have been hugely successful (Michael Frayn's brilliant comedy *Noises Off* started off at the Lyric).

The Bush Theatre (Shepherd's Bush Green, W2; 01-743 3388), above a pub, has always been a theatre without frills, a theatre in which excellent writing and acting talent can be seen at very close quarters, British talent predominating. Its reputation has been consistently growing under its present management.

286

Hampstead Theatre Club (Swiss Cottage Centre, NW3; 01-722 9301) has tended to concentrate on starry casts in literate plays with more than an outside chance of a transfer. Civilised, but none too radical.

The Tricycle Theatre (269 Kilburn High Road, NW6; 01-624 5330), originally formed by actors from the Pindar of Wakefield pub (see under Music Halls), is one of the pleasantest of the fringe theatres, but the choice of plays and casts is, to put it politely, whimsical.

The Latchmere (503 Battersea Park Road, SW11; 01-228 2620) has a handsome restaurant attached to its small theatre. The menus complement the plays. Thus, when I saw the apocalyptic piece, *The Bed Sitting Room*, I ate baked potato skins. God help us if they mount *Titus Andronicus*. The pub in which it is established is a handsome Victorian pile.

Exhibitions and plays at the *ICA* (The Mall, W1; 01-930 3647) often excite hostility from the press and other guardians of our morality (dirty nappies in a feminist exhibition caused a furore) and the theatre itself ('like a VD Clinic', comments a friend) cannot always be relied upon for a comforting night out for a family party from Penge. However, the snack bar is one of the best and the bookshop stocks some interesting radical paperbacks.

Of the newer fringe theatres the *Man in the Moon* (392 King's Road, SW3; 01-351 2876) is one of the jolliest with an eclectic programme ranging from Toussaint L'Overture to Marie Lloyd.

There are four theatres in London principally devoted to Theatre in Education, but where splendid visiting companies such as *Shared Experience*, *Portable Theatre* and *The People Show* may sometimes be found. These are the *Cockpit Theatre* (in the north), the *Curtains Theatre* within Toynbee Hall (in the east), *Oval House* (in the south) and the *Questors*, Ealing (in the west). Of these the *Questors* (Mattock Lane, W5; 01-567 5184) is the handsomest, the *Cockpit* (Gateforth Street, NW8; 01-402 5081) the best equipped and the most professional, the *Curtains* (Arts Workshop; 01-247 3633) has the greatest community concern, and *Oval House* (54 Kennington Oval, SE11; 01-582 7680 and 735 2786), with its agreeable tattiness, the most energy. Among its many activities – putting on plays is only a small part of what fringe theatre occupies itself with – it has recently organised a course in Epic Acting.

The *Young Vic* (66 The Cut, SE1; 01-928 6363) has a marvellously versatile acting area (two, if you count the studio), an excellent atmosphere, but no very clear policy and a diffident approach to getting audiences to come. Set in what was once a butcher's shop, it has marvellous tiles and Dickensian offices.

The *Albany Empire* (Douglas Way, SE8; 01-691 3333) in

Deptford is a power-house of talent in an under-privileged area. In the modern and intelligently designed main hall you can eat and drink while watching anything from Feminist Cabaret to Rastafarian rapping. It is a noticeably young theatre, but allow plenty of time to find it.

At the *Half Moon Theatre* (213 Mile End Road, E1; 01-790 4000) a production of *Trafford Tanzi* by Claire Luckham, which deservedly transferred to the Mermaid, was all that fringe theatre ought to be. The enthusiasm at the box office was infectious in contrast to the surliness that greets you at most West End theatres. I rang to inquire about tickets. 'You've *got* to come,' they said. The *Half Moon*, having built two new theatres on the site of the old one, enjoys great local support. It remains to be seen whether the new artistic director can continue the success of Robert Walker (twenty-stone, shaven-headed and determined) but early signs are promising.

The *Orange Tree Theatre* (45 Kew Road, Richmond, Surrey; 01-940 3633) run by Sam Walters (genial, cultured, and fraught-looking) also draws most of its support locally, and the character of the place reflects life in Richmond as the Half Moon reflects life in the East End. In a tiny ninety-seat room above a pub, local actors perform plays by local authors to local audiences, but cosiness is avoided by excursions into the classics (*King Lear* and *Peer Gynt* in miniature); the place respects the intelligence of its clients. Here lunch-time performances have been discontinued but the summer festival of children's plays has become something to look forward to. Here too a new and enlarged theatre is imminent.

Tickets for many fringe productions can be centrally booked at the *Fringe Box Office*, Duke of York's Theatre, St Martin's Lane, EC2; 01-379 6002. For a fuller survey of fringe theatre see the excellent publication: *The British Alternative Theatre Directory* by Catherine Itzin (John Offord).

Best fringe theatre: *The Almeida.*

Theatres (Open Air)

Occasional theatre performances take place against the backcloth of *Holland House*, a Jacobean mansion, much restored, in Holland Park (no advance booking), but although this romantic ruin would be ideal for a number of plays (*Nightmare Abbey*, *The Cenci*, *Thieves Carnival*), no impressario has yet taken it upon himself to set up a regular company there. Performances of Shakespeare in the galleried yard of the *George Inn*, Southwark (77 Borough High Street, SE1; 01-407 2056) attract tourists and Sam Wanamaker has plans to build on Bankside a facsimile of Shakespeare's Globe Theatre. In recent years the *Tower of London* has been used as scenery for an open air performance of *The Yeoman of the Guard* during the London Festival, but this is all prevarication, because there is really only one full-time (well, summer-time) professional, open air theatre in London, and that is David Conville's outfit in *Regent's Park*. Competition from Concorde, thunderstorms and bike boys is fierce, but the actors manage to make themselves heard most of the time, especially now that they're acting in a 1,200-seat, steeply-raked amphitheatre. Snacks are excellent. On my last visit I enjoyed worst sausages and loganberries and cream. Ticket prices are modest (£2-£6) but the standard of productions varies alarmingly. As a general rule choose Shakespeare plays set in forests and avoid productions by Richard Digby Day in favour of Conville productions. But increasingly Shakespeare is giving way to other theatrical classics. The theatre faces west so, even if the play isn't worth watching, the setting sun behind the fine trees is. Blankets may be hired, but remember to bring cushions, thermos flasks of coffee or something stronger. Despite the bugs there cannot be many pleasanter ways of passing a fine summer's evening.

Best open-air theatre: *Regent's Park*.
Worst open-air theatre: *The Beating of the Retreat*.

Theatres (West End)

There are London theatres which actors dread. The *Phoenix* is one and the *Piccadilly* another – especially since no one can find it. Actors are not over the moon about playing in the Westminster Theatre either. It can mean that they are being employed by Moral Rearmament, and a morally rearmed audience is not a barrel-load of laughs. I find it impossible to enjoy anything at *Sadler's Wells Theatre* with the exception of Lindsay Kemp. But now there are plans to turn this historic theatre into a massive glass-fronted complex. Could be interesting. The *Prince of Wales* is hideous (the theatre, that is); the *Prince Edward Theatre* has the rudest box office staff (or had) which is saying something, bearing in mind how much competition there is for this award, and at the *Queen's* and *Aldwych* Theatres the attendants always chatter and bang doors before the interval. This habit is spreading to other theatres and can wreck a carefully contrived coup de théâtre. The *Shaftesbury* has a crowded foyer but a charming front of house manager. The *Vaudeville* has been nicely renovated inside and out with *Mousetrap* money, but the façade of the *Adelphi* has been ruined, although you can still see in the lettering of 'Royal Adelphi' a touch of genuine deco wit. Somebody must visit the *Strand Theatre*, but nobody has ever been seen going in or, more ominously, coming out. The *Cambridge Theatre* unwisely mounted an elaborate magic show and promptly became invisible.

The *Haymarket* is a gloriously theatrical building and backstage it has the loveliest star dressing room in London. The *St Martin's* is special because it's where I had my only West End play performed. ('You and you alone, sir,' wrote one of my fans, 'have been responsible for the disintegration of the British Empire.') And the *Savoy Theatre*, the first to install electric lights, kept my wife happily employed for nearly a year. The *Duke of York's* reeks with charm; it is usually host to a classy and successful play. The *Palladium* is expensive enough mid-week and charges an extra £2 on Fridays and Saturdays. The *Aldwych*, where Ben Travers farces ran so successfully during the twenties and thirties, is acoustically difficult; I worked on *London Assurance* there; a happy time in a happy place. Now its been decked out in dark green and gold. The renovated *Old Vic* is even more handsomely rejuvenated. 'Honest Ed' Mirvish spent a fortune on it, and beautiful it is. Unfortunately it has mounted some of the tattiest old rubbish seen for years and the subscription policy has not proved successful with London audiences who are predominently touristic. The upstairs rehearsal rooms are light and airy; a pleasure to work in. Indeed it's wonderful that the money was spent not only on the audiences, but that the interests of the actors were also considered. The coat of arms facing down the Waterloo Road stands out very proudly in silhouette.

The *Royal Court* lives in the shadow of its history. Those who remember the regime of George Devine and the sense of occasion which informed each new play there, have little time for Max Stafford Clarke, but he is not a negligible figure. He has kept the theatre open in difficult days. A few of his productions have been superb. And, in liaison with Methuen's the *Royal Court* publishes the text of all its new plays – then sells them to playgoers; an excellent service. The Theatre Upstairs at the *Royal Court* (Sloane Square, SW1; 01-730 1745 for downstairs, 01-730 2554 for up) mounts socially concerned productions which can be stunning, or which can be bullshit. It enjoys excellent houses for the bullshit.

Cut-price tickets (half the regular price plus 50p service charge) for some West End plays are available at the *SWET* Theatre Booth in Leicester Square (2.30 p.m.-6.30 p.m. non-matinee days; 12 noon-6 p.m. matinee days – no telephone). Cut-price tickets for the Royal Shakespeare Company at the *Barbican* are sometimes available on the performance day after 10 a.m. at £4; for the *National* after 10 a.m. at £4.50; previews and midweek matinees £3.50.

Best West End Theatres: the *Duke of York's* (for atmosphere); the *Haymarket* (for architecture).
Worst West End Theatres: the *Prince of Wales* and the *Apollo*, Victoria.

See also Arts Centres, and Theatres, Fringe.

For full details of London theatres – useful when booking tickets – I recommend: the *Playgoer's Companion* by Barry Turner and Mary Fulton (Virgin Books).

Ticket Offices

See under Theatres (fringe) and Theatres (west end) for details of booking theatre tickets. It is often expensive and unnecessary to use the special credit card hot lines; much simpler to try the theatre box office first.

If the show you've set your heart on is sold out, you could try *Sidi*, in Drury Lane (opposite the New London Theatre); tickets for most events are mysteriously available there. If money is no problem phone *Obtainables* (01-839 5363) and they may be able to fix you up.

And the *BBC Ticket Unit* (Broadcasting House, London W1A 4WW, send SAE) or the equivalent for *Thames TV* (01-387 9494), or *London Weekend Television* (01-261 3434) will provide you with free tickets for audience participation shows. *Channel Four* (01-631 4444) will put you in touch with the producer of the Channel 4 show you would like to attend.

Best London Ticket: *Wimbledon Men's Final.*
Worst London Ticket: *The same when it's rained off.*

Tiles

While excavating in the crypt of *St Etheldreda's* in Ely Place, archaeologists, amongst whom was Father Cunningham, the estimable parish priest, made a sensational discovery – a Monk's Walk comprising many lovely old blue and yellow Flemish tiles laid down nearly 700 years ago. Another discovery is what can be done with London's underground (q.v.) stations, many of which are being adorned with tiles and mosaic designs commissioned from contemporary artists (Eduardo Paolozzi at Tottenham Court Road, for instance). The most beguiling tiles are to be found in the foyer of the *Whitechapel Public Library*, Whitechapel High Street; they were removed thither from a building demolished in 1963 to make way for the new traffic roundabout. The tiles form a mosaic of Whitechapel Haymarket in 1878. Amongst the vignettes two young men, one a townee, one a rustic, are about to indulge in a meaningful relationship while a merchant in a purple hat is passing a posy of flowers via his riding crop to a girl in orange stockings on a hayrick. One can understand his partiality. Since this delightful mis-en-scène (the horses are wearing ear muffs) is next door to Bloom's kosher restaurant and the Whitechapel Art Gallery and opposite the City of London Polytechnic, a detour is obviously called for.

Other good tiles may be seen in the *Young Vic*, in numerous butcher's (q.v.) shops, in the *Martinez Restaurant* (25 Swallow Street, W1; 01-734 5066), decorating the *Michelin Building* in the Fulham Road, and in the *Princess Louise* pub (208 High Holborn, WC1; 01-405 8816), which also has fine engraved glass ceilings, but has replaced its original cubicles.

Best tiles: *Whitechapel Public Library.*

Toll Gates

Only one toll gate remains, but it's a beauty. The toll gate in *College Road*, Dulwich, was built in 1789 by Mr Charles Morgan of Penge, who needed easy access to some fields he had rented from Dulwich College, and he could see no reason why others who wished to use it should not pay for the privilege. The college took it over on Morgan's death, continued to charge travellers and still do. The table of tolls on a board beside the road charges for every 'horse, mule or donkey drawing any vehicle' as well as for 'lambs, sheep or hogs, per score', but it also taxes motorists 5p, though not at night. Between 1901 and 1958 the tolls were collected by the same loyal lady.

In *Barnes High Street* I spotted 'Ye Old Toll Gate Antiques' and I can believe that the pretty house was indeed a toll house, but it isn't now.

Best toll gate: *College Road, Dulwich.*

Toys

The children I know best are just as happy cutting a hole in the side of a cardboard box or climbing a tree and creating a tree house than playing (for more than a few minutes) with the latest electronic video game. But an old cardboard box and a pair of scissors don't make much of a birthday present.

Robert Louis Stevenson wrote: 'If you love art, folly, or the bright eyes of children, speed to Pollocks', and *Pollocks Toy Museum* (1 Scala Street, W1; 01-636 3452) is still there. Not only can you study the old theatres and plays, but you can also buy equivalents of the antique – usually Victorian – toys. A magical place. *Pollocks* has opened a second branch (Unit 44, The Market, Covent Garden, WC2; 01-379 7866) and it too is a delight. Beatrix Potter postcards are cheaper here than at W. H. Smith.

Also to be found in the new Covent Garden complex (Unit 32 – 01-379 7681) is *Eric Snook*, who concluded a remarkable coup when he secured the rights to marketing ET spin-offs. His best traditional lines are his rag dolls and his mechanical chicks and rabbits. He took back a defective pencil box with very good grace. (Incidentally there is a Doll's Hospital at 16 Dawes Road, SW6; 01-385 2081.) Eric Snook stocks some Galt toys, which are extremely ingenious and popular with children, but for the best selection you should hop along to *Galt's* (84 Fortis Green Road, Muswell Hill, N10; 01-444 0282).

The toughest toys of all are Tonka trucks and tractors; they are indestructible. For teddy bears try *Carrie's* (32 Pembridge Road, W11; 01-727 4805). For collectable toys – not to be played with – try *Stuart Cropper* (Stand 1/14 Grays Mews Antique Market, 1 Davies Mews, W1; 01-629 7034). I can powerfully recommend *Tridias* (44 Monmouth Street, WC2; 01-240 2369 with a branch in Richmond), *Tigermoth* (166 Portobello Road, W11; 01-727 7564) for stocking fillers as well as trendy clothes, *Tiger Tiger* (219 King's Road, SW10; 01-352 8080) for dolls houses, puppets, and jokes, *John Turnbull* (Hercules Road, SE1) for model soldiers, *Bagatelle Toys* (79 High Street, Wimbledon, SW19; 01-946 7981) for general toys.

What about *Hamley's* (188 Regent Street, W1; 01-734 3161), the largest toy shop in the world, and *Selfridges'* toy department (Oxford Street, W1; 01-629 1234)? Between them they stock just about every toy ever made, but go there in the run-up to Christmas and it's like walking into the world of Hieronymus Bosch.

There are over 100 toy libraries in London, a full list of which may be obtained from the *Toy Libraries Association* (Wyllyotts Manor,

Darkes Lane, Potters Bar, Herts; 0707 44571), which also produces a Good Toys Guide.

The *London Toy and Model Museum* is a must. For details look under Museums.

Best toys: *Pollock's Toy Museum.*

Trees

> Poems are made by fools like me,
> But only God can make a tree.

Joyce Kilmer (1888-1918)

The interesting question is why God also made the beetle which carried Dutch Elm Disease, thus killing more than 9,000 matured elms in the royal parks alone. Students at Chelsea College of Art have transformed three of these into an abstract sculpture (between the Magazine and Rima in Hyde Park), but I would have preferred the trees. Now a nasty new bug is attacking the plane trees.

London is full of arboreal wonders, from the oaks in *Greenwich Park*, which would have been 300 years old when Shakespeare admired them, to the superb oak on the Green at *Northolt Village*. There's a plane tree on the banks of the Wandle in Festival Walk, *Carshalton* which, at 125 feet, is the tallest plane in Britain. A yew in the Old Vicarage Garden at *Enfield* is reputedly over 400 years old, and in the *Chelsea Physic Garden* (see Gardens) grows the biggest olive tree in the country, an *olea europaea*, which also ripens fruit in December – seven pounds were harvested in 1976. Also in this garden a cork oak, a pomegranate, a fine Chinese Willowpattern tree, a maidenhair tree, an Indian bean tree, a cucumber tree, and many other varieties, including a black mulberry (*morus nigra*). Many mulberries grow in south London, and from their leaves came the caterpillars which made the silk which made the dress which Lady Di wore on her wedding day. South London is also notable for its box elders.

There's a wild cherry in *Highgate Woods*, which is said to have inspired Housman ('loveliest of trees, the cherry now . . .'); there's a fully matured palm in *Isleworth Cemetery*, beneath which lie victims of the Great Plague – the burial ground itself has been vandalised; there's a black walnut in *Marble Hill Park*, which is of vast circumference and considerable dignity, and there is a huge horse-chestnut in the middle of *Richmond Terrace Gardens*, perfect for playing under after your picnic. Growing out of the stone of that fine

Wren church, St Magnus the Martyr, *Billingsgate,* is one of those twisted old trees which have long since, like an old dog, forfeited any claims to pedigree; but it is much loved. So is the tree which grows through the middle of the PEN Club headquarters in Glebe Place, *Chelsea*; and the beech tree at *Kenwood.*

But it is not merely single trees which so delight the eye. There's that avenue of limes giving a vista to Holy Trinity, *Brompton*, and a superb avenue of planes in *Chingford Mount Cemetery.* Around the *Albert Memorial* and in Queen Mary's Gardens, *Regent's Park*, are such generous agglomerations of trees that it scarcely matters what they are; what matters is that they survive to give us all, or those of us who are not past caring, a moment's reflection, 'a green thought in a green shade'.

For vines, see under Vines. Of course.

Best tree: *The oak at Northolt.*

P.S. If you wish to endow a tree to commemorate a person or a special event contact *The Tree Council* (35 Belgrave Square, SW1X 8QN; 01-235 8854) who will welcome your interest.

P.P.S. Of the ten million trees planted in 1973 ('Plant a Tree in '73') between a half and two-thirds survived.

Tropical Fish

See under Pets.

Tunnels

Under the Thames in London is a warren of tunnels. The most romantic is the *Thames Tunnel* (Rotherhithe to Wapping). For nineteen years after a company had been formed by Marc Brunel (Isambard Kingdom Brunel's father) disasters attended the project. There were floodings in which six men drowned, and bankruptcies, and many workers suffering from 'tunnel disease' went blind. Brunel spent his savings and those of his wife on this dangerous and speculative venture, until at last the tunnel was opened in 1843. Within a year, two and a quarter million people (more than the population of London) had passed through it, but without vehicular traffic it could never pay its way, and in 1864 the tunnel which had cost a million pounds to build was sold for £200,000 to the East

London Railway Company. Still in use, the *Thames Tunnel* carries the Wapping to New Cross trains.

Tower Subway (Tower Hill to Tooley Street – completed August 1970), originally carried a sub-aqueous omnibus service – 'the twopenny tube' – but it proved unreliable. Closed to the public in 1897, it now serves as a duct for pipes and cables. It is entered by green pillar boxes at Tower Hill, and Vine Lane on the south bank. Access is via steel ladders through cast iron cylinders, but you need to have a steady head and a resolute spirit. It is privately owned.

The *Blackwall Tunnel* (Blackwall to Greenwich 1890-1897) was the first to be lit by electricity. This required a special power station to be built but the light was sufficient for a gentleman to read The *Times* in any part of the tunnel. It took 17,000 lbs of iron, 1 million tiles and 7 million bricks in the building. A second tunnel became necessary and this was opened in 1966.

The two *Dartford Tunnels* (opened 1963 and 1980 and costing £6 million and £36 million respectively) currently carry between twenty-five and forty thousand vehicles a day. The walls are faced with vitreous mosaic designed to reflect the light without causing glare. But even taking into account the £7,000,000 toll plaza extension the tunnels remain hopelessly inadequate for the amount of traffic, and a Dartford bridge, opposed by local residents, 250 of whom will lose their homes, is being considered.

The *Greenwich Subway* (Island Gardens, on the Isle of Dogs, to Church Street, Greenwich – opened 1902) is for pedestrians only and well worth a visit. The domed entrance halls, the lifts, the staircases are all original and designed on the grand scale. The view from the Island is the best in London.

Quite unexpected is the *King William Street Tunnel* with its phantom tube station of King William Street. To get down there take a lift from Regis House, by London Bridge, then walk through a nightmarish sequence of tunnels until you arrive at the platform. Here 100,000 people sheltered during the Blitz. (There are in fact seven deep-level shelters, built to withstand German rockets, still empty under the Northern Line). There are also underground stables for pit-ponies underneath the main line at *Euston* (access from the waste ground at the back of Camden Lock Market). For details of these and other subterranean surprises, I can recommend two excellent books *Tunnels Under London* by Nigel Pennick (Electric Traction Publications, Cambridge) and *London Under London* by Richard Trench and Ellis Hillman (John Murray 1985).

Best Tunnel: *Greenwich Subway.*

Worst Tunnel: *Central Electricity Board tunnels at Deptford and Barking.*

Umbrellas

> The rain it falleth every day
> Upon the just and unjust fella
> But more upon the just because
> The unjust hath the just's umbrella.
>
> Anon.

For more than 55 years Mrs May O'Sullivan hand-sewed umbrellas for *James Smith and Sons* (53 New Oxford Street, WC1; 01-836 4731). The art of applying the shade to the ribs with just the right amount of tension is no small matter, and is partly why James Smith – he of the amazing window displays – has cornered so much of the market. The firm sold brollies to Gladstone, Bonar Law and Lord Curzon; also hundreds of thousands of swagger sticks to officers in the Great War. Once the firm supplied ceremonial sun-shades to African chiefs, now golf umbrellas are more popular, though just as ritualistic. Most designer umbrellas, marketed by such all-right names as Cardin, Givenchy, Knirps and Marco Valentini are manufactured by *Schaverien Growy*, down the East End in Bethnal Green.

The royal umbrella warrant is held by *Swaine, Adeney, Brigg and Sons* (185 Piccadilly, W1; 01-734 4277). Here you can select a model to suit your height and specify whether gold or silver rings, and rosewood, ash or maple for the handle. A sword-stick umbrella (about £500) is also available, though whether that is also supplied to royalty we may never know. Swaine etc is the only firm still making silk umbrellas.

In the forecourt of *Westminster City School* (Palace Street SW1) is a statue in memory of Sir Sydney Waterlow, former chairman of the Board of Governors, and philanthropist who endowed Waterlow Park (see under Parks). He carries a trilby hat and umbrella.

Best Umbrellas: *James Smith & Sons.*
Swaine, Adeney, Brigg & Sons. (Jointly).

Underground Lines and Stations

The *Victoria Line* (opened between 1968 and 1972) is the best underground line in London. Where other lines have scheduled speeds of between 16 and 23 mph, the *Victoria* rolling stock can roll along much faster by virtue of 'longer station spacing', as they say. Only on the new Heathrow extension of the *Piccadilly Line* and on the suburban sections of the *Metropolitan Line* is it possible to travel faster, although paradoxically on the countrified stretches of the *Metropolitan* you would not wish to. Apart from its speed and regularity, the *Victoria Line* adopted the imaginative scheme of having tile murals at each station so that regular passengers could get their bearings with a shock of friendly recognition. The trains on the *Victoria* and *Jubiliee Lines* are automatically controlled which means that, if you have greater faith in computers than in human beings, you should feel safer on these lines than on the older ones.

But while the *Victoria* and the *Jubilee* are all sweetness and light, weepings, wailings, and gnashings of teeth may be heard the length of the notorious (and dirty) *Northern Line*, while the *Bakerloo* is a law unto itself. The *Circle* trains always come when you want the *District*, and vice versa. In 1973 the *Piccadilly Line* replaced its electro-pneumatic braking system with the Westcode electrically-controlled mechanism, which is why you no longer hear that poignant sigh just before the train pulls out of the station. The average length of a traveller's journey on the underground system is 4.7 miles, a journey which takes him or her less than fifteen minutes; not, all things considered, bad.

The stations are idiosyncratic. *Earl's Court* has a greengrocer (not cheap), a fine Victorian overhead roof, an overhead duct which carries a river, and handsome veteran destination boards. You can drink at *Kew, Baker Street, Sloane Square* and *Liverpool Street* stations; you can buy antiques at *Edgware Road* and stamps at *Waterloo*. At *Bank* station, which connects with *Waterloo* via 'The Drain' (the Waterloo and City Railway and the oldest surviving part of the underground system), there is a travolator, similar to the one at Heathrow. The *Barbican* station (formerly Aldersgate Street and Barbican) is most elegant, while *Uxbridge* is aggressively bold in an uncompromising thirties style. *Baker Street* has a cinema and Sherlock Holmes on the walls; *Bond Street*, which has the best dressed ticket collector – he even sports a pocket watch – is like a modern shopping precinct – damn it, it *is* a modern shopping precinct – suave and expensive looking – damn it, it *is* expensive, while *Goodge Street* and *Hampstead* (once South Kentish Town) are little architectural revolutions in the tiled neo-Georgian manner. *Goodge Street* has new lifts replacing the chaotic old ones. *Marble Arch* and *Hyde Park Corner* escalators have been out of order since early 1983; not a great advertisement for London Transport. *St John's Wood* station (c1940) is curved and low and pleasantly bricked; entering it is like walking into the mouth of a friendly fish. *Great Portland Street, Hanger Lane* (1947 but tatty), and

Arnos Grove (1933) are circular. *South Kensington* is all red tiling and witty iron scrollwork, a bit arty but fun, just what *South Kensington* ought to be. At *Holborn* you have to walk miles for your interline connection. The *Angel, Islington* is worth walking several miles to avoid. Do so. Walk to *Highbury and Islington* – a pleasant walk and preferable to the vertiginous squalor at the *Angel*. *Highgate* and *Barons Court* are nasty, *Chalk Farm* and *Gunnersbury* and *Mornington Crescent* worse. *Camden Town* is the draughtiest station in London. But worst of all must be *Oxford Circus* in a wet afternoon rush hour; almost unendurable.

A hint to strap-hangers. Supposing you have to make the daily trek from *Victoria* to *Wimbledon* on the *District Line* at 5.30 p.m. It is worth while travelling east for a few stops, say to *Blackfriars*, and then west, thus ensuring a seat for the journey home.

The London transport map of the London Underground is, of course, a triumph of graphic art, clear and satisfying. It must also have been looked at longer and with greater concentration than the Night Watch, the Mona Lisa and the Laughing Cavalier together.

Best line: *Victoria*.
Best station: *Baker Street* (renovated to something like its original state).
Worst line: *Northern*.
Worst station: *Chalk Farm* (also *The Angel* and *Oxford Circus* in the rush hour).

P.S. Read *The Story of London's Underground* by J. R. Day (1972).

Underwear

> Lottie Collins has no drawers,
> Will you kindly lend her yours?
> She is going far away
> To sing Ta-ra-ra-boom-de-ay!
>
> Playground song

With the alarming announcement, supported by all the authority of the opinion polls, that it is men's bottoms first, their eyes second, that women find most arousing, men should obviously look more carefully at their underpants.

Marks and Spencer's Y-fronts which have kept me going for all these years may have to be reassessed. It is interesting, though, that – perhaps as a result of women's stated preference – *Calvin*

299

Klein has started marketing traditional men's underpants for women. There is just one question I should like to ask *Calvin Klein* . . .

Meanwhile men will continue to get their pants at *Marks and Sparks*, and women for special occasions will continue to visit *Chic* (78 Heath Street, NW3; 01-435 5454), and *Sue Ellen* (16 Kingswell, Heath Street, W3; 01-435 8800).

As for *Janet Reger*, the shops have gone – the end of an era.

Universities, Colleges, Polytechnics, etc

Good ones: The *Royal College of Defence Studies* in general, and the pink gins in the officers' mess in particular. Also the *Institute for Strategic Studies*. Do these two have war games together and, if so, who wins? The *City of London Polytechnic*, the *North East London Polytechnic*, *Imperial College*, *Goldsmiths' College*, *City Lit*, *King's College*.

At the *South Bank Poly* brilliant and cheap language laboratories may be found. The *South Lambeth Evening Institute* is celebrated for its pottery courses at the *Elmwood Pottery*, and I have heard nothing but good of the Drama and English faculty at *London University*.

Not such good ones: *The Architectural Association* (it produces, says a friend who may have an axe to grind, 'smooth talking con-men with little or no architectural interest'); *University College*, Gower Street; *South West London College*, Tooting.

As for the *London School of Economics* (LSE) moving to the right these days, what can I possibly say that has not already been said about an institution that has already produced both my mother and Mick Jagger, bless them.

Unusual Shops

The following are all recommended. I have excluded from the list unusual shops featured elsewhere in the book.

Astroturf, and avant-garde technological furniture and effects, from *Astrohome*, 47/49 Neal Street, WC2; 01-240 0420.
Beautiful Bodies from *City Gym* (Murray's), New Union Street, EC2; 01-628 0786.
Beehives complete with bees (£45+) from *John Davies*, 66 Embercourt Road, Thames Ditton, Surrey; 01-398 3277.
Capes from *Born and Bred*, 85 Bourne Street, SW1.

Designer jewellery for men and women from *XYZ*, 74 Heath Street, NW3; 01-794 3242.

Electric Art from *Argon*, 3 Theberton Street, N1; 01-359 3845.

Ephemera from *Dodo*, 185 Westbourne Grove, W11; 01-229 3132.

Flying Ducks, and kitsch generally from *Schram & Scheddle*, 262 Upper Street, N1; 01-226 4166.

Frozen Reindeer from *The Swedish Shop*, 7 Paddington Street, W1; 01-486 7077.

Holograms from *The Light Fantastic Gallery*, Unit 48, Covent Garden, WC2; 01-836 6423. Also a shop in Sheen.

Home Wine Making and Brewing Equipment from *W. R. Loftus*, 1/3 Charlotte Street, W1; 01-636 6235.

Hoods for 2CVs from *Wendy Chamberlain*, 2 Tremaine Road, SE20; 01-778 7997.

Interpreters from *Ethnic Switchboard*, 01-993 6119.

Keyboard Hire from *Keyboard Hire*, 8 Thornhill Road, N1; 01-607 8797.

Lavatory Seats from *Sitting Pretty*, 131 Dawes Road, SW6; 01-381 0449.

Left-Handed Goods from *Anything Left-Handed*, 68 Beak Street, W1; 01-437 3910. Most popular sellers: scissors, potato peelers, can openers, pens with left-handed nibs.

Lighting from *Christopher Wray*, 591/593/600/602/606/613 New King's Road, SW6; 01-736 8008 and from *Roger of London*, 344 Richmond Road, Twickenham; 01-891 2122, and very cheap from *Mr Resister*, 267 New King's Road, SW6; 01-736 7372.

Magic from *Davenport's*, 51 Gt Russell Street, WC1; 01-405 8524.

Movie Memorabilia from *The Cinema Bookshop*, 13 Gt Russell Street, WC1; 01-637 0206.

Personalised Presents (your name or monogram on almost anything) from *Eximous*, 12a Maddox Street, W1; 01-629 3152.

Sci-Fi Magazines etc. from Al Reuter, *Reedmore Books*, 1 Midland Crescent, NW3; 01-435 4634 and from *Forbidden Planet*, 58 St Giles High Street, WC2; 01-379 6042.

Murals (commissioned, mainly for children) from *Hippo Hall*, 65 Pimlico Road, SW1; 01-730 7710.

Painted Furniture (for adults) from *Shop for Painted Furniture*, 95 Waterford Road, SW6; 01-736 1908, (for children) from *Dragons*, 25 Walton Street, SW1; 01-589 3795.

Patchwork from *Patchwork Dog and Calico Cat*, 21 Chalk Farm Road, NW1; 01-485 1239.

Polo Sticks etc. from *Holbrow's*, incorporated within *George Parker & Sons* (saddlers to the Queen Mother) 12 Upper St Martin's Lane, WC1; 01-836 1164.

Posters from *Poster Shop*, 168 Fulham Road, SW10; 01-373 7294.

Saxophones (and other brass instruments) from *Paxman's* 116 Long Acre, WC2; 01-240 3647.

Scaffold Furniture from *One Off*, 31 Shorts Gardens, WC2.

Shells (very beautiful) from *Eaton's Shell Shop*. 16 Manette Street, W1; 01-437 9391, (opposite Foyles).

Spectacles (fantastic frames) from *Cutler & Gross*, 18 St Christopher's Place, W1; 01-486 4079.

Stained Glass (ready made, DIY or made to measure) from *Lead and Light*, 15 Camden Lock, Chalk Farm, NW1; 01-485 4568.

Stoves from *Stove Shop*, Camden Lock, Chalk Farm, NW1; 01-969 9531.

Swizzle Sticks (and cocktail paraphernalia) from *The Cocktail Shop*, 5 Avery Row, W1; 01-493 9744.

Tapestry from Ehrman, 21-22 Vicarage Gate, W8; 01-937 4568.

Translations from *Eurolingua*, 15 Newman Street, W1; 01-323 1118/0645.

Uniforms (for chefs, waiters, butchers etc) from *P. Denny & Co.*, 39 Old Compton Street, W1; 01-437 1654.

Vegetarian Restaurants

A useful telephone number first: *The Vegetarian Society* (53 Marloes Road, W8) may be reached on 01-937 7739. They will be able to give you the very latest gen on vegetarian and vegan restaurants. And a useful book, although not absolutely up to date, is *The Guide to Good Food Shops* by S. Campbell (Macmillan).

But really things have improved significantly for vegetarians, as they have for Non-Smokers (q.v.). Most restaurants of any pretensions will now serve at least one specialist dish in this category rather than the depressing and ubiquitous omelette. An example is *Inigo Jones* (14 Garrick Street, WC2; 01-836 6456) which offers a menu potager, of exceptional variety and interest at an exceptional prix fixe (£23.50 plus service at 15%). But then *Inigo Jones* had a Michelin star; only briefly, but it did have one. The emphasis is slightly different at *The Garden* (616 Fulham Road, SW6; 01-736 6056), where Charles Brodie, entrepreneur of *La Poule Au Pot* (see French) and *Maggie Jones* (see English), runs a restaurant principally for vegetarians but with a meat dish or two – with a guarantee that the bird or animal was killed with kindness.

Now a few of the real things:

Cherry Orchard (241-5 Globe Road, E2; 01-980 6678). Buddhist-run. See under Budget Restaurants.

Cranks (9-11 Tottenham Street, W1; 01-631 3912). The newest of the stable, which opened in compensation for the closure of the Heal's branch. A take-away counter and a self-service counter. Soups and potato fillings excellent. The self-service doesn't work if you order hot food. By the time you get to your table it's cold. Very popular; slightly on the expensive side. Other branches at Unit 11, Central Avenue, Covent Garden, WC2 (01-379 6508) and 8 Marshall Street, W1 (01-437 9431) – the original.

Diwana Bhel-Poori House (121 Drummond Street, NW1; 01-387 5556). Go for the Thali (£3), comprising lentil soup, rice, two vegetables, one farson (savoury dish), papad, mango pickle, 3 chapatis or 4 puris and a sweet. Must be the best value in London.

Earth Exchange (213 Archway Road, N6; 01-340 6407). Also a bookshop, herbalist and clinic. Not too solemn however, and agreeable food.

Food for Thought (31 Neal Street, WC2; 01-836 0239). Occasionally a set three-course meal for £12.50. At other times excellent cooking with the emphasis on stir-fried vegetables and nourishing puds.

Green Cottage II (122a Finchley Road NW3; 01-794 3833). See under Chinese Restaurants.

Hare Krishna Curry House (1 Hanway Street, W1; 01-636 5262). An extremely cheap Gujerati vegetarian restaurant.

Manna (4 Erskine Road, NW3; 01-722 8028). Old established, imaginative cooking, cheerful atmosphere.

Neal's Yard Bakery and Tea Room (6 Neal's Yard, Shorts Gardens, WC2; 01-836 5199). Closed Wed and Sat evenings. Soups, pies, cakes, and a vast selection of aperients.

Rani (3/5 Long Lane, Finchley, N3; 01-349 4386) and *Shanti* (185 Battersea Park Road, SW11; 01-720 9928). Both new. Both serve excellent dosa (crisp pancakes) and avial (spicy vegetable stew) as well as much else. More reports please.

Slenders (41 Cathedral Place, Paternoster Square, EC4; 01-236 5974) closed evenings and week-ends. Popular, large, self-service restaurant near St Paul's. Cheap. Non-trendy.

Wholemeal Café (1 Shrubbery Road, SW16; 01-769 2423). Menu changes daily but always including a bake of the day and puddings. Those who know go down on their knees in front of the hot banana pudding.

Wilkins Natural Foods (61 Marsham Street, SW1; 01-222 4038). With a take-away department at 53 Marsham Street. Opposite the depressing Department of the Environment; cheap, unassuming, small, recommended.

Best vegetarian restaurant: *Food for Thought*.

Vets

When Magpie, my much lamented Geordie mongrel bitch, was a mere pup-in-arms and was taken for her first ride on the London Underground, all hell broke loose. Leaping from my arms she caught her paw in the Oxford Street escalator. She howled. A middle-aged lady trotted up, brandishing a handkerchief. 'Don't worry', she cried, 'I'm a midwife.'

Having bandaged the paw, she directed me to an animal clinic where the paw was set, but upside-down, and I was instructed to keep the bandage on for at least a week. Long before then the putrefaction was such that a local vet in New Cross had to repair the damage as best he could.

This was the same bitch, whose pregnancy at the age of seven was wrongly diagnosed by a vet as 'a phantom', So we starved the poor creature (she had always been greedy) when we should have been feeding her up.

But there are competent vets, and the best is *Bruce Fogle* (Portman Veterinary Clinic, Seymour Street, W1). I can also heartily recommend *Andrew Carmichael* (7 Addison Avenue, W11; 01-603 4407/4094). *Peter Cronin* (5c Bedford Corner, South Parade, W4; 01-994 2387). The *Elizabeth Street Veterinary Clinic* (01-730 9102) is open 24 hours a day.

There is a herbal and homeopathic vet in London, *John Rohbach* who grows all his own plants and has a stock of 800 home-made essences and extracts. 'I try to form a relationship with the animals that is conducive to healing,' he says. 'The animal must believe I am going to help him.'

There is also a veterinary dentist who will cap dog's teeth for cosmetic purposes, but I shan't give you his address.

Views

It's nature versus art. Nature is represented by the view from the first floor room of the Roebuck Pub at the top of Richmond Hill. In fact you don't need to be in the Roebuck, because the view looks splendid in all weathers and at all times of the year from any vantage point, but the Roebuck is ideal. Nor am I alone in thinking this. Turner, amongst numerous other artists, thought it a fit subject for his palette and it is known as *Turner's View*.

And art is represented by the wonderful view which I've mentioned elsewhere from the *Isle of Dogs* across the river to the Royal Naval College, Greenwich.

Other justifiably famous views include the palpitatingly romantic view from the *Rennie Bridge* over the Serpentine, especially on a summer's evening: the silhouette view of towers and spires and upended matchboxes from *Primrose Hill* or *Parliament Hill* looking south into the distant smoke; the view from *Westminster Bridge* ('Earth has not anything to show more fair,' said Wordsworth, and he was an authority), but the view from *Hungerford Bridge* runs it close; the view from *Battersea Old Church* looking west along the river – Turner was there too! The Haymarket Theatre at night from *St James's Square*; the view from William and Mary's bedroom in *Kensington Palace* along the Serpentine, which is why the Serpentine was moved to its present position; the view from *Greenwich Observatory* towards the river; the view down *George Street* from the north side of Hanover Square to the portico of St George's Church; the view up *Fleet Street* to St Paul's (partially obscured by a crass development), the view from the dome (q.v.) of *St Paul's*; the view of *Cannizaro Park*, Wimbledon from the big house; the view from the top of the *NatWest Building* – but you're only allowed to see it if you're a big executive; the view of *Hertford House* across Manchester Square; the view south along *St James's*.

Best Views: *Turner's View.*
Royal Naval College. (Jointly).
Worst view: *from the dressing rooms of the National Theatre.*

Vines

Everybody knows about the *Great Vine of Hampton Court*, which was planted in 1768 and has survived everything, including tourists. But a vine planted in his back garden in *Dartford* by Les Stringer in 1977 is even more remarkable. Growing through the neighbour's fence the vine had to be trimmed back. The trimmings lay disregarded behind a shed for a couple of years, when Les popped one of them into a hole in some concrete. It went berserk. Within a month it was in bud; within two months it had two bunches of grapes. Now it has entirely covered the factory of Sandix Street Metal Industries. In 1983 it gave

7620 bunches of grapes weighing over 1000 pounds where Hampton Court's giant vine only produced 200 pounds of grapes. The grapes from Les's vine are put to the profit of the local hospital; so are the cuttings. By the time you read this the whole of Kent and South London may be a mass of glossy purple grapes. Let's hope so.

Best vine: *The Dartford Vine.*

Wall Writings

Old graffiti date you dreadfully. Remember 'Marples Must Go'? Long after he went it is still faintly visible on the *Cromwell Road* extension, as well as on the M1 bridges. 'Springboks out' survives in *Isleworth*, and George Davis is still innocent down the *East End*. Then we have 'Rambo is a Mother's Boy' which sprang up everywhere spontaneously as though pre-ordained; maybe it was.

Intellectual wall writings tend to be self-conscious. In the *Charing Cross Road:* 'The Grave of Karl Marx is just another Communist plot' sounds artful rather than spontaneous, but at the *Festival Hall:* 'Colin Davis can't tell his brass from his oboe' is witty enough to be excusable. At the *LSE* 'Lateral thinking is a con.' 'Honest?' 'Yes, straight up.' I still don't understand those old favourites: 'Cats like plain crisps' and 'It's only Rock 'n Roll'. Since graffiti have recently been so widely anthologised (by Nigel Rees among others) it could be more interesting to study advertising slogans. In the *Commercial Road* I spotted a placard requesting: 'Boys Wanted for Plastics' and nearby in *Black Lion Yard*, E1, could be seen (and maybe still can) on some doors: 'J. D. & J. Evans, Cowkeepers' with a Hebrew inscription insisting that the milk is properly kosher. On the gasometer at the *Oval* (the most celebrated gasometer in the world) it warns: 'Use Gas Well' and on the wall of a café in the *Waterloo Road* one could/can read: 'The Sunday Referee. Most Enterprising Paper of the Age'. One genius inscribed his entire philosophy of life and critique of social revolution on a convenient wall along the approach to *Paddington Station*, where the commuter trains linger, and where it had once innocently announced: 'Virol – Nervous Girls Need It!'

In several places I have spotted the healthily cynical: 'If voting changed anything, they'd make it illegal'. Facing commuters travelling east on the M4: 'Good morning, lemmings'. But my favourite has been on public display in *Dean Street* – the Soho Square end – for as long as I can remember . . .

Best wall writing: (though it is in fact a hanging sign board):
Hospital for Women
Please Go Quietly.
Worst wall writing: *Skinhead graffiti* (usually grossly racist).
Examples may be seen on the side walls of the London Pavilion in
Great Windmill Street and around London football grounds.

Weather

The meteorological variations within Greater London from Ruislip,
Barnet and Southgate in the North to Epsom and Dartford in the
south are significant. It is *foggiest* in the London parks, along the
Thames and at Heathrow; it is *snowiest* on the borders of London and
Kent, and it is noticeably *warmer* within the central London enclave.
The absolute temperature range over the last 100 years at Kew is from
22.2°F (−3.4°C) on January 5th, 1984 to 93.9°F (43.4°C) on August
9th, 1911, but on that same August 9th the temperature reached an
official 100°F at Greenwich.

In hot weather the *hottest* places in central London are iron railings
exposed to direct sunlight, and the *coldest* places in cold weather are
the conductor rails of the London Underground network. The
average annual rainfall at Kew is 23.95 inches. The *driest* month is
March, the *wettest* months are July and November, the *coldest* month
used to be January but is now February, while the *hottest* month is
July; the *sunniest* month is April, the *cloudiest* is December, and the
foggiest is November. The *hottest* time of the year, consistently over the
years, is between 3 and 4 p.m. on 29th July. Letters to the *Times* have
claimed mysteriously and with authoritative backing from statistics
that Thursdays are much *wetter* than other days of the week.

In short, one has only to visit other capitals, such as Washington
DC, Kampala, Port Stanley, Bahrein, or Moscow, to realise just how
lucky we are.

P.S. Serious students should study: *The Climate of London* by T. J.
Chandler (Hutchinson 1965) or *London Weather* by J. H. Brazell
(1968).

Weather Vanes/Weather Cocks

There is a fine fat ram on top of *Young's Brewery* in Wandsworth High
Street, and there is an ethereal flying horse above the *Inner Temple*.
Cocks may be spotted all over the shop, notably on *All Hallows By The*

Tower's steeple, and *19 Cheyne Place*, Chelsea. There is a ship, as you might expect, above *Trinity House*, Trinity Square, EC3; less predictably ships float above *Liberty's* in Great Marlborough Street and *Tooting Public Library* (a Viking vessel). But the best ship sails proudly over the restored *St Nicholas Cole Abbey* in Queen Victoria Street, having been removed from the vanished church of St Michael, Queenhithe. *Battersea Library* features an old man dozing over his books, while *Lambeth Palace* has an arrow and a crown in the finest of iron tracery. The weather cock on the roof of the *Banqueting House* (all that remains of Whitehall Palace) was placed there by James II to establish the direction of the winds when William of Orange was preparing to sail.

But the best has to be . . .

Best weather vane: *Old Father Time* with his sickle at Lord's Cricket Ground.

See also under Art Nouveau.

Weddings

Smart London weddings are solemnised at the *Guards Chapel*, St James's, Piccadilly, *St George's*, Hanover Square, or – to get maximum coverage from the papparazzi – *Caxton Hall Registry Office*. The most improbable wedding in recent months was at the first named of these and brought together in holy matrimony Mr Richard Plunkett-Ernle -Erle-Drax, Coldstream Guards, and the golden-haired Miss Zara Legge-Bourke. Among the guests were Lady Lees and Lady Lock, Dreda Lady Tryon, Mrs David Dollar, Mrs John Thomas – I promise you – Mr and Mrs Wellesley-Wesley, Mrs Jacqueline McChynchy, nanny Van Cutsem, nanny Phillips, and nanny Henderson, among many others. Presumably if Zara was strong willed and determined not to lose her maiden name, she would by now be Mrs Zara Plunkett-Ernle-Erle-Drax-Legge-Bourke. Try getting that on an Access card!

Wildlife

Salmon have returned to the *Thames*, house-martins to the eaves, and hedgehogs to the London hedgerows. Foxes, which eat rats and mice creep into the inner suburbs at night along the railway embankments and even occasionally make it to the *City*. The only harm they do –

except to poultry – is to howl at night. A vixen in *Blackheath* used to wreck what I laughingly called my beauty sleep.

Also using the railways to hunt for mice and voles are tawny owls (q.v.) and kestrels, while magpies are everywhere, and black redstarts are not uncommon. Butterflies (q.v.) add bezazz to many city gardens.

Twenty-six Sites of Special Scientific Interest (SSSIs) have been opened (contact the *London Wildlife Trust* for details). A prime example, no more than a falcon's stoop away from Tower Bridge is the *William Curtis Ecological Park*. Hunt it out – but not all of you at once. Less encouragingly a strain of botulism in the filthy Italian Garden in *Hyde Park* resulted in the death of almost all the ducklings hatched during the spring of 1985. *St James's Park* and *Regent's Park* have professional bird-keepers, but *Hyde Park* does not. A Mrs Anna Green has taken it upon herself with a band of helpers to do what she can for the birds of *Hyde Park*, taking them home and giving them a chance to recover in clean water.

Wheelchairs

Happily the authorities are slowly waking up to the clumsiness of wheel-chairs and the thoughtlessness of architects. Something is being done. But in one of London's biggest and smartest cinemas, the Classic, Haymarket, wheelchairs are still not admitted.

For details of where else you or your friends may not be allowed to go get *The Wheelchair Guide to London* from the London Central YMCA (phone 01-637 1333 x 4299).

Windows

One of the most elaborate windows in London must be the Ruskin window at the east end of Sir Gilbert Scott's Church of *St Giles*, Camberwell. Designed when Ruskin was really only a kid – well, twenty-five – it is imaginatively coloured in ultramarine, cobalt and crimson and depicts incidents from the Old and New Testaments set in scholarly opposition. 'The purest and most thoughtful minds', said Ruskin 'are those which love colour the most', and he certainly lived by this dictum. An interesting comparison may be made with William Morris's three-lancet east window in *St John the Apostle*, Whetstone, N20, and with the fine John Piper window in *St Margaret's*, Westminster. But the most impressive modern church window is

Hugh Easton's vision of the Risen Christ above blitzed Stepney in the beautiful church of *St Dunstan and All Saints*, Stepney High Street.

In *Southwark Cathedral* is a stained glass window (Christopher Webb, 1954) featuring characters from the plays of Shakespeare, the adopted local lad, whose brother Edmund Shakespeare is buried in the cathedral. Also a fine west window by the Victorian Henry Holiday. Not far away is the skeletal rose window – sad but beautiful – all that remains of the old Palace (q.v.) of the Bishops of Winchester. The glass in *St Paul's* was destroyed by bombs in 1941, but some old armorial glass may be found in the *Great Hall of Lambeth Palace* and in the fine hall of *Gray's Inn*. The *Great Hall of Guildhall* has new stained windows with scrolls detailing 663 mayors and lord mayors. *St Katherine Creechurch* in Leadenhall Street has 17th-century glass designed as a catherine wheel, of course, in its fine east window.

The windows in Horace Walpole's Gothic extravaganza at *Strawberry Hill* might as well be in a church; other fine Gothic windows may be seen in the *House of Commons*, at *48 Park Lane*, and, of course, at *St Pancras Station*. I have great fondness (because I have passed them so many times) for those huge and heavily leaded studio windows along the *Cromwell Road* extension, overlooking what used to be playing fields until bureaucrats decided they had a better idea.

Christopher Wren designed some Mozartian windows in Fountain Court at *Hampton Court Palace*, and Nash's row of little windows, like aircraft propellers, above the portico of the *Haymarket Theatre*, are delightful. But then London is full of charming little windows and fanlights (q.v.).

Best windows: *St Dunstan and All Saints*, Stepney.

Worst windows: (jointly) The *Senate House*, London; *Dulwich College Great Hall* ('So ugly', says my nephew, 'that it's permanently covered by a curtain') and the ground level windows along the north side of *William IV Street*, WC2. From these vile smells emanate.

Wines

It's been quite a few pages since I gave you any statistics so here goes. Average yearly consumption throughout the country of the 26,300,000 people who drink wine in Britain is 23 bottles per year. In 1984 we bought 600 million bottles compared with 380 millions in 1980. In 1984 we also spent £1,865,000,000 on wine, most of which came from France and Germany. Women drink more wine – usually white – than men, and most of those women are between 25 and 34. The average cost of these bottles is a very modest £2.12 and the most popular wine is Peter Dominic's Piat d'Or – statistics by courtesy of . . . Peter Dominic.

Currently the most fashionable wines are Sancerre and Muscat de Beaumes-de-Venise. Moving up fast are Cahors and Madiran from France. Wines from New Zealand and Western Australia are increasingly popular. And no-one outside Oxford colleges drinks German wine any more.

Here, thanks to Andrew Barr, who is a most reliable source for much of this information, is a list of best buys:

Plonk: Pavion Vin Rouge (Oddbins) – £2.99 per 1½ litres.
Germanic: Bulgarian Riesling (widely available and guaranteed free of anti-freeze) – £1.89.
Claret: Château Les Barreyes 1982 (Cullens) – £2.19.
White Burgundy: Rully (André Delorme available from The Winery) – whatever year you can find – about £4.
Sauternes: Clos St Georges (Sainsbury's) – £2.80.
Spanish Red: Raimat Abadia (Victoria Wine) – £3.15. Better than any Rioja.
Italian: Vino Nobili di Montepulciano (Majestic Warehouses) – £3.29.
Champagne: Cuvée Grand Siècle, Laurent Perrier (Harrods and elsewhere) – about £23.
Pink Champagne: Pol Roger 1975 (Selfridges & The Champagne House) – about £12.

Of the wine warehouses, the best are *Majestic Warehouses* (Albion Wharf, Hester Road, SW11; 01-223 2983) or *Bibendum* (113 Regent's Park Road, NW1; 01-586 9761). Bottle for bottle, the best value comes from Geoffrey Harrison at *London Wine Brokers* (Chelsea Wharf, 15 Lots Road, SW10; 01-351 6856). There is a £4 delivery charge in Greater London. Also recommended: *Berkmann Wine Cellars* (12 Brewery Road, N7; 01-609 4711). *Christie's* and *Sotheby's* (see Auctions) are best for cheaper wines – always taste them first – for burgundies or for non-vintage champagnes. But I'm getting ahead of myself; see below under Wine Merchants.

Best wine for all occasions: *Vino Nobili de Montelpulciano.*
Worst wine for all occasions: *Mateus Rose.*

P.S. In a reputable restaurant the house wine will usually be excellent value – why else should they put their name to it?

Wine Bars

At the last count – and it's not easy to count them when they won't stand still – there were more than 250 wine bars in London. Wine is no longer significantly more expensive than beer, and women are said to be safer from unwelcome attentions in wine bars than in pubs, but this is only true of the nicer wine bars and the nastier pubs. In many City wine bars women are not welcomed. In others, especially in South Kensington, they are regarded as fair game.

The king of the London wine bar scene is John Davy, who owns more than twenty of the things. His first was the *Boot and Flogger* (10-26 Redcross Way, SE1; 01-407 1184). At a Davy wine bar you get a choice of six house wines, and twenty-four more select wines, with ports, sherries and a cold buffet. The *Balls Brothers* chain (almost all in the City) offers a choice of some seventy wines, but is a bit clubby and predictable.

The *Cork and Bottle* (44-46 Cranbourne Street, WC1; 01-734 7807) is to be found underneath Chez Solange and the adjoining stamp shop just off the Charing Cross Road. It's not always easy to get served, but the wine available (details on blackboards) are varied and interesting. Don and Jean Hewitson, who also run other wine bars, organise regular festivals of wines from different regions at the *Cork and Bottle*, and always stock Antipodean wines. Expect to pay between £1 and £2 a glass. For £1.65 I enjoyed a Laboure Roi Chablis. The glass was not very full, and it would have been better value to have bought the bottle at £6.50. However the homemade snacks are tasty and, if you choose your evening, you can watch Juan Ramirez plucking with his plectrum. Unluckily, I had to settle for some turgid, taped Matt Monroish stuff.

Best in the City – where the first and the best wine bars are to be found – are:

Corney and Barrow (118 Moorgate, EC2; 01-628 2898). Beautifully designed, excellently varied menu, superb cheeseboard, very large glasses of sophisticated wines, and *Fenchurch Colony* (next to Fenchurch Street Station, and 14 New London Street, EC3; 01-481 0848) spacious, friendly and well stocked. A choice of 55 wines to go with your turkey and cranberry pie sandwich.

Elsewhere I'm particularly keen on:

Daly's (210 The Strand, WC2; 01-583 4476) where over-paid lawyers mingle with under-paid sub-editors from Macmillans. Excellent snacks and reputable wines. Visit the splendid cheese shop next door.

Julie's Bar (137 Portland Road, W11; 01-727 7985) is currently very fashionable – which doesn't mean much in the brittle world of wine bars, but it has plenty to offer the well-heeled customer. Beleaguered producers from Television Centre seek solace here, and the gossip is classy. So too is the food. There is a small back garden used for lunches in the summer; they serve cream teas when the wine bar is closed, and the service is cheerful.

Hoult's (20 Bellevue Road, SW17; 01-767 1858) is extremely lively and even more so when Julie Kirk is around. Excellent food and wine; a party that spills out onto Wandsworth Common.

Draycott's (114 Draycott Avenue, SW3; 01-584 5359). Where the privileged few are fattened up for the revolution. Wines from the *Bow Wine Vaults*, which is always encouraging. Owned by the Ebury Wine Company, who run two other recommended wine bars – *Bolton's* (198 Fulham Road, SW10; 01-352 0251) and *The Ebury* (139 Ebury Street, SW1; 01-730 5447), which was the first of the trendy wine bars and has just celebrated its 25th Anniversary. French food by Madame Yvonne Ottet and a Mongolian director. But the customers are rude.

The Wine Gallery (49 Hollywood Road, SW10; 01-352 7572) is the Good Food Guide Wine Bar of the Year. Give it a try.

Les Amis du Vin (and variations) have received mixed reports.

Best wine bar: *Corney and Barrow*. (Sole agents for Dudet's Beaujolais, Leroy's Burgundy. Also fine clarets and vintage port.)
Worst wine bar: *El Vino's*.

Wine Merchants

For Warehouses and Auctions see the entry under Wine.

If the price is your concern and you can't get to an auction, or warehouse you should buy your wine at *Oddbins* (various branches). In 1979 *Which* reported that *Oddbins* was the cheapest off-licence chain, and it has remained so. The best branches are 141 Notting Hill Gate, W1 (01-229 4082) and 142 Fulham Road, SW10 (01-373 5715), where the staff are particularly amiable. In the same edition of *Which* the most expensive chain was *E. J. Rose & Co Ltd* (various branches).

Although *Oddbins* remains the cheapest chain, the cheapest single shop is *Del Monico's* (64 Old Compton Street, W1; 01-437 2738). Their window display is a work of art and contains their entire stock. The most expensive shop in London would be the *Curzon Wine Co* in Curzon Street, were one not to include *Fortnum's*, whose prices for single bottles seem to resemble what other people are quoting for cases.

At the *Camden Wine and Cheese Centre* (214 Camden High Street, NW1; 01-485 5895) you can select from fifty champagnes, at *The Vintner's Main* (14 Buckingham Palace Road, SW1; 01-828 3967) from sixty English wines, and at *Harrods* from eighty-five malt whiskies (but see Milroy's below). The antique *Berry Brothers & Rudd* (3 St James's Street, SW1; 01-930 1888) is worth a visit for the sake of nostalgia and *au recherche du temps perdu*.

Bottoms Up (various branches) is challenging *Oddbins* for the cheap and cheerful end of the market. The best of their house clarets is Harvey's Medoc AC, the worst Findlater's Côtes de Bourg. *Marks & Spencers'* Vinho Verde is a trusted favourite if you can get the cork out; it's good value. The best wine cellars in London restaurants are at the *Connaught* (Carlos Place W1; 01-499 7070), *Oslo Court* (Prince Albert Road, NW8; 01-722 8795) and the *Tate Gallery Restaurant* (Millbank, SW1; 01-821 1313).

Also recommended:

The Champagne House, 1/15 Dawson Place, W2 (01-221 5538).

Moreno, Norfolk Place, W2; for Spanish wines.

The *Wine Studio*, 9 Ecclestone Street, SW1 (01-730 7596) for Californian wines.

Alex Findlater, Abbey Road, NW9 for Australian wines.

Sookias and Bertant, Putney for the wines of South West France.

Milroy's, 3 Greek Street, W1 (01-437 9311/2385) for malt whisky – over 130 varieties.

La Vignerons d'Aquitaine, 36 Kensington Church Street, W8 (01-937 9132) for obscure wines, including the best Russian wines.

The Winery, 4 Clifton Road, W9 (01-286 2733) suave with a blazing fire in winter.

Best wine shop: *La Vignerons d'Aquitaine*.

Zoos

Henry I was one of the earliest zoo-keepers. He had a collection of lions, leopards, an elephant, and a white bear from Norway. The Norwegians also provided 'four pence daily, with a muzzle and iron chain, to keep him when extra angry and a stout cord to hold him when a-fishing in the Thames'. Henry I was accused of extravagance. Another famous zoo-keeper was George Wombwell who brought two boa-constrictors straight off the boat at Tilbury, exhibiting them to such effect that he was made for life. He became a man of substance with several travelling menageries to his name.

Chessington Zoo has perked up a bit but features a circus and fun-fair and is not a serious zoo (that is to say one concerned with genetics and endangered species) at all.

London Zoo, now owned by Lord Zuckerman, is in the process – and a very painful one – of transforming itself into an Animal Theme Park. It has applied for permission to demolish many of its most loved buildings and terraces. Yet it rejoices in some excellent architecture. The original buildings were by the great Decimus Burton, and the more recent buildings have enhanced what had been deteriorating. The Snowdon Aviary, the Charles Clore Mammal Pavilion, and the impressive Lion Terraces all pay tribute to Sir Hugh Casson, who was in charge of the developments. But all that is now at risk.

The children's zoo at *Battersea Park* is also at risk. Zoo Check, organised by Virginia McKenna, whose efforts succeeded in closing down *Southampton Zoo*, regards this menagerie as offering totally inadequate accommodation for the animals. Another modest children's zoo is in *Golders Hill Park*.

Whipsnade, some little way up the M1, sets animals as far as possible in their natural environments, and is enjoyable.

The GLC organise a mobile zoo which tours the parks throughout the summer (details 01-633 1728). Pony rides always provided.

Best zoo: *Whipsnade*.

Bibliography

Besides the specialist volumes mentioned in the course of the text, the following are a few of the books I have found enlightening. A full bibliography would run to the length of a Tolstoy novel. (In the London Library there are 200 feet of shelves devoted to the history and topography of London.)

Annual Publications and Multi-Editions
Alternative London by various authors (Otherwise Press)
The Good Food Guide ed. Christopher Driver (Consumer Association)
A Guide to London's Best Restaurants (Virgin Books)
A Guide to London's Best Shops by Charlotte duCann (Virgin Books)
Let's Lunch in London by Corrine Streich (Papermac)
London Pub Guide (Robert Nicolson Publications)
The Time Out Guide to Eating in London (Time Out Publications)
   Weekly listings magazines are invaluable. I have stolen shamelessly from *Time Out* and *City Limits*.

The Best Comprehensive Guides
Dickens's Dictionary of London 1879 by Charles Dickens (Howard Baker Press Ltd 1972)
London: The Biography of a City by Christopher Hibbert (1977)
The New Penguin Guide to London by F. R. Banks (Penguin 1972)
London: The Unique City by S. E. Rasmussen (1948)
The Face of London by Harold P. Clunn
   I'm told there is an excellent guide published by American Express, those great philanthropists, but I have yet to see it.

The Best Anthologies
The London Anthology by Hugh and Pauline Massingham (Spring Books)
The Pride of London by Walter and Sidney Scott and Joan Stevenson (John Green 1947)
Authors to look out for: Geoffrey Fletcher, Ivor Brown, V. S. Pritchett, H. V. Morton, E. B. Chancellor, Charles G. Harper, William Kent and Ian Nairn.
The Streets of London by David Benedictus (Thames/Methuen 1985) is of some small interest.

Further Information
The London Tourist Board (LTB), National Tourist Information Centre, Victoria Station Forecourt, London SW1 (01-730 3488). Open seven days a week.

The London Index

The London Index is an at-a-glance guide to the subject entries in this book, but organised by London borough and postal district. One of the criticisms of the first edition of the book was that although it made fascinating browsing, it was difficult to 'use as a guide'. Therefore, the London Index organises the entries (e.g. jazz, Indian food, all-night eating) by London district. It is then possible to see immediately if a particular area has any recommended facilities and then simply read the relevant subject entry in the text to find it.

The best of each is listed in italics; the worst is not listed. You'll have to read the book to find out what you should avoid!

The London Index

NORTH

N1
All-Night Petrol
Cemeteries
Chapels
Cinemas
Cottages
Crescents
Drama Schools
Driving Schools
Emergency Services
Epitaphs
Fancy Dress
Fanlights
Fish and Chips
Fishmongers
Jazz
Lions
Music Halls
Pasta
Pipes
Pubs
Pub Signs
Records/Tapes
Schools
Squares
Stationers
Street Markets
Street Names
Swedish Food
Tailors
Talent Shows
Theatres (Fringe)
Unusual Shops

N2
Pubs
Tennis

N3
Fish Restaurants
Street Names
Synagogues
Vegetarian
    Restaurants

N4
African Food
Art Deco and
    Art Nouveau
Discos
Friezes
Parks
Peacocks

N6
Cats
Cemeteries
Chickens
Churches
Cottages
Domes
Epitaphs
Estate Agents
Ghosts
Golf
Hills
Hostels
Houses
Parks
Pillar Boxes
Roofs/Chimneys
Statues
Steps/Staircases
Surprises
Swimming
Tennis
Trees
Vegetarian
    Restaurants

N7
Butchers
Concert Halls
Farms
Jazz
Skating
Wines

N8
African Food
Drama Schools

N9
Children's London

N10
Hills
Records/Tapes
Toys

N11
Obelisks

N12
Auctions
Cemeteries
Statues

N13
Pasta

N14
Chinese
    Restaurants

N16
Birds
Frames and
    Framing
Gates
German Food
Surprises

319

320

Shoes
Street Names

326

Hairdressers
Kites
Roofs/Chimneys
Signposts
Skating
Synagogues

SW17
*Art Deco and
    Art Nouveau*
Auctions
Weather Vanes/
    Weather Cocks
Wine Bars

SW18
Auctions
Breweries
Children's London
Delicatessens/
    Grocers
Horse Troughs
Pubs and Pub food
Rivers/Streams
Weather Vanes/
    Weather Cocks

SW19
Arches
Birds
Children's London
Dog Tracks
Driving Schools
English
    Restaurants
Estate Agents
Fancy Dress
Frames and
    Framing
Parks
Ponds
Queues
Stores

Sundials
Tennis
Toys
Views

EAST

E1
All-Night Eating
Art Nouveau
Art Galleries
Arts and Crafts
Beigels
Blue Plaques
Bollards
Breweries ·
Churches
Delicatessens/
    Grocers
Epitaphs
Façades
Farms
Fishmongers
Fountains and
    Drinking
    Fountains
Gardens
Indian Restaurants
Kosher Food
Murals
Museums
Poetry
Protection Agencies
Pubs
Pub Signs
Shop Fronts
Squares
Statues
Steps/Staircases
Street Markets
Synagogues
Theatres (Fringe)
Tiles

Tunnels
Wall Writings
Windows

E3
Birds
Talent Shows

E2
Auctions
Breakfasts
Budget Restaurants
Garden Centres
Hospitals
Libraries
Open-Air Eating
Parks
Pubs
Roofs/Chimneys
Shoes
Street Markets
Vegetarian
    Restaurants

E4
Dog Tracks
Street Names
Trees

E5
Discos
Farms

E7
Cemeteries
Football
Ghosts
Pub food

E8
Budget Restaurants
Cinemas
Fish and Chips
Lavatories

329

330

Knitwear
Lebanese
  Restaurants
Mews
Mexican Food
Museums
Pubs and Pub food
Records/Tapes
Signposts
Skating
Surprises
Swimming
Synagogues
Tea Houses/Cream
  Cakes
Theatres (Fringe)
Wine Merchants

W3
Car Parks
Hostels
Obelisks

W4
Alleys
All-Night Petrol
Chess
Estate Agents
Fancy Dress
Hamburgers
Houses
Ice Cream
Pillar Boxes
Pubs
Surprises
Vets

W5
Betting Shops
Driving Schools
Indian Restaurants
Theatres (Fringe)

W6
Arts Centres
Bridges
Budget Restaurants
Chess
Dancing
Dragons
Housing Estates
Lions
Music Halls
Organs
Poetry
Polish Food
Pubs and Pub food
Records/Tapes
Schools
Street Lights
Theatre (Fringe)

W8
Alleys
All-Night Eating
Children's London
Delicatessens/
  Grocers
Discos
Embassies
English
  Restaurants
Estate Agents
Fancy Dress
Fish and Chips
Fountains and
  Drinking
  Fountains
Frames and
  Framing
Free Entertainment
Garages
Gardens
Gates
German Food
Hostels

Indian Restaurants
Italian Restuarants
Kites
Knitwear
Lions
Mews
Model Boats
Palaces
Parks
Pasta
Peacocks
Pets
Schools
Squares
Statues
Streets
Tea Houses/Cream
  Cakes
Unusual Shops
Views
Wine Merchants

W9
Bicycles
Budget Restaurants
Darts
Emergency Services
Fishmongers
Free Entertainment
Garden Centres
Gardens
Pub Food
Shirts
Streets
Wine Merchants

W10
Bicycles
Cemeteries
Epitaphs
Ghosts
Obelisks

331

W11

Bookshops
Butchers
Cinemas
Florists
French Restaurants
Greek Restaurants
Hotels
Japanese
  Restaurants
Parks
Pubs and Pub Food
Records/Tapes
Street Markets
Swimming
Toys
Vets
Wine Bars
Wine Merchants

W12

African Food (Take
  Away)
All-Night Petrol
Budget Restaurants
Driving Schools
Football
Murals
Records/Tapes
Swimming
Tennis

W14

Blue Plaques
Fancy Dress
Friezes
Squash Clubs
Streets
Tennis
Theatres
  (Open Air)

WC1

All-Night Eating
All-Night Petrol
Art Galleries
Ballet
Betting Shops
Bicycles
Bookshops
Brasseries
Budget Restaurants
Canteens
Children's London
Cinemas
Clocks
Cocktails
Coffee
Concert Halls
Crescents
Domes
Dragons
Drama Schools
Emergency Services
English
  Restaurants
Fanlights
Fish and Chips
Friezes
Ghosts
Libraries
Lions
Modern and
  Commercial
  Buildings
Most Confusing
  Street
Museums
Music Halls
Pizzas
Poetry
Publishers
Pubs
Records/Tapes
Sandwiches

Shoes
Shop Fronts
Solicitors
Squares
Statues
Streets
Tiles
Umbrellas
Unusual Shops
Wine Bars

WC2

African Food
Alleys
All-Night Eating
Art Galleries
Arts and Crafts
Auctions
Banks
Bicycles
Blue Plqeus
Bollards
Bookshops
Brasseries
Breakfasts
Bridges
Budget Restaurants
Buskers
Butchers
Buttons
Cabaret
Car Parks
Cats
Chapels
Characters
Cheese
Children's London
Chinese Restaurants
Chocolates
Church
Cinemas
Clairvoyants
Cocktails

333

Broxbourne,
Herts
Birds

Carshalton,
Surrey
Trees

Chertsey, Middx
Farms

Chessington,
Surrey
Peacocks
Zoos

Cobham, Surrey
Golf Course

Cockfosters,
Essex
Delicatessens/
Grocers

Croydon, Surrey
Birds
Concert Halls

Dartford, Kent
Tunnels
Vines

Enfield, Middx
Alleys
Gates
Hills
Rivers/Streams
Trees

Epping, Essex
Birds

334

Hampton Court,
Surrey
Clocks
Gardens
Palaces
Pillar Boxes
Roofs/Chimneys
Vines
Windows

Hanwell, Middx
Cottages

Harrow, Middx
Fish and Chips

Ilford, Essex
Roadsweepers

Isleworth
Art Deco and
Art Nouveau
Pubs
Street Lights
Trees
Wall Writing

Kew, Surrey
Art Galleries
Bridges
Chinese
Restaurants
Cottages
Cricket
Fishing
Gardens
Lions
Tea Houses/Cream
Cakes
Weather

Kingston-on-
Thames, Surrey
Alleys
All-Night Petrol
Auctions
Bicycles
Darts
Fishing
Fishmongers
Stores
Swimming

Long Ditton,
Surrey
Synagogues

Luton, Beds
Football

Mitcham, Surrey
Epitaphs

Northolt, Middx
Trees

Petersham,
Surrey
Farms
Garden Centres
Surprises

Pinner, Middx
Bicycles
Epitaphs

Richmond,
Surrey
Arches
Art Deco and Art
Nouveau
Bookshops
Bridges
Car Parks

Reader's Contribution Form

Return to David Benedictus, Sphere Books Ltd, 30-32 Gray's Inn Road, London WC1X 8JL

I should like to nominate:

Nominee's name ....

Address ....

Phone number ....

In existing category ....

or in new category ....

Comments ....

....

....

....

Note: any establishment in the Greater London area may be considered. Contributions from those with vested interests not welcomed! Feel free to take issue with existing entries.

My Name ....

My Address ....

....

My phone number ....

I would/would not like an acknowledgement in the book (please delete).

All nominations will be checked before being included in or excluded from future editions of this book. Thanks.

337

Reader's Contribution Form

Return to David Benedictus, Sphere Books Ltd, 30-32 Gray's Inn Road, London WC1X 8JL

I should like to nominate:

Nominee's name ....

Address ....

Phone number ....

In existing category ....

or in new category ....

Comments ....

....

....

....

Note: any establishment in the Greater London area may be considered. Contributions from those with vested interests not welcomed! Feel free to take issue with existing entries.

My Name ....

My Address ....

....

My phone number ....

I would/would not like an acknowledgement in the book (please delete).

All nominations will be checked before being included in or excluded from future editions of this book. Thanks.